# THE PLOTS AGAINST HITLER

DANNY ORBACH is a senior lecturer in the Hebrew University of Jerusalem. A veteran of Israeli intelligence, he studied for more than ten years in Tel Aviv, Tokyo and Harvard Universities. As a historian, commentator and political blogger, he has published extensively on German, Japanese, Chinese, Israeli and Middle Eastern history, with a special focus on military resistance, disobedience, rebellions and political assassinations.

# THE
# PLOTS
# AGAINST
# HITLER

# DANNY
# ORBACH

HEAD
*of* ZEUS

First published in 2017 by Head of Zeus Ltd

1 3 5 7 9 10 8 6 4 2

A catalogue record for this book is available from the British Library.

ISBN (HB) 9781786694577
ISBN (E) 9781786694560

Printed and bound by CPI Group (UK) Ltd, Croydon, CR0 4YY

Head of Zeus Ltd
5–8 Hardwick Street
London EC1R 4RG
WWW.HEADOFZEUS.COM

*This book is dedicated to my dear teacher Itzik Meron (Mitrani),*
*who accompanied this project from the outset*
*but did not have an opportunity to witness its publication.*

# CONTENTS

## Note on Ranks

Many of the protagonists in this book were officers in Third Reich military organizations: Wehrmacht, Navy, and SS. A number of them advanced in rank between 1938 and 1944—the years covered here —and often more than once. Many books on the German resistance, especially in English, mention consistently the last and highest rank each individual obtained. Claus von Stauffenberg, for example, usually appears as a colonel, though he received this rank only in July 1944. In this book I mention the relevant rank for each time period. So, Henning von Tresckow is referred to as a colonel in chapters dealing with his assassination attempts in March 1943, but as a major general in later chapters. Two of the ranks of general officers in the Wehrmacht, "general of infantry/artillery ext." and "colonel-general," do not have a clear equivalent in English-speaking armies. Therefore, for simplicity's sake, I translate both to "general." The SS had its own special ranks, which I convert to American military equivalents; for instance, Brigadier General Nebe instead of Oberführer Nebe.

# INTRODUCTION

*And when the cries of misery have reached my ear*
*I warned, indeed, not hard enough and clear!*
*Today I know why I stand guilty here.*
— ALBRECHT HAUSHOFER, 1945

GUILT. NO OTHER word carries so much significance when considering German history. Even the drama of the July 1944 plot to kill Hitler, staged by Col. Claus von Stauffenberg and his confederates in the anti-Nazi resistance movement, is fraught with guilt and a maelstrom of other emotions, which we view through the thick fog of myth and memory.

The story of the anti-Nazi underground in the German army and its various attempts to assassinate Hitler has been cast and recast in books, movies, screenplays, and TV shows. That is hardly surprising, as the story contains elements of a thriller: nocturnal meetings in frozen fields; the elaborate drama of military conspiracies; bombs hidden in briefcases and liqueur bottles; and the dramatic day of July 20, 1944, with its abortive assassination and final, desperate attempt at a coup d'état.

Drama apart, the story of the German resistance has a crucial moral component. After all, the Nazi era is still viewed around the world, and most of all in Germany itself, through the lens of collective guilt, historical responsibility, and the burden of National Socialist crimes. Traditionalist German historians, from the 1950s to today, have tended to view the story of the German resistance as a "spot of light" in the darkness of the Nazi era, therefore easing the burden of historical guilt. The resistance fighters were portrayed as upright, deeply moral people set to "confront the dark forces of the age," in the words of Hans Rothfels, the founding father of resistance historiography in Germany.[1] The narrative presented by traditionalist German historians, most subtly by Peter Hoffmann, is rich in detail and highly sympathetic to the German resistance fighters. The coup attempt of July 20, 1944, according to Countess Marion von Dönhoff, was a "revolt of conscience." The motives of the conspirators, she wrote, were moral.[2] Their purpose, states Peter Hoffmann, was first and foremost to stop Nazi crimes, including the Holocaust. It was a humane goal, in the sense that its purpose was to uphold the principle of "life and the preservation of life."[3] They were patriotic Germans, for sure, who hoped to save their fatherland from destruction, but nationalism was always secondary to morality.

Come the boisterous sixties, and the political climate in Germany changed dramatically. Young historians, like other educated Germans of their age, began to mercilessly examine the "myths" of the past. The German resistance did not survive the new critical climate unscathed. From the late sixties on, critical, left-leaning historians such as Hans Mommsen, Christoph Dipper, and Christian Gerlach cast doubts on the integrity of the German resistance. To them, the conspirators, most of whom were conservative bureaucrats and military officers, were dubious figures to begin with. True, Count Stauffenberg tried to assassinate Hitler and paid for it with his life. But had he not cooperated with the Nazi regime for many years beforehand? What about the other conspirators? Were they really moral men and women, anti-Nazis to the core, who tried to stage "a revolt of conscience," or rather were they opportunistic figures who cooperated with the Nazis until the war was no longer winnable?

Gradually, laurel after laurel was removed from the heads of previously revered conspirators. They may have slowly learned to hate the Nazi regime and opposed most of its crimes, argued Hans Mommsen, but they were also antidemocratic reactionaries.[4] They harbored strong anti-Semitic sentiments, wrote Christoph Dipper in a highly influential study published in 1984. They may have been against the Holocaust, but most of them wanted the Jews out of Germany and supported "legal" and "nonviolent" discrimination.[5] They weren't merely anti-Semites but also murderers and war criminals, argued Christian Gerlach in 1995. Many prominent conspirators, first and foremost Maj. Gen. Henning von Tresckow, willingly took part in the mass murders of Russians, Jews, and Poles. Traditionalist historians, Gerlach contended, had whitewashed the conspirators' crimes and written "nonsense" about their supposedly unimpeachable record. The sad truth was that they resisted Hitler not because of his crimes but because they disagreed with him about the "best way to win the war."[6]

The debate goes on. The German resistance to Hitler, it seems, is a field in which historical arguments are not purely academic but shot through with passion. People are elevated to Olympus by one scholar, only to be condemned to the darkest hell by another. Professional and even personal accusations are hurled back and forth. I myself, as the following pages will demonstrate, am far from a neutral spectator. In the first days of my interest in the resistance, as a young student in Israel, I was impressed by what I saw as the selfless bravery of the German conspirators. As a third-generation child of Holocaust survivors, I was deeply moved to read about the conspirators' sympathy for the persecuted Jews. I was equally disappointed to discover their supposed anti-Semitism and complicity in war crimes in Dipper's and Gerlach's accounts. I decided to delve into the sources and form my own opinion.

In ten years of research prior to the publication of *Valkyrie*, my Hebrew-language monograph on the resistance, I examined every primary and secondary source I could find.[7] My research took me to some thirteen archives in Germany, England, Russia, and the United States. At times, I was shocked by my own findings. Gradually, I became more and more disillusioned with the left-leaning, "critical" school of resistance studies. Seemingly critical scholars, I found, blamed German resistance fighters for opportunism, anti-Semitism, and war crimes based on skewed evidence, distortions, and misreadings of primary sources. The representation of the resistance by such scholars is often a caricature, a "crooked mirror" that teaches us more about the political bias of the scholars than about the German resistance itself.[8]

However, I could not return to the cozy, heroic picture presented by many traditionalist historians. True, some of the critical historians were sloppy, but the questions they asked were worthwhile. Gradually, I came to believe that one must transcend the current moralistic debate, redraw its terms, and reframe it altogether.

This book is an attempt to do that. It retells the story of the resistance, shedding new light on its psychological, social, and military dynamics, as well as on the reasons behind its decision to assassinate Hitler. I use the German resistance as a test case to draw specific insights with general implications: Why are certain people, and not others, drawn to active resistance despite the mortal risks involved? Who is most likely to become a resistance fighter? What can we learn about the complex and fluid motives that may lead people to resist? When one steps out of the moralistic debate, even without disavowing it entirely, a whole new world of meaning may be discovered. In it, motivations and intentions are more properly seen as slippery and difficult to pin down. As the medievalist Aviad Kleinberg wrote in his study of Catholic saints,

> The question of what really motivates the ascetic is meaningless, as is the question of whether a "true" saint really exists. If "true" means perfectly pure, the response will always be negative. Nothing in the world is pure. Does this mean that everything in the world is completely impure? There again the response will be negative. In this world we are always dealing with relative values . . . Furthermore, what makes a person act at one moment is not necessarily what makes him act at another. People sometimes do things without intending to do them; sometimes honor, power, habit, or fatigue can alter the purest intentions. People rarely conform to clear and precise models, just as they rarely have feet that perfectly fit size 11 shoes. They fit, more or less. They fluctuate and shift from one model to another. At any given moment their actions reflect the balance of drives and contingencies that result from a unique situation which cannot be reproduced.[9]

Indeed, what sense does it make to ask whether the resistance fighters had "moral" or "patriotic" motives without deciphering what morality and patriotism meant to them? Is it possible to draw a line between morality and patriotism, and if so, did the conspirators consciously do so? Can one build a more convincing model of their motives? These questions will be explored throughout the book, and concluded upon in chapter 20.

The story of the German resistance conspirators, however, was essentially a military one. The following chapters will chronicle the dramatic history of the schemes, assassination attempts, and bomb plots they were involved in. We will follow the conspirators from 1938 to 1944, uncovering assassination plots, some famous and some little known, in an attempt to treat the rarely discussed issue of conspiratorial networks. Previous studies have tended to focus on groups or individuals in the resistance, but almost none of them, as far as I have been able to establish, have adequately analyzed the interactions between the members of these groups.[10] How were new fighters recruited to the resistance? How did the conspiratorial networks operate in reality, and how did different leadership styles affect the outcome of the plots and their chances of success? Most importantly, we shall see how certain individuals, whom we shall call brokers and connectors, kept the networks alive by ensuring that information flowed within them.

In addition, we shall deal with the complexities involved in the decision of the German resistance fighters to assassinate Hitler. On one hand, such an action offered the enormous temptation to change the course of history with one stroke. On the other, murdering one's sovereign leader was, for most conspirators, ideologically, legally, and morally problematic. How did the leaders of the resistance, devout Christians as they were, justify the killing of their hierarchical superior, to whom they swore an oath of allegiance? Such questioning teaches us a lot not only about the resistance but also about problems of obedience and disobedience in Nazi Germany and beyond.

I base my narrative on primary sources—diaries, letters, memoirs, and testimonies—as well as on German, American, British, Finnish, and Soviet documents. I also make use of the records of Gestapo interrogations and of Nazi court proceedings, as well as interviews with the conspirators and members of their families. A particularly important source is the almost inexhaustibly rich trove of documents collected by the late professor Harold C. Deutsch and preserved among his papers at the U.S. Army Heritage and Education Center in Carlisle, Pennsylvania. I have also made extensive use of the private archives of two other prominent historians, Eberhard Zeller and Bodo Scheurig, both kept at the Institute for Contemporary History in Munich.

Many of the documents I have used have been examined little (if at all) by the existing literature. For example, the fascinating diaries of Hermann Kaiser, the broker who connected the different resistance groups in Berlin and the east, offer a rare glance into the inner circle of the conspiracy. I have also made extensive use of interviews that Harold C. Deutsch and his team conducted with participants in the September 1938 coup attempt, an episode that remains relatively obscure to this day. These interviews cast new light on the frame of mind of senior members of the resistance movement on the eve of and during World War II. Likewise, French sources that until now have not received the attention they deserve enabled me to uncover the story of the negotiations conducted in the summer of 1944 between agents of the German resistance movement and Free French espionage officers. Another important source, also cited here for the first time, is the transcript of the interrogation, by Soviet intelligence, of Col. Hans Crome, a member of the resistance movement who was taken prisoner by the Red Army in 1944. This document, written in Russian, is preserved in the Russian Federation's state archive, in Moscow. Its significance lies in the information it includes about the resistance movement's recruitment methods, its undercover communications procedures, and its internal structure.

In addition, I have made critical use of the substantial body of research on the German resistance movement published between 1945 and 2015 in English, Hebrew, and German. My findings point out the severe failings of some of the most influential and accepted works on the subject. The breadth of these sources, primary and secondary, has enabled me to present a full account of these events, including moments of crisis and decisive junctures, while reaching new insights valid beyond the bounds of this specific story. In our world of revolutionary "springs," civil wars, occupation regimes, and brutal tyrannies, questions of resistance are more important than ever.

# THE PLOTS AGAINST HITLER

# 1

# OPPOSITION IN FLAMES

B Y JANUARY 30, 1933, the eve of the Nazi takeover, it was still unclear whether Hitler and the National Socialists would rule Germany without a fight. The two anti-Nazi opposition parties, the Communists and the Social Democrats, still held far-reaching networks of
activists, many of them armed. They boasted millions of loyal supporters, clubs, and labor unions, and more than enough young men willing
to fight. Within a year, all of these seemingly formidable networks of
opposition would disappear, consumed by fire.

On the evening of February 27, 1933, two pedestrians and a policeman were walking by the Reichstag, the impressive home of the German parliament in Berlin, when something unusual suddenly caught
their eyes. A light, some strange flicker, was dancing behind the windows, followed by a swiftly moving shadow. The policeman knew immediately he was looking at arson, and called for reinforcements. Police entered the Reichstag together, moving through a screen of thick,
black smoke. Quickly, they noticed the mysterious trespasser sneaking
from the chamber, half-naked, covered in sweat, with a beet-red face
and unkempt hair. A passport found on him indicated that his name
was Marinus van der Lubbe, a Dutch citizen. He had used his shirt
and a can of gasoline to start a fire. When asked for his reasons, he answered, "Protest! Protest!"[1]

Few of the many Berliners who witnessed the flames in horror
imagined that the new Reich chancellor, Adolf Hitler, would use the
fire as an excuse to uproot all opposition networks, organizations, and

parties in Germany. The chancellor, appointed only one month earlier, on January 30, destroyed in less than one year political parties of all persuasions, the autonomy of the German states, and the powerful trade unions. Dramatic changes also swept the civil service, the judicial system, schools and universities, and, most importantly, the army. By late 1934, Hitler and his Nazi Party were the sole masters of Germany, unobstructed by any effective form of active or potential opposition.[3]

The politicians of the new regime were quick to arrive at the burning building. First among them was Hermann Göring, one of Hitler's paladins and speaker of the Reichstag. The commander of the firefighters gave him a report on the attempts to extinguish the fire, but Göring was more interested in extinguishing something else. "The guilty are the Communist revolutionaries," he said. "This act is the beginning of the Communist uprising, which must be promptly crushed with an iron fist." Hitler and his propaganda master, Josef Goebbels, were not far behind. "From this day on," declared the new chancellor, "anyone standing in our way will be done for. Softness will not be understood by the German people. The Communist deputies have to be hanged tonight."[2]

The Reichstag, one of the last relics of the dying Weimar Republic, was reduced to a blackened shell. Alarm swept the country, fed by sensationalist headlines in the morning papers. "AGAINST MURDERERS, ARSONISTS AND POISONERS THERE CAN ONLY BE RIGOROUS DEFENSE," read one of them. "AGAINST TERROR, RECKONING THROUGH THE DEATH PENALTY." Alarm soon became hysteria. "They wanted to send armed gangs to the villages to murder and start fires," noted Luise Solmitz, a conservative schoolteacher, in her diary.[3] "So the Communists had burned down the Reichstag," wrote Sebastian Haffner, a young jurist and one of the few remaining skeptics.

> That could well be so, it was even to be expected. Funny, though, why they should choose the Reichstag, an empty building, where no one would profit from a fire. Well, perhaps it really had been intended as the "signal" for the uprising, which had been prevented by the "decisive measures" taken by the government. That was what the papers said, and it sounded plausible. Funny also that the Nazis got so worked up about the Reichstag. Up till then they had contemptuously called it a "hot air factory." Now it was sud-

denly the holy of holies that had been burned down . . . The main thing is: the danger of a Communist uprising has been averted and we can sleep easy.[4]

Neither the government nor the Communists were sleeping easy. On the eve of the Reichstag fire, Hitler had yet to win support from the majority of Germans. The National Socialist Party was still far from a Reichstag majority. The opposition parties from the left, the Social Democrats and the Communists, were still major political powers.[5] Now, the Nazis used the red scare to rally large parts of the German public to their cause. Many people, even if cold to Hitler and his radical ideas, began to consider him the lesser evil. Others, especially adherents of the National Conservative right, turned to the Nazi leader as a redeemer. The teacher Luise Solmitz, though married to a converted Jew, was one of them. "The feelings of most Germans are dominated by Hitler," she confided in her journal. "His fame rises to the stars. He is the savior of a wicked, sad world."[6] The fears of the public were exploited to kick off a half-planned, half-improvised campaign for total political, cultural, and ideological subjugation of Germany. Needless to say, the charged atmosphere made it easier to neutralize all centers of power from which prospective opposition might arise.

Who really burned the Reichstag? Was it a National Socialist sham, or an act of solitary lunacy committed by van der Lubbe? Scholars have debated this question ever since.[7] In any case, the Nazis were the only winners. When they formed the government, they demanded only two portfolios apart from the chancellorship: the Ministry of Internal Affairs of the Reich and the corresponding ministry in Prussia, the largest and most important German state. They knew what they were doing. These two ministries gave them total control over the police, the secret police, and internal security apparatus all over the Reich. Using their newly won power, they set out to destroy the opposition root and branch by way of propaganda, temptation of Germans who were not yet convinced Nazis, and terror against remaining members of the opposition.

Resistance became ever more dangerous. One of the founding fathers of the German resistance movement, Hans Bernd Gisevius, wrote bitterly later, "Was it the Reichstag alone? Was not all Berlin on fire?"[8] The campaign to eliminate the opposition and its institutions was a part of a larger process, which was later called *Gleichschaltung* (bringing into line). Its intention was to take full control of German society by injecting National Socialist ideology into all aspects of life, accompanied by lucrative carrots for collaborators and sharp sticks for anyone who dared to resist.

On February 28, one day after the Reichstag fire, the constitutional barriers were broken. The new government passed emergency decrees "for the protection of people and state," allowing it to monitor letters, telegrams, and phone calls, and to restrict the freedom of speech and the press. More importantly, the right of habeas corpus was suspended, so enemies of the regime could not even expect proper redress by law.

The first victims were the Communists. The Nazis blamed them for the fire and ordered the arrest of their Reichstag section leader. In just a few weeks, the party disintegrated: its newspapers closed, organizations were banned, and all leaders were placed under arrest. The Communist force, deemed a mortal threat by so many Germans, was paralyzed. Its ranks in disarray, it offered almost no resistance. Its swift disappearance surprised its supporters and many ordinary Germans alike; they had once thought of it as an armed and violent revolutionary force. By contrast, no one anticipated anything from the Social Democrats. Haffner wrote,

> A Communist attack was what we expected. The Communists were determined people, with fierce expressions. They raised their fists in salute and had weapons—at least, they used guns often enough in the everyday pub brawls. They boasted continually about the strength of their organization, and they had probably learned how to do "these things" in Russia. The Nazis had left no one in doubt that they wanted to destroy them. It was natural, indeed obvious, that the Communists would retaliate.[9]

But they did nothing of the kind.

Why did the Communist Party go down so quickly in spite of long preparations for violent action against both democracy and fascism? Peter Hoffmann has argued that its leaders were fettered by their own dogmatic ideology.[10] They and their patron, Soviet leader Joseph Stalin, believed that the rise of the Nazis was nothing but the death rattle of the liberal bourgeoisie, that is, the Weimar Republic. The Communist Party, said a Russian diplomat in Berlin to Friedrich Stampfer, editor of the Social Democratic journal *Vorwärts*, would surely take the government, but only after Hitler had destroyed democracy to clear the way.[11] This false confidence led the Communists to make disastrous decisions, above all their refusal to join the Social Democrats in a united anti-Nazi front. Finally, the Communist Party's predictions of a popular revolution failed to materialize, and its politicians were surprised by a determined and peremptory rival. As a party, it ceased to exist.

The Social Democratic Party, known as the main rival of the Nazis and the strongest political mainstay of the Weimar Republic, was paralyzed as well, though for very different reasons. Its leaders were fixated on "legality," even when their rivals trampled every law in their quest for absolute power. Somehow, the Social Democratic leaders believed, they would be protected: by the police, by the courts, by the state, by someone. They believed this until it was too late.

The Social Democratic Party had not always been so lethargic. During the stormy year of 1920, in response to a monarchist coup d'état by conservative politician Wolfgang Kapp, the party mobilized the workers for a general strike. The mass protests forced Kapp and his lieutenants to give up power, and practically restored the Weimar Republic. But in 1933, after the Reichstag fire, the Social Democratic leaders did not call for a general strike, the most effective weapon they had. Instead, they opted to comply, in order not to give the government "excuses" to ban them, as if the Nazis needed any.

The National Socialists, meanwhile, were constantly moving. In March, using the crisis to bolster their hold over the state, they drafted the so-called Enabling Act, which allowed them to pass legislation without parliamentary approval. That law, carefully drafted, laid the legal basis for the future dictatorship of the Third Reich. The parties of the center and the right decided, foolishly enough, to vote for the act. Still not knowing Hitler well enough, they thought that would give them enough credit with the Nazis to survive. Hitler himself did everything he could to soothe them: he promised to use his newly won power only rarely, against a Communist revolution and only after due consultation with the president. Still, he lacked the parliamentary majority of two-thirds, required to approve the new law. The Communists and the Social Democrats still held a blocking majority. The Nazis, though, would not be stopped by such trifles. On March 5, all Communist deputies were arrested. Göring, president of the Reichstag, made it clear that if necessary, Social Democrats would be kept out of the chamber to secure the right number of votes.

The left-wing deputies who did make it into the provisional chamber of the Reichstag, located in a Berlin opera house, discovered an atmosphere far from amiable. The SA, the private militia of the Nazi Party, filled the galleries and intimidated the deputies with loud interjections, boos, and singing. Still, the Social Democrats did not give up. Their leader, Otto Wels, delivered the swan song of the parliamentary left in Germany. "We, the German Social Democrats," he said, "pledge ourselves to the principles of humanity and justice, liberty and socialism. No enabling act will give you the power to destroy these indestructible, eternal values."[12] Hitler was not impressed: "You are late, but still you come! . . . No one needs you anymore . . . The star of Germany will rise, and yours will fall. Your death bells are already tolling . . . I am not interested in your votes. Germany will be free, but not through you."[13]

The death bells of the Social Democratic Party were indeed tolling, to the cheers and applause of their rivals. On June 22, 1933, National Socialist Minister of the Interior Wilhelm Frick declared the party "an enemy of state and nation," and ordered it dissolved forthwith. The biggest party of the German left ceased to exist.

The parties of the center and the right did not fare any better, in spite of their previous cooperation with Hitler. On June 21, police and SA forces stormed the headquarters of the Nationalist People's Party. The party leader, Alfred Hugenberg, was a political ally of Hitler and shared many of his ultranationalist, imperialist, and anti-Semitic views. He even served as a cabinet minister. But the Nazis showed no mercy to the person whose close cooperation helped them to win power. The party was forced to dissolve itself, and on June 26, Hugenberg resigned from the government. One week later, on July 4 and 5, the two Catholic parties were forced to disband as well. Their fate was sealed on July 14, when the government issued the following act, turning Germany officially into a one-party state: "The German National Socialist Workers' party is the only political party in Germany. Any individual taking upon himself to form an organization of another political party, or to establish another political party, is subject to imprisonment for up to three years, or detention from six months to three years."[14]

That was the end of the political parties, the most natural, most important source of legal opposition in Germany. The *Gleichschaltung*, however, did not stop there. Now Hitler turned to the other centers of national power, and swept them aside without resistance.

That outcome was far from obvious. Germany had a strong tradition of regionalism, going back to the preunification era. Before 1871, the German-speaking territories were divided into numerous independent principalities with their own currencies, governments, and armies. When these principalities saw the need, many did not hesitate to fight each other or to form alliances with outside powers. Some, like Prussia, were considered world powers. After the unification, under Bismarck, the newly formed German Empire did not abolish the principalities but instead rearranged them under its own political authority. Even in 1918, when a wave of revolution swept through the principalities and turned them into republics, the federal structure of the country was kept intact and the states retained local governments of their own. One of them, Bavaria, had been on the verge of separatism in the early 1920s.

Now things were different. The local governments kowtowed to the regime, only to be tossed out one after another. Instead of elected prime ministers, the new rulers appointed National Socialist governors (*Gauleiter*), who answered not to their constituencies but only to the Nazi Party in Berlin. Only Bavaria, the southern Catholic state with its strong local identity, resisted, before a coup solved that problem. National Socialist militiamen, working in close cooperation with the police, stormed local prime minister Dr. Heinrich Held's office. Held was removed and replaced by one of Hitler's lieutenants. Now, Bavaria, too, had been integrated in the *Gleichschaltung*.

The trade unions, which boasted millions of members from all over the Reich, were also quick to fade away. To the surprise of some of their more ardent supporters, the scenario of 1920 did not repeat itself, and a general strike against the new regime was not even considered. The trade-union leaders believed that by going along with Hitler, they might reach a modus vivendi with the regime. Therefore, they competed with one another to declare the most ardent loyalty to Hitler. That didn't help them. The Nazi leadership did not tolerate competing power centers, let alone ones hitherto associated with the left.

In this case, the Nazis resorted to a ploy. Hitler declared May 1 to be Workers' Day, a National Socialist holiday, and the trade unions were invited to celebrate it along with the party. The festivities were boisterous, with an impressive parade held by both National Socialists and trade unionists. Years later, Communist activist Franz Jung bemoaned the fact that he and his comrades "marched thickly surrounded by SA, SS, and Hitler Youth." An ideal picture of class harmony, indeed.[15]

The scheme worked as planned. The leaders of the trade unions felt warm and secure, only to be mortally surprised the next day. The brouhaha of the parades had not quite died down when the trade unions were confronted by an all-out attack. Their offices were stormed, documents were seized, and they—who had really tried to prove their loyalty to the new regime—were duly led to concentration camps. With the trade unions all but gone, the German workers were quickly swallowed in the maelstrom of the *Gleichschaltung* and reorganized in a countrywide Nazi organization called the Labor Front.

Other power centers were also easily neutralized. From April 7, 1933, onward, government ministries were purged of Jews and political undesirables. Sweeping purges were also made in courts, police forces, schools, and universities. Most intellectuals did not even try to protest on behalf of their demoted colleagues. In fact, most of them, including some luminaries such as the philosopher Martin Heidegger, closed ranks behind the new regime. Resistance also failed to come from industrial, economic, and financial circles. After overcoming some initial misgivings, the leading industrialists, businessmen, and financiers quickly joined in to grab a piece of the pie. Hitler and his close colleagues knew how to seduce them: the banning of strikes and trade unions, a moratorium on the unpopular democratic regime, and most importantly, large-scale rearmament, which carried the potential for enormous profits.

"It cannot be denied, he has grown. Surprisingly for his opponents, the demagogue and party leader, the fanatic and rabble-rouser seems to be developing into a real statesman." That was the March 21 entry in the diary of novelist Erich Ebermayer, who was by no means a Nazi.[16] He was not alone. Many other Germans were enchanted by

Hitler's charisma and found their place among the masses marching for *Gleichschaltung*. On November 12, 1933, general elections were held again. The turnout was massive, reaching more than 95 percent. Only the National Socialist Party had been allowed to run, so Hitler "won" in a landslide: 92.11 percent voted for him, with only 7.89 percent daring to dissent or abstain.[17] These elections, of course, were held under dictatorial conditions, with no competition, and were fueled by massive government propaganda. The secrecy of the ballot was also not ensured. Still, the massive turnout suggested that most Germans were sympathetic to the new regime.

Hitler and his advisers wisely avoided some obvious pitfalls. When faced by demands of Nazi radicals to stage a second social revolution, the chancellor flatly refused, an effective way to win support among the revolution-wary upper classes. This was especially true for the army. This proud, stiffly conservative organization had a long tradition of autonomy and claiming political power. Many saw it as an independent force, the only refuge from Nazi lawlessness. However, from early on, it was clear to keen observers that this was an illusion. Unlike the Social Democrats and the Communists, the army was not a rival but an ally of the Nazi regime. True, some of Hitler's top commanders looked down on his barbarism, but even they were ready to cooperate with him. The higher echelons of the Reichswehr (later to be renamed the Wehrmacht) were hoping for a compromise regime, led by Hitler but dominated by themselves. Most young soldiers were loyal to the regime, as were many other German youths. Even senior officers began, in growing numbers, to abandon the dominant cautious approach to become dyed-in-the-wool Nazis. Dissenters were mostly silenced or made to retire. Foremost among them was Gen. Kurt von Hammerstein, the commander in chief and an implacable rival of Hitler. In 1934, a handful of officers still tried to fight the incorporation of racial theory into military regulations, but their resistance faded quickly, too. The army slowly but surely bound itself to Hitler's leadership.

The alliance with the army was sealed in June 1934, after Hitler crucially decided to dismiss his own militia, the SA. The leaders of this violent organization did not make a secret of their intention to remove the hated, aristocratic military leadership and to build instead a National Socialist people's army. The generals could not live for long with such a threat. In the end, Hitler had to choose a side—and he did. In a burst of terrifying cruelty, later known as the Night of the Long Knives, Hitler ordered the entire SA leadership massacred. Several conservative opponents of the regime were also murdered, including two senior officers: former Reich chancellor Gen. Kurt von Schleicher, and intelligence officer Maj. Gen. Ferdinand von Bredow. But this did not keep the military leadership from celebrating, and the two main military leaders of the country, commander in chief Gen. Werner von Fritsch and chief of the General Staff Gen. Ludwig Beck, failed to even lodge a protest. The army's victory was, of course, illusory. The SA was pushed to the sidelines in favor of the SS, the elite army of the National Socialist Party. It was more organized, and it posed a much greater threat to the army in the long run.

To show gratitude for the elimination of their SA rivals, some senior generals, led by War Minister Field Marshal Blomberg, proposed that from then on, every soldier would swear loyalty not only to the nation and the Reich but personally to Hitler. (From 1934 onward, he held both chancellorship and presidency, and was simply called the Führer—leader.) And so it was: "I swear by God this holy oath, to unconditionally obey Adolf Hitler, the Führer of the German Reich and people and the supreme commander of the Wehrmacht. As a brave soldier, I will be ready to risk my life at any time for this oath."[18]

A pro-Nazi shift also began in the working class, traditionally a mainstay of the Social Democratic Party and the Communist Party. The government's increased public spending, monumental public projects, and rearmament brought about a massive decrease in unemployment. Though strikes were banned and real wages stagnated, few went hungry as they had in the last years of the Weimar Republic.[19] The National Socialist recreation service, Strength through Joy (Kraft durch Freude), organized vacations, excursions, and athletic and cultural events for workers and civil servants. A growing propaganda machine spread Nazi doctrine at schools, universities, and workplaces, and in journals and cinemas. Many went along with it. In his memoirs, Sebastian Haffner described these temptations:

> The effect [of the propaganda] was intensified by the way one was
> permanently occupied and distracted by an unending sequence of
> celebrations, ceremonies and national festivities . . . There were

mass parades, fireworks, drums, bands, and flags all over Germany, Hitler's voice over thousands of loudspeakers, oaths and vows . . . The colossal emptiness and lack of meaning of these events was by no means unintentional. The population should become used to cheering and jubilation, even when there was no visible reason for it. It was reason enough that people who distanced themselves too obviously, sshh! — were daily and nightly tortured to death with steel whips and electric drills.[20]

The other side of the happily united *Volk* was "the Jew," the eternal bête noire of the National Socialist Party. This relatively unpopular minority was pitched as the enemy against which the newly formed nation must unite. Yet things did not go smoothly from the start. For example, the cooperation of the public with the anti-Jewish boycott of April 1, 1933, was limited, in spite of venomous propaganda from the government and local organs of the Nazi Party.[21]

However, the impact of anti-Jewish propaganda, which catalyzed existing anti-Semitic sentiments, was growing, especially in the younger generations. In fact, it was an essential part of the "togetherness" of the collective shaped by the regime. Sebastian Haffner, who was dating a Jewish girl in those days, recalled that on the day of the boycott, he went hiking with her in a forest near Berlin. En route, they met some groups of schoolboys accompanied by their teachers:

> Every one of these classes, as they passed, shouted "Juda verrecke!" to us in their bright young voices, as though it was a sort of hiker's greeting. It may not have been aimed at us in particular. I do not look at all Jewish, and Charlie (who was Jewish) did not look very Jewish either. Perhaps it was just a friendly greeting . . . So there I sat "on the springtime hill" with a small, graceful, vivacious girl in my arms. We kissed and caressed each other, and every so often a group of boys went past and cheerfully told us to perish.[22]

Under these circumstances, very few opposition activists dared to keep on protesting, and many of those who did were violently tossed aside. In the first year and a half after the takeover, SA thugs developed the habit of kidnapping "bad elements" and beating them to death in torture cellars. After the decapitation of the SA in June 1934, this sporadic, unorganized terror became much more efficient under the leadership of the SS. Throughout Germany, there were more than fifty concentration camps, where hundreds of thousands of Germans were interned. The prisoners were by no means exclusively resistance fighters. Most of them were citizens who had dared to criticize the government in public or even (in some cases) had cracked a joke at Hitler's expense. Behind the barbed wire, prisoners faced starvation and backbreaking daily labor. Any violation of the rules could be punished by death, and many who passed through the electric fence into a camp never returned. A popular ditty went thus: "Please, dear God, make me mute, / lest in Dachau I'll set foot" (*Lieber Gott, Mach mich stumm, / dass ich nicht nach Dachau kumm*).[23]

Outside the concentration camps, opponents of the regime were also isolated and living in constant terror. Even if they weren't arrested, they could be arbitrarily fired from their jobs. The long arm of the government could reach them, their family, and their friends at any moment. No one could be trusted. Anybody, close as he or she might be, could be an informer of the Secret State Police, known by its shortened name, Gestapo. Actually, there were relatively few professional Gestapo agents around, many fewer than most contemporaries imagined.[24] Most informers were ordinary people who gave tips to the Gestapo of their own free will: children brainwashed at school or at Hitler Youth meetings, neighbors, friends, and colleagues. These informers were motivated not only by ideology—though it certainly mattered—but also by personal gain. Currying the favor of the authorities could take one a long way, perhaps securing a promotion in the workplace, thus oiling one's way through the corridors of power.

But that was not the full picture. Opponents of the regime were not merely passive victims. In fact, many of them were brave, resolute, and dedicated. Immediately after the disaster of 1933, Social Democratic and Communist groups started building on old party networks to form resistance cells in neighborhoods, clubs, and factories. Many of these groups distributed their own propaganda through leaflets, newspapers, and other kinds of underground media, coordinated by both insiders and exiled leaders. The Communists, especially, tried their hand at well-organized Bolshevik-style underground activity. Yet, according to Peter Hoffmann, by 1935, "the period of large-scale underground activity was over. The Gestapo had annihilated the various organizations."[25] In fact, by that year, most active members and leaders of the meticulously crafted Communist networks were in concentration camps, exiled, or dead.

The reason was not stupidity or lack of experience but a structural problem. The Communists, true to their belief in mass action and popular resistance, worked to build a mass network. There was ample talk of "united fronts," cooperation between different cells, and broad national distribution in factories and workplaces. But as a network expands, the ability of its experienced cadres and leaders to filter newcomers becomes more limited, and very quickly the whole organization grows out of control. Such decentralization may be a blessing under democratic conditions, but not under a totalitarian dictatorship. Every recruit is potentially dangerous; every newcomer could be an informer, or a Gestapo agent. The fact that most Germans were sympathetic to the regime made that danger even more acute. With every new member, the chance to be penetrated by the security service grew, as even loyal recruits could unintentionally speak to informers. An arrested member could always be tortured until he identified others, thus allowing the Gestapo to follow the links in the network all the way back to its leaders.

Therefore, a network that was too large, like the Communist network, was bound to be destroyed. The Gestapo just had to wait for an opportune moment. The only model that could work for a coup d'état under totalitarian conditions would be an elitist underground with access to arms, and a very limited number of powerful members. Such groups were all but nonexistent in 1935. They would be formed only two years later, not from among Hitler's rivals but from the ranks of his allies, under very unusual and surprising conditions.

## 2

# "THAT DAMNED MARE!":
# THE ARMY TOP-BRASS SCANDAL

O N  A  C H I L L Y  day in September 1937, a political snowball started
rolling from the green expanses of the Tiergarten in Berlin. As
scandal followed scandal, the ensuing months witnessed a domino fall
of several prominent figures in the German General Staff, foreign service, and government ministries.[1] Heinrich Himmler, the commander
of the SS, and Hermann Göring, Hitler's right-hand man, were the
quickest to exploit and co-opt these events, using them to orchestrate
far-reaching purges in the ruling elites of the Third Reich. Their met-
aphorical fingerprints were discovered in a series of sensational in-
cidents, in which dubious, shadowy figures played fleeting roles and
then disappeared again into the night. Rumors and half-truths, inven-
tions and distortions were used in fierce political arm wrestling between the top brass of the SS and the Wehrmacht. The struggle, which
ended in clear victory for the former party, also led to the development
of an embryonic network of dissidents, which would eventually take
part in the July 20, 1944, plot to kill Hitler.[2]

It began when Field Marshal Werner von Blomberg, Hitler's minister of war, was forced to resign because of an embarrassing affair. "It's
all because of that damned mare!" said a General Staff colonel when
explaining its origin later. On that cold September day, Blomberg discovered to his dismay that his usual morning ride could not take place,
as his mare was suffering from paralysis. Like many officers, Blomberg

took great pleasure in the equestrian arts, and was used to riding every morning in the Tiergarten before the beginning of his busy daily schedule.

Hitler, ostensibly, did not have much reason to complain about Blomberg and his work. The general, an appointee of the late president Hindenburg, was nothing but a staunch party sympathizer who worked enthusiastically to further the Nazification of the German army. Far from being the moderate, responsible general imagined by some contemporaries, Blomberg was taken in by Hitler and the new National Revolution.[3] In the first years after the Nazi takeover, he even supported the arming of the SA. Thus, under a thin "apolitical" guise, he was one of the architects of Germany's Nazification.

However, from the party leadership's point of view, Blomberg had one substantial shortcoming: he was cold to Hitler's aggressive foreign policy. Just like Gen. Werner von Fritsch, the commander in chief of the army, Blomberg didn't have principled objections to war. His main concern was timing. He and Fritsch expressed the fear that the German army was not yet ready for a large-scale conflict. Hitler, never too happy to work with independent subordinates, was eager to co-opt the dramatic events of late 1937 and early 1938 in order to get rid of both men. Their undoing would prove to be the birth of an organized conspiracy against Hitler.

Blomberg decided to walk in the park without his horse and encountered a young woman named Eva Grün in a chance meeting that was to develop into a stormy love affair. The field marshal was fifty-nine years old, a widower glad to find a remedy for his loneliness. "He was crazy about me," Grün proudly recalled.[4] Blomberg asked, and received, the Führer's blessing for the union, and Hitler even volunteered to serve as a witness at the couple's wedding. After the ceremony, the happy couple traveled to Italy for their honeymoon.

Then, mysterious events began taking place. Senior officers in the General Staff received phone calls from giggling young women, congratulating the army for accepting "one of their own" into its ranks. At the same time, rumors of Frau Blomberg's complicity in pornographic modeling and prostitution had reached the Berlin Police Bureau. The chief of police, who did not know what to do with the hot potato, handed it over to Hermann Göring, the powerful "number two" in the Nazi hierarchy. Göring was quick to translate the incriminating evidence into political capital, and gave the file to Hitler.[5] The rumors quickly spread through the General Staff.

Army commander in chief General Fritsch and his chief of General Staff, Gen. Ludwig Beck, were furious. They petitioned Hitler to demote Blomberg without delay, as it was "inconceivable that the first officer in the army marry a whore." One officer interpreted his duty in somewhat broader terms. He traveled to Capri, Italy, where the Blombergs were spending their honeymoon, placed a loaded pistol on the field marshal's desk, and ordered him to end his own life. Blomberg did not comply with that order, but his career was over, and, on January 27, 1938, he was forced by Hitler to resign.[6]

Little did Fritsch know that his righteous anger would pave the way for his own professional undoing. Widely assumed to be Blomberg's natural successor, he was fiercely opposed both by Göring, who had set a greedy eye on the war minister portfolio, and by SS leaders Himmler and Reinhard Heydrich, who dreamed of shaping their organization as an alternative National Socialist elite army. In the preceding years, Fritsch had shown some opposition to the enlargement of the SS, and tension had been growing even among the lower echelons of the two military organizations. "Wait, you pigs," young SS soldiers threatened their Wehrmacht counterparts. "Soon, Himmler will become war minister, and then we'll show you who's the boss here."[7]

The idea to appoint Fritsch as the new minister was, hence, highly unattractive to Himmler and his SS colleagues. In order to stop the appointment—which was supported by Hitler—Himmler, Göring, and Heydrich hatched a plot to implicate Fritsch in homosexuality, a very serious charge in those days.

At the center of the plot stood one Otto Schmidt, a convicted criminal who made his living by seducing and extorting homosexuals. When arrested in 1935 and brought to the Gestapo, Schmidt gave away all of his contacts, incriminating hundreds of homosexuals, including prominent people. A grateful Gestapo official portrayed him as the "biggest expert on the homosexual scene in Berlin."[8] One of the victims was an elderly, sick cavalry captain named Frisch.

Someone, Schmidt or one of his interrogators, decided to add one letter to the name of this military homosexual, and thus Frisch was rechristened Fritsch. His rank was also upgraded from captain to general. The file reached Himmler and gave him the perfect opportunity to fabricate evidence on the "perversions" of the unsuspecting commander in chief. An investigation was promptly opened by the Gestapo, and its results, which implicated Fritsch in "unnatural sexual acts," was duly submitted to Hitler.

Thus, in summer 1935, Otto Schmidt's sensational testimony was as juicy as any yellow-press article could have been. At the end of 1933, declared the witness, he was strolling in the Wannsee train station when he suddenly saw an "evidently homosexual" rich old man, dressed in a dark coat with a collar made of fur and a black hat, white scarf, and monocle. The last item was important, as it was General Fritsch's trademark in the Third Reich's military elite.

The witness further testified to noticing the old man sneaking into the men's room along with a homosexual known as Bayern Seppl (Bavarian Joe). After some time the old man emerged, only to find Schmidt waiting for him at the door. The extorter introduced himself as police officer Krüger and ordered him to identify himself. The old man gave the name "General von Fritsch" and paid the "officer" five hundred marks, the first installment in a long chain of hush-money payments.

Hitler was initially unresponsive to the accusations. Himmler, who had long wished to get rid of Fritsch, submitted the investigation portfolio in 1935 but was all but ignored by his Führer. At that time, his relations with the army commander in chief were smooth, and the swift rearmament of Germany required close cooperation with the General Staff. Hitler, always a pragmatist in sexual questions, ordered the file to be promptly burned.

However, in 1938 things were different. The cautious Fritsch was not as esteemed in the Führer's headquarters, and the Blomberg scandal had made Hitler very suspicious regarding the personal lives of the Wehrmacht top brass. The Schmidt file, never burned but only stored on a dark shelf, was quickly produced. Hitler did not think initially to get rid of Fritsch, but when presented with the opportunity by his SS lieutenants, he didn't hesitate to use it to overhaul the leadership of the Wehrmacht.[9]

Fritsch was astounded to find himself in Blomberg's shoes. The

only difference was that he enjoyed the strong support of many senior generals, foremost among them his friend and admirer Chief
of the General Staff General Beck. The latter, though never a Nazi,
was a loyal adherent of Hitler at this point, but the cruel demise of
Fritsch created the first breach between him and the regime. In time,
Beck would become the leader of the German resistance movement.

# 3

# THE OFFICER, THE MAYOR, AND THE SPY

THE INVESTIGATION AGAINST Fritsch and the proceedings of the court-martial moved some younger, stauncher supporters of the general to rally to his defense. Naturally, some of these people were critical of the regime, especially of the arbitrary, dirty games of the SS and the Gestapo.[1] One of them was more than critical. A senior officer in the Amt Ausland/Abwehr, the military secret service, Lt. Col. Hans Oster was a closet anti-Nazi. The Fritsch affair gave him the perfect opportunity to unite like-minded people—from the army, the bureaucracy, the foreign ministry, and the conservative establishment —to fight for a legal, legitimate cause: to prove Fritsch's innocence, reinstate him as the commander in chief of the army, and lay bare the crimes of the Gestapo.[2]

Oster, a rising star of German military intelligence, was born in 1887, the son of a Dresden pastor. He was educated from an early age as a devout Protestant Christian, and as a staunch patriot and royalist he chose to embark on a military career. He was decorated for bravery during the Great War and, like many others, was disgusted by the democratic revolution of 1918–1919. He agreed to serve the republic, or the "frail, multi-party state" as he called it, only with great reluctance.[3] In the army, Oster was known as a talented, handsome officer, a good cello player, a lover of the equestrian arts, and a gregarious womanizer.

In January 1933, when the National Socialists took over the country, Oster was mired in his own affairs. A few days beforehand, on December 31, the army had discharged him because of a relationship he had had with the wife of a well-known professor. With his promising career in tatters, Oster spent several months hunting for work in vain. Salvation eventually came from unexpected quarters. Adm. Wilhelm Canaris, a senior officer in the Abwehr and an old friend, answered Oster's desperate pleas and petitioned for his case. The supreme command refused to reinstate him to active service, but thanks to Canaris he was appointed a civilian adviser in the secret service. Now, he was responsible for counterespionage and for monitoring subversive activity in government ministries. From this vantage point, Oster recognized the full extent of the terror, violence, and corruption in the new Nazi regime. He witnessed with disgust the persecution of the Jews and the "struggle" against the church. "I feel responsible before God for the Jews of Germany," he allegedly told a friend.[4] His religious sentiments were only part of the story. After his good friend the intelligence officer Ferdinand von Bredow was murdered by the Nazis in the Night of the Long Knives (June 1934), he started personally hating Hitler and his "gang of brigands."[5]

By 1938, Oster was growing in prominence in the Abwehr, and he was able to make small, gradual steps toward the implementation of his old dream: the establishment of a clandestine opposition movement. In his first two years of service, his commanders had looked down on him as an untrustworthy type who was forging connections for his own ends and flirting with the secretaries in the hallways. But in 1935, his luck changed.[6] His old friend and confidant Adm. Wilhelm Canaris became the new Abwehr chief and appointed Oster director of the Central Division—number two in the hierarchy of the Abwehr. The demoted officer was also reinstated to active service and eased back into uniform. Canaris ordered that nothing would be done in the Abwehr without Oster's knowledge.[7]

Oster was quick to use his new power to weave a network of contacts both in the Abwehr and throughout the military and civilian elites. No one was more skilled at pushing his way into prominent circles. Ever watchful for dangers and opportunities, he shared his real sentiments only with a handful of trusted friends. One of these men, who became Oster's eyes and ears in the Nazi security service, was Hans Bernd Gisevius—a Gestapo agent turned staunch enemy of the Nazi regime.

Gisevius was a schemer whose fingerprints could be seen all over the early anti-Nazi opposition. "His appearance was as stiff as the collar he wore," write Walter Laqueur and Richard Breitman. "A man of towering height, he looked like a caricature of a senior Prussian civil servant. He was so ostentatious in his behavior that few chose to believe at first that this strange creature was a bona fide secret agent. Some thought him a buffoon; others, an impostor putting on an elaborate act. Many believed he was a dyed-in-the-wool Nazi trying to hoodwink the Swiss and the allies."[8] His behavior gave the impression that he was a clown or a pompous windbag, who couldn't really be involved in illegal activity. Under the cover of this partly natural and partly fabricated persona, Gisevius gave a great service to the crystallizing opposition. He became an anti-Nazi secret agent and one of Oster's closest friends.

Contrary to what he wrote in his memoirs, Gisevius began his career as an adherent of National Socialism. Before Hitler's rise to power, he was a nationalist student leader, quick to lend his support to the new government. He won a coveted post in the Prussian police and elbowed his way up the hierarchy through ploys and manipulations. After several months, he was transferred to the Gestapo headquarters in Berlin. However, his stormy character and taste for schemes had made him unpopular in influential circles, and he was quick to make enemies in the Gestapo and beyond. Slowly, his power started to wane. In 1934, the head of the Gestapo delivered the coup de grâce, ordering him transferred to a marginal job at the Prussian Ministry of the Interior.

Gradually, Gisevius had turned against the Nazi regime in toto. The hatred he felt for the Gestapo leaders who marginalized him spread to the SS, Himmler, and finally the Führer himself. And contrary to the impression of many, his actions were not those of a mere selfish opportunist: as a Gestapo official he became privy to the full extent of Nazi terror, and though he could not care less about the fate of the Communists, he was troubled by the persecution of the Jews and nonconformist clergymen. Oster, who became known to him during his time at the Gestapo, had him transferred to the Abwehr in 1938 as a special civilian adviser (*Sonderführer*). Gisevius used his new job and contacts in the police top brass to supply Oster with secret information from inside the system. From then on, he became an important member in the Oster circle and developed a radical oppositionist ideology: the Nazi regime had to be crushed by any means. If violence and murder were necessary, so be it. "A friend de-scribed him as a gangster fighting for a good cause," write Laqueur and Breitman. "Very self-centered, a strong proclivity toward con-spiracy led him to plot not only against the Nazis but also sometimes against his own side."[9] It is quite possible that through Gisevius's me-diation, Oster came to meet a third key figure, former lord mayor of Leipzig Dr. Carl Friedrich Goerdeler.

Goerdeler had nothing of Oster's cunning and sleekness, nor of Gisevius's predilection for schemes and manipulations. With his gray hair, great height, and irritating tendency to preach, he came across as a humorless bureaucrat tied heart and soul to the establishment. This persona seems incongruous with his decision to go in for illegal op-position. Nevertheless, he went all the way from reluctant coopera-tion with Hitler to unrelenting resistance. For many high-placed ci-vilians and officers, he became the resistance embodied. What could have moved such an upright person to cross the line so emphatically?

Carl Friedrich Goerdeler was born in Schneidemühl, a village in the then German province of Posen (now in Poland). After graduat-ing in law and economics, he served in the Great War as an officer in the reserves. Then, he embarked on a successful municipal career in several localities, including the important urban center of Königsberg. In 1931, he reached the climax of his career, serving simultaneously as lord mayor of Leipzig and Reich price commissioner. In the stormy years preceding the Nazi takeover, President Hindenburg even con-sidered appointing him a chancellor.

Goerdeler devoted much of his energy and attention to the town of Leipzig. There he was known as a diligent mayor with authoritar-ian tendencies. In 1933, he supported Hitler's rise to power and will-ingly worked with the new government, but his relations with the local Nazis were already unsteady. Conflicts arose, for example, over Goer-deler's refusal to fly the swastika flag over the town hall or to change "Jewish" street names. He did harbor prejudices against German Jews, but (as his daughter told the author of this book) he supported the "clean" anti-Semitism of the Nuremberg Laws, because he thought they would restrain the party "radicals" from practicing anti-Semitic violence. As early as April 1933, to protest the boycott of Jewish shops, he "went in formal dress to a Jewish quarter of his city to protect Jews and their businesses, and he used the city police to free Jews who had been detained and beaten by SA storm troopers."[10]

Step by step, though, municipal-council Nazis undermined Goerdeler's position. Nazi anti-Semitic legislation, such as the prohibition of Jews' using public swimming pools and other communal bathing facilities, applied also in Leipzig, and Deputy Mayor Haacke's pressure presumably forced Goerdeler to endorse this bylaw.[11] He was also troubled by the persecution of the church, the aggressive foreign policy, and what he saw as irresponsible fiscal policy. The lord mayor, whose authority was slipping from his hands, became increasingly embittered.

In 1936, Goerdeler was heading to the point of no return. The American historian Harold C. Deutsch, then a young journalist, recounted the following meeting in Goerdeler's office:

> [Goerdeler said that] the foremost German problem today is the re-establishment of ordinary human decency. To his amazed visitor he then rapidly detailed a formidable list of iniquities he perceived in Hitler's Germany, mentioning also some of his troubles with the local Nazis. Rising at the end to conduct his visitor to the door, he passed a large window looking out on the space before the city hall. Pointing in the direction of the famous Gewandhaus, before which stood a statue of Mendelssohn, he said: "There is one of my problems. They [the brownshirts] are after me to remove that monument. But if they ever touch it I am finished here."[12]

Many future members of the resistance had similar "here and no further" moments. For Goerdeler, the monument issue was a matter of principle. He saw himself as the real protector of German *Kultur* and was disgusted by the National Socialist disregard for the tradition he cherished. The monument was also a matter of principle for the local Nazi leaders. After all, for how long could the party tolerate a mayor who rejected the fundamentals of its policy, particularly on the "Jewish question"? Members of the municipal council even complained about Goerdeler's wife, "who is known as a Jew-lover throughout the town, and is even not ashamed to drive an official vehicle to go shopping in

Jewish shops."[13] Deputy Mayor Haacke wrote to the authorities that Goerdeler was estranged from virtually all aspects of National Socialist ideology. In particular, he could not understand the party's hatred of German Jews:

> The Mendelssohn monument affair clearly reflects Dr. Goerdeler's approach to the Jewish Question. As my letter indicates, Goerdeler made things enormously difficult whenever [it was demanded] to change a Jewish street name. Even if he is now using the monument as a pretext for resigning, I am sincerely convinced that the reasons for [that step] go much deeper ... He came to understand that the days of his worldview were numbered due to the growing success of National Socialism, and drew the final conclusion.[14]

The monument was removed in November 1936 when Goerdeler was away at a conference in Helsinki. Haacke used the opportunity to get rid of the statue in order to "spare the lord mayor the unpleasant decision."[15] When Goerdeler returned, he promptly resigned from his post: "Thus I decided without hesitation not to take responsibility for the desecration of culture [*Kulturschande*]. All of us listened to Mendelssohn's songs with great pleasure and sang them as well. To deny Mendelssohn, is nothing but an absurd, cowardly act ... I still hope to go back to serving the nation, when its atmosphere is purer and cleaner. By my resignation I protested against the removal of the Mendelssohn monument in front of the entire world."[16]

One year after his resignation, Goerdeler had finally joined the cause of Oster and Gisevius, with whom he was well acquainted. This strange trio—the secret service colonel, the former Gestapo official, and the retired lord mayor—became a rallying point for the remnants of the German opposition. Together they formed the first network of resistance in the German army, which was destined to undergo dramatic structural shifts and waves of expansion and collapse from 1938 to 1944.

The first incarnation of their network is called a "clique" in network-analysis theory, defined as "an informal association of people among whom there is a degree of group feeling and intimacy and in which certain group norms of behavior have been established."[17] Gisevius's memoirs indicate that most or all members were friends or close acquaintances who met often. Rules of compartmentalization (every member knowing only the minimum required to carry out his tasks) were all but nonexistent: only in rare cases did members withhold information from their coconspirators. Division of labor was also minimal, and the roles of the founders and members were vaguely defined, if at all. However, even in this early incarnation of the movement, one can follow some patterns that characterized it to the very end.

The first and most important guiding pattern defined here is the rule of revolutionary mutation. As the Gestapo later observed, "The recruitment of new members and confidants was mostly done on the basis of previous ties of friendship and acquaintance."[18] This corresponds to the observation of network analyst David Knoke that networks of insurgency are usually created on the basis of existing legal networks. In this way, Knoke has written, "an insurgency can more easily attach these loyalties to the movement itself. Rather than arduously building new commitments from scratch, activists can persuade potential supporters that the movement organization offers a natural expression of their current solidary sentiments . . . Recruitment to any social activity requires a preceding contact with a recruiting agent, more often a social intimate than an impersonal actor."[19]

To keep their revolutionary effectiveness, such networks have to be relatively autonomous and protected from the suspicious eyes of the security services. Under the conditions of National Socialist Germany, they were able to exist in half-autonomous social "islands," such as certain segments of the working class, the high bureaucracy, the conservative right, and above all the army. The Gestapo investigators were again on the mark when they observed that the rise of a military resistance movement was possible only because the officer corps had historically seen itself as autonomous from the "civilian authorities" and subject only to "its own rules." More importantly, the SS and the Gestapo were not allowed to quickly penetrate it or interfere in its internal affairs.[20] Even though many officers were National Socialist by conviction and their numbers increased over the years, most hesitated to "inform" on their "comrades" to the civilian police. Without such an autonomous tradition, the efforts of Oster and company to recruit new members at the officer corps would almost certainly have landed them in prison.

Inside these autonomous islands of the bureaucracy, nobility, conservative right, and officer corps, there existed complicated networks of kinship, marriage, and social ties, many of them based on joint schooling or military service. The solidarity in these networks was strong enough to limit the extent to which "strangers" could penetrate them. Most of the networks were never involved in opposition to the Nazi regime, but a tiny portion went through a process of revolutionary mutation in the opening months of 1938. Under the auspices of Oster, Gisevius, and Goerdeler, they morphed from social networks into conspiratorial ones.

One of the main venues for this mutation was a prestigious Berlin club named the Free Society for Scholarly Entertainment, popularly known as the Wednesday Society (Mittwoch Gesellschaft). This venerable social institution had its roots in the nineteenth century and held strictly observed rules of scholarly elitism. Only a handful of people, each of them a respected expert in his field, were allowed to join the club. The assembly met every second Wednesday at the house of one of its members. The host had to give a lecture in his field of expertise, which was recorded in the protocol. After each lecture, there was ample time for discussion and socializing. The Wednesday Club was never a resistance group as such, and some of its members, like the race scientist Eugen Fischer, were virulent Nazis.

However, the general atmosphere in the club was critical toward the system, and several of its prominent members, among them Ludwig Beck and Ulrich von Hassell, ended up in the inner circle of the German resistance. Generally speaking, the club was an ideal venue for revolutionary mutation: it was strictly private, strangers were not allowed into meetings, and criticism of National Socialist ideology was tolerated. Most importantly, the strong solidarity between members decreased the risk of denunciation. Goerdeler, who was not a club member but a friend of many who were, found it an especially promising recruitment ground.[21]

Goerdeler, Oster, and Gisevius fulfilled different functions in the fledgling clandestine network. Goerdeler and Oster were "salesmen," to borrow the typology of Malcolm Gladwell. Namely, they moved to mutate preexisting social networks, to import the idea of resistance, to inflame it, and to keep it intact. Just as in other social networks, those created by salesmen were maintained by "connectors," people with unusual social skills and contacts in various social circles who were able to disseminate the subversive ideas of the salesmen. Gisevius and Oster were certainly important connectors in the early resistance, though Goerdeler also fulfilled that role to some extent. At this early stage, anyway, the roles were far from being clearly defined.[22]

In winter 1938, the network was mainly intended to undermine the SS by defending General Fritsch.[23] That esteemed cause won some qualified support from Chief of Staff Gen. Ludwig Beck. At this stage, he was not even close to being a resistance fighter, and wanted only to help his friend and commanding officer. True, during the Fritsch crisis he came to distrust the Nazi leadership, but to stage a coup d'état would have run contrary to everything sacred in the Prussian military tradition. "Conspiracy and mutiny do not exist in the lexicon of the German officer," Beck allegedly told General Staff officer Franz Halder, in response to Halder's proposal to organize a violent reprisal against the Gestapo.[24]

Practically, Oster and his friends were tilting at windmills. Whatever the results of his trial might be, Fritsch was gone for good as far as Hitler was concerned. Meanwhile, he had already appointed a new commander in chief, an unimpressive compromise candidate named Walther von Brauchitsch.[25] Worse still, contrary to the perception of Oster and his friends, Fritsch was never a closet resistance fighter, not even an oppositionist. Although he did become embittered, he continued to admire Hitler to his last day. Yet the quest to defend him was not completely futile, as it helped to draw the conspirators together.

Simultaneously with Brauchitsch's appointment, Hitler established his control over the army. Taking the war portfolio for himself, he appointed Gen. Wilhelm Keitel as his chief of staff and head of the Supreme Command of the Armed Forces (OKW). Keitel, who during the war was often nicknamed Lakeitel (a pun on his name, *Lakai* can be translated as "lackey"), was no more than a petty bureaucrat.[26] The man who was expected to represent the interests of the army to Hitler rarely dared to question or to doubt, let alone to criticize, his leader. Keitel, according to Constantine FitzGibbon, was "obsequious to his seniors and hectoring to his juniors, [and] would have well become the head waiter in an expensive and squalid night club."[27] In a way, Keitel's appointment symbolized the new, weakened position of the Wehrmacht after the 1938 reshuffle. Fritsch was loyal to Hitler, but he could speak his mind. Keitel did not even pretend to have an independent voice. Far from being the "second pillar of the state," alongside the party, the Wehrmacht of Keitel and Brauchitsch became a tool to be used by the Führer at will.

The reshuffle was not limited to the military. Hitler used the opportunity to deepen the Nazification of some major government ministries, too.[28] The purge created a more solid National Socialist bureaucracy in preparation for war, but simultaneously some of the demoted gravitated to the opposition clique of Oster, Gisevius, and Goerdeler. In addition to their personal embitterment and joint aspiration to protect Fritsch, many of the newly won members were deeply concerned with Hitler's irresponsible foreign policy and incessant use of violence.

The first venue for the purges was the foreign ministry. Hitler replaced the conservative minister Constantine von Neurath with his sidekick Joachim von Ribbentrop. Neurath, like Blomberg and Fritsch, was a loyal follower of Nazi policy but still a bit too cautious for Hitler's taste. Ribbentrop's appointment, which was taken badly by some conservatives at the foreign ministry, gave a pretext for establishing a minuscule opposition group in the diplomatic corps. The central actor in the cell was Erich Kordt, a young, bespectacled adviser known as a rising star in the ministry. Ironically, he was trusted even by the new Nazi minister, who relied on his expertise in international affairs and entrusted him with top-secret documents. Officially, he was a party member; he even held a high honorary rank in the SS.[29]

Kordt, however, was a closet anti-Nazi and a confidant of Hans Oster. From his privileged position at the ministry, protected by Ribbentrop and his SS uniform, he was able to supply the opposition with valuable inside information. As usual, ties of kinship and friendship in the ministry were used to bring about a revolutionary mutation. Kordt's most loyal ally was his older brother Theo, a promising young diplomat serving at the London embassy.

Another key figure in the incumbent conspiracy at the foreign ministry was Ulrich von Hassell, the German ambassador to Italy—an old-school diplomat, a well-educated conservative, and a patriot. Hassell, too, supported Hitler right after the takeover but was later horrified by the Gestapo reign of terror, the persecution of the Jews, and the harassment of the church. In addition, he had strong professional reservations against National Socialist foreign policy, especially the alignment with Italy and Japan against the Western powers.[30] He was finally sacked as part of the reshuffle of 1938, maybe as a result of his nonconformist views.

Capitalizing on his influence in conservative circles, Goerdeler spread the message of resistance among old-school politicians and noblemen. One of his closest allies in this endeavor was the colorful aristocrat Ewald von Kleist-Schmenzin, a major landholder and politician in rural Pomerania. Kleist, renowned for his honesty and bravery, was an implacable enemy of the Nazi regime from January 1933 onward.[31] The staunch conservative, monarchist, and antidemocrat was one of few members of the German National People's Party to believe that the real enemy was not on the left but on the right.[32] National Socialism, a new pagan religion, was bound to destroy Germany, as its race cult was diametrically opposed to Christianity and the values of the German-Prussian tradition.[33] For the biblically minded Kleist, Hitler and his followers were a new reincarnation of the worshipers of Ba'al and Ashera, the old Canaanite idols. To oppose them, the true champions of faith and nation would have to be rallied, "All the knees which have not bowed unto Baal" (1 Kings 19:18).[34]

Kleist's hatred of fellow conservatives who turned into Nazis knew no bounds. The leaders of the German right, he claimed, betrayed their fatherland, religion, and nation. Therefore, in the future, people would say, "As godless as a Protestant pastor, as characterless as a Prussian civil servant, and as honorless as a Prussian officer." He himself refused to donate money to the Nazi Party, not even a mark, and flatly declined to fly the swastika flag over his manor house. A special role awaited his son and follower Ewald-Heinrich, one of the few would-be assassins of Hitler.[35]

From then on, the German resistance movement began to take shape. Lieutenant Colonel Oster connected the officers and the civilians, and through Goerdeler he came to know Ewald von Kleist-Schmenzin and his conservative friends. The thrust of his efforts, though, was directed at the army itself. The biggest fish to catch was the chief of the General Staff, Ludwig Beck. The tactic was to surround him with enemies of the regime. For that purpose, Oster formed a contact with Gen. Franz Halder, a General Staff officer known as a Beck confidant and a staunch anti-Nazi. At the same time, Oster applied increasing pressure on his commander, secret service chief Adm. Wilhelm Canaris, and gradually convinced him to support the conspiracy. "Until our last breath," Oster wrote, "we shall stand firm, according to our education as children and later as soldiers. We have nothing to fear but the wrath of God."[36]

But what does it mean to "stand firm"? Forming oppositional networks is all very well, but Oster had no clue how to overthrow the regime. He did have some key military allies, first and foremost Halder, but Halder could do nothing without the support of General Beck, his hesitant commander. In any case, the formidability of the Nazi regime and the weakness of the army precluded most options for active insurgency. The conspirators had to work slowly and carefully, as even one informer would be enough to obliterate the movement altogether. In addition, civilians could not arrange coups d'état by themselves, and only a small number of generals were even slightly sympathetic to the conspiracy.

While Oster's tiny network was slowly expanding, Hitler reshuffled the political cards. On March 12, 1938, following formidable diplomatic bullying, the German army entered Austria, and Hitler's own homeland was united with the Reich. Support for the Anschluss in Austria was anyway skyrocketing, and most Austrians loudly welcomed the invading troops. The first overt act of Nazi international aggression was an astounding success, and not a shot had been fired.

The newspaper headlines celebrated the Anschluss, and it became the major topic of discussion in the elites and the officer corps. With all the brouhaha, the ugly plot against Fritsch was forgotten. The general was acquitted by a court-martial chaired by Hermann Göring, but he never resumed his position as commander in chief. In a conversation with the Wehrmacht leadership, Hitler expressed his personal sympathy for Fritsch's fate but insisted that as a leader, he could not go back on his word.[37] The frustrated Fritsch was angry, but he consistently refused to cooperate with the opposition. "Hitler is Germany's fate, for better or worse," he told Hassell, the former ambassador who tried to win him over to the network.[38]

The recruitment efforts of the network, however, were focused not on Fritsch but on the chief of the General Staff, Beck, whose internal break with the Nazi regime was drawing ever closer. Like his fellow officers, he was a firm Anschluss supporter, but unlike them, he opposed the way in which this fruit was plucked: through Hitler's military bullying. When ordered by the Führer to draw plans for Case Otto, the code name for a German invasion of Austria, he agreed to do so only reluctantly, arguing that Germany was not yet ready. After the Anschluss, he praised the Führer for his ability to fulfill his dream without shedding blood, but the gap between him and the government was widening. The chief of the General Staff began to believe that this would be only the beginning of Hitler's military adventures, and the result might be a disastrous world war. The unrelenting Oster, ever watchful, was quick to notice the cracks in Beck's defenses, and turned him into a personal project. Shortly afterward, he noticed an opportunity, a large-scale international crisis that was to transform Beck's theoretical critique of the regime into a practical one.

# 4

# "IN THE DARKEST COLORS": THE DECISION OF GENERAL BECK

B Y SUMMER 1937, Field Marshal Blomberg was working on "Case Green," a plan for the invasion of Czechoslovakia. It was clear to the generals that Hitler was striving to crash the Czech state by occupying the German-speaking Sudetenland. By doing that, he hoped to swallow the region's formidable border fortifications, mines, iron ore, and other natural resources. The meek response of the Western powers to the Anschluss had removed the last barriers to action, and the great Sudeten crisis was on the horizon.

Czechoslovakia, a creation of the Treaty of Versailles, was a multiethnic democracy suffering from incessant feuds between the Czech majority and the minorities.[1] The most troublesome minority was the three-million-strong German community, concentrated mainly in the Sudetenland. After 1933, many of the Czech Germans had become ardent Nazis, and their leaders received orders straight from Berlin. The local Nazi offshoot, the Sudeten German Party, demanded full separation from Czechoslovakia and union with the Reich. The party chairman, ·Konrad Henlein, summarized his agenda in a secret 1937 memorandum: to win large parts of Czechoslovakia, not only the Sudetenland, for the German Reich.[2] Hitler had applied increasing pressure on Czechoslovakia, while Britain and France, ever fearful of a new European war, were doing nothing tangible to stop him.

On Saturday, May 20, 1938, only two months after the Anschluss, General Keitel submitted Case Green to Hitler. The scheme presupposed the annexation of Austria to the German Reich. It read, "It is my [Hitler's] irrevocable decision to crush Czechoslovakia by military action in the near future . . . Using the opportune moment is required for success."[3] According to this plan, Germany was to occupy Czechoslovakia by use of a diplomatic provocation in order to justify, in the eyes of some European states, a military "response" and occupation. More than a few officers were uncomfortable with the plan, but very few were brave enough to show open dissent. Gen. Ludwig Beck, chief of the General Staff, was the most prominent member of this tiny group.

A former approver of the Nazi regime, Beck had praised the 1933 takeover as the "first ray of light since 1918." Now, however, he was horrified at the possible consequences of Hitler's foreign policy.[4] To a great extent he felt like a military Cassandra, the only one who could clearly see the approaching abyss. As a quiet, restrained, and educated officer well versed in strategy and military history, Beck believed the Clausewitzian dictum that war is the "continuation of policy by other means" and therefore must be preceded by careful political deliberations. A war is not an adventure, and a leader should never start one without a truly justified cause. In addition, Beck was one of the few officers in the General Staff who saw the army high command not only as a military tool but also as a full partner in shaping security policy. This view was completely foreign to Hitler, who saw himself as the omnipotent leader and the generals as his military yes-men.[5]

When Blomberg had asked him to draft a theoretical study, codenamed Schulung, on a military advance into Czechoslovakia in 1935, Beck had expressed opposition to the invasion. The chief of the General Staff was reluctant to draft such a plan, theoretical or not. At the time, his resistance was not principled but practical. Germany might invade Czechoslovakia, but only after diplomacy was exhausted, and by no means before 1940.[6]

The misunderstanding between Beck and Hitler was profound. Beck certainly applauded the "breaking of the shackles of Versailles." He, too, strove for territorial expansion and German hegemony in central Europe. He also recognized the German need for "living space" (Lebensraum), but his interpretation of the term was different from the Führer's: not unlimited expansion in the east but, rather, limited takeovers (peaceful, if possible) of German-speaking territories, mainly Austria and the Sudetenland. Unlike Hitler, Beck recognized the principle of self-determination and was unenthusiastic about controlling "non-German" nations. After Germany had seized its "rights" and expanded to the 1914 borders (plus Austria and the Sudetenland), further expansion should be economic, not military. Hitler, by contrast, envisioned a large-scale European war, leading to the defeat of France, the crumbling of Russia, and the occupation of coveted Lebensraum in the east. Beck was opposed to such policy for moral and practical reasons. For him, though war was "part of the divine order," a real statesman should never start one unnecessarily. He was particularly opposed to an aggressive war against Britain and France. "The three nations share Europe together," he wrote in 1937, "and their problems are therefore to be solved diplomatically, taking the balance of power into account."[7]

Indeed, Beck's worst nightmare was a head-on clash between the three nations on the Sudeten question. His dread over such a confrontation and its aftermath was expressed in a stream of memoranda sent to his superior, General Brauchitsch. These memoranda were written in a military, professional language, and did not challenge the basic premises of the political leadership. On May 30, 1938, for example, Beck wrote that "although Czechoslovakia in its current boundaries is intolerable for Germany, Britain and France will not tolerate further transitions in the balance of power in favor of the Reich, which is not ready for a new conflict." Therefore, if the Führer's plan is to be implemented, "it is impossible to portray the fate of Germany in a future war except in the darkest colors."[8]

Beck's grievances were naturally ignored, and he became more isolated and embittered by the day. Still, he convinced himself that Hitler was redeemable, if only one could show him the way of reason by keeping the party radicals at bay. At the same time, his contacts with Goerdeler, Oster, and critics of the regime in the Wednesday Club meetings made him more and more susceptible to revolutionary mutation. As Beck became increasingly isolated from the leadership, his resistance to such mutation gradually eased.

In July 1938, Beck was outsmarted by his rivals. Pro-Nazi officers in the General Staff, above all Walther von Reichenau and Ernst Busch, showed enthusiastic support for the Führer's plans, and even generals who sympathized with Beck were reluctant to openly take his side.

For years Beck had been an advocate for greater political influence for the General Staff, seeing his struggle against Hitler as a campaign for institutional independence. Therefore, he felt deeply hurt to see his comrades defecting one by one.[9] In his despair, he suggested that the generals resign en masse. Only such a threat, he believed, could bring Hitler back onto the path of reason. He himself was adamant: never would he take responsibility for a disastrous European confrontation, setting Germany against all the other Western powers. His intentions were evident in a memorandum he wrote on July 16, 1938, later to become a seminal text of the German resistance: "Critical decisions about the future of the nation are at stake. History will cast blood guilt on these leaders [of the Wehrmacht], if they refuse to act according to the dictates of their conscience and their professional, political knowledge. Military obedience finds its limits when their knowledge, conscience and responsibility forbid following an order . . . Unusual times require unusual actions."[10]

It is easy to imagine how it tormented Beck, a man who had grown up in an atmosphere in which obedience was a paramount value, to reach a point where "military obedience finds its limits." Only a few months before, during the Fritsch crisis, he had told Halder that "conspiracy and mutiny do not exist in the lexicon of the German officer." Now, his attitude was changing. Suddenly, it was not only opposition to foreign and security policy that was on the line; the Gestapo's regime of terror must be held in check, too. If only the Führer could be liberated from the Nazi radicals, Beck convinced himself, a total reform in Germany could and should be implemented. Shocked by his own insights, Beck communicated to the generals the essentials of his new program: "For the Führer; against war; against the rule of party functionaries; peace with the church; freedom of speech and the end of Cheka [Soviet secret police] style terror; . . . restoration of the rule of law; an end to the construction of palaces; housing for the common people; Prussian decency and simplicity."[11]

Caught up in his idealism, Beck still failed to understand that the Führer himself was the driving force behind the ills he described. Like many others, his political education came at the cost of a devastating personal blow. On August 4, he submitted an antiwar speech to General Brauchitsch, to be delivered to the leading generals. Brauchitsch, too, understood that a world war would be disastrous for Germany. At first, he accepted Beck's plan, only to get cold feet at the eleventh hour. He did not use the new, more critical speech, but instead read Beck's old memorandum from July 16. The generals, except Reichenau and Busch, agreed in principle but refused to take practical measures. Hitler, who had had enough of Beck's endless, tedious memoranda, seriously considered dismissing him. The chief of staff perfectly understood his position and resigned on August 18. As his successor he recommended Gen. Franz Halder, whose criticism of the regime was much more radical than his own. Whether because of Beck's recommendation or not, Halder was indeed appointed by Hitler as the new chief of the General Staff.[12]

Beck was deeply disappointed with his army comrades. "Brauchitsch [has] left me in the lurch," he said in disgust. The Wehrmacht leaders were nothing but "mediocrities, fools and criminals," and Hitler was no better. The Nazi regime, he confessed to Halder, could never reform itself. In another remark, he declared that he would never participate in "National Socialist adventurous wars."[13] The man who refused to rebel to protect his friend and superior during the Fritsch crisis had undergone a change when exposed to Hitler's adventurism in the Sudetenland.

Lieutenant Colonel Oster realized that Beck was ready for a revolutionary mutation. Oster visited Beck again and again in Goethestrasse, wrote Nicholas Reynolds, "urging, pleading, persuading. If any one man can be said to have enlisted Beck in the resistance, it was Oster."[14]

Now, relieved of his command, Beck was finally free to rethink his former life and principles. He devoted most of his time to military history, and gravitated more and more toward Oster, Gisevius, and Goerdeler. After a few months, in 1939, he admitted that there was no choice, and a coup d'état might be the only way. The word *mutiny*, it seems, had entered the lexicon of the German officer. Beck's revolutionary mutation was complete.

It is uncertain whether Beck gave his consent to the coup plans, which were secretly drafted at the time. In the dark, General Halder held long talks with the leading conspirators and forged a secret agreement with Lieutenant Colonel Oster: the moment Hitler ordered the army to invade Czechoslovakia would be the moment to stage the coup d'état.[15]

# 5

# THE BIRD AND ITS CAGE:
# FIRST ATTEMPT AT COUP D'ÉTAT,
# SEPTEMBER 1938

SEPTEMBER 1938 WAS a stormy month in Europe. The Sudeten crisis reached its peak, and the tension between Germany, England, and France was growing by the day. The fear of war was spreading throughout the continent. The conspirators, however, were full of
hope. On September 5, it seemed that their coup would soon be realized. Hopes were high mainly because of the appointment of Gen.
Franz Halder—known for his anti-Nazi sentiments—as chief of the
General Staff. Hans Oster, the main strategist and connector of the
resistance clique, was certain that the new chief would be a better
partner than his hesitant predecessor, General Beck. Halder, after all,
seemed determined to prevent a continental war at whatever cost, as
he was certain that such a war would bring about the end of Germany.
Thus, Oster hoped that a move against the war could develop into a
full-scale revolt against Hitler and the Nazi regime. Gisevius was not
so certain:

> When I rang the doorbell of Halder's apartment, the master of
> the house himself opened the door. Even a chief of staff could
> not be sure of the reliability of his servants. He avoided the usual
> polite phrase and allusive circumlocutions and plunged directly
> in medias res. For several hours we talked with what was to me
> such singular frankness that I involuntarily thought: Isn't this man

the general? . . . My astonishment was boundless on meeting him, for before me sat a colorless, bespectacled schoolmaster, his hair combed back, with somewhat taut features in an inexpressive face . . . The whole impression he gave was that of the so called "little man." "Hitler had picked out an obedient functionary," I thought to myself, and I could not understand how others could consider him determined and eager to act.[1]

Gisevius was pleasantly surprised to find appearances deceiving. He listened to the general attack Hitler more radically than he himself ever had. When, for example, Gisevius raised the possibility that Hitler's evil deeds were related less to his personality and more to the inevitable dynamics of revolution, Halder cut him short: "That madman, that criminal," he said, "was consciously steering Germany into war, possibly because of his 'sexually pathological constitution' which created in him the desire to see blood flow."[2] Halder made it very clear that he was determined to prevent war by any means, and he even called the Führer a "blood sucker." Still, he and Gisevius couldn't agree about timing. Gisevius, probably representing Oster's position, urged Halder to order a coup immediately. He promised Halder support from senior police and Wehrmacht commanders.

Halder remained unconvinced, and he took Gisevius's promises and predictions with understandable skepticism. He reminded the younger man that the army itself was in a difficult position, and insisted (correctly) that most young soldiers and officers supported the Führer. No, a coup could not be declared here and now. It could be done only once the regime had been beaten or at least humiliated by an external power. As most officers believed that war would be disastrous, Halder saw the trigger as a Franco-British declaration of war. In such a case, the army could overthrow Hitler and be hailed by the public as the savior of the peace. Many Germans, after all, still remembered the horrors of the Great War, and only the fear of a renewed European conflict could free them from Hitler's charms. Therefore, Halder concluded, he would delay the order for the coup until the last moment before the war. Gisevius returned to Oster somewhat disappointed, so he was surprised to hear that Halder had instructed the conspirators to plan the coup down to the last detail. When Hitler ordered the army to invade Czechoslovakia, Halder would issue the orders. Instead of Prague, the Wehrmacht would march to Berlin.[3]

Meanwhile, National Socialist foreign policy was working at full speed, and the invasion of Czechoslovakia was drawing nigh. On August 3, Foreign Minister Ribbentrop wrote with self-assurance to all Reich ambassadors in Europe that "no third side will be so reckless as to attack Germany." That document indicates that Hitler and his closest associates were unafraid of interventions by Great Britain, France, or the Soviet Union. Czechoslovakia was isolated, they thought, and would be easy prey.[4]

Oster, Goerdeler, and Gisevius did not agree. They trusted England and France. According to their political reasoning, France could not abandon its Czechoslovakian ally, because that would severely harm its reputation in Europe. They were also certain that Britain, mindful of the balance of power, would not permit Hitler to dominate central Europe. Dr. Hjalmar Schacht, the head of the Reichsbank and a close collaborator of Oster and Gisevius, boasted about his expertise on British foreign policy. He promised his associates that Britain would never let Hitler occupy the Sudetenland unchecked.[5] The conspirators knew that only a resolute British "no" to Hitler, backed by a force of arms, might motivate Halder to stage a coup. Oster, though, was not content to wait for British cooperation. He tried to ensure it by sending his own emissaries to London to inform Downing Street of the potential coup. He knew he was involved in treason and that each one of the emissaries would be subject to the death penalty. Still, they were ready to take the risk.[6]

The first volunteer was Dr. Carl Goerdeler. After his troubles with the Nazis at Leipzig, the authorities were suspicious of his intentions and initially refused to give him back his passport. Goerdeler overcame this difficulty with a ruse: he promised Göring that he would send him reports on the public mood in Britain and France. That covered up the true nature of his mission: to warn leading circles in Britain that Hitler was going to war and that any attempts to appease him would be fruitless.[7]

With financial help from rich friends and benefactors, Goerdeler could freely travel around Europe and beyond. In Britain, he had to reckon with a sophisticated National Socialist propaganda machine, spreading around the world a glittering vision of the new, peace-loving German nation. Goerdeler's daughter, Marianne Meyer-Krahmer, recalled many years later,

> The National Socialists were masters of propaganda. The "world youth" was invited to a gigantic "peace festival in Berlin" [the Berlin Olympic Games of 1936]. Hundreds of dignitaries came, and honored not only the sport, but also the Führer of the host country. One of the teams even greeted the leaders at the gallery with "Heil Hitler." The party had staged the games aptly, and the event was really splendid, with sky-illuminating projectors and the first Olympic village built in Berlin, as a meeting place for athletes from all countries ... The reactions were particularly positive. Upon returning to their countries, the athletes enthusiastically reported their impressions from "New Germany"—clean streets, settled social relations, happy people—that was the picture intended to be portrayed through them. The press, too, reported favorably ... People did not want to understand or guess that behind the glittering image crime and barbarism lurk.[8]

Goerdeler, therefore, had to calculate his steps carefully. Still, he didn't just warn his British counterparts of Hitler's foreign policy, he also took pains to disclose the violence and terror of the regime inside German borders. By doing so, he hoped to convince his counterparts that Hitler was not a legitimate politician who could be parleyed with, but a dangerous adversary with whom no compromise was possible.

Goerdeler had visited Britain in June 1937 and had given a speech at the Liberal Club in London. His host, the industrialist Arthur Young, related later,

> Goerdeler impressed us all with his forceful, humorous, and likeable personality; superb moral courage dominated the man. He left no doubts in our mind about the evil things that Hitler and his associates were doing and would continue to do with increasing speed if no checks were applied. He felt that Britain could exert such a check by being more forceful in her negotiations with Hit-

ler and his associates. He pleaded most earnestly for a firm policy in dealing with Hitler as being the only one that Hitler would understand aright; and the only policy likely to retard his evil purposes. We must in all our doings be firm, and call "black black and white white," as he put it. Any equivocation or appeasement would be interpreted as weakness; would inflame Hitler's megalomaniac propensities; and would discourage the liberal forces inside Germany who had no illusions about the Hitler regime and who, as Goerdeler contended, were anxious to co-operate with us to find a solution to the Hitler problem.[9]

One of the dinner guests was a British politician who had arranged for Goerdeler a one-on-one meeting with Sir Robert Vansittart, undersecretary at the Foreign Office and one of the most formidable opponents of appeasement toward Germany. Vansittart agreed to accept a memorandum from Goerdeler and to pass it on to the cabinet, but there the matter rested. Foreign Minister Anthony Eden rejected the memorandum out of deep mistrust for the German conspirators. Like many other British statesmen, he was reluctant to cooperate with subversive politicians from other countries, whose motives and intentions were unclear to him. Consequently, His Majesty's Cabinet never knew about Goerdeler's visit.

In April 1938, when the Sudeten crisis was still in its initial stages, Oster was already beginning to envision with his confidants a coup d'état. Goerdeler was sent again to London to secure British guarantees for firmness against Hitler, this time traveling with his wife and daughter. He did not join them, though, on their excursions to Kew Gardens, the British Museum, and Buckingham Palace. Instead, he met again with British politicians, repeating his warnings about the Führer's real intentions. Now, he also raised the issue of German Jews, whose horrific treatment he had witnessed himself as the lord mayor of Leipzig. The British, he argued, should boycott the Nazi leaders altogether until they reversed their anti-Jewish policy. As Young described, "X [Goerdeler] fears catastrophe. He is greatly perturbed that there is not yet in evidence any strong reaction throughout the democracies, in the press, the church, and in Parliament against the barbaric, sadistic and cruel persecution of 10,000 Polish Jews in Germany.

These poor creatures are driven like wild animals, with machine guns behind them, over the Rhine into Switzerland and over the Polish frontier. Ten thousand of these people are in despair."[10]

Desperate, Goerdeler even made contact with the Zionist leader Dr. Chaim Weizmann, the future first president of Israel, and submitted a strongly worded memorandum with a "detailed exposé of conditions in Germany." Weizmann was shocked, and tried to share the document with Prime Minister Chamberlain:

> I showed the document to a friend of mine in the cabinet, and asked him to get Mr. Chamberlain to read it. He failed. I then went to see Sir Warren Fisher, one of the heads of the Civil Service, a close friend of Mr. Chamberlain, with a room adjacent to his in Downing Street. I showed him the document, and explained that undoubtedly Herr Gördler [sic] had risked his life several times to accumulate the information it contained. Sir Warren Fisher opened his desk and showed me an exact copy of the document. "I've had this," he said, "for the last ten days, and I've tried and tried again to get Mr. Chamberlain to look at it. It's no use."[11]

Goerdeler's mission ended in failure. Acceptance of his demands would mean a complete volte-face in British appeasement policy, which was unthinkable from Chamberlain's point of view.[12] The prime minister wanted above all to avoid war, owing both to his moral abhorrence of bloodshed and to a more practical assessment of the inadequacy of British military power. He also relied on the professional opinion of the chiefs of staff, that Britain would probably lose if forced to confront Germany.[13]

Another problem was Goerdeler's own nationalism. In his talks with Sir Robert Vansittart, for example, on the one hand, he insisted that the Sudetenland was a German territory that must be annexed to the Reich. On the other hand, he implored the British to be firm against Hitler's attempts to annex it by force. That was unfathomable for the British. If the Sudetenland should be part of Germany, why not give it to Hitler? Why make such a dramatic change in policy, taking risks to support a group of conspirators whose effectiveness had not yet been validated, in order to face a new regime and encounter the very same demands? Alexander Cadogan, undersecretary in the Foreign Office, wrote in his diary that Goerdeler's demands must be rejected, because they were too close to those of *Mein Kampf*.[14] Goerdeler's desperate argument that, for Hitler, the Sudetenland was only an excuse for further territorial expansion was also rejected. The belief that Hitler was a rational, though radical, politician with whom business could be done was, after all, the cornerstone of appeasement.

After Goerdeler's failure, Oster and his colleagues sent many other emissaries, only to face the same replies. Ewald von Kleist-Schmenzin, who carried the most valuable information about the coup, left for London on August 18, when the conspirators were already planning the military operation. Contrary to Goerdeler, who had made more general statements, Kleist told the British explicitly that a military revolt was in the works and that he represented senior generals from the General Staff. Everything, he said, depended on His Majesty's Government. If it would be firm, Hitler would fall.[15] Kleist's friend British journalist Ian Colvin arranged meetings for him with prominent opponents of appeasement, among them Vansittart and Churchill. But Vansittart was already a marginalized official with waning influence, and Churchill was as yet only a conservative backbencher. Prime Minister Chamberlain met Kleist as well, on August 19, but did not take him seriously. Apart from his considerations already noted, interference in the sovereign affairs of another country was out of the question for him: "I take it that von Kleist is violently anti-Hitler and is extremely anxious to stir up his friends in Germany to make an attempt at his overthrow . . . I think we must discount a good deal of what he says."[16]

Meanwhile, Oster continued to apply pressure on Halder. On August 12 (or 26, according to Halder's version), the conspirators met the chief of staff again. The resistance was represented by Gisevius and Schacht. This meeting, though, was far less pleasant than the first one, Gisevius recounted: "The interview was a stormy one. From the very beginning there was a certain mood of dishonesty. Schacht and I had the distinct feeling that Halder was not as brave as he had been a few weeks ago. For some reason he was looking for a line of retreat . . . It was clear that the chief of staff was trying to convince us that everything might turn out well after all, that the Western Powers might present Hitler with a free ticket to the east."[17]

On August 12, the conspirators were exposed to the fundamental weakness of their network. In order to stage a coup, they had to obtain the approval of Halder, who was never really one of them. In order to gain his approval, substantial British cooperation was required. The conspirators, thus, were completely dependent on two major power factors outside their own control: they had to convince the British to fundamentally change their foreign policy, and they had to urge the hesitant Halder to act. The resistance network of 1938 was a small circle of friends, no more. This had many advantages, among them an atmosphere of trust, crucial in such undertakings, and relative security from Gestapo informers. The biggest disadvantage was that in order to succeed, the resistance clique had to hope that outsiders, both in Berlin and in London, would do exactly as they asked. And these outsiders, in both capitals, had much more pressing concerns than complying with the wishes of a small group of German conspirators.

A partial solution to this problem was for the conspirators to hedge their bets by expanding the circle of insiders. Particularly, Oster was interested in enlisting more cooperative generals: military leaders who would be not merely cautious partners, like Halder, but full-fledged members of the conspiracy. Such generals might have military forces under their own control, and, if close to Halder, they could apply even more pressure on the chief of staff. The problem of utter dependence on British foreign policy, however, stayed as it was, as it was hard to imagine a revolt without Halder, who was completely dependent on a firm British stand against Hitler. Hence, on the British question the conspirators had no choice but to hope for the best.

More generals were indeed won over. One of Halder's deputies in the General Staff, Qm. Gen. Karl-Heinrich von Stülpnagel, became an active member of the conspiracy and was to remain loyal until the end. In addition, Oster was able to recruit his direct superior, Abwehr chief admiral Wilhelm Canaris, and Lt. Gen. Georg Thomas from the economic section of the General Staff. All three gave their full consent to cooperate, but none had troops directly under his command.[18]

Hence, a field commander was urgently required to secure loyal troops in the capital. For that purpose, Oster and Gisevius had an eye on the commander of the Greater Berlin defense district, Gen. Erwin von Witzleben, who was known for his hostility to the regime. In conversations with other officers, he often refused to recognize Hitler as Führer, calling him instead "your headman" or "Adolf."[19] To test the waters, Oster arranged a meeting between the general and Gisevius. The rapport between the two men was instantaneous:

> Witzleben was a refreshingly uncomplicated man. He had no bent for the kind of political finesse so dear to a bureaucratic general such as Halder. The Berlin commander was a typical front-line general, who had his heart in the right place. Probably not too well read and certainly not inclined towards the fine arts, he was nevertheless a man firmly rooted in the chivalric traditions of the old Prussian officer corps. He liked country life and was a passionate hunter; there was nothing of the schoolmaster about him, as there was about our chief of staff. Oster had only to hint at the delicate matter at hand. Witzleben understood at once and placed himself unconditionally at our disposal.[20]

Unconditionally? Not really. The uncharacteristic fondness shown by Gisevius, usually a basher of generals, to Witzleben should not hide the fact that even the most anti-Nazi of generals conditioned his participation, just as Halder did, on Britain's and France's having a firm attitude toward Hitler. The real difference between Halder and Witzleben lay more in their basic attitudes toward the question of coup d'état. For Halder, an impending war, which Germany could not win, was the reason for the coup. For Witzleben, war was a trigger that made a coup possible. Witzleben would stay loyal to the resistance until the bitter end. The conspirators knew that, unlike the cautious, sophisticated Halder, Witzleben could be believed and relied on.[21]

In early September, a first meeting took place. Witzleben visited the country estate of Dr. Schacht, who would take it upon himself to lead the civilian government after the planned coup d'état.[22] The Berlin commander came with one of his officers, the commander of the Potsdam Division, Lt. Gen. Walter von Brockdorff-Ahlefeldt. Just like his commander, he was an anti-Nazi and was fully committed to the conspirators. Following the meeting, Witzleben started to work on the military planning of the revolt and tried to win over new partners with even more troops under their command. Witzleben, in a way, filled a crucial gap in the network of the conspiracy. So far, the Berlin clique was mainly made up of intelligence and staff officers, whose circles of confidants overlapped. Witzleben connected them to a whole new world: that of the field commanders in Greater Berlin. Through him, the conspirators could tap military forces completely unavailable to them otherwise.

Witzleben, who openly told Halder about his involvement, had two main supporters in Berlin: Lieutenant General Brockdorff, mentioned earlier, who was supposed to lead the uprising in Berlin itself, and Maj. Gen. Paul von Hase, a junior commander who had more troops at his disposal. Another ally was Lt. Gen. Erich Hoepner, commander of an armored division in Thuringia. Witzleben understood that for a military revolt, infantry units were not sufficient. Tanks were required in Berlin in order to safeguard the conspirators in the capital. According to one version, Hoepner's task was to block SS reinforcements from Munich to Berlin. According to another, which seems more plausible, he was to move with his tanks to the north, to support the conspirators in Berlin itself.[23]

Hitler, meanwhile, continued to conspire against Czechoslovakia. It seemed he did not suspect for a moment that a coup was being planned in the highest military circles. Determined to take the Sudetenland, and maybe even more Czech territory, with or without British and French consent, he had briefed Keitel and Brauchitsch on the planned invasion in early September. The operation was scheduled to begin one month later. The Czechoslovakian leaders were cowed. On September 7, President Edvard Beneš summoned the Sudeten leaders and promised to fully meet their requirements. "My God," said one of them, "he's given us everything!"[24] But the Nazis, who were eager for a military confrontation, were becoming more and more bellicose by the day. The German incitement against Czechoslovakia had reached new heights, and Goebbels's headlines were screaming about horrendous Czech atrocities visited on Sudeten Germans. On September 10, in a kind of macabre warm-up for Hitler's fateful speech at the party rally at Nuremberg, Göring fulminated against Czechoslovakia: "A splinter of a nation, its origins unknown, is continuously repressing a cultured people . . . we know who is standing behind it: Moscow and the Jewish-Bolshevik devil."[25]

The American journalist William Shirer, who spent these frantic

days in Prague, met the crestfallen Edvard Beneš, who well understood that he was being cornered. True, Czechoslovakia had a strong,
resolute army, fortifications, and a modern air force, but it was doubtful whether it could stand up to an assault by the German Reich.
Moreover, after the annexation of Austria, Hitler's empire surrounded
the Czechs on three sides. Shirer wrote that both train station and airport "were full of Jews scrambling desperately to find transportation
to safer parts."[26]

Neville Chamberlain, clinging to his appeasement policy, was still
hoping for a reasonable compromise. On September 14, an urgent letter from Downing Street arrived at Hitler's office: "In view of the increasingly critical situation I propose to come over at once to see you
with a view to trying to find a peaceful solution. I propose to come
across by air and am ready to start tomorrow. Please indicate earliest
time at which you can see me and suggest place of meeting. I should
be grateful for a very early reply."[27]

Theo Kordt, a minister in the German embassy in London and the
resident agent of the resistance, failed in his attempts to warn the British about Hitler's "true intentions" and to convince them to play along
with the conspiracy. In Berlin, his brother Erich reported to his coconspirators that Chamberlain proposed to meet Hitler immediately to
solve the Sudeten question. He also updated them on the prime minister's position. Oster and his friends, who started to despair as far as
Britain was concerned, still trusted their own Führer. Some of them,
at least, believed that he was so seized by megalomania that he would
reject all British proposals, however moderate they might be.

One can imagine their dread, therefore, when Hitler accepted
Chamberlain's proposal and offered to meet him in Berchtesgaden,
at his palatial chalet in the Bavarian Alps. In the meeting itself, however, the Führer kept his belligerent mood. He would not tolerate any
violence against his people in the Sudetenland. In any case, his intention was to solve the problem one way or the other.[28] The disputed
territory had to be annexed by Germany. No other solution was possible.

The British prime minister, again, took a peaceful, soft approach.
The war, which he dreaded both morally and practically, was knocking
at the door. Chamberlain tried to buy time, telling Hitler that before

accepting his demands, he must consult his cabinet. The Führer, certain that Britain would not raise a finger for Czechoslovakia, was reinforced in his belief. Now it was time to raise the stakes, as noted in a circular sent by the German Foreign Office:

> The Führer told Chamberlain yesterday ... that his decision is to shortly put an end, in one way or the other, to the intolerable state of affairs in the Sudetenland. There are no more discussions to be had on autonomy for the Sudeten Germans, only on annexation to the Reich. Chamberlain has given his personal consent. Now he is consulting the British cabinet, and staying in touch with Paris. A second meeting between Chamberlain and the Führer is planned for the next few days.[29]

The last development was still unknown to the conspirators. Oblivious for a while of the discussions between Hitler and Chamberlain, they still hoped that Britain would not surrender to the new, more radical demands presented in Berchtesgaden.

The next two weeks, between September 15 and 29, involved frantic planning, bordering on panic, at both political and military levels. Two main questions remained open. The first concerned the new regime after the overthrow of National Socialism. General Halder, always keen on pointing out difficulties, was deeply concerned by what he saw as the negligence of the conspirators on that crucial issue: "The putsch and the assassination that will remove Hitler is only the negative side. Every person interested in the fate of his nation has to be concerned also with the positive side. What will happen afterward? No one told me anything about it. The soldiers were only asked to 'clean the place,' like housemaids, but what will be in the room afterward? I heard nothing about it, neither from Beck nor Goerdeler. That was the decisive weakness of the resistance movement as a whole."[30]

Still, most conspirators agreed at least on some basics. After Hitler's removal, the country would be run by a military dictatorship for a short transition period, followed by the restoration of the rule of law. The SS and Gestapo would be declared illegal, and a short while afterward elections would be held according to the old Weimar constitution. Schacht even mentioned a parliamentary government at some point, though most conspirators favored an authoritarian regime, perhaps even a restoration of the monarchy.

A second, no less pressing issue was Hitler's personal fate. Here, the conspirators were not of one mind. Halder strongly opposed an assassination (maybe because he feared a new "stab in the back" legend that would stigmatize him as a murderer) and proposed instead arresting the Führer and putting him on public trial. Goerdeler, who opposed assassination on religious grounds, probably supported the public-trial option as well. Dr. Hans von Dohnanyi, an anti-Nazi jurist and prominent Abwehr conspirator, had been collecting incriminating documents on the Nazis for years—and promised to publish them all after the coup. Dohnanyi had a slightly different plan: to stage a medical committee that would declare Hitler insane and order him to be locked up in a mental institution.[31] Some of the conspirators, though, held a different view. They understood that Hitler's charisma was the cement binding the Third Reich together and that as long as he was alive, Nazism would survive. Therefore, a new plan was hatched: a "conspiracy within the conspiracy," to murder Hitler during the military operation without Halder's knowledge.

The initiator of the plan was Lt. Col. Hans Oster, the founding father of the military resistance and one of its most radical conspirators. As he was busy with the overall planning of the coup, he left the operational details to two of his younger agents, Friedrich Wilhelm Heinz and Franz Maria Liedig. These young officers, ardent resistance fighters and former members of a right-wing Freikorps militia, were prepared to do anything to put an end to the regime. Heinz began his career as a notorious terrorist during the Weimar Republic and became a fanatical Nazi thug. During the 1930s, however, he was expelled from the National Socialist Party and turned his revolutionary zeal against the new regime. The methods he espoused remained the same: the regime could be changed only through violence, terror, and assassination. Unlike most members of the Oster clique—loyal civil servants who found their way to the resistance after much hesitation and misgiving—Heinz was a born revolutionary. For him, the underground was a way of life.

Oster stayed in touch with Heinz and Liedig throughout September, and on approximately the tenth he ordered Heinz to form an elite shock troop. "Commando Heinz," fifty to sixty men in all, was assembled at breathtaking speed, its soldiers armed by Oster from Abwehr supplies. Supervised by Abwehr officers, they encompassed all types: armed civilians, right-wing activists with revolutionary pasts, student leaders, and soldiers. Around September 15, the unit was finally formed, deployed in safe houses around Berlin, and waiting for a sign from Oster. Its job was to arrest Hitler and the Nazi leaders after Witzleben's troops took over the capital. Heinz and Liedig, with Oster's consent, planned to shoot Hitler to death during the operation under the pretext that he would try to avoid arrest. (Ironically, many people in the Third Reich perished for the same reason.)[32]

Most historians believe that only three people were privy to the plot: Oster, Heinz, and Liedig.[33] However, a rare document unearthed from the archive of the U.S. Army in Carlisle, Pennsylvania, indicates that Witzleben, too, knew about the plan and lent his support. Ursula von Witzleben, a relative of the general, recalled that on September 12, she and her husband were invited by Erwin and his wife to a private party:

> It was a disgusting day: cold, rainy and windy. After we drank tea, I wondered why my cousin [Erwin] decided to take a walk in the General Staff's park at Kurfürstenstrasse ... Around six, the square was full of people. Officers, soldiers and NCOs were passing by, at least in partial earshot of our conversation. Then my cousin turned on a narrow road in the park and stopped ... "We cannot speak in the apartment, because I believe it is full of microphones." Then he looked at me and kept on: "What I am going to tell you now, requires trust and great responsibility on your part ... Hitler has to go, because the leadership of the army cannot agree by any means to implement his grandiose schemes ... I will go to his office, speak with him man to man, as a responsible commander, and tell him that this is no leadership ..." I was alarmed, because the plan was impossible. Consequently, I was able to tell my cousin only the following: "I am afraid you do not understand the situation. You are no longer a general bound to the Prussian king. You are going to see Adolf Hitler. You will enter the chancellor's office, but will never return alive." My cousin looked at me and said: "The others think the same, and therefore we have only one option: assassination." "Is there no other way?" I asked. "No,"

he answered. "Hitler wants war, he provokes it, and that will be the end of Germany."

Here Witlzeben added a prophetic remark:

The people will have to carry a burden of collective guilt, but they will not understand it and will not be able to bear it.[34]

So it seems that Witzleben was privy to Heinz's plan and approved of it, though not without reservations. For him, as well as for Oster and Gisevius, it was clear that any possibility of success required meticulous military planning. Gisevius, for his part, was working to obtain police cooperation, for which he relied on the support of two old friends: Berlin police commandant Count Wolf von Helldorff and his counterpart from the Reich criminal police, SS Col. Arthur Nebe.

These police officers both had a sullied past of Nazi crimes. Helldorff, a former SA leader and National Socialist "old fighter," became notorious as a bon vivant and a corrupt and greedy police commander. During the 1930s, he was responsible for incessant violence against and blackmail of Jews. A close confidant of the Nazi leadership, he used to boast of his ties with Foreign Minister Ribbentrop.[35] Nevertheless, in 1938 he began to look for alternatives. The reasons are not clear, but from that year on, he joined the conspirators, never to leave them. Now, he promised Oster that his policemen would at least keep neutral in case of a coup.[36]

Just like Helldorff, Arthur Nebe, chief of the Reich criminal police department, was and remains an unsolved mystery. He was an SS commander, complicit in the most abominable crimes of the Nazi regime. Between June and November 1941, he was responsible for Einsatzgruppe B, one of the murder units that orchestrated the mass shooting of Jews on the eastern front. However, like Helldorff, he worked with the conspirators from 1938 onward. His cooperation was especially vital, as he supplied Gisevius, his contact person, with information on key government buildings, camps, and secret SS facilities.[37]

Using the vital information given by Nebe, the conspirators began to plan the details of the military operation. In chapter 3, we saw how the complicated ties of family, kinship, and friendship shared by many conspirators of aristocratic background served as a basis for the conspiratorial networks of the Berlin clique. Now, those ties were used for camouflage. Witzleben, taking a considerable risk, gave Gisevius an office in his military headquarters, under the pretext that he was a distant relative working on his "family papers." It is hard to imagine an officer with a nonaristocratic background using such a ploy. Gisevius was indeed working on papers, just not dynastic ones. In fact, he was studying a detailed map of Greater Berlin, marking key points, central facilities, and routes for troop movement.

On one of the days after September 12, Witzleben decided to send Gisevius and Lieutenant General Brockdorff into the field. They met near a suburban train station and were picked up by a car. The driver was a lively woman named Elisabeth Strünck, whose husband, a prominent insurance agent, was Goerdeler's confidant and a member of the inner circle. The two passengers, civilian and officer, stepped into the car, and Elisabeth started the engine. The three "harmless sightseers" drove by all the strategic sites bound to be occupied on Day X, studying especially escape routes through gardens and back doors. Brockdorff "wrote steadily and calculated the minimum number of troops necessary." It was decided that particularly large units would have to be employed for three critical tasks: the liberation of the Sachsenhausen concentration camp, and the occupation of both the radio station at Königwusterhausen and the guard regiment headquarters at Lichterfelde.[38]

Thus, a plan involving close cooperation between soldiers, shock troops, and (it was hoped) policemen was taking shape. In his talks with the conspirators, Halder predicted that the mobilization plans would be laid before him at least three days before the outbreak of the war. As soon as the final order to march was given, he would instruct Witzleben to start the coup. The troops of Brockdorff and Hase would occupy the capital, laying siege to the government quarter. In the best-case scenario, the police would cooperate. If Helldorff could not ensure that, his men would at least remain neutral. The shock troops of Heinz would spring out of their hideouts, storm the government buildings, and arrest the Nazi leaders. As mentioned, Heinz and Oster had quietly agreed to take Hitler down under the pretext of his attempting to escape arrest. Simultaneously, Witzleben would contact Hoepner to secure the vital armored units for the coup.

Following these military measures, the conspirators would take over the radio stations. Their broadcast to the people would explain that they were only keeping public order and repressing a revolt of SS and Gestapo elements. A provincial martial law would be declared, followed by a new government, possibly a monarchy. Heinz, whose early career had been devoted to the cause of the former imperial family, was in touch with the former crown prince, Prince Wilhelm. According to several accounts, the latter showed some interest in the plans, corresponding with the conspirators in coded letters. On September 15, Witzleben told one of his officers that the plans were ready, and now the conspirators only had to wait for the final order to invade Czechoslovakia. The days ticked by, and on September 20, the leading members of the clique met again in Oster's apartment. After they had left, Oster met privately with Captain Heinz and gave his final okay for the plan to assassinate Hitler.[39] Now, everyone waited for the Führer, and for Chamberlain.

But what about Himmler and his secret police? Taking into account the immense risks faced by the conspirators, it is astounding that the Gestapo knew nothing about this conspiracy, even many years later. That had to do, in part, with the close-knit structure of the conspiratorial network. In 1938, the group was a small, dense circle of friends and relatives, mostly of elite background. This made betrayal very unlikely. It also had to do with unbelievable negligence on the Gestapo's part as far as traditional elites—the nobility and the army—were concerned. Most of its resources were spent on endless persecution of the networks of the beaten left, which they still considered the greatest threat to the regime. The right and the traditional elites were not considered such a menace, even though that was where the real danger to National Socialism lay. This negligence of the dreaded Nazi secret police was to be a persistent phenomenon that allowed the conspirators to survive and work until July 20, 1944.

Everyone knew that the fate of Germany and Europe was now balancing on a knife-edge. On September 22, Chamberlain traveled again to Germany for negotiations, and he met Hitler in Bad Godesberg, near Bonn. As well as feeling the strain of foreign policy, Chamberlain also had internal political worries. He was told by some of his advisers that domestic opposition to his policy of appeasement was growing. Hitler was by no means calmer. William Shirer, who came to Godesberg to cover the conference, described the tense atmosphere in that town on the Rhine:

> Hitler was in a highly nervous state. On the morning of the twenty
> second I was having breakfast on the terrace of the hotel Dressen,
> where the talks were to take place, when Hitler strode past on
> his way down to the riverbank to inspect his yacht . . . Every few
> steps he cocked his right shoulder nervously, his left leg snapping
> up as he did so. He had ugly, black patches under his eyes. He
> seemed to be, as I noted in my diary that evening, on the edge of a
> nervous breakdown. "Teppichfresser!" [carpet eater] muttered my
> German companion, an editor who secretly despised the Nazis.
> And he explained that Hitler had been in such a maniacal mood
> over the Czechs the last few days that on more than one occasion
> he had lost control of himself completely, hurling himself to the
> floor and chewing the edge of the carpet.[40]

These were days of immense pressure not only for Hitler and Chamberlain but also for the conspirators, who were waiting eagerly for a crisis in the Godesberg talks.[41] Hitler raised the stakes at the last moment, as was his habit. To Chamberlain's horror, the German leader roundly rejected his offer to cede the Sudetenland to Germany without a referendum. Hitler now wanted not only to annex the Sudetenland but to do so through a military occupation. "With the most profound regret and disappointment, Chancellor," Chamberlain told Hitler on the morning of the twenty-third, "I have to state that you have made no effort to assist my attempts to secure peace."[42]

What disappointed Chamberlain lifted the spirits of the German conspirators. Now, they could once more hope that Britain would not surrender and that Hitler's radical demands would be met with a declaration of war. For a while, Oster was worried about the fact that Hitler stayed in Godesberg. He had to be in Berlin to allow the conspirators to arrest or kill him. "The bird," according to Oster's metaphor, "has to come back to its cage."[43] And indeed it did come back, on the afternoon of September 24.

The events in London offered some encouragement. Chamberlain's behavior in Godesberg had been so conciliatory that it had evoked opposition even among his closest associates. On the night of September 24, while driving from the Foreign Office to his home, Foreign Secretary Viscount Halifax had a serious conversation with his friend and confidant Undersecretary Sir Alexander Cadogan. For the last few days, the latter had insisted that Hitler was not interested in a reasonable peace and that war, after all, was inevitable.[44] Halifax, formerly an avid supporter of appeasement, was close to being convinced. At a decisive cabinet meeting on the morning of September 25, he echoed the sentiments of Kleist and other emissaries of the conspiracy, and expressed his new ideas before Chamberlain and the other ministers. Hitler, he argued, would not be content with a solution to the Sudeten question. In fact, "so long as Nazism lasted, peace would be uncertain ... For this reason [Halifax] did not feel that it would be right to put pressure on Czechoslovakia to accept ... If they rejected [Hitler's proposal] he imagined that France would join in, and if France went in we should join with them ... If [Hitler] was driven to war the result might be to help to bring down the Nazi regime."[45] Chamberlain could not believe his ears. In one of the notes he exchanged with Halifax during the meeting, he wrote, "The complete change of view since I saw you last night is a horrible blow to me. But of course you must form your opinions for yourself. It remains however to see what the French say. If they say they go in, thereby dragging us in, I do not think I could accept responsibility for the decision."[46]

The two statesmen continued to exchange heated notes throughout the cabinet meeting. Halifax apologized to Chamberlain for his sudden change of mind, and confessed that he'd been kept awake all night by his anguish over the Czech question. The prime minister answered sardonically that "night conclusions are seldom taken in the right perspective." For a moment, it seemed that Chamberlain's policy was about to collapse. But it did not. Most ministers, apart from Halifax, First Lord of the Admiralty Alfred Duff-Cooper, and two or three others, were still behind the prime minister. Another surprising turn took place that same night, when Chamberlain convened the cabinet again and told the ministers that the French were determined to stand by the Czechs.[47]

On September 26, an encouraging development also took place in Berlin. Admiral Canaris, the chief of military intelligence and Oster's boss, finally decided to support the anti-Nazi uprising. He and Oster both knew that Hitler had rejected Chamberlain's proposals at Godesberg. The coup was closer than ever.

Events in London were no less dramatic. Chamberlain was distressed to hear that the mission of his close adviser Horace Wilson had ended in failure. Hitler had yelled at him and was not ready even to listen to Chamberlain's letter. Wilson warned the Führer that "if France, in fulfillment of her treaty obligations, should become actively engaged in hostilities against Germany, the United Kingdom will feel obliged to support France." Hitler's response was furious: "If France and England strike, let them do so! It's a matter of complete indifference to me. Today is Tuesday. By next Monday we shall be at war."[48]

The next day, the moment of truth came. Hitler, in an attempt to foment warlike spirit in the populace, ordered General Witzleben to march his armed soldiers in the streets. Witzleben had to obey, but he later told Gisevius that "he would have liked best to march his men right into the Chancellery."[49] Hitler watched the parade from the balcony of his office. A veteran of the Great War, he remembered well the popular enthusiasm with which marching soldiers were received. Now, however, he was disappointed and frustrated in the extreme. Relatively few bothered to line the streets, and most who did, did not linger for long. Even party members were not as enthusiastic as expected. In some working-class districts, braver souls greeted the soldiers with clenched fists. "I had not been standing long at the corner," wrote William Shirer in his diary, "when a policeman came up the Wilhelmstrasse from the direction of the Chancellery and shouted . . . that the Führer was on his balcony reviewing the troops. Few moved. I went down to have a look . . . Hitler looked grim, then angry, and soon went inside, leaving his troops to parade by unreviewed. What I've seen tonight almost rekindles a little faith in the German people. They are dead set against war."[50]

The conspirators were increasingly nervous. On the day of the parade, a noisy quarrel broke out between Gisevius and Oster. Oster told his friend that Hitler would, in the end, prevail and that the "Western powers would yield." Gisevius told him that he "deserved a post in the propaganda ministry." The two ringleaders, torn between hope and fear, were waiting at Abwehr headquarters. Loyal coconspirators were posted in other key positions: the Wehrmacht high command, the Ministry of the Interior, police headquarters, and the foreign ministry. All were on high alert and regularly reported new developments to Oster.

In London, preparations for war had already begun. In the cabinet, Chamberlain found himself increasingly isolated. His last proposal, to send a telegram to Prague with a request to accept Hitler's demands, was rejected by most ministers, led by Duff-Cooper and supported by Halifax. Chamberlain still believed that war was not inevitable, as he declared in a statement to the nation that day:

> How horrible, fantastic, incredible it is that we should be digging trenches and trying on gas masks here because of a quarrel in a far-away country between people of whom we know nothing . . . I am myself a man of peace to the depths of my soul. Armed conflict between nations is a nightmare to me; but if I were convinced that any nation had made up its mind to dominate the world by fear of its force, I should feel that it must be resisted. Under such a domination, life for people who believe in liberty would not be worth living; but war is a fearful thing, and we must be very clear, before we embark on it, that it is really the great issues that are at stake.[51]

On September 28, early in the morning, Heinz ordered his men to leave their safe houses and gather in the army high command. He distributed rifles, ammunition, and hand grenades, which he had received from Oster and Canaris. Everything was ready for the final assault. Heinz knew that when his men stormed the chancellery, they would be greeted by Erich Kordt, a resistance agent in the foreign ministry, who would open the doors for them. According to Terry Parssinen, "The silence of predawn Berlin was broken by the click-click-click of ammunition being loaded in carbines and automatic weapons. Now, before he could turn his young lions loose on Hitler's Reich Chancellery, he had only to hear word that Brockdorff's twenty-third division was on the march from Potsdam [to Berlin]."[52]

The atmosphere seemed especially ripe for an insurgency. The leaders of the army were no less tense than ordinary Germans. On the evening of September 27, Oster gave Gisevius the Führer's reply to Chamberlain, which was understood by the conspirators as a German refusal to negotiate over Czechoslovakia. The next morning, Gisevius raced with the letter to Witzleben, and he gave it to Halder as the final piece of evidence. Halder was furious. Taking advantage of his indignation, Witzleben pressed him to see Brauchitsch and win him over to the putsch. After a while, Halder returned with good news. Brauchitsch was furious, too, and would most probably support the conspirators.[53]

Gen. Walther von Brauchitsch, commander in chief of the army and usually an obedient servant of the Nazi regime, understood that a war would mean the end of Germany. He told Halder that he would like to check the situation again before deciding, and drove to the Reich Chancellery to find out the truth. Everything was ready for the putsch. Witzleben rushed into Gisevius's office. "Gisevius, the time has come!" he exclaimed.[54]

When Brauchitsch entered the chancellery, he faced a completely unexpected development. At 11:00 a.m., the phone rang in the office of Erich Kordt. The Italian foreign minister was on the line, and he asked to be connected with his ambassador, Bernardo Attolico. Mussolini then took charge from Rome, and ordered his ambassador in Berlin to invite Hitler to a "peace conference" in Munich along with Chamberlain, in order to sort out the Sudeten question.

Chamberlain's capitulation was far-reaching. After Hitler had accepted Mussolini's proposal to organize the peace conference in Munich, the British prime minister gave a jubilant speech before his parliament. As far as he was concerned, he had prevented a major disaster not only for Britain, which was unprepared for war, but for Europe as a whole: "I have something further to say to the house yet. I have now been informed by Herr Hitler that he invites me to meet him at Munich tomorrow morning. He has also invited Signor Mussolini and Monsieur Daladier. Signor Mussolini has accepted and I have no doubt Monsieur Daladier will accept. I need not say what my answer will be."[55]

The "peace conference" took place in Munich between September 29 and 30. Chamberlain and Édouard Daladier had accepted without much debate the Italian proposal, actually a slightly softened version of Hitler's conditions at Godesberg: the Sudetenland would be given to Germany, through military occupation. The Czechs were not allowed to take anything out of the area, not even cattle or agricultural equipment. So the fate of Czechoslovakia was sealed while Chamberlain probably continued to believe that this would be Hitler's last territorial demand, as he had promised it would be again and again.[56] But, as a popular German joke of the time went, only in his tomb would Hitler's last territorial demand be met. When Chamberlain returned to the balcony of his office in Downing Street, he waved the Munich memorandum in front of cheering crowds: "We, the German Führer and Chancellor and the British Prime Minister, have had a further meeting today and are agreed in recognizing that the question of Anglo-German relations is of the first importance for the two countries and for Europe. We regard the agreement signed last night and the Anglo-German Naval Agreement as symbolic of the desires of our two people never to go to war with one another again."[57]

"I believe it is peace in our time," he declared. The crowds waved and cheered. During the next days, Chamberlain's bureau was flooded with endless letters of support from Britain and all over the world. But praise was not the only reaction. Halifax was still skeptical, and First Lord of the Admiralty Alfred Duff-Cooper resigned from his cabinet post in protest. Winston Churchill gave a characteristically prophetic warning:

> We are in the presence of a disaster of the first magnitude which has befallen Great Britain and France. Do not let us blind ourselves to that. It must now be accepted that all the countries of central and eastern Europe will make the best terms they can with the triumphant Nazi power. The system of alliances in central Europe upon which France has relied for her security has been swept away, and I can see no means by which it can be reconstituted. The road down the Danube Valley to the Black Sea . . . has been opened . . . It seems to me that all those countries of Middle Europe, all those Danubian countries, will, one after another, be drawn into this vast system of power politics . . . radiating from Berlin.[58]

After a short moment of hesitation, the Czech president, Beneš, decided to give up. He resigned, and his successor allowed the Germans to occupy the Sudetenland unhindered. In a stroke, Czechoslovakia had lost its fortifications, two-thirds of its coal mines, and its natural, geographical protections. It was dying, and the coup de grâce was only a matter of time. "We are abandoned. We are alone," said Beneš's successor in an address to the nation that night.[59]

Almost as miserable were the conspirators in Berlin. After the high hopes that their time had come, they had been blocked by Britain's inability to curb Hitler's foreign policy. "Never, since 1933," bemoaned Erich Kordt in his memoirs, "was there such a good chance to free Germany and the world."[60] Now the heartbroken conspirators met in Witzleben's apartment and put the plans for the coup in the fireplace. There they burned, along with a great deal of the young Berlin clique's hope and self-confidence. Never again would they have at their disposal an armored division, a friendly commander in Berlin, shock troops, and a sympathetic chief of staff.[61] The independence of Czechoslovakia had almost gone, the last chance of peace in Europe was missed. The conspirators were angry and vengeful. Naturally, they heaped their scorn on Chamberlain. More than six years later, Halder told the international tribunal at Nuremberg, "I had already passed the order to Witzleben for starting the coup when the information reached us that Chamberlain and Daladier were coming to Munich and, therefore, I had to withdraw my order ... The coup d'état was justified before the people by saying that Hitler was provoking a war and that without a violent coup d'état war could not be prevented. Now that wasn't possible any longer."[62]

The conspirators did not merely fail, they also made fools of themselves in front of their erstwhile collaborators from the army. Had not Schacht said to any general who was ready to listen that Britain would never abandon Czechoslovakia? After the war, he, too, was still furious and unforgiving:

> It is clear from the chain of events that this first attempt of Witzleben and myself to stage a coup d'état was the only one that could substantially change the fate of Germany ... In autumn 1938 it was still possible to try Hitler before the Supreme Court, but all subsequent attempts presumed an assassination ... I planned a revolt at an opportune moment and brought it to the verge of success, but history was against me. Intervention of foreign statesmen is something I could not have taken into account.[63]

Gisevius and Oster had to quietly dissolve Commando Heinz's shock troop unit. They would never be able to reassemble it. Its soldiers dispersed all over the country and later performed various military functions during the war. Lieutenant General Brockdorff, Witzleben's partner in the conspiracy, withdrew from the resistance for good. The Nazi mood in the Wehrmacht, he conceded, left the movement no chance.[64] Gisevius summarized the feelings of the conspirators then and later: "The impossible had happened. Chamberlain and Daladier were flying to Munich. Our revolt was done for. For a few hours I went on imagining that we could revolt anyway, but Witzleben soon demonstrated to me that the troops would never revolt against the victorious Führer . . . Peace in our time? Let us put it a bit more realistically. Chamberlain saved Hitler."[65]

Had Chamberlain saved Hitler? Perhaps. What is clear, and more interesting, is that the failure of the conspirators had nothing to do with any mistake they had made. In fact, they did not have the time to make any. Instead, their failure may have been directly related to the structure of their network, especially its character as a small, dense clique of friends. This was a source of strength in one sense, keeping the network relatively safe from the Gestapo and making it easy for the leaders, such as Oster, to control and orchestrate it. However, its size also meant that in order to function, it had to obtain the cooperation of outsiders such as General Halder and Prime Minister Chamberlain. Its leaders had to hope that decisions taken in London would turn out to be favorable. When they did not, the conspirators lost the best chance to stage a coup against Hitler and the Nazi regime. As we will see in the next chapter, a single man, without a network, would come closer to killing Hitler than the highest echelons of the German military ever would.

# 6

# WITHOUT A NETWORK:
# THE LONE ASSASSIN

U NTIL THE END of 1944, an unusual German prisoner named
Georg Elser lived within the notorious concentration camp
Sachsenhausen, in a special facility separate from other inmates. He
was polite but taciturn, and he kept himself busy mostly by carving
wooden artifacts for the SS guards who watched him. He also built his
own zither and played it well.[1]

Unlike many other prisoners in Sachsenhausen, he was not a Jew,
a homosexual, a criminal, nor a leftist political activist. Rather, he
was a German carpenter and watchmaker, short in stature, with his
black hair combed backward. His simple German, which he spoke in
a thick Swabian accent, disclosed a limited education and south German roots. "He does not have a typically criminal face," wrote the Nazi
newspaper *Völkischer Beobachter* on November 22, 1939. "His eyes are
wise . . . and he thinks long and carefully before he answers . . . When
one looks at him, it may be forgotten for an instant what a satanic
monster he is, what guilt, what terrible burden his conscience carries
with such intolerable ease."[2]

In Nazi eyes, Elser's guilt could hardly have been heavier. He had
staged a highly sophisticated assassination attempt on Adolf Hitler,
all by himself. In the history of the Third Reich, no assassination attempt—not even Stauffenberg's famous bomb plot on July 20, 1944
—was so meticulously planned and so nearly successful. However, unlike Stauffenberg, Oster, and other would-be assassins from the resis-

tance movement, Elser had no network to support him: no allies, no contacts in the military, no political friends. No one supplied him with cover, bombs, safe houses, or know-how. He never even eased his psychological burden by telling a friend about his terrible mission.

Georg Elser was born in 1903, the oldest of five children; he had three sisters and one brother. He grew up in Königsbronn, a small rural community in the Swabian Alps. His parents made their living from carpentry and agriculture and, like many other rural Germans, could hardly make ends meet. At some point his father took to drinking, and would come home intoxicated every night and beat up his wife.[3] Elser's childhood was not a happy one. At school his achievements were mediocre, and he was relatively isolated from his classmates. Like many other rural boys, he spent the time after school doing house chores and agricultural work. Following the outbreak of the Great War, in 1914, the family's finances deteriorated even further. Georg left school and set out to find a job, first in ironworks and then in carpentry. In 1917, at age fourteen, he left home.

Georg was interested in little beyond his job and his close friends and relatives. He never read books or, until the late 1930s, even newspapers. During the Great War, he spent all his days in hard physical labor, his free time devoted to his only hobby: music. Elser was a talented player, especially of the harmonica and flute. Upon completing his apprenticeship in carpentry, he became greatly valued by successive employers, who understood that here was no normal worker. Elser was a technical genius, with an unusual understanding for complicated machines. Still, his wages were low, and, restless as he was, he could not find peace of mind in any single workplace. He moved between different workshops, walking from village to village, all the while earning and saving money. In 1922, his journeys finally brought him across the border to Switzerland. There, he worked in several carpentry workshops, played in dance clubs, and had some fleeting romances with German and Swiss women.[4]

In 1929, Germany was hit by the Great Depression, and Elser's family, destitute even at the best of times, came close to the brink. His alcoholic father was worse than useless. To afford his drinks and to cover his numerous debts, he started selling the family's land. In 1932, in spite of the bad blood between him and his family, Elser responded to his mother's urgent plea and came back to Königsbronn. He did his best to help, but in the Depression it was hard to find steady work. Two years before, following an affair with a local woman, his only son, Manfred, was born. His partner left immediately afterward and married another man. Elser never saw her, or his son, again.[5]

The young carpenter was not interested in the stormy politics of the times. Still, for practical reasons he voted for the Communist Party. Like many other workers, he believed that the Communists would obtain better wages and more affordable housing for the working class. In January 1933, when Hitler took over the government, Elser was still largely indifferent to politics, though he never liked the Nazis. But time turned his initial indifference into hostility. Years later, Elser related to his Gestapo interrogators the hard feelings he had toward life in Nazi Germany: low wages, high taxes, and limited personal freedom. For born individualists like himself, it was hard to adjust to life in a totalitarian regime.[6]

There was also the problem of religion. Elser, a devout Protestant, did not like the church policy of the Nazi regime. "I believe that God made the world and all men ... and in Heaven and Hell, just as I was taught in Bible class," he said.[7] He was not interested in theological debates, but he didn't like the attempts of the Nazi regime to change tradition by force. Nevertheless, his route to active resistance would be long and tortuous.

His fateful decision to "do something" was, in the end, precipitated by the impending European war. Unlike General Beck, Elser understood immediately that Hitler himself was more responsible for the warmongering than the "radicals in the party." He understood that Nazi policy would lead to a total destruction of the German fatherland. This was not only a theoretical, patriotic concern: Who, if not the workers, would be the first to suffer? Who would be the first to fight and die? "I am convinced that the Munich Agreement will not hold," he said, "and Germany will continue to raise claims and annex other countries. Therefore, war is inevitable."[8] His conclusion was terrible, but clear as ice: "My hope was to prevent a bigger bloodshed ... I understood that the state of affairs in Germany could be changed only by taking down the leadership. By 'leadership' I mean the bosses: Hitler, Göring and Goebbels ... I hoped that after eliminating these three other people will come to power ... without plans to annex other countries, [people] who will take care to improve the life of the workers."[9]

Elser's mission seemed unrealistic in many respects. All by himself he had to obtain explosives, build a bomb, gain access to Hitler (not easy for a senior officer, let alone a simple worker), and get past the Führer's bodyguards. He had to obtain precise intelligence, which was almost impossible to collect, without agents or confidants. Yet Elser was able to achieve all this because of his background, his unusual talents, and a fortuitous set of circumstances.

Elser was never "normal," by most definitions of that word. Coming of age in the 1920s, a time of both freedom of movement and economic trouble in Germany, the restless wanderer covered many miles on foot and acquired a diverse set of skills. He worked in carpentry and watchmaking, and became skilled in ways that would later benefit his bomb-building project. Moreover, around 1938, he worked in a munitions workshop and later in a quarry, and was therefore able to acquire explosives and practical experience with detonation.[10]

All of that was not enough, though. Elser could have all the knowledge in the world about watchmaking and bomb manufacturing, but he still had to get close to Hitler despite his formidable personal security. Here, a set of events outside Elser's control came to his aid: "So I decided to kill the leadership myself. I thought it would be possible only when all of them were in a ceremony of some sort. I read once in the newspaper that the next time all of them would come together would be 8–9 November 1938 at the beer hall Bürgerbräukeller in Munich."[11]

Unwittingly, the carpenter hit upon the best possible occasion to assassinate the Führer and his inner circle. The ceremony he mentioned was the anniversary of the Beer Hall Putsch, Hitler's failed attempt to overthrow the Weimar Republic in 1923. This abortive uprising, long a seminal legend of the National Socialist Party, was celebrated by the "old fighters" every year in Hitler's presence. Proud of their heritage and tradition, the veterans insisted on keeping the Munich police out of the building. If they could protect Hitler with their own bodies in 1923, couldn't they still handle his security? Hitler, probably for sentimental reasons, sided with them. "Here in this gathering," he instructed, "I am protected by the old fighters led by Christian Weber. Police responsibility ends at the entrances."[12] Consequently, there was a heavy SS and security presence in the streets leading to the building during the ceremony, but not months beforehand. And the two veterans responsible for the security inside, both SS officers, were unbelievably negligent.[13] This resulted in a quadruple coincidence: Elser's resourcefulness, his decision to choose this ceremony, Hitler's sentimentality, and the veterans' hubris.

Elser was a meticulous planner. In 1938, he came to the ceremony to check the ground and decided to plan the operation for the following year. Thus, on November 8, 1938, at around 7:00 p.m., a short, simply clad man arrived at Munich's main train station, holding a wooden suitcase he had made himself. The station was crowded with passengers, many of them wearing brown National Socialist uniforms. Veterans from all over Germany, accompanied by many curious citizens, came to take part in the ceremony and to see their dear leader again.

At 8:00 p.m., Elser reached his rented room and asked the landlord for directions to the beer hall. He traveled there on foot, a considerable distance along the river, until he saw the dense crowd and, far away, the double doors of Bürgerbräukeller. He pushed his way through the crowd, entered the building, and crossed the drinking hall to the portal of the great hall: "I went from the entrance to the middle of the hall, looked around and noticed where the podium was . . . Still, I hadn't yet decided how to best carry out the assassination in this hall . . . I went out of the great hall through the dressing room to the small drinking hall . . . There I sat at the first table and ordered dinner. The time was around 23:00."[14]

Then he came back to his room, deep in thought. The assassination plan was still forming in his mind. The next day, as Hitler was about to give his speech, he also spent in the beer hall. Now, the negligent work of the veterans was evident to him. His observations indicated that security measures in the building were almost nonexistent. He promptly made his decision: "This hall is the right place to assassinate the leadership." The act itself, Elser concluded, could be done through one means alone: a bomb. He decided to install it in the pillar behind the podium, hoping the explosion would topple the roof and kill both Hitler and other Nazi leaders.

Upon his return to Königsbronn, Elser began to plan the device. He had twelve months to prepare. During the nights, he sneaked unnoticed into the munitions workshop and stole explosives, a little every day. A short while afterward, he resigned and found work in a quarry, where dynamite was often used to break up the stone. At night, he would go to the warehouse, open the primitive lock with his self-made key, and steal what he needed. No one ever noticed his suspicious behavior.[15]

During the summer, Elser took sick leave and traveled again to Munich to draw the hall and measure the pillar behind the podium. During his reconnaissance, he supported himself with his savings. In Munich he rented an apartment close by, and dined every day at the beer hall, his sharp eyes observing the structure, dimensions, and distances. Quickly, he found that the great hall could be reached through the dressing room, and that its double doors were open throughout the day until closing time. Moreover, he found a back door in the great hall providing access to the street through the garden.[16]

Elser went up and down the deserted great hall, drew the pillar, and examined it closely. He took several photographs with a camera he had received as a birthday gift ten years earlier. His gentleness and his camera made him a favorite of the waitresses. Once, he even took a group picture of them. He drank beer with the caretaker and learned that the caretaker was soon to be recruited into the army. Quick to notice opportunities, Elser asked his new friend to cajole the owners on his behalf. Might it be possible for him to become the new caretaker? The caretaker promised to speak with the boss, but did nothing. In response, Elser started to buy him beer and bribe him with money. Finally, when he had to return to Königsbronn, he asked the caretaker to write and tell him when he was going to leave. The fellow broke his promise again, and Elser never got the job. He came back home, his purse much thinner.

He went back to work at the quarry. In the evenings, he sat in his room and studied the drawings of the beer hall. Without any previous formal experience, he designed a highly sophisticated bomb, based on two watches, explosives, a battery, and a system of cogwheels. The hour hand of one watch was linked to a handle, which triggered a device hidden behind the clock face. When the hour hand made half a revolution, the handle turned an internal cogwheel thirty degrees.

A second watch with a similar mechanism was installed to back up the main one. When the cogwheel turned to a certain point, a firing pin would strike the detonator, causing the device to explode. Because of the watches, the system didn't need a fuse, and Elser could leave the beer hall before the blast. For two months, Elser experimented in his parents' garden, finally drafting a detailed plan for his device. He never consulted experts or professional literature.[17]

On May 19, 1939, a colleague accidentally dropped a heavy rock on Elser and smashed one of his feet. During weeks of convalescence, he lay in his room and elaborated the drafts of the bomb to completion. When he was fit again, around the end of June, he decided to leave work for good, and from then on he lived only on his savings. "From that moment," he later told his interrogators, "I lived only for one purpose—preparing for the assassination."[18]

On August 5, the curtain rose for the final act. Elser traveled to Munich. Again he rented an apartment close to the beer hall, dined there every evening, and sneaked into the great hall near closing time. There, he hid in a corner among a pile of cardboard boxes and waited for night to come. When the door was locked, he began to work. Using a scalpel, he painstakingly carved a cavity in the massive pillar, hiding it through a secret "door" that he could close and open when he needed to. He used metal, lest anyone knock on the pillar and become aware of its hollowness. Every night he worked until around 2:00 a.m. and then lay down, exhausted, on his pile of boxes. When the clock struck 6:30, he woke up and left the hall through the emergency door to the garden.[19]

Elser spent the days in his apartment. Behind a locked door, he studied his drawings and assembled the device itself. He told the landlord that he was working on a secret invention, which would one day make him rich and famous. Between August and November, that invention took shape. Unexpected difficulties occasionally arose. In September, after the outbreak of the war, civil-defense observers were watching for enemy airplanes from the roof of the hall. Elser described what happened one night: "When the hall was opened . . . a man came into view just before I was about to leave my hideout. He wanted to take a box from the hideout, and therefore noticed me. He took the box and left the hall without a word. A short while later he returned with the owner—he came to the gallery from the left, and the owner from the right. Meanwhile I climbed to the eastern gallery, sat at a table and conducted myself as if I was writing a letter." To avoid raising suspicions, Elser probably pretended to be drunk: "To the owner's question I replied that I had a boil on my thigh and I wanted to squeeze it. To his question what I was doing in the backroom, I said that I wanted to squeeze my boil there. I also told him that I wanted to write a letter. He told me to write it in the garden . . . I sat in the garden of the beer hall and to avoid suspicion drank a coffee."[20]

Meanwhile, Hitler and his senior officers were facing difficult decisions. Many of his generals deemed the plan to invade western Europe —most notably France—suicidal. Few believed that Germany, strong as it might be, could defeat France and the Low Countries.[21] The plan was strongly opposed by General Brauchitsch, commander in chief of the army, and even a Nazi officer as staunch as Walther von Reichenau didn't back his Führer. Because of the tense circumstances, Hitler decided not to attend the ceremony at the beer hall that year, and he sent his deputy Rudolf Hess in his place. On the evening of November 2, 1939, Elser went again to the beer hall, this time taking the bomb in its wooden suitcase. Before leaving his apartment, he set the two watches. The bomb was set to explode on November 8, in six days, or exactly 144 hours.

Over the next three nights, Elser installed the device in the hollowed pillar. On the morning of November 6, he checked the system one last time. It worked splendidly. Then he returned to his apartment, gathered his things, and hurried to the main train station. Back in autumn 1938, when he made the decision to kill Hitler, he understood well enough that he ought to leave Germany before the explosion. He planned to escape the Gestapo by fleeing to Switzerland and working there as a carpenter. Not wanting others to be convicted in his stead, he intended to write a detailed letter to the authorities in Germany, declaring that he alone was responsible for the assassination. He also intended to give the Swiss a small "gift" for accepting him as a political refugee: a document specifying everything he knew about the munitions workshop where he had worked in Germany. If he wasn't given asylum in Switzerland, he planned to go on to France. Paris was already at war with the Reich and would surely be happy to protect the man who had killed its sworn enemy.

But on November 6, it wasn't yet time to escape. Final arrange-

ments had to be made. First Elser traveled to Stuttgart to say farewell to his beloved sister, Maria, the last family member to whom he
was close. Her husband, Karl, a kind-hearted butcher, was fond of his
mysterious brother-in-law. When Elser arrived at the station, at noon,
he headed to the hotel where Karl was working. Maria's husband welcomed him, left work right away, and helped him carry his suitcase
from the train station to their apartment: "During my short stay at
Stuttgart, my sister and my brother-in-law always asked me where I
was going. 'Must cross the fence [the border],' I said. When they asked
me time and again why, I just said: 'I must.'"[22]

Elser stayed with Maria and Karl for one night only. On the afternoon of November 7, he took leave of his sister for the last time. However, on a whim, he decided not to head for the Swiss border but to
go back to Munich instead. Fears were haunting him, and he just had
to check the system one last time. All his worldly possessions were a
suitcase with clothes, half a sausage, a little money, working tools, and
some spare parts. At 9:30 p.m., he reached Munich and headed to the
beer hall, which was still open: "Immediately upon my arrival at the
hall I climbed the gallery . . . Putting my ear against the pillar, I heard
the clock ticking softly. Then I opened the secret door with a knife . . .
[and] checked with my pocket watch whether the clock was running
too fast or too slow. Everything was fine."[23]

Elser was happy. His masterpiece, laboriously assembled through
those long, lonely months, was ticking away undiscovered. He left
Munich and took the first train to Konstanz, near the Swiss-German
border.

The next day, Elser benefited yet again from factors outside his control. Hitler changed his plans abruptly and decided that he would speak
at the anniversary of the Beer Hall Putsch after all. On November 8,
while Elser's train was pulling into Konstanz, Hitler left his Munich
residence and traveled in a black Mercedes to the beer hall. There, he
was greeted by an electrified crowd of veterans. Hitler stepped into the
great hall and climbed onto the podium. The time was 9:00 p.m., and
just behind the Führer, Elser's two clocks ticked away.

In his speech, Hitler attacked the capitalist West and contrasted
Britain's warmongering with the peaceful foreign policy of National

Socialist Germany. This time, England was the main target of his abuse:

> The lies of that time [1914] are identical to the lies of today. Why did England join the war? Already in 1914 they said: England is fighting for the small nations ... Later we have seen how ... her statesmen treat the liberty of these small nations, how they are repressing minorities, abusing nations ... Moreover, they said: England is fighting for justice ... For three hundred years England has been fighting for justice, and has therefore taken 40 million square kilometers of this Earth ... They declared: the British soldier does not fight for his own interests, but for the right of self-determination of other nations. England has also fought for civilization, which exists of course in England alone. Only where miners live, in Whitechapel and the other neighborhoods of the miserable masses, only there one can find civilization and social degeneration.[24]

The veterans applauded and cheered. Then, at 9:05 p.m., rather than rambling on for hours, as was his habit, Hitler abruptly finished his speech. He had barely said farewell to the veterans before he was gone —ordering his driver to hurry to the main train station. He had some pressing duties in Berlin and wanted to get there as quickly as possible. The way to do so was to board his special train (the weather did not allow a plane), and considering the traffic in Munich that day, he had to leave early in order to catch it. Elser's plan had been saved again and again by chance. This time chance betrayed him.[25]

The veterans were in no mood to leave the hall. They went on drinking, chatting, and relating stories from their glorious past. The waitresses hurried about carrying trays full of Bavarian beers. One of them, Maria Strobl, passed by the pillar at exactly 9:20 p.m.

The watch ticked for the last time. The cogwheel took a final turn, triggering the pin. One strike on the charger and the device went off. The pillar exploded, burying Hitler's podium under two tons of rubble. The poor waitress was severely wounded, a colleague of hers was killed, and seven veterans died on the spot. Screams pierced the hall. People pushed their way outside. Many believed it was an air raid.

Near the doors, uniformed women were weeping loudly. All looked pale and anxious. Ambulances were dashing past, and police appeared. Arrested persons were being taken away. The power of the blast was enormous.[26] Elser's masterpiece went off as planned, and on time. Had Hitler stayed just a little longer, he would have died.

A few minutes earlier, while the Führer was still speaking at the beer hall, Elser was trying to steal across the border. The night was freezing, and the young would-be assassin, in his torn clothes, was tired and scared. He forgot to get rid of the remnants of the bomb and some spare parts, and, worst of all, he still had the drawing of the beer hall in his coat pocket. Around 8:45 p.m., he passed a dark garden near the border customs office. Inside the bright building, two officials were sitting and listening to Hitler's speech. One of them looked through the window and saw Elser sneaking by in the direction of the border. He called out to him to halt. "I stopped right away," he recalled later, "and if I'm asked what my first thought was that very moment, I must say I was angry at myself, and my own recklessness."[27] The policemen searched him and found the incriminating evidence. A short while later, a telegram came to all border stations, informing them of the assassination attempt, with instructions to look for infiltrators. One of the policemen, a former soldier, inspected the spare parts and recognized them immediately as bomb components.[28]

Hitler heard about the blast on his way to Berlin, when he stopped in Nuremberg for a short break. When he reached Berlin, Göring and his other close associates congratulated him on his good luck. The Führer viewed the episode as yet another "proof" of the divine protection he believed he was under.[29]

Elser was brought to the police in Konstanz, and quickly became the main suspect in the assassination attempt. The bomb components and the drawing of the beer hall found in his jacket did not leave room for much doubt about his guilt. The Gestapo headquarters in Berlin ordered Konstanz to hand him over to the Gestapo station at Munich. There, he was interrogated by a special committee chaired by the commander of the criminal police, Brig. Gen. Arthur Nebe. Nebe had been a major player in the September 1938 conspiracy, which included a plan to assassinate Hitler. In this surreal scene, then, a person who tried to assassinate his head of state was interrogated by a senior police officer who had tried to do the same thing a short time before.

In any case, Elser confessed that he had tried to assassinate Hitler and insisted that he had no accomplices. This true statement was accepted by Nebe and his committee, but not by their superiors in Berlin.[30] On November 9, two British intelligence operatives were kidnapped from a town called Venlo on the German-Dutch border. Hitler and Himmler guessed that these were Elser's "operators." The contact man, it was presumed, was a German anti-Nazi exile in Switzerland. Otherwise, how did Elser have the know-how and financial resources to build his elaborate bomb?[31]

Elser was moved to Gestapo headquarters in Berlin for yet another round of interrogations. There, he was beaten up, tortured, and abused to try to squeeze out the names of his accomplices. He insisted again and again that he had worked alone, moved only by his belief that he was doing the right thing. When the Gestapo officials confronted him with his mother, he wept, but his story remained unchanged. Finally, the Berlin Gestapo, too, adopted Nebe's conclusion, that Elser was a lone wolf. But the interrogators went on, asking Elser about his religious and political beliefs, through his sexual and drinking habits, to the assassination attempt and the structure of the bomb. When asked whether he knew that Jewish organizations offered money for the Führer's head, Elser replied, "No," and that in any case he had never hoped to enrich himself.[32]

The interrogation protocol indicates that Elser was almost always calm, even unmoved by the interrogators' questions. The only time that he was really upset was when his interrogators told him that innocent people had died in the explosion. "I wanted to kill the leadership," he said. "Today I wouldn't have done it again ... because the goal wasn't reached." Afterward, he told the interrogators that his failure might have been ordained, "because the intention was wrong."[33]

Once the interrogation was concluded, Elser was moved yet again, this time to Sachsenhausen. There, he was jailed with the two kidnapped British intelligence operatives, who some still believed were his operators. He enjoyed relatively good conditions in return for some requests—for example, to rebuild the bomb—and he was allowed to fashion things from wood and to play his zither to while the time away. In early 1945, he was moved to the Dachau concentration camp.[34]

Elser's luck ran out only when it became clear even to the most fanatical Nazis that the war was lost. One of his SS guards later recounted that Elser knew that his days were numbered. "I do not regret what I did," he told the guard. "And anyway there is no use. I believe I have done something good, but it failed, and I must suffer the consequences. Yet I am afraid. Day and night I think how my death will be." Then, he played the zither one last time, his eyes wet with tears.[35] On April 9, 1945, the air raid sirens were sounded yet again in Dachau. Elser was taken by guards to an unknown location near the camp and shot to death.

Elser's story shows that a conspiratorial network is not a precondition for a promising assassination attempt. However, such a "near hit" relies on other factors: an individual who is well traveled, highly talented, and diversely skilled and who enjoys the benefits of a dense network of employers and technical educators, and a fortuitous, unexpected set of unrelated circumstances. Only such a set of coincidences could have created the breach in Hitler's personal security that Elser exploited so skillfully.

But luck, which helped him get so close to his target, failed Elser in the end. When one is part of a network, teamwork can remedy many of the unexpected challenges posed by ill luck. Inside information may be obtained about the target's plans; a partner may help to fix the problem; a new assassination attempt may be planned. When an assassin works alone, without any intelligence on his target or cooperation with its inner circle, unexpected circumstances are almost impossible to work around. He must have perfect luck all the way. Elser had this luck until the final throw of the dice, when all his efforts were brought to naught.

# 7

# THE POINT OF NO RETURN:
# POGROM AND WAR

O N NOVEMBER 7, 1938, a young Jewish refugee named Herschel
Grynszpan walked into the German embassy in Paris and demanded to see an official. The desk clerk directed him to a junior diplomat, Ernst vom Rath. When asked why he had come, he pulled a gun
and shot vom Rath in the abdomen. Grynszpan was arrested by the
French police and questioned. He told them that he had committed
the act in "revenge for the Jewish people." Only a few days earlier, his
sister had written to tell him that their parents, Polish Jews who lived
in Hannover, had been expelled, along with several thousand of their
coreligionists, to the Polish border. On October 26, Nazi authorities
had ordered seventeen thousand Polish Jews to leave Germany immediately without their property (which was left to be looted by the
government and private citizens). The refugees, rejected by both Germany and Poland, were languishing at the border. Among them were
the Grynszpans.[1]

Dr. Josef Goebbels, Hitler's minister of propaganda, was quick to
use the opportunity to reach both ideological and personal ends. A rabid Jew hater, even by the standards of the National Socialist leadership, he wanted to strike out at the Jews—the more, the better. Moreover, his personal standing was somewhat compromised following a
racially problematic love affair with a Czech actress. Hitting the Jews,
the common enemy of all Nazis, was an efficient way to rehabilitate

himself. Vom Rath finally died on November 9, and on the same day the entire Nazi leadership came together to celebrate the Beer Hall Putsch at Bürgerbräukeller in Munich. (Unbeknownst to any of them, Georg Elser was also there, planning his assassination attempt for the following year.) Goebbels gave a speech of incitement, calling all but explicitly for violent riots.[2] Even before his intervention, "spontaneous" pogroms had begun in the Magdeburg region. Nazi thugs, abetted by large segments of the population, had burned synagogues, destroyed Jewish shops, and violently harassed local Jews. Goebbels saw the assassination in Paris as a chance to turn the local riots into a nationwide tsunami of violence. On November 9, all hell broke loose. Reinhard Heydrich, chief of the security police, orchestrated the pogrom and issued detailed instructions to its executors. According to historian Leni Yahil,

> A pogrom that burgeoned into a mass frenzy of destruction spread around the country. According to figures that Heydrich issued on November 11 in a preliminary report to Göring, 191 synagogues were set ablaze and another 76 were completely destroyed ... The next day Heydrich reported that seventy-five hundred Jewish businesses had been demolished. The debris of the shattered shop windows gave the pogrom its name [the Night of Broken Glass] ... In his first report Heydrich related that thirty-six Jews were killed and another thirty-six severely injured; eventually the number of murdered reported was ninety-one. Thirty thousand Jews or more were arrested and incarcerated in Dachau, Buchenwald and Sachsenhausen, as planned in advance, and hundreds of Jewish-owned apartments were looted and ruined.[3]

The Nazi leadership used the pogrom as a starting point for further blows against German and Austrian Jewry. Under special decrees of Göring and Heydrich, the Jews were expelled from nearly all sectors of the German economy. The community had to pay one million marks as blood money for vom Rath and rebuild the ruins of the Night of Broken Glass by itself. Insurance policies were unpaid. Jewish children were expelled from German schools, and almost all public places were closed to them and their families. For the first time,

Jews were incarcerated in concentration camps only because they were Jews.[4]

The cruel pogrom found the anti-Nazi conspirators shocked and unprepared, fueling their motivation but also their deep feeling of impotence. They had still not recovered from their failure in September, when the coup had seemed to be around the corner. They could hardly keep pace with events. Contrary to their predictions, Hitler did not fall into disgrace. Rather, his star rose even higher. Goerdeler, for one, was also shocked by the cooperation of many common Germans with the rioters. He understood—partially, reluctantly, and maybe for the first time—that he and his friends were a tiny drop within a Nazi ocean. Others were deeply disappointed by the silence of the generals.[5] At the same time, the Night of Broken Glass, or Kristallnacht, was the point of no return in their struggle against the Nazi regime. For Goerdeler, all bridges had been burned, all chances for future reconciliation gone forever. Hitler, he said to a British friend, was "beyond redemption."[6] His confidant and later biographer Gerhard Ritter related the feelings shared by the former lord mayor and his closest circle: "We loved Germany; we were proud of Germany. But so far had we come, as to be forced to be ashamed for her in front of the entire world. Anyone who did not experience these dark November weeks as a German cannot fully comprehend the extent of the humiliation and helpless despair evoked in countless German hearts. Now, even for the many among us who still hesitated, there was no possibility for reconciliation with the tyrannical regime."[7]

Kristallnacht influenced not only consistent opponents of the regime, such as Goerdeler, but also people who were sympathetic to some aspects of National Socialist policy. Prof. Johannes Popitz, for example, served as the finance minister of Prussia. As an intellectual with Nazi sympathies and ingrained hostility toward the Jews, he had so far not opposed the "removal of the Jews from German public life." Now, however, he felt that things were going much too far; such inhuman violence should not be tolerated, as it violated both "law and morality."[8] Unlike most German high officials, who supported the pogrom or remained silent, Popitz decided to do something. He went to see Göring, and demanded the arrest and prosecution of "those responsible" for the pogrom. "Popitz, my dear," answered the stout

*Reichsmarschal,* "do you want to prosecute the Führer?" That was his turning point. A member of the Wednesday Society, he already had good relationships with fellow members and resistance fighters such as Ludwig Beck, Ulrich von Hassell, and Prof. Jens Jessen.

Kristallnacht, in a clear example of the phenomenon of revolutionary mutation discussed in chapter 3, helped to turn strictly social relations into conspiratorial ones. Popitz decided to break with the regime and became a member of the inner circle of the resistance.

Goerdeler, for his part, did not blame the Nazis alone. True, he said, "Germany is controlled by 10,000 of its worst elements . . . a gang of thugs and murderers who recognize no human or moral law." Hitler desired to destroy "Jews, Christianity and capitalism" in order to take over the world.[9] Yet the British were also responsible for Kristallnacht, as they did nothing to protect the Jews. They had given in to Hitler in Munich and indirectly fueled his sense of impunity.

Goerdeler prophesied that the "persecution of the Jews will continue with even greater ferocity. The persecution of the Christians will be intensified, and an onslaught on the capital will follow."[10] Ulrich von Hassell, too, was close to despair:

> I write under the gloomy impression of the abominable persecution of the Jews . . . Our international reputation has never been compromised so badly, not since the Great War . . . Still, my main concern is not the international consequences . . . but that our life in Germany is being controlled ever tighter by a system capable of such things . . . Actually, there is no doubt that here was an organized, formal anti-Jewish persecution campaign, set to take place simultaneously, on the same night, all over Germany. Truly a disgrace.[11]

The only conspirator who did something tangible was the deputy commandant of the Berlin police, Fritz von der Schulenburg. Upon hearing that Jews had been arrested after Kristallnacht, he immediately released those under his charge, declaring that they had violated no law. "A small bureaucrat," Goebbels spitefully called him in response.[12]

A few months elapsed. The winter was almost over, and war was drawing nigh. Luck did not favor the conspirators: Gen. Erwin von Witzleben, their most powerful ally in Berlin, was transferred to command an army in western Germany. Other conspirators found themselves pushed to the margins. General Halder was unresponsive to communications from the resistance. Now, as Hitler scored success after success, was no time for a coup d'état. The conspirators, still fixated on the strategy of 1938, could not imagine a revolt without Halder's cooperation. Witzleben, too, seemed deep in despair. Hitler's policy, he confided to one of his officers, would lead to a world war and the destruction of Germany. Yet one should not look for easy solutions such as retiring from public life.[13] According to the pattern of September 1938, the conspirators still hoped for a diplomatic defeat, a setback, something to push Halder over the fence.

In contrast to the disoriented conspirators, who lacked initiative and concrete plans, on March 15, Hitler occupied the rest of Czechoslovakia, in gross violation of the Munich agreement. Czech independence was taken, and the occupied country turned into the "Protectorate of Bohemia and Moravia." Emil Hácha, the last sovereign Czech president, was forced to sign the death sentence of his country. On the same day, the Wehrmacht marched in Prague. Hitler declared: "The provinces of Bohemia and Moravia were part of German living space for a millennium . . . Czechoslovakia, showing a lack of basic capability to exist, is disintegrating . . . The German Reich cannot tolerate incessant chaos in these regions, which are vital for its own, as well as for general, peace and security. Therefore, in tandem with the laws of survival, the German Reich decided to interfere and to take reasonable action to restore basic order in central Europe."[14]

The British public was outraged. Foreign Secretary Halifax, already skeptical about appeasement, called on the prime minister to change his policy forthwith.[15] Even Chamberlain himself could not remain indifferent to this violation of the Munich agreement. Reluctantly, he declared that Britain and France would not tolerate further German aggression, especially toward Poland, the next prospective victim of National Socialist foreign policy: "In the event of any action which clearly threatened Polish independence . . . His Majesty's Government would feel themselves bound at once to lend the Polish Government all support in their power. They have given the Polish Government an assurance to this effect. I may add that the French Government have authorized me to make it plain that they stand in the same position in this matter."[16]

Chamberlain's position was weak. He knew that Hitler had unabashedly lied to him when saying that the Sudetenland would be his last territorial demand. Czechoslovakia was conquered, the Munich agreement violated, and Chamberlain had done nothing in spite of his guarantee of Czech territorial integrity. In the same speech, he justified his behavior on practical grounds: Czechoslovakia would have been ruined in a war, and Britain would have had no chance to save it. His own private notes reveal the distress he felt and his desperate attempts to justify the betrayal of Czechoslovakia before his own conscience.[17] The prime minister was no naive fool, however. Though he yearned for peace, he had also prepared for the worst. Now, much more rapidly than in 1938, the British were rearming. War was approaching.[18]

In his modest house at Goethestrasse in Berlin, General Beck was following events by radio, realizing that his dark prophecies were all about to be fulfilled. Germany was close to another world war. He opposed the occupation of Czechoslovakia, a violation of an international agreement not justifiable by any real German interest. Goerdeler and Oster were of the same opinion. The latter, still holding his powerful position in the Abwehr, kept working toward one goal: the prevention of an international disaster. Even now, with the conspiracy at its nadir, Oster skillfully filled the role of connector, constantly orchestrating the flow of information, orders, and instructions inside the conspiratorial clique.[19]

In order to reinforce the opposition in the Abwehr itself, Oster recruited a "special adviser" (*Sonderführer*), a rank reserved for civilians working inside the Wehrmacht. The new recruit was the anti-Nazi jurist Dr. Hans von Dohnanyi. After Dohnanyi was expelled from his previous workplace, the justice ministry, for his openly anti-Nazi views, Oster installed him in the Abwehr.[20] Formally tasked with briefing Oster and Canaris on international developments, he in fact devoted all his time to underground activity, assisting persecuted Jews and systematically documenting Nazi crimes. He collected evidence on corruption and murder, including documents indicating Goebbels's personal responsibility for Kristallnacht. After the hoped-for coup, he and Oster planned to publish these documents, to prove to the German people that they had overthrown not a legitimate government but a criminal gang.[21]

Meanwhile, Oster was trying to reinforce the old Berlin clique, win over new members, and open new channels to work within. As Halder's cooperation was still seen as a necessary condition for the coup, the most important thing was to surround him with loyal confederates. For that purpose, Oster arranged for yet another conspirator, the head of the Abwehr sabotage section, Lt. Col. Helmut Groscurth, to be the liaison officer between himself and the army high command. An unrelenting enemy of Hitler and the regime, Groscurth looked with horror on the prospect of Nazi victory in a world war. A triumph for Hitler, testified a colleague many years later, was for him intolerable.[22] Now, on the eve of war, he used his close working relationship with Halder to apply increasing pressure on the chief of staff. Nevertheless, Halder still refused, and he certainly did not recognize the occupation of Czechoslovakia as a good enough reason to overthrow the regime. The frustration of Oster and his friends mounted when they understood that Halder would not move unless he was convinced that Britain and France would fight Germany.

Oster's third important measure was to appoint an official leader for the movement. He and his lieutenants agreed that only a distinguished person such as General Beck, well regarded in the higher echelons of the army, could serve as the supreme leader of the conspiracy. Beck, fully disillusioned with the regime, was ready. Oster referred to him, at least formally, as his superior officer and commander. In 1939, for example, Oster gave the following instructions to Dr. Josef Müller, an Abwehr conspirator sent to negotiate with the Allies through the Vatican in Rome:

> Dr. Müller, you are now in the central headquarters of the German Abwehr . . . serving also as the directorate of military opposition under General Beck. If you work with us . . . you'll never get your orders from the Abwehr. Even Admiral [Canaris] will tell you that you are no longer bound to obey his orders. For us the wishes of General Beck are equivalent to orders, and if you work with us—you have to accept General Beck as your commander . . . The tasks I give you—are the tasks given to you by General

> Beck . . . Our—that is, General Beck's—request for you, is to get
> in contact with the Pope. You should ask him if he is ready to con-
> tact the British government and clarify whether they will enter
> peace negotiations with the German opposition.[23]

Oster clearly distinguished the normal military chain of command
from the clandestine network of the resistance. Müller should always
prefer the latter over the former. General Beck was portrayed as the
supreme commander, whose authority represented the entire organization ("we"). Oster's instructions to Müller reflect the slow transition
that the Berlin clique was undergoing after the 1938 failure. The network expanded, slowly but surely, beyond the intimate circle of friends
formed by Goerdeler, Oster, and Gisevius two years before. As it did
so, an image of a supreme commander was necessary to impress newcomers and to create a feeling that they were joining a secret organization led by a distinguished authority figure. The image of "the General" was supposed to inspire confidence and awe, while day-to-day
power remained with Oster as the most important connector in the
network. Beck was far from being a puppet, and gradually did demonstrate leadership, but as far as the network was concerned, he was
never at the center. In the German resistance, as in many other organizations, there was a huge difference between formal power ("the
tasks given to you by General Beck") and actual power ("the tasks that
I [Oster] give you").

At the same time, the network was expanding in the civilian, political sphere. Oster surmised that it was better for the resistance to be
backed by a broader political base, so it could win at least some popular support after a coup d'état; not only officers and civilians associated with the conservative right should be won over but also politicians from the moderate left, the Social Democratic Party, and the
former labor unions. Witzleben, for example, was afraid that the workers might crush an incumbent revolt by way of a general strike, just as
they had in 1920 (but not in 1933!). Accordingly, he told Goerdeler,
active support from labor leaders was a very important requirement.[24]

This was the background for the contact created by Oster and
Goerdeler with Wilhelm Leuschner, former minister of the interior of
the state of Hessen and a member of the Social Democratic Party. Already in 1938, he knew about the plans and was keen to work with con-

servatives against Hitler and the Nazi regime. A moderate, easy-going politician, he was able to transcend old party rivalries and cooperate closely with Goerdeler, Oster, and Beck. As a man of compromise, he even agreed to grant his conservative colleagues the restoration of the monarchy if they conceded as far as labor and social rights were concerned. His sphere of influence attracted other Social Democratic activists and politicians–turned–resistance fighters, among them Prof. Adolf Reichwein, a director in the Berlin Folklore Museum, and Dr. Julius Leber, a former Social Democratic parliamentarian.

Leber came to the resistance fresh from a concentration camp, where he had been interned for four years. Instead of breaking him, he later testified, the tortures he endured gave him the ability to know, see, and judge himself better.[25] After his release, in 1938, he owned a small business, which the conspirators would use during the war as a hideout (in addition to Leuschner's beer-can factory and Reichwein's office in the Berlin Folklore Museum). Beck took care to visit Leuschner often, wearing black sunglasses for camouflage, to keep communication channels between conservatives and Social Democrats open.

In tandem with the old strategy of 1938, the conspirators attempted not merely to ensure Halder's support but also to reach understandings with London, with equally disappointing results. In 1939, there were no concrete plans for a coup d'état. Witzleben, the only conspirator with control over troops, was isolated in Kassel and could not do much alone.[26] Still, Oster hoped that British cooperation might give Halder the impetus to change his mind. Perhaps it was still possible to remedy the debacle of Munich. These negotiations, though, were even more farcical than they had been the year before. The envoys of the conspiracy, for one, were uncoordinated and contradicted each other. Even worse, they all wanted to keep many of Hitler's territorial acquisitions, and they were seen more and more by the British as rabid German nationalists no different from the Nazis. Josef Müller, in Rome, didn't fare any better, and the credibility of the conspirators in British eyes, very low to begin with, steadily deteriorated. The best the emissaries could get was an equivocal statement of support from Chamberlain, which failed to impress Halder or any other high officer.[27]

On August 23, 1939, Nazi Germany and the Soviet Union signed a nonaggression pact, ensuring among other things the partition of Poland between the two dictatorships. Hitler's star was again on the rise, Halder avoided the conspirators, and even Oster understood that no one would agree to revolt against Hitler now, after such a tremendous achievement. The conspirators could only sit and watch Germany and the rest of Europe drift toward a second world war.[28]

As German nationalists, the conspirators found themselves in an uneasy position. On the one hand, they advocated, like most other Germans, restoring the territories "stolen" from Germany in the wake of the Great War. But they did not want these territories to be taken by Hitler. Goerdeler and Hassell understood that Hitler would not be satisfied with these territories but would go on to occupy all of Poland and, if unchecked, the entire European continent. They had no plans, few allies in the high command, and no cooperation with the British. Witzleben, disgruntled and isolated, had to be updated by Gisevius on developments in Berlin. Halder and Brauchitsch were in the mood for war, not resistance. On August 31, the Germans staged a final ploy to excuse the impending attack on Poland. One hundred and fifty concentration camp inmates, clad in Polish uniforms, were led to "attack" a German broadcasting station on the Polish-German border. The Nazi reaction was, of course, swift and brutal.

Admiral Canaris watched the events in horror, unable to change the course of history. On the afternoon of August 31, one day before the invasion, he foresaw a dark future for his beloved fatherland. Gisevius, who encountered him at the Wehrmacht high command, was taken to a dimly lit side corridor. "That is the end of Germany," Canaris told him, his voice choked with tears.[29]

The resistance of the Polish army was heroic but short-lived. The German armies stormed Warsaw from the north, south, and west. Göring's Luftwaffe bombed Poland ruthlessly, grinding fortifications, military camps, factories, and towns into dust. Countless civilians were pulverized from the air. Warsaw was destroyed in a cruel bombardment, which did not stop even after the city had surrendered. SS squads marched with the army, leaving blood and destruction behind them. Under Hitler's orders, the invaders massacred the Polish nobility and intelligentsia, along with Jews and other "undesirables."[30]

This time, the British were not ready to give up. On September 1, the British ambassador in Berlin delivered a formal note from his government: "Unless the German Government are prepared to give His

Majesty's Government satisfactory assurances that the German Government have suspended all aggressive action against Poland and are prepared promptly to withdraw their forces from Polish territory, His Majesty's Government will without hesitation fulfill their obligation to Poland."[31]

Britain and France were ready for war. General Beck, following the events from his home, was expecting the worst. To him, there was no chance that Germany would survive an armed conflict with the Western powers.[32] At 9:00 on the morning of September 3, Viscount Halifax gave the final ultimatum to the German government: "I have accordingly the honor to inform you that, unless no later than 11 a.m., British summer time, today September 3, satisfactory assurances to the above effect have been given by the German Government and have reached His Majesty's Government in London, a state of war will exist between the two countries as from that hour."[33]

The British ultimatum was rejected. At 12:06 p.m., Neville Chamberlain declared war on Germany.

That same day, at 9:00 p.m., Germany turned the declaration of war into reality. A German submarine sank without warning the British passenger liner SS *Athenia*. In all, 120 civilians, including 28 Americans, perished in an act that violated international law. The Second World War had begun.

# 8

# THE SPIRIT OF ZOSSEN:
# WHEN NETWORKS FAIL

THE CONSPIRATORS WERE paralyzed. In September 1938, they had hoped for war. Now that it had come, they were completely unprepared, their networks perhaps a little denser but lacking any operational power.[1] During the autumn months, they kept meeting and working on hypothetical plans. The dark prophecies of Ludwig Beck, who foretold a French attack on the exposed western front, were unfulfilled for now except for a halfhearted French offensive, which was easily blocked. The French and British declared war but were slow to move and did very little for seven months. This period was nicknamed Sitzkrieg (the Sitting War, also known as the Phony or the Twilight War). The conspirators decided that their next opportunity would come before the "real" war, namely, when Hitler ordered the army to march westward. The generals were thrilled by the easy conquest of Poland, but many of them were still afraid of open war with England and France.

Then, a new window of opportunity suddenly opened. Gen. Kurt von Hammerstein, commander in chief of the army prior to 1934 and a staunch anti-Nazi, was called from retirement to command an army at the western front. Through the years, he became isolated and bitter, forced to helplessly watch Nazi barbarism and irresponsible foreign policy. Hammerstein, known as the "Red General" because of his good contacts in the German left, was not bound by dogmatic values of obedience and honor like most of his military colleagues. He recognized the part he had played in allowing the Nazi takeover and was resolute about doing everything possible to remedy his mistake. Now, he believed, Providence had given him a second chance.

On September 9, Hammerstein took charge and moved to his new headquarters, in Cologne. Soon afterward, he invited Fabian von Schla-brendorff, an emissary of the resistance, for a meeting, and concluded a plan for rapid action. Hammerstein would call Hitler to visit Co-logne to "demonstrate the military might of the Third Reich in the west at the same time as the Polish Campaign was being fought in the east."[2] Upon his arrival, the Führer would be arrested and neutralized. Hammerstein was ready to suffer the consequences and hoped that his example would serve as a trigger for a general insurgency. Schlabren-dorff promised to do his best. For a few hopeful days at the beginning of September 1939, the networks of resistance awoke again into life. Schlabrendorff recounted in his memoirs that "it became my job to inform the British on Hammerstein's plan. The British embassy had already been vacated, but I succeeded in reaching Sir George Ogilvie-Forbes, the counselor of the British embassy, around lunchtime in the Hotel Adlon."[3]

The Adlon, tall and luxurious, towered above the linden trees of Unter den Linden, the main thoroughfare of Berlin, a few steps from the Brandenburg Gate. Schlabrendorff entered the lobby and found the British diplomat waiting for him. While they were chatting in the lounge, two SS officers approached them. Schlabrendorff, as he testi-fied later, had "most uncomfortable moments," as he believed the offi-cers came to arrest him for dining with a British diplomat hours after the outbreak of the war. Luckily, however, they were oblivious to his presence and came merely to arrange with Sir George some details re-lated to the imminent departure of British embassy staff.[4]

For a moment, hopes were high. For the first time since Witzleben's departure from Berlin, the conspirators found a senior commander ready to cooperate with them. Even better, unlike anyone else with whom the conspirators had worked before, Hammerstein demanded assurances neither from Halder nor from Britain. He was ready to act against Hitler unconditionally, and alone.

Now the plan was ready for the next stage. Hammerstein dispatched the invitation to Hitler's headquarters. But the Führer refused to come. He probably didn't trust Hammerstein, whose anti-Nazi sympathies were well known, to the extent of putting his personal safety in Hammerstein's hands. Worse, a few days later, the Red General was removed from his post and retired. Hammerstein, sad and embittered, had failed to take his second chance. In 1933, he had not stopped the National Socialists from taking power, and now he could not stop them from waging war. In the next few years, before he succumbed to cancer in 1943, Hammerstein spoke bitterly of the leaders of the Wehrmacht, of their narrow-mindedness and cowardice. "These people turn me, an old soldier, into an anti-militarist," he told a friend upon hearing that Halder and Brauchitsch would not support a coup, not even after the National Socialist atrocities in Poland.[5]

The months of October and November, after Hammerstein's sudden departure, were a prolonged nightmare for the conspirators. Still, even in the midst of their despair, the networks of resistance slowly expanded: some joined, and even more became ripe for recruitment. The atrocities of the SS in Poland convinced several young officers who had not yet been politically involved to turn against the regime. Thus, for example, Maj. Helmuth Stieff, from the organization section at the army high command, became anti-Nazi following the massacres in the first months of the war: "Uprooting whole generations, including women and children, could be done only by sub-humans who do not deserve to be called 'Germans.' I am ashamed to be a German. Such a minority, with its murder, pillage and arson . . . will bring disaster on us all unless rapidly stopped."[6]

Hermann Kaiser, a captain in the reserves, who was later to fill a crucial role in the resistance networks, was also moved by the atrocities in Poland. He wrote in his diary in May 1941, "The army is hungry for pillage. Situation in Warsaw: The population is starving, so that women and children collapse and die in the street. Provincial Labor Leader [*Gauarbeitsführer*] Faatz: The Polish must perish, be exterminated . . . Destruction of churches: altars are being destroyed with firearms, and crucifixes are being slashed with axes . . . Property is being redistributed."[7] Even more radical was Fritz von der Schulenburg, deputy commander of the Berlin police, drafted into the army after the beginning of the war: "These acts will be stopped only through shooting. A change can be made only through an armed revolt. Only the forced removal of the omnipotent man can bring about a healing change."[8]

Irrespective of their will to act, Stieff and Schulenburg could do nothing against the regime. Everything was dependent, yet again, on Halder and Brauchitsch. Lieutenant Colonel Groscurth, on a visit to Poland right after the invasion, was also horrified by the massacres of Jews, noblemen, and intellectuals. Accordingly, he gave detailed reports to Oster, Beck, and his direct superior, Halder. The chief of staff, however, was not interested in horror stories and refused to consider them as a good enough reason for a coup d'état. He even forbade Groscurth from dispatching these reports to the military commanders on the western front, in order "not to burden them with details."[9]

Canaris's desperate attempts to end the atrocities did not fare any better. In the first months of the war, he issued protest after protest, only to be ignored by all. Just like Hammerstein, he began to hate the senior generals for their criminal indifference. "There is just no point in trying to convince them," he told Hassell.[10]

Dramatic developments stirred the high command yet again on October 9. Hitler convened the senior commanders of the Wehrmacht and gave them what many of them feared most: the order for a German offensive in the west: "If, in the near future, it turns out that England and its French satellite do not intend to end the war, I have reached a decision to act aggressively and without delay . . . An offensive is to be prepared . . . through the territories of Luxemburg, Belgium and Holland. This offensive should be executed with full force, as quickly as possible."[11]

Most generals in the high command were strongly averse to the western campaign, scheduled by Hitler for November 26. Brauchitsch was certain that Germany would be soundly defeated. Gen. Ritter von Leeb, commander of the Third Army Group, sent an impassioned memorandum against the offensive and called for peace, and even a radical Nazi general such as Reichenau denounced the plan as "criminal." He did not mean the breach of sovereignty of the Netherlands, Luxembourg, and Belgium, but rather a crime against the army, which might be destroyed as a result of such a dangerous adventure.[12]

Groscurth, eager to take advantage of this new opportunity, turned again to Halder. This time, the chief of staff was more attentive. His quartermaster general, Karl-Heinrich von Stülpnagel, promised Halder to "lock Brauchitsch up" if he refused to cooperate. In addition, he promised the chief of staff to tour the fronts to find new allies among the senior commanders in the field. On October 29, General Halder gave his final okay, and a few days later he instructed Oster to re-create the 1938 plans. For one week, the Wehrmacht high command in Zossen, near Berlin, turned into a hub of clandestine subversive activity.[13]

Again, Oster and his friends were busy planning. Contact was made with Heinz, the commando leader from 1938, and he was told to stand on high alert. In Rome, Dr. Josef Müller approached the British for assurances that they would not take advantage of the situation in case of a coup. Loyal commanders, such as Witzleben, agreed to put their troops at the disposal of the conspirators. Erich Kordt was even ready to assassinate Hitler simultaneously with the coup. He asked Oster for explosives in order to blow Hitler up during one of the daily briefings.[14]

But this coup attempt was no more than a phantom of the conspiracy of 1938. To paraphrase the French thinker Alexis de Tocqueville, it seems that Halder was "staging a play on the revolt of 1938" instead of repeating it. He never stopped raising obstacles and flatly refused to move on without Brauchitsch's consent. In addition, he complained to an emissary of the resistance, Lt. Gen. Georg Thomas, that Britain was waging war "not only against Hitler, but also against the German people." There was no other great man to replace the Führer, most young officers supported the regime, and the nation needed a guiding idea such as National Socialism. But still, Halder never said no, and left the conspirators in suspense. Would he act at the decisive moment? No one could tell. The agents of the resistance fared even worse with General Brauchitsch. When Thomas tried to brief him on the secret negotiations with Britain, he was silenced and threatened with arrest.[15]

On November 5, the army was ordered to stand on high alert, ready to march westward against Belgium, Holland, and Luxembourg. The conspirators believed they had reasons to be optimistic. The most important commanders were against the offensive, and the chance of winning their support for the coup was therefore substantial. Halder ordered Beck and Goerdeler to be ready for immediate action. Again, their hopes were high. Meanwhile, Brauchitsch drove to the Reich chancellery to convince Hitler to give up the offensive.[16] If the meeting failed, the conspirators believed, Brauchitsch would surely back them with his support. Beck, Oster, and the other leaders were putting their trust in Zossen, the center of resistance to the offensive in the west. Goerdeler, optimistic by nature, had begun to prepare cabinet lists for a new government. Beck and Schacht were more skeptical. Everyone was anxious to hear news from the crucial meeting between Hitler and Brauchitsch.

And news did come. The bizarre meeting between the Führer and the commander of his land army put an end to the conspiratorial farce of Zossen. After Brauchitsch mumbled something about the bad weather and possible insurgency among the troops, Hitler thundered at him, "In which units? What measures have you taken? How many death sentences did you give in response?" In his fury, Hitler said that he was quite familiar with the "spirit of Zossen"—a spirit of subversion, mutiny, and treason. One day, he would squash that spirit once and for all.[17]

Brauchitsch came back to Zossen trembling with fear. Hitler's remark about the "spirit of Zossen" convinced Halder and the conspirators that their plot might have been exposed. In a momentary panic, the chief of staff ordered all documents to be burned and the plan canceled. "It is not possible to avert the western offensive," he told Groscurth with tears in his eyes. "I simply cannot do it."[18]

Beck, meanwhile, received a detailed report from Groscurth on the atrocities of the SS in Poland: fifteen hundred Jews, including women and children, had been intentionally frozen to death while being transported in open trucks. The former chief of staff was horrified. These atrocities, he wrote to General Brauchitsch, would disgrace the German army for eternity. Brauchitsch did not even bother to respond. "The baleful character of the regime, especially ethically speaking, is ever clearer to Beck," wrote Hassell in his diary.[19] But what could the former chief of the General Staff do to help the Jews and the Poles, and to stop his country from being both morally corrupted and militarily defeated? The only solution was to cajole Halder again. Beck was reluctant, but when Stülpnagel, who held both men in high esteem, organized a meeting, the leader of the resistance could not refuse.[20]

The two met again on January 26, 1940. To avoid the Gestapo, they walked together in the empty streets of Dahlem, a quiet suburb of Berlin. Beck lectured Halder on the urgency of a revolt: Hitler was bringing doom on Germany. Halder, as usual, pointed out difficulties: the nation stood behind Hitler, and the conspirators had failed to make adequate political preparations. In these circumstances, it was not possible to stage a coup. Beck, in response, accused Halder of cowardice. "As an experienced rider," he said, "Halder must know that one had first to throw one's heart over the obstacle." This remark, noted Nicholas Reynolds, turned the rest of the meeting into an "exercise in name calling."[21] Beck must have remembered that, in the past, it was Halder who had tried to convince him to move against Hitler. Now, the roles were reversed. It seems that it was less the personality of either Beck or Halder that mattered, and more the role of the chief of staff, which invested its bearer with a sense of responsibility and caution. Beck and Halder parted on the "worst of terms."[22] They never saw each other again.

One ray of hope remained. Erich Kordt, the young diplomat in the foreign ministry, was ready to go ahead with the assassination plan. Maybe, he thought, Halder would change his mind if the Führer were dead. But, on November 8, it became clear that the plan couldn't be carried out. As a result of Georg Elser's assassination attempt, all security organizations were on high alert, and it was virtually impossible to get explosives except for strictly authorized, well-defined reasons. The last chance appeared to have gone.[23]

As if that were not enough, the conspirators suffered another blow from the outside. On November 9, the SS kidnapped two British agents, S. Payne Best and Richard Stevens. The pair were in touch with two colonels from the resistance, who promised to connect them with a general. After a few meetings, an interview was scheduled in Venlo, on the Dutch-German border. Unfortunately, the two "colonels" were Gestapo agents, and their commander was none other than Walter Schellenberg of SD (SS security service) counterintelligence. When the agents arrived at the meeting point, in a café a few meters from the German border, they were attacked by machine-gun fire. Their companion, a Dutch intelligence operative, died, and they themselves were bundled into Germany.[24] As is mentioned in chapter 6, Hitler and Himmler both suspected that Best and Stevens were the wire-pullers behind Elser's assassination attempt. That was not true. Nevertheless, the event was detrimental for the conspirators. Now, the British were ever more careful when in touch with German anti-Nazis, and the negotiations, never flowing anyway, turned into a trickle.[25]

In 1940, the German resistance had reached an impasse. The conspiracy, though somewhat larger, was completely impotent, with most of its senior allies lost. The powerful generals, Halder and Brauchitsch included, were unreachable; grim predictions of German defeat looked hollow; and negotiations with the British were going nowhere. The strategy of Beck, Goerdeler, and Hassell, presuming the cooperation of outside forces, cajoling and imploring Halder and Brauchitsch to act, had gone nowhere, along with the belief that a legal, "bloodless" revolution was a realistic option. September 1938 was long in the past, and it seemed futile to try to repeat the same strategy over and over again. More and more conspirators accepted Oster's opinion that Hitler must first be removed by assassination, and only then should the generals be approached. Oster had had enough of attempts to convert Halder and Brauchitsch. Along with many others, he liberated himself from the incompetent "spirit of Zossen."[26]

But that was not enough. Oster understood that the reliability of the conspirators, himself included, had been irreversibly compromised in the eyes of the British. To remedy that, he made a decision considered by many Germans, even after 1945, to be unforgivable. In late September 1939, he called his old friend Colonel Sas, the Dutch military attaché, and leaked to him the exact timing of the German offensive in the west. He knew that German soldiers might die because of it, but then maybe the war would be brought to a quick end. Under these circumstances, who knew? Perhaps coup d'état would become a distinct possibility again. From conspiracy, Oster moved to collaboration with the enemy.

"One may say I am a traitor to my country," he told the Dutch officer when giving him the information, "but actually I am not that. I regard myself as a better German than all those who follow Hitler. It is my plan and my duty to free Germany and thereby the world of this plague." Oster knew well that he had crossed the Rubicon. "There is no going back for me anymore," he told his friend and confidant Franz Liedig, one of the co-organizers of the 1938 shock troops. Later on, he continued to sabotage the German war effort by tipping off officers from Belgium, Norway, Denmark, and Yugoslavia about impending German attacks on their countries.[27]

It was to no avail. Both the Dutch and the Belgians refused to believe Oster's information, and they were certain that the German informer was nothing but a provocateur.[28] Very few believed, indeed, that Germany would attack the western countries at all. On May 10, 1940, when Hitler finally gave the orders to march, the western armies were mortally surprised. The Wehrmacht turned to France through the Low Countries, occupying Belgium and the Netherlands. To the astonishment of Beck and the other ringleaders of the resistance, the French army and the British Expeditionary Force were soundly beaten. France was exposed to German attack, and its army, already weakened by the Belgian debacle, was hardly able to slow the Wehrmacht at all. In spring 1940, it was only a matter of time before France fell.

The conspirators were agape once more. Beck refused to believe that England and France were so weak. He was still certain that Hitler was bound to lose the war. Hitler could not win; he should not win. In early 1940, Beck met with one of his friends, a pastor, who was optimistic about the war. He told Beck that Germany would win. The general gave his military counterarguments and explained to his friend why the Reich would finally lose. Once the conversation had ended, Beck escorted him out of the garden. When he opened the gate, the former chief of staff provided an afterthought. "I have seen the man," he avowed, "and I can assure you that he is one of the most evil men ever to walk the face of the earth."[29]

At the end of September 1939, Beck found out that his close friend, Gen. Werner von Fritsch, who had been removed from his post on fabricated charges of homosexuality, had been killed on duty. While walking in a field near the front, he had been spotted by a Polish machine-gun crew and was shot to death. Beck was certain that the death amounted to suicide. Fritsch could not bear his humiliation.

A little later, in early October, Beck invited Goerdeler to his house in Goethestrasse. The two of them agreed not to waver in their resistance against Hitler, no matter the costs. They were in constant touch with Oster, who was still working on expanding the clandestine network. Beck also maintained close contact with the Social Democratic leaders Leuschner and Leber, who had joined the resistance in late 1939.

In Goethestrasse, following the German atrocities in Poland, Beck and Goerdeler listened to the BBC. The announcer introduced a British general, a veteran of the Great War. The old officer asked where the upright Prussian officers he knew from the last war were. He lamented the death of Fritsch, who symbolized the proper spirit in his mind. The BBC played a German military funeral song: "Once I had a comrade / a better one you could not find." Goerdeler turned to Beck. His eyes were wet with tears.[30]

## 9

# SIGNS IN THE DARKNESS:
# REBUILDING THE CONSPIRACY

**D**OROTHY THOMPSON WAS an influential American journalist during the Second World War. She hosted an important radio show and was considered a distinguished expert on all things German. Contrary to others in the American elite, she sympathized with the German opposition and was familiar with it. In a series of shortwave broadcasts to Germany in summer 1942, she called from New York to a German acquaintance—a mysterious oppositionist known only as Hans—imploring him and his political friends to stop hesitating, rise up, and act. It was time to get rid of Hitler once and for all: "The last time we met, Hans, and drank tea together on that beautiful terrace before the lake, you told me: 'Listen, Dorothy, there will not be a war' . . . I said that one day you would have to demonstrate by deeds, by drastic deeds, where you stood, if the salvation of Germany depended on the answer to that question. And I remember that I asked you whether you and your friends would ever have the courage to act."[1]

But the mysterious Hans (on whom more later) and his fellow resistance fighters were unable to do "drastic deeds," and not necessarily because of insufficient courage. The failures of the German resistance in 1938 and '39 had led it into a crisis related to basic structural constraints. As we saw in chapter 8, the network structure of the conspiracy, tailored to the reality of September 1938, did not fit with the altogether different world created by the war. Too small to do anything on its own, the network led by Oster, Goerdeler, and Beck did not have access to Hitler and was still dependent on Halder's goodwill. Now, under the conditions of the escalating global conflict, cooperation from the higher echelons of the army was increasingly unrealistic. They were busy with the war, intoxicated with victory. Some of them were even bribed with promotions, medals, and enormous sums of money.[2] In order to overcome their dependence on unreliable outsiders, the conspirators had to acquire an ability to stage a coup d'état mainly by themselves. For that to happen, the network had to be much larger and also had to undergo some important transitions in structure and strategy. Though Oster and others were constantly working to expand the network, by 1940 the transitions were still far off in the future.

It was hard to recruit new rank-and-file members while Hitler was scoring breathtaking victories in the west. In May 1940, German panzers stormed into France through the Ardennes Forest, considered by many to be impregnable to armored units. Large parts of the French army were destroyed in Belgium, along with the British Expeditionary Force. Between May 27 and June 4, the remnants of the beaten British troops—hundreds of thousands of them—were evacuated to England from Dunkirk in France. Paris was occupied eleven days later, and French prime minister Paul Reynaud resigned. By June 21, the game was up. Hitler forced the French to sign an armistice in Compiègne Forest, in the same rail carriage where Germany had signed its humiliating armistice terms at the end of the Great War. Germany took vast French territories, Paris included, under its control. What was left was entrusted to the puppet regime of Vichy.

Hitler's victories were confusing for die-hard German patriots like Beck, Goerdeler, and Hassell. They, too, remembered Germany's humiliation after the Great War, but they could not bring themselves to rejoice in the military triumph of their country. It was, after all, the triumph of Adolf Hitler. Ulrich von Hassell, who became the de facto foreign minister of the resistance, poured his feelings into his diary: "No one can deny the magnitude of Hitler's achievement, but they cannot cover up the real nature of his actions and deeds and the terrifying danger looming over all the sublime values ... The weight of this tragedy can move one to despair, making it impossible to rejoice in the greatest national achievements ... The masses are ruled by idiotic indifference, a result of seven years of being ordered around by loud-speakers."[3]

Hassell, Beck, and Oster were still waiting for a military setback that might convince the generals to reconsider their support for the regime. Meanwhile, Hitler's enemies abroad were having difficulties as well. The United Kingdom still stood upright, badly beaten, while its French ally was no more. In summer 1940, Britain was left alone, a small island of democracy confronting Hitler's mighty Reich. The Nazi empire stretched from Poland in the east to France in the west, and ruled also Norway, Denmark, Belgium, and the Netherlands. But Winston Churchill, Chamberlain's successor as prime minister, was not ready to surrender.

Upon realizing that Churchill would continue fighting, Hitler made up his mind to invade the British Isles. The main struggle would be in the air, as the Royal Air Force and the British fleet had to be destroyed as a precondition for an amphibious invasion. Britain was hit hard, and some of its towns were badly damaged by the air raids of the Luftwaffe. But by autumn 1940, the RAF was still in the air and Hitler understood that an invasion was not feasible. The amphibious assault, code-named Operation Sea Lion, was canceled.

Unable to win over Halder or other senior generals, or to do something by themselves, Oster and his men were still trying to grow their network, readying it for independent action. They did most of their recruitment through liaison officers, many of them civilians scanning the fronts to locate potential recruits from those with anti-Nazi sympathies. When a likely person was found, an initial conversation took place, and then he was directed to one of the commanders, or "connectors," for further clearing. Most new recruits were ordered to expand the network further, thus achieving what is called in network-analysis theory a "viral effect," namely, a state of affairs in which every new recruit recruits others, and the network grows exponentially. Needless to say, the ever-present danger of exposure by the Gestapo, the wartime conditions, and the Nazi sympathies of most officers dampened such an effect. But still, the network grew.

For reasons of security, new recruits were given partial information only, and were in some cases told that the movement had been established only recently, in order to keep hidden the coup plans of 1938

and '39. Col. Hans Crome, an anti-Nazi officer and member of the resistance, told his Soviet captors how he was recruited:

> In October 1941, an old friend of mine, Dr. Jessen, a professor of
> economics at Berlin University, arrived in Paris. Dr. Jessen had
> met me several times before arriving in Paris and knew my nega-
> tive attitude toward Hitler. For that reason he informed me with-
> out any fanfare that an illegal organization had been established in
> Berlin in 1941, whose goal was to remove Hitler and his political
> system and to stop the war . . . When Dr. Jessen asked me to join
> the organization, I naturally agreed without hesitation.[4]

Now, Crome had to justify the trust given to him, while obeying strict
procedures of information security:

> Discussing practical issues about the organization, we decided
> that I would actively recruit new members to the organization and
> assume the role of liaison officer between the Berlin headquarters
> and General Field Marshal Witzleben . . . In conclusion, Dr. Jes-
> sen suggested that I come into contact with Generals Oster and
> Olbricht, who were in charge of the organization's practical issues
> and whom he informed of my joining the organization upon re-
> turning to Berlin . . . I agreed with Dr. Jessen in summer that year
> that an SS man named Langbehn would arrive in Crimea to con-
> tact me and provide a secret password with Jessen's signature. We
> also agreed that I would inform General Oster about new recruits
> [using code words] via official correspondence.[5]

Recruitment, however, was not enough. The network had gotten
bigger, but in the first two years of the war, it was as yet unclear what
it could do—what the point of it was. Bereft of support from senior
generals, operational capabilities, or access to Hitler, the resistance resorted to waiting patiently as well as diving into an ocean of plans,
hopes, and dreams.

# 10

# ON THE WINGS OF THOUGHT: NETWORKS OF IMAGINATION

**B**EING UNABLE TO do anything tangible against the regime, leading members of the resistance spent the first few years of the war in meticulous preparation for a post-Nazi Germany, something that seemed remote but still inspiring. After all, the resistance had to be engaged in some sort of positive activity other than recruitment, and if a coup d'état was not feasible, what was there to do apart from plan? Opinions were exchanged, memoranda written, cabinet lists and shadow governments formed. With the building of a clandestine network in the real world being slow and frustrating, the conspirators turned also to networks of imagination. This intellectual work was a means for friends to exchange ideas about the future of the country, to re-create the conspiracy as an imagined political community with its own president, prime minister, cabinet posts, laws, regulations, and constitution. It may seem absurd in retrospect, considering that the war and its atrocities were raging all around them, but for the conspirators it was vital. Had not General Halder, for instance, complained in 1938 and '39 about the conspirators' failure to adequately prepare a political basis for a new regime?

The first proposal for an "alternative governmental structure" was written by Ulrich von Hassell, after long deliberations with Goerdeler, Beck, and Popitz. Hassell proposed the replacement of the totalitarian regime with a *Rechtsstaat*—a conservative state in which the rule of law would reign, based on fairness, justice, and Christian values. After the overthrow of the Nazi regime, the conspirators would establish an interim military dictatorship followed by an authoritarian regime, most probably a monarchy. Hassell, never a democrat, did not want to restore the Weimar Republic or anything similar. He desired a strong government not responsible to an elected parliament, whose role would be to ensure basic rights such as life, property, honor, and justice. The Nazi Party would be dissolved and banned, nor would other parties be allowed. Instead, the country would be ruled by a coalition of government, army, and business elites. Germany would propose a "just peace" to its enemies and would consequently leave all "non-German" territories. It would, however, keep Austria, the Sudetenland, Danzig, and the Polish Corridor. The Reich would still strive for hegemony in Europe, but peacefully, not militarily, as a natural outcome of its geographical, economic, and cultural power.[1]

The plans drafted by Dr. Carl Goerdeler, the dominant figure in the conservative part of the resistance, were more complicated and influential than those made by Hassell. They were most thoroughly expressed in "The Goal" (Das Ziel), which he probably wrote at the end of 1941. The document depicts in detail Goerdeler's vision concerning all spheres of life in "New Germany." It is divided into a philosophical introduction and three main topics of discussion: foreign policy, internal policy, and constitutional structure. The philosophical introduction is the key to the document and is, in fact, a discussion on human nature and reciprocal relations between citizen and state, under the curious slogan "the totality of politics." On the one hand, wrote Goerdeler, man is a selfish creature, struggling and competing against others to promote private interests. On the other hand, he carries a divine, spiritual spark, which may lead him to achievements for the benefit of society. The role of the state is to create a balance between these two poles and to form a peaceful space in which people would be able to compete without doing harm to their neighbors. Meanwhile, society must cultivate the good elements in human nature through spiritual and moral support, allowing human beings to peacefully and freely develop their talents. The state should be not artificial but rather "organic," a term Goerdeler repeated again and again in "The Goal." It must be based on a confederation of "natural" communities, an alliance between localities and families united to ensure the collective good. In that sense, Goerdeler incessantly wavered between Enlightenment ideas, such as natural rights, individualism, and the power of reason, and anti-Enlightenment, conservative ideologies perceiving the state as an "organism" and putting stress on "natural" communities. An ardent disciple of the European Enlightenment, and a critic at the same time, he oscillated between these two poles throughout his life.

Holding this hybrid view, Goerdeler abhorred the idea of a totalitarian, ever-meddling government, out of a liberal concern for human and civil rights and a worry that such a government would enforce a "nonorganic" order, the worst enemy of human freedom and dignity. This indicated Goerdeler's animosity to National Socialist totalitarian ideology, with its methods of coercion, deprivation of freedom, and an education system intended to turn human beings into obedient machines. However, in a more conservative spirit, he maintained that modern democracy would fail as well. Its underlying materialism distanced man from God and, just as bad, subordinated citizens to the artificial rule of mass parties, which had nothing to do with the real interests of voters. Goerdeler's solution was a hereditary monarchy led by an emperor who would appoint a Reich chancellor, who in turn would lead the state as long as he enjoyed the emperor's confidence. At the same time, Goerdeler wanted to avoid dictatorship by significantly curtailing the authority of central government. Its role should be mainly restricted to foreign policy, national security, public order, justice, and infrastructure. Most decisions related to the life of the citizens would be taken by mayors and local parliaments, elected by votes from all Reich citizens of both genders. Citizens would vote only for candidates from their immediate environment, whom they knew and respected, instead of for political demagogues on the national level, known to them only through stupefying propaganda and mass rallies.

Compared to Hassell's unabashed authoritarianism, Goerdeler's vision was liberal: full freedom of speech, of religion, and of the press, and property rights would be ensured. All would be allowed to speak their mind, and no party would be banned—not even the Nazi Party. Nevertheless, the criminals among the party leaders would be prosecuted, and the property looted by party organs would be restored to its rightful owners. All civil servants appointed because of their Nazi affiliations would be reviewed, and might be demoted. However, Goerdeler did not agree to deprive any person, even a Nazi, of basic rights such as freedom of speech. As far as foreign policy was concerned, his plan was very similar to Hassell's: peace would be made, and Germany would withdraw from most occupied territories, except for Austria, the Sudetenland, Danzig, and the Polish Corridor. It would also form an alliance with Great Britain and the United States, thereby restoring its lost African colonies from the Great War. (It would not exploit these colonies economically but rather develop them for the indigenous peoples.) Nazi criminals would face the full force of the law, and the state would compensate all victims of Hitler.[2]

The two proposals, both Hassell's and Goerdeler's, may seem authoritarian from today's point of view. Some scholars have argued that there was no real difference between the German resistance and the Nazi regime, or that the "resistance was fighting a regime with which it essentially concurred."[3] This argument is problematic, not only because its definitions of both democracy and Nazism are simplistic and inaccurate but also because it ignores the crucial issue of interaction between the different groups in the conspiracy. The proposals of Hassell and Goerdeler were not "platforms" of the resistance but merely two opinions among many. The Social Democratic leaders in the conspiracy had naturally different ideas, and so did the Kreisau Circle, discussed in detail later in this chapter. As the draft cabinet list of the conspiracy shows, the future regime would have been a coalition between all of these different groups. Regardless of their viewpoints, the mere fact that there were many groups required a certain degree of pluralism, which was likely to lead to a regime that was at least somewhat democratic. This is true regardless of the pressure the Western Allies would likely have applied against an authoritarian regime in post-Nazi Germany.

Furthermore, even authoritarian proposals such as Hassell's differed greatly from the Nazi regime itself. Almost all conspirators, regardless of political orientation, agreed to liberate the inmates of the concentration camps, to give up on unbridled territorial expansion in both east and west, and to withdraw from most occupied territories. The ideas of "living space" (Lebensraum) and genocidal anti-Semitism —two cornerstones of Nazi ideology—were completely absent from their proposals.[4]

But what about legal, "civilized" anti-Semitism, which was well accepted in wide circles of the German conservative right and beyond?

The proposals of Hassell and Goerdeler differed also in their respective solutions to the notorious "Jewish question." Both agreed that Hitler's Jewish victims must be compensated, but their opinions regarding Jews' civil status differed greatly.

Surprisingly, Hassell's proposal was the more liberal of the two. According to his memorandum, immediately after the downfall of the regime, all laws enacted by the National Socialist Party and its affiliate organizations would be nullified, "especially the Jewish laws."[5] That definition included, of course, the notorious Nuremberg Laws. The new regime would safeguard the rights of the Jewish minority and ensure full civil equality.

The position taken by Goerdeler was certainly less liberal, but it was more complex, and in certain respects more farsighted. As we have seen in previous chapters, Goerdeler was a sworn enemy of National Socialist anti-Semitic persecution. He denounced all expressions of racist violence, especially Kristallnacht, and even implored the British to refuse to negotiate with Hitler until he stopped persecuting Polish-German Jews. During the war, he was horrified about the transport of German Jews to the extermination camps in the east. He wrote,

> On January 19 and 27 [1942] ... Jews from Leipzig were again evacuated. Outside it was freezing, minus 15 to 20 Celsius. The Jews had/to hand their woolen clothes over ... They were loaded into open trucks, men, women and children ... In the transport there was a 64-year-old woman whose brother, a professor in the University of Leipzig, had been severely wounded in the last war and won a medal for extraordinary courage ... They were sent to the east in cattle trucks ... It horrifies the soul, when one imagines the hearts of fathers and mothers, seeing their children freezing and starving before their own eyes. I cannot imagine any German with a heart, who does not understand that such horrors must bring revenge upon our people ... Such intended inhumanity is unprecedented in the annals of human history.[6]

As a reaction to these "unprecedented horrors," already under way when "The Goal" was written, Goerdeler desperately tried to remedy the problem at its root, providing a solution that would ensure such things never happened again. He proposed "a general reform of the status of the Jews in the entire world." As a die-hard nationalist with pro-Zionist sympathies, he believed that the only solution for the Jewish people was national independence: establishing in Palestine, or parts of Canada and South America, a Jewish state in which citizenship would be automatically granted to all Jews in the world. Such a state would allow the Jewish people to lead a normal, sovereign life, like any other nation on earth, and would protect world Jewry from anti-Semitic regimes, pogroms, and riots, not only by giving sanctuary but also insofar as the Jews would have diplomatic power and a sovereign presence at the League of Nations. This was far from being unreasonable. As is argued by the jurist Fritz Kieffer, in the prewar years even the Third Reich hesitated to violate the rights of Jews with foreign passports, out of fear of reprisals by their governments.[7] It was, therefore, the mere citizenship of Jews in anti-Semitic countries which turned them into an "internal problem" for these countries and denied them effective protection. A Jewish state was, according to Goerdeler, the only real, enduring solution.

In an influential article written in 1984, historian Christoph Dipper wrote that Goerdeler planned to cancel the citizenship of most German Jews. This article, though often quoted uncritically by other scholars, is based on an erroneous reading of Goerdeler's writing. In fact, Goerdeler never called for the expulsion of Jews, nor for the sweeping withdrawal of their citizenship. Though, in principle, Jews were supposed to be citizens of "their" state, in practice, around 80 percent of German Jews would keep their current citizenship: everyone whose family became naturalized with the emancipation decree of 1871 (and not before the emancipation, as Dipper suggested) and those who had converted to Christianity, in addition to all Jewish veterans of the Great War and their direct descendants. The rest would be considered citizens of a foreign country (the Jewish state) and would be able to stay and work in Germany just like any other foreigner.[8]

It is no wonder that Goerdeler considered himself pro-Zionist. In fact, when touring Palestine and other Middle Eastern countries with his son, his warmest praises were reserved for the Yishuv, the Jewish-Zionist community in Palestine. "The vegetable fields and fruit orchards of the Jews," he wrote, "are among the most fertile I have seen in the Levant and North Africa . . . The town of Tel Aviv is especially interesting, and is planned according to modern principles. It has neat shopping streets, good shops, a nice beach and handsome villas ... The streets are clean and covered with asphalt." He especially appreciated Jewish technological innovation, for example, in irrigation canals, and the combination of advanced scientific research and physical labor. He also praised the kibbutzim, the Hebrew education system, and the Hebrew University of Jerusalem.[9]

The proposals of Goerdeler and Hassell enjoyed some currency in the conservative circles of the resistance, but no less important was the work of a special think tank, established separately around 1940. It was called the Kreisau Circle, after the estate of its founder, Count Helmuth James von Moltke. This unusual resistance fighter, identified later as the mysterious "Hans" whom Dorothy Thompson referred to in her radio broadcasts, was an international lawyer and a scion of one of the most important Prussian noble families. His great-uncle Gen. Helmuth von Moltke was the famed Prussian strategist of the Franco-Prussian War. Another relative was the German chief of staff in the early days of the Great War. Helmuth James was born in 1907 and inherited the estate in Kreisau, Upper Silesia, which had been given to his great-uncle as a present from the kaiser. He took charge of the estate while still young and immediately began working on a plan to settle its debts. He was successful as a lawyer, landlord, and economist.

A liberal and generous man, though at times cool and haughty, Moltke was admired by many of his German and international acquaintances—so said his two British friends Michael Balfour and Lionel Curtis. Their account has a touch of hagiography about it, common in many postwar reminiscences, but it is still both touching and valuable:

> It often appeared as though the ordinary pleasure of life meant little to him: he never smoked, seldom drank, and generally seemed indifferent to what he was eating ... Unsparing of himself, he looked critically on people reluctant to make a similar effort ... but his slightly dour concentration on the subject in hand was moderated by a lively sense of humour, puckish rather than cynical: no matter how much Helmuth loathed the things for which his opponents stood, he was much more likely to laugh at them

than lose his temper . . . Underlying all of his strength of character and intellect was a deep love for the simple things of life, flowers and the country-side, his home, his children, his friends.[10]

An unusual left-leaning liberal among Prussian landlords, Moltke was also a supporter of the Weimar Republic. Unlike many others, he chose to give away most of his lands to peasants, as he believed that in modern times land should belong to its cultivators. During the 1920s, he was mainly disturbed by social problems, especially the poor conditions in Silesian working-class neighborhoods, and joined an initiative of the jurist Eugen Rosenstock. Together with other friends, some of whom became members of the Kreisau Circle, he helped to create summer camps for young Silesians of all classes, combining physical labor, liberal education in law, history, economics, and culture, and a variety of musical and recreational activities.

Prof. Adolf Reichwein, one of the lecturers in the Silesian summer camps, was to fulfill a major role in the Kreisau Circle and the German resistance as a whole. He was a Social Democratic Christian intellectual, tall, with fiery red hair. As an avid supporter of the republic, he joined the Social Democratic Party. In the late twenties, he traveled around the globe, building his reputation as a scientist, scholar, educator, and adventurer. As part of his journeying, he crossed the United States and Canada in an old Ford car, reached Lapland and the North Pole, and traveled on to East Asia, where he was deeply influenced by Chinese philosophy and mysticism. As a declared rival of the Nazi regime, he was fired from the university in one of the post-1933 purges, but he rejected a tempting offer of an academic teaching post in Istanbul. Unlike many others, he did not want to find shelter abroad, preferring to fight the Nazi regime from within.[11]

In 1933, the educational work of Moltke, Reichwein, and others came to an abrupt end. The new regime was now unwilling to tolerate humanistic educational initiatives, and the summer camps of Silesia were dissolved. Unlike many other Germans, Moltke had no illusions about the new regime. Upon hearing a friend say, "It is good that the Nazis took over, because soon they will get tired of government and will be replaced," he became enraged. He advised other friends, mainly Jews, to leave Germany as soon as possible. "Get out! Get out!" he told them emphatically. "This man [Hitler] will do everything as he wrote in his book [*Mein Kampf* ]." That was a frighteningly accurate prophecy, but not many people took it seriously at the time.[12]

Moltke's resistance to the Nazi regime increased with the passing years: the Night of the Long Knives; the persecution of churches, Jews, and the left; the Nuremberg Laws and Kristallnacht, all reinforced his original belief: Hitler was implementing his master plan as laid out in *Mein Kampf.* Moltke did his best to help. More and more of his time was devoted to assisting Jews who were trying to emigrate from Germany, and he even went to the Viennese Gestapo to help two of them.[13] In the late 1930s, along with his wife, Freya, he weaved a dense network of resistance fighters—noblemen, intellectuals, high officials, and labor-union leaders. Moltke's group was in contact not only with Beck, Goerdeler, and Oster but also with the Western Allies and anti-Nazi underground movements in Holland, Denmark, France, and Norway. That was the group that the Gestapo later nicknamed the Kreisau Circle.

In 1938, Moltke stumbled upon the German resistance network by contacting Hans von Dohnanyi and, through him, Hans Oster. The latter recruited him as a legal adviser to the Abwehr, the usual cover for resistance activities. As part of his new duties, Moltke was able not only to subvert criminal orders, save victims, and reduce the severity of war crimes, but also to be in touch with leading oppositionists. He didn't take part in planning the 1938 coup, but he knew something of it. His group, though connected with the German resistance, all the while maintained its own separate, independent network.[14]

In fact, Moltke was less interested in coups than in what he perceived as more basic, underlying problems with the anti-Nazi cause. As is mentioned in chapter 5, General Halder had complained that the conspirators never planned anything substantial for the "day after," and merely asked the soldiers to "clean the room" like "housemaids." Moltke would have agreed with this complaint. For him, planning for a future Germany was an absolute necessity, regardless of whether the Nazi regime was overthrown by the conspirators or by military defeat. In the first years of the war, he was very skeptical and ambivalent about the mere idea of a coup, though he never ruled it out completely and was ready to cooperate with its initiators.

A breakthrough in the plans occurred when Moltke met a distant relative, Count Peter Yorck von Wartenburg, destined to be his closest friend and associate in the Kreisau Circle. He discovered that Yorck, too, had formed a small group of anti-Nazi activists, with a mind to plan for the future of Germany. Now, the two small groups united into a single network.[15] All members were naturally well aware that they stood in mortal danger. From the regime's point of view, their intellectual activity constituted high treason punishable by death.

Moltke and Yorck divided the twenty-odd members of their network into small groups and gave them research tasks, such as church-state relations, economics, law and constitution, local government, security, foreign policy, and prosecution of war criminals. At times, external experts were consulted, but they were not told about the project as a whole. The groups met separately, once a month or more often, in Moltke's estate at Kreisau or in Yorck's place at Klein-Oels. There were also three important plenary meetings of the entire circle in May 1942, October 1942, and June 1943.

The few surviving testimonies on the meetings at the Kreisau estate tell us something about the clandestine, mysterious atmosphere that prevailed. When members came to the meetings, they didn't stop at the Kreisau railway station but rather at an obscure little station in the nearby countryside, built long before for a visit of Emperor William II. Understandably, they did not want to cross the village, where they would be exposed to the curious eyes of the locals. Moltke waited for his guests at the little station and led them through lanes, forests, and lakes to the "mountain house," a small abode near the castle used by him, Freya, and their children. Even inside the house, security precautions were tight. In the dining room, only social matters could be discussed; politics was for the locked conference hall alone. Moltke, it seems, couldn't trust even his servants. In this curious atmosphere, surrounded by the lush landscape of rural Silesia, the Kreisauers imagined Germany's future.

The state they imagined was a federation of small and large communities with considerable authority for self-government, united by a loose federal structure to maintain justice, order, freedom, and the rule of law. In many respects, this was similar to the plan of Carl Goerdeler. Just as in his plan, the citizens' influence inside their communities would be greater than their power over the federal government. Eligible voters—every citizen twenty-one years old or older— would elect their representatives to the council of the region (*Kreis*).

These councils would elect representatives to the state parliament (*Landtag*), and only the *Landtag* deputies would elect the Reichstag, the highest legislative body of the Reich. The parliament in every state would elect senators (*Landesverweser*), and the members of the Senate (*Reichsrat*) would elect the head of state (*Reichsverweser*) for a term of twelve years. The *Reichsverweser* would have wide powers: to appoint and demote the prime minister and other cabinet members, and to ratify laws with his signature.

Unlike Goerdeler, the Kreisau Circle saw the "Jewish question" as an issue of German citizenship that must be resolved inside Germany, not internationally, according to principles of liberalism and civic equality. The draft constitution explicitly maintained that "all laws and acts discriminating against an individual for reasons of belonging to a certain nation, race or creed are void. All discriminating bylaws deriving from such acts are to be cancelled as well."[16] The new government would denounce racism and racial thinking and, just as Goerdeler had planned, would compensate the victims of National Socialism—both Jews and others. A special emphasis was put on educational reform. New textbooks would be written as quickly as possible, but even before they were ready, all existing National Socialist textbooks would be removed from the curriculum.

In matters of foreign policy, the Kreisau plan departed radically from both Goerdeler and Hassell, and was certainly less colored by realpolitik. Far from being based on nationalism, the Reich policy would strive to limit the sovereignty of the nation-state and would integrate Germany in a new federal structure, a "United States of Europe." All Nazi leaders would be removed from power, and the war criminals among them would be tried before an international tribunal of six judges: three from Allied countries, two from neutral countries, and one from Germany. That structure was intended to frame the future war-crimes trials as an endeavor of international justice, rather than as petty revenge against the German people.[17]

Planning for the future of Germany was a common, even a fundamental, activity of the German resistance up to 1942 and even beyond. However, Goerdeler, Beck, and Hassell were also trying to work toward a coup d'état. In the Kreisau case, things were more ambiguous. Theoretical discussions, interesting and important as they were, may seem to an ex post facto observer somewhat detached from reality.

Until 1942, Moltke and his friends were flying on the wings of thought, dealing with theoretical questions and building networks of imagination, while the war was raging before their eyes. Moltke himself abhorred violence of all kinds, at least until 1942. In 1940, most members of his circle held similarly pacifist views. Some of them worked with Goerdeler and were ready to contribute their talent to the post-Nazi state, but their Christian idealism prevented them from joining the coup plans until later.[18]

In addition to Julius Leber and Fritz von der Schulenburg, both of whom always advocated a violent coup, Peter Yorck was gradually being won over toward a more violent, activist line. Unlike Moltke, he saw himself not as a citizen of the world but as a Christian and a German in body, heart, and soul. As a nobleman, he felt it was his duty to resist the wickedness and crimes of the Nazi regime. "I am not and could never be a Nazi," he said many years later to his National Socialist judge, when accused of resistance to the "National Socialist concept of justice, that the Jews have to be uprooted." "The vital point running through all of these questions," he said, "is the totalitarian claim of the state over the citizen to the exclusion of his religious and moral obligations toward God."[19] Yorck obtained information on the "final solution" and distributed it to both the Kreisau Circle and the main network of the German resistance. The extermination of the Jews probably convinced him that the Nazi regime must be resisted by force, even by deadly violence.

Moltke, as we shall see later, was drifting tortuously toward this view as well. Meanwhile, he helped to save Jews, supported European undergrounds, undermined criminal orders, and served the conspiracy as a diplomat, using his excellent contacts with British and American notables. Like Oster, he was willing to assist the Allies in their war effort against Germany. "We are ready to help you to win both the war and the peace," he assured a British contact in 1942.[20]

Around late 1941, some of the conspirators again planned to kill Hitler. Field Marshal Erwin von Witzleben, the commander in chief of the Wehrmacht at the western front, reluctantly allowed some of his staff officers to plan another assassination attempt. It is possible that the detailed information on the atrocities of the SS in Poland given to him by Canaris in spring 1940 influenced his decision.[21] Again, a coup was not, and could not really be, planned. The resistance network was still too small and lacked operational strength.[22]

The two would-be assassins, Capt. Alexander von Voss and Capt. Count Ulrich Wilhelm Schwerin von Schwanenfeld, were both close associates of Field Marshal Witzleben. Schwerin belonged to the tiny minority of young, deeply religious officers horrified by the atrocities in Poland.[23] The route of Voss into the resistance, however, was more complicated, a clear example of revolutionary mutation. Voss was a nonpolitical Prussian conservative, with a nationalistic and military mind-set. His letters are a mixed bag of optimism and eagerness for German victory, and a growing critique of the National Socialist system's corruption, abuse of the French, and failure to end the war with a fair peace agreement. His wife testified that, like Schwerin, he was horrified by the atrocities in Poland. This criticism, however, did not lead him into the resistance until he joined Witzleben's staff, in October 1940. There, as he rubbed shoulders with die-hard resistance fighters, his doubts and criticism crystallized more and more into active resistance. Witzleben, he wrote, was like his father, and the two had lengthy daily conversations. The field marshal told him "what he otherwise does not tell anyone else." It was the father-son relationship with Witzleben that mutated Voss into an active resistance fighter.[24]

When Voss and Schwerin heard, in late 1941, that Hitler had planned a military parade in Paris, they recruited a handful of conspirators to form a sharpshooter squad. According to another version of the plot, Count Schwerin was supposed to throw a hand grenade at the Führer. Voss and Schwerin probably knew they would be shot shortly afterward (the former even wrote farewell letters to his family), but both still decided to go ahead with the plan. Unfortunately, it soon became clear that the rumors of a planned parade were baseless. Hitler didn't even intend to visit Paris. He was usually reluctant to visit the fronts, and when he did so, he took care to change his schedule frequently and without notice.[25]

Beck was even more pessimistic than usual, owing both to the conspirators' latest failure and to the deteriorating military situation in North Africa. "Who will save us?" he wondered in despair to his confidant, the teacher and reserve captain Hermann Kaiser.[26] The echoes of despair even reached the Finnish ambassador in Berlin, who wrote to the foreign ministry in Helsinki that the opposition was merely a medley of disgruntled citizens, who posed no threat to the regime and should not be taken seriously.[27] Still, Beck and Oster kept waiting for their chance. In January 1942, they agreed, with Witzleben's consent, to make Hitler's death, through an assassination, the precondition for any future coup attempt.[28]

All the while, the conspirators, Kreisauers, Social Democrats, and conservatives alike continued to weave their networks of imagination: papers, memoranda, draft constitutions, and prospective cabinet lists. One such list proposed Witzleben as president, Beck as war minister, and Goerdeler as minister of the interior, but it was quickly forgotten.[29] Oster continued to recruit new members, and he especially looked for a charismatic, capable field commander to plan the assassination attempt. Halder failed him, Brauchitsch failed him, Britain and France failed as well, and Hitler was stronger than ever. Still Oster persisted, even in his darkest, most despairing days.

After Germany's invasion of the Soviet Union, in June 1941, Oster finally decided that Henning von Tresckow, a senior operations officer in Army Group Center, was the right man for the job. The focus of the conspiracy moved to the eastern front, entailing a dramatic transition in both network structure and strategy.

# 11

# BROKERS ON THE FRONT LINE: THE NEW STRATEGY

O N THE MORNING of June 22, 1941, the German ambassador to Moscow, Count Friedrich-Werner von der Schulenburg, walked into the office of the Soviet foreign minister, Vyacheslav Molotov, in the Kremlin. He found his host stunned and confused by the news of a German incursion deep into the USSR, in gross violation of the Nazi-Soviet pact that the two countries had signed less than two years before, in August 1939. The Germans had assembled huge forces on the border, consisting of three large army groups supplemented by thousands of tanks and fighter planes, in preparation for one of the largest military campaigns in history. Schulenburg read to the bewildered Molotov a communiqué that had been dictated to him by Foreign Minister Ribbentrop in Berlin:

> In 1939 the Reich government sought, ignoring vigorous opposition deriving from the fundamental contradictions between National Socialism and Bolshevism, to achieve understandings with Soviet Russia . . . The Reich government pursued a friendly policy toward the Soviet Union . . . As a result of this policy, the Soviet Union enjoyed major advantages in its foreign policy . . . The Reich government assumed that the two peoples would achieve abiding neighborly relations, and that each nation would respect the regime of the other and would not intervene in its internal affairs. Unfortunately, it quickly became clear that the Reich gov-

ernment erred fundamentally in making this assumption . . . The Soviet government has violated the agreement it signed with Germany and is about to attack Germany from the rear in a life-or-death struggle. The Führer has ordered the German Wehrmacht to resist this threat with all the means at its disposal.[1]

Schulenburg, who had devoted most of his diplomatic career to improving relations between the two countries, was himself in shock. "I believe," he told Molotov, "that we are talking about war, and there is nothing more that I can add." The Soviet foreign minister then asked, "Why did Germany sign a non-aggression pact only to violate it so casually?" The ambassador kept his silence.[2]

Hitler's decision to attack the Soviet Union, in Operation Barbarossa, triggered a major shift in the German resistance movement. As we have seen, the setbacks that the conspirators suffered between 1938 and 1941 had proved to all that the Berlin clique of Beck, Goerdeler, Hassell, and Gisevius was ineffective. These setbacks gradually bolstered the view held by Colonel Oster and others that attempts to convince the high command to stage a revolution from above were all but futile. Instead, Oster argued, the conspirators had first to kill Hitler to trigger the coup, and only then could they convince the senior generals to get on board.

However, this new strategy required an altogether different mode of operation. During the war, it was hardly possible to assassinate Hitler in Berlin, the capital of the Third Reich, where his security arrangements were almost impregnable. And a fortuitous security breach, like the one used by Georg Elser in 1939, was unlikely to recur. The only possible course of action was to kill Hitler when he was on the move during a visit to one of the fronts. To do that, one needed intelligence, coordination, and a network of couriers and collaborators outside of Berlin.

As we saw in the preceding chapter, some conspirators had planned to assassinate Hitler in Paris in late 1941. This isolated scheme lacked the military force it needed to back it up. Even if it had been successful, the conspirators had no means to follow up with a coup d'état. Only the dramatic military expansion of the Nazi empire into Soviet territory, from 1941 onward, gave the conspirators the opportunity to properly plan assassination attempts. Once resistance cells were formed there, the eastern front proved to be a much better stage for saboteurs and conspirators. Unlike the crowded and closely monitored urban center of Paris, it had vast expanses on which to experiment with bombs, and few watchful eyes. The matter was still complicated, though: resistance cells had to be created and, just as crucially, Hitler had to be lured to visit a place where the assassins were ready.

Meanwhile, the old Berlin clique had morphed into a network of small, connected cliques. The network built by Goerdeler, Oster, and Gisevius in 1938 had been a dense social circle, in which most members were concentrated in one place (Berlin) and knew each other very well. By the end of 1941, the resistance was gradually taking the shape of an alliance between two main cliques, one in Berlin and one at the eastern front, with some offshoots elsewhere as well. The conspiracy became much more complicated and entangled, and its day-to-day operations required more effort, talent, and, most of all, leadership and social-networking capabilities. As a result, notwithstanding Beck's nominal leadership, the resistance was overseen not by one military figure but rather by a coalition of coconspirators constantly negotiating with each other.

In order to link one clique to the other, a new function became essential. A "broker" is a kind of superconnector who enjoys good contacts in other groups as well as in his or her own social circle. The broker's job is to bridge remote groups whose members don't know each other, and to coordinate their activity so as to facilitate joint operations.[3] That function, from late 1941 on, was fulfilled by Hermann Kaiser, a history teacher and captain in the reserves. As the officer responsible for the war diary of the commander in chief of the Home Army, Kaiser had formed a dense web of contacts with senior officers. Under the pretext of frequent work trips, he was able to coordinate between the different cliques, groupings, and cells of the resistance.[4] Gradually, even Beck became dependent on him. For the elderly, lonely, and ailing leader of the resistance, Kaiser was not only a liaison but also a friend who accompanied him to concerts and engaged him in political, military, and aesthetic discussions.[5]

Kaiser's diary documents not only his frequent trips and meetings with senior officers but also the reason he was so well liked by them. Through highly placed contacts, he had access to a generous supply of good wine and was always happy to share bottles with thirsty friends.[6] During the austerity of the wartime regime, that was unusual. Amid the intoxicating bottles, the former teacher brokered the dangerous idea of resistance to the Nazi regime.

Kaiser, one of the most active conspirators, has not garnered much attention in conventional resistance literature. His diary, an invaluable source for the history of the conspiracy, was published only in 2010. This relative neglect is unsurprising, given the tendency of resistance literature to focus its attention on the plots and their leaders without paying due attention to the connections and interaction between them. Yet Kaiser's role coordinating between the Berlin clique and the anti-Nazi resistance at the eastern front was crucial.

Just like many other conspirators, Kaiser began his career as a nationalist right-winger. An initial supporter of the Nazi revolution, he even joined the party. But when a friend of his was murdered on the Night of the Long Knives, he began to distance himself from Hitler and his henchmen. His two brothers, both of them critics of the regime, also influenced him to tread the path of opposition. Furthermore, along with other conspirators, he was unhappy about the German atrocities in Poland and was especially incensed when churches were destroyed. "As an enthusiastic idealist and devout Christian," wrote his acquaintance, historian Friedrich Meinecke, "he saw Hitlerism as a sin against God."[7] Later, he was disgusted by atrocities against Russian POWs and civilians at the eastern front. The murder of the Jews also troubled him, but it seems that, in comparison to other leaders of the resistance, the Holocaust was not as important to the final balance of Kaiser's motives.[8]

In any case, his opposition didn't immediately manifest itself as active resistance. In accordance with the rule of revolutionary mutation, it was a professional, not a clandestine, contact that drew him to the circle of the conspirators. Kaiser, an amateur historian, was studying the life of a general from the Wars of Liberation against Napoleon. As part of his research, he frequently met both scholars and officers. On January 16, 1941, he came into contact with Gen. Ludwig Beck, the leader of the German resistance movement. The content of the meeting is mostly unknown to us, but it is clear from Kaiser's diary that Beck initiated him into the resistance, telling him that their mission was to "cut the Gordian knot," namely, to overturn the regime. "We agreed on everything," wrote Kaiser in his diary. "[Beck] is a very wise man with character, a sense of responsibility and broad education. [He said] that the boundaries must be delineated only by responsibility to nation, conscience and God." After two more meetings, both in September 1941, Beck and Goerdeler had successfully won him over to the conspiracy. "Y [Goerdeler] is a man with character, nerves for action, integrity and sincerity," he noted. No stone was left unturned: the gloomy situation at the eastern front, the possibility of obtaining a fair peace for Germany after the war, and the atrocities against civilians and prisoners in Russia were all discussed. Kaiser's conclusion was that "not one day is to be lost. We must act now." The die was cast. From then on, he became a full-time conspirator.[9]

Through Fabian von Schlabrendorff, Hermann Kaiser came into contact with Lt. Col. Henning von Tresckow, a senior operations officer in Army Group Center at the eastern front. Tresckow, a former adherent of the regime, was horrified at the Nazi crimes of the 1930s. A consistent supporter of the German Jews, he deplored both legal discrimination and violent persecutions. Kristallnacht, especially, was, to him, an unforgivable act of barbarism. The aggregate impact of these events, along with the plot against General Fritsch and the atrocities in the Polish campaign, turned him into an implacable enemy of Hitler.[10]

Around 1941, Tresckow was won over to the conspiracy by Schlabrendorff, an aristocratic lawyer and veteran of the German resistance. In the months following the onset of Operation Barbarossa, Tresckow became a focal point for local critics of the regime. Though he was disliked by some as an overambitious, arrogant officer, his influence on others was extremely strong. "A leader one would wish to have," wrote a superior, oblivious to Tresckow's anti-Nazi activities.[11] "He had a personality that simply bowled you over," recalled his friend, admirer, and coconspirator Margarethe von Oven. "He had an incredible gift for connecting with you and winning you over. He had something—how shall I put it? Have you seen pictures of him? He exercised a very strong immediate influence on his surroundings; he had a great personal charm—charm and the ability to convince. You trusted him."[12] Quickly, Tresckow became the rising star of the

conspiracy. He promised Schlabrendorff that he would build an organized resistance cell at the eastern front using the first major military
setback as a pretext to act against Hitler.[13]

According to Schlabrendorff, Tresckow was "one of National Socialism's natural enemies. His unflagging zeal in his fight against Hitler
made him one of the outstanding figures of the resistance."[14] Tresckow
indeed viewed himself as an exemplar of the Prussian military tradition, which was separated from Nazi totalitarianism by an abyss. In the
confirmation ceremony of his sons, he said that their Prussian heritage
was "a synthesis of duty and freedom . . . of strictness and compassion."
This tradition, so often misunderstood, "demands a commitment to
truth, inward and outward discipline in carrying out one's duty to the
last moment." But most importantly, "it is impossible to separate freedom from the true Prussian spirit . . . and without it there is a danger
of degenerating into a soulless soldiery and narrow-minded self-righ-
teousness."[15]

Tresckow kept his word. In the following months, he formed an
anti-Nazi cell that, in addition to Schlabrendorff, included Rudolf
von Gersdorff, the army group's intelligence officer, who had turned
against the regime because of the massacres in Poland and Russia; Alexander Stahlberg, a cousin of Tresckow's; Eberhard von Breitenbuch,
who would later try to assassinate Hitler; and Col. Bernd von Kleist,
one of the staff officers. Kleist, a sharp-witted and cynical man, fore-
cast the outcome of Operation Barbarossa. "The German army attacking Russia," he told his fellow conspirators, "is like an elephant treading on an anthill. The elephant will kill thousands, tens of thousands,
perhaps millions of ants, but in the end the [ants'] numerical superiority will win out, and they will climb up him and consume him to the
bone."[16]

Tresckow's cell did not begin as a group of plotters. Rather, according to the rule of revolutionary mutation, it began as a legal, tight
social network that granted these young and idealistic officers, all of
them critics of the regime, a sense of belonging within a hostile political environment. "We, the younger people, respected and revered
[Tresckow] . . . ," recalled Breitenbuch. "His heart was open even to
the domestic worries of each one of us—and how rare that was! I have
never met another person who could win you over to his views with
such clarity and common sense."[17] The group liked to shut themselves

up in a room with a roaring fireplace, where they feasted on steaks and wine and discussed social, military, and political matters over long chess games. Such an atmosphere helped the charismatic Tresckow to gradually consolidate a group of loyal comrades and "mutate" it into a revolutionary cell.[18]

# 12

# WAR OF EXTERMINATION:
# THE CONSPIRATORS AND THE HOLOCAUST

H ITLER NEVER CEASED to stun Tresckow and his friends with his
brutality. On March 30, 1941, the dictator announced his infamous
Commissar Order, in which he declared that the officers who served as
political attachés in each Red Army unit must be shot when captured
rather than taken prisoner. The war in Russia would not be conducted
chivalrously: "This war is a war between worldviews—Bolshevism has
been doomed to die. We must therefore free ourselves of the idea of
the brotherhood of soldiers. The Communist is not our comrade and
never was. This is a war of extermination . . . and we do not conduct a
war in order to keep the enemy alive."[1]

Except for mounting some meek protests, the senior generals did
nothing. On May 13, some six weeks later, Field Marshal Wilhelm
Keitel, chief of staff of the Supreme Command of the Armed Forces,
issued a second order, according to which the military justice system
was not required to prosecute cases against soldiers involving civilians,
even when the soldiers had committed crimes and violated military
regulations.[2] Rudolf von Gersdorff, Tresckow's intelligence officer,
immediately understood the implications: it was a license to murder, loot, and rape. Tresckow and Schlabrendorff also saw what was in
store. Tresckow decided to act without delay. On a sunny day at the
beginning of June, Tresckow and Gersdorff went to see Field Marshal
Fedor von Bock, the army group's commander. They were determined

to prevent the two orders from being carried out. On the way there, Tresckow halted and told his good friend,

> Gersdorff, if we don't succeed in persuading the field marshal to fly immediately to Hitler and to bring about a revocation of these orders, the German people will assume a guilt that the world will not forget for centuries. Not only Hitler, Himmler, Göring, and their gang will be responsible, but you and I as well, your wife and my wife, your children and my children, the old woman who just went into the store over there, the man riding his bicycle over here, and that little boy playing with a ball. Think about what I just said.[3]

Bock, who was Tresckow's uncle on his mother's side, was a weak-willed man, unreservedly loyal to the Führer. Tresckow used the clearest possible language with him. "Fedi," he said, "I've had your plane made ready. You must fly immediately to Hitler, not alone but with [Field Marshal Gerd von] Rundstedt and [Field Marshal Wilhelm Ritter von] Leeb [commanders of Army Groups South and North, respectively]. You must put a pistol to Hitler's chest and demand the immediate revocation of the orders . . . If you refuse to obey him now, he will have to give in."[4]

Bock interrupted. "What if he dismisses us?" he asked. "Then," Tresckow told him, "you will at least exit the stage of history honorably." Bock responded heatedly, "Hitler will send Himmler as my replacement." Tresckow shot back, "We'll know how to deal with him."[5]

It was useless. Bock refused to fly himself. Instead, he sent Gersdorff to Berlin to lodge a protest with the army's commander in chief, Field Marshal Brauchitsch. As one might expect, Gersdorff's trip was a total failure. He was blocked by a lower-ranking general who said that Brauchitsch had already made every effort to cancel the order and that there was no more to be done. Brauchitsch was not even at headquarters at the time, so Gersdorff couldn't meet him in person. He returned to Field Marshal Bock empty-handed. "Have it be noted, gentlemen," the army group commander instructed, "that Field Marshal Bock protested."[6]

At dawn on June 22, the order Barbarossa was issued, and the German army launched a massive artillery barrage. For the Russians, it came as a total surprise. During the invasion's early hours, Stalin refused to believe that Hitler had really violated the Molotov-Ribbentrop pact. Many of the Red Army units on the border fell to pieces, and their soldiers, maltreated by their superiors and lacking motivation, simply fled or surrendered, abandoning weaponry that had hardly been used. Army Group North, under Field Marshal Leeb's command, surged toward Leningrad, while Rundstedt's Army Group South moved into Ukraine. Army Group Center, led by Bock, advanced in a pincer movement into Belorussia and besieged Minsk. During its early months, Barbarossa was a huge success. The armored divisions advanced at great speed and flattened the Russian defenses under their treads. Field Marshal Bock took Minsk and dealt the Red Army a decisive defeat near Smolensk. Rundstedt wiped out the Red Army in Ukraine and conquered Kiev.

Behind the advancing Wehrmacht lines, the Einsatzgruppen, the SS's operational formations, slaughtered Jews and other "undesirables." They followed a standard protocol. After surrounding a Jewish village or town, they forced all the inhabitants out of their homes. Then, they led the Jews to a forest or other isolated spot, gave them shovels, and ordered them to dig huge pits. They then murdered them all—men, women, the elderly, children—by shooting them in the back of the head or with machine-gun fire. The most notorious of these massacres took place at Ponary (Punar), then just outside Vilnius, and at Babi Yar in Ukraine. Rivka Yosselevska, a Jewish woman who survived the slaughter, lived to testify at the Eichmann trial about the Germans' systematic murder policy:

When we arrived at the place, we saw naked, undressed people. We still thought that this was just torture. But I still wanted to see and be sure, to be certain. I turned around and looked at what was under the hill, that platform, what was in the ditch, the pit. Then it was clear to me. I saw that several lines of people who had been shot to death were lying there . . . And I want also to mention here that my girl told me when we were still in the ghetto: Mother, why did you dress me in my Sabbath clothes? They are taking us to shootings and death, after all. And when we stood by the pit she said: Why are we standing and waiting, let's run away . . . I turned my head away and he said to me: Who should I shoot first, your daughter or you? I did not answer. I felt how my daughter was torn away from me, I felt her final scream and I heard how she was shot. Afterward he came to me. I turned my head away. He grabbed my hair to shoot me. I remained standing. I heard a shot, but I remained standing. He turned me back. He began to load his pistol again. He turned me and shot and I fell.[7]

More than a million and a half Jews were murdered by the Einsatzgruppen, by army units, by Nazi police, and in some cases by Wehrmacht units. The army's leaders were, from the start, passive and sometimes active partners in the extermination campaign. Gen. Franz Halder, who only two years previously had been prepared to take part in an anti-Nazi coup, bore the largest measure of responsibility for the army's acceptance of these criminal orders, with Brauchitsch not far behind.[8] Other important generals, such as Erich von Manstein, the brilliant strategist of the German invasion of France, competed in issuing venomous anti-Semitic orders that mandated "cruel but justified revenge against Jewry." The most energetic of these was Field Marshal Walther von Reichenau, commander of the Sixth Army and later commander in chief of Army Group South, who gave his blessing to "the severe but justified acts of revenge against these sub-humans, the Jews."[9] Wehrmacht units supplied logistical assistance to the Einsatzgruppen, surrounding villages and towns. In some cases, soldiers volunteered to take part in the massacres.[10]

Tresckow and his friends knew all about these crimes, and there is a stormy debate among historians about their involvement. In their capacity as staff officers, they had to initial reports on war crimes, pass on commands with atrocious content, and participate in campaigns against partisans, which were often accompanied by massacres against Jews and Russians. Credible evidence shows that Tresckow, Gersdorff, and the others opposed such crimes from the outset, but their opposition became vigorous when the massacres in their front escalated.[11] From June to October, most civilian victims in the operational theater of Army Group Center were men. But in late October, the massacre became wholesale: women, children, and the elderly began to be slaughtered in large numbers as well. Tresckow, a staff officer who commanded no forces, confronted the slaughter of Jews in his jurisdiction for the first time on October 20, near the army group headquarters in Borisov (Barysaw), in Belorussia. Rudolf von Gersdorff later related,

> The SS men drove to Barysaw and surrounded the ghetto ...
> They gave instructions to the Lithuanian SS units to eliminate
> the Jews ... They first forced the Jews to dig deep pits, and they
> were then divided into groups of a hundred, thrown naked into
> the pit, and mowed down with machine gun fire from the Lith-
> uanian SS men. To verify who was dead and who was still alive,
> they forced the next group of Jews to step on the bodies and then
> to share the same fate. One SS man was seen lifting small chil-
> dren onto their feet, shooting them in the head, and throwing
> them into the grave. A few Luftwaffe soldiers who had come out
> of curiosity from a nearby airfield were overcome by a murderous
> fervor and shot at the Jews packed in the graves. Blood-curdling
> scenes played out at the edges of the pits — desperate attempts to
> escape, entreaties by young Jewish women who wanted only to
> save themselves and their children, but to no avail. All ended up in
> the SS's mass grave.[12]

Tresckow was furious that Jews were being murdered all along the front, and when the crimes took place on his watch, he was even more enraged. He went immediately to Field Marshal Bock and demanded he use military force to halt the slaughter. "This must not happen again," he said, "and therefore we have to act. In Russia we are in possession of power. If we act against [the SS] now without restraint, we can make an example out of it."[13] Bock categorically refused. Later, when Tresckow pleaded with him to join the efforts to overthrow Hitler "to save the situation," the field marshal berated his operations officer. "I shall not tolerate any attack upon the Führer," he shouted. "I shall stand before the Führer and defend him against anyone who dares to attack him."[14] But, even if Bock had collaborated, it is hard to believe that Tresckow would have been able to eject the Einsatzgruppen from the army group's rear, or even to curb their actions. The most he could have done was to thin out their numbers somewhat, as he apparently tried to do. He argued that it was technically difficult to deploy so many SS units, "because it is not clear whether it is possible to send them [in time]."[15]

Gersdorff, risking his career, set off to tour the front, where he sought to persuade young officers to oppose the massacres. Just like the commando officer Wilhelm Heinz (commander of the shock troops in the Oster conspiracy of 1938), who denounced the massacre of the Jews of Lvov in his order of the day to his troops, Gersdorff hoped to foster resistance in the lower ranks. In the official war log of the army group, he wrote, "During all the long talks I conducted with officers, I was asked about the shooting of Jews, without raising the subject myself. I received the impression that nearly all the officers opposed shooting Jews, prisoners of war, and Commissars ... This shooting was perceived as breaching the honor of the German army, and especially that of the German officer corps."[16]

But Gersdorff saw what he wanted to see. Even though not all soldiers and officers were cooperating with the murders—some even objected to their superiors or the higher echelons—brutality, on the whole, dominated the eastern front. Millions of POWs starved to death. German soldiers slaughtered Russian and Ukrainian villagers just as they did Jews, stole boots and warm clothing, and evicted many civilians from their demolished homes to die in the freezing winter. The German war against the partisans served as a cover for massacres of the local people, especially Jews. Tresckow was horrified. "Should we wonder that there are partisans," he asked, "when the population is treated so disgracefully?"[17] An anti-Nazi coup, the only way out of the impossible situation in which Tresckow and his friends found themselves, was still out of reach. That situation would not change for another year.

# 13

# "FLASH" AND LIQUEUR BOTTLES: ASSASSINATION ATTEMPTS IN THE EAST

THE GERMANS' MOMENTUM ran out at the end of 1941. Army Group North failed to take Leningrad. The famine-stricken populace in the besieged city refused to surrender. In a controversial decision, Hitler declined to allocate all possible forces to the conquest of Moscow, instead ordering Army Group Center to transfer much of its armored force to north and south for the engagements at Leningrad and Stalingrad. When he changed his mind, it was too late. "If we do not make a resolute advance to Moscow now," Tresckow said, "we'll have lost the campaign."[1] He was right: Hitler's soldiers, like Napoleon's more than a century before, were not prepared to fight it out during a Russian winter. Heavy rains began in the autumn, and German tanks had difficulty moving on Russia's narrow, muddy roads. When winter began, engine oil solidified, and the German troops, who were malnourished and lacked winter gear, began to freeze. "The German soldier of the winter war of 1941–1942 has undergone a transformation . . . ," Gersdorff wrote. "He has lost his feeling of superiority."[2] Many German generals began doubting whether victory was possible.

Adolf Hitler, always adept at casting the blame on others, dismissed the commander in chief of his ground forces, Field Marshal Brauchitsch, and appointed himself to the position instead. From this point on, he intervened in nearly every military operation and decision, from the number of machine guns deployed at specific locations to the state of the trenches. On the same day, he also relieved the commander of Army Group Center, Field Marshal Fedor von Bock, replacing him with Günther "Hans" von Kluge.

Tresckow underwent a change that winter. As he had promised Schlabrendorff before Operation Barbarossa began, he planned to exploit the Wehrmacht's setback and stage a coup. He wanted to save Germany from a searing defeat at the hands of Russian Bolshevism and to preserve the German army after the war. But this was not the primary reason he acted. "This war that you still believe has a chance is irrevocably lost," Tresckow told Lt. Alexander Stahlberg, his cousin and fellow conspirator, "and we serve an arch-criminal, I repeat, an arch-criminal. According to reliable information, SS units are committing massacres beyond anything you can imagine."[3]

Schlabrendorff took it upon himself to become the link between Tresckow and the conspiracy's headquarters in Berlin. Under cover of military business, he traveled frequently to the capital, relaying messages from Kaiser, Oster, and the leaders in Berlin. His reports about Tresckow's willingness to take action revived the conspiracy. The connection between Schlabrendorff and the members of the resistance revealed to Tresckow that the movement was in contact with a powerful ally, the chief of the General Army Office in the army high command, Gen. Friedrich Olbricht.

Olbricht, who would play a vital role in the conspiracy, was a balding, bespectacled man of average height. As the commander of the General Army Office, one of the top leadership positions in the Home Army, he took on the role of administrator of the resistance movement. He devoted himself to myriad details, technical and tiresome, but critical to running the underground movement. Coming from a middle-class family (his father was a school principal), he had grown up in the enlightened German Protestant tradition of the nineteenth century and was known as a lover of philosophy, opera, and classical music. A German patriot from his youth, he had nevertheless always avoided political extremism and abhorred German hypernationalism no less than Communism. As an officer, he maintained close ties with the common people, and with Jews, Social Democrats, and even Communists. His ideology of soldierly behavior was certainly unusual. In 1943, when confronted with the notion of absolute obedience, he told his commanding officer that for every ninety-nine orders he received, a soldier could say no to one.[4]

That, however, was not enough to turn him into a conspirator. Whether Olbricht, as his biographer has argued, was involved in the early coup d'état attempts or not, it is clear that by the opening months of 1941, he was still not considered a full-fledged member of the conspiracy.[5] In mid-November that year, Hermann Kaiser, who worked closely with Olbricht as part of his military duties, arranged a meeting between the general and Dr. Carl Goerdeler. However, contrary to some later myths, Olbricht was "very careful" and hard to convince.[6] More pressure was required. Kaiser, who believed that time was short and every hour precious, did not despair. He kept on pushing, and in December 1941 his efforts were crowned with success: Olbricht finally joined the conspiracy. It is reasonable to assume that the loss of his beloved son on the front influenced his decision.[7]

However, the real prize the conspirators sought was not Olbricht but his commanding officer, Gen. Friedrich Fromm. The usual bête noire of the resistance literature, Fromm was the almighty commander of the Home Army, usually described unflatteringly as short, fat, and sleek, a cunning opportunist whose habit was to "sit on the fence" and always look out for his personal interest. This description has some merit, but it is also somewhat unfair. Far from being universally hated, Fromm was respected by many as a highly competent commander and the "strong man of the home front."[8] Still, he was certainly disliked by the resistance fighters operating within his command. This was not because he was an enthusiastic Nazi. Had he been one, then conspirators like Kaiser, Olbricht, and, later, Stauffenberg would have early on found themselves in a prison cell. It was only Fromm's willingness to harbor the conspirators that gave them some breathing space.

In fact, it was Fromm's reluctance to commit himself to one side or the other that infuriated the conspirators so much.[9] His military role made him crucial to their plans. Not only could he have them arrested, but his central role in the military command hierarchy would be invaluable during a coup. If he cooperated, the forces of the Home Army would naturally stand under the conspirators' command, with the junior officers obeying his every word. But Fromm refused to pick a side —and it was this ambivalence that made him so intolerable.

Throughout the lifetime of the conspiracy, Fromm seemed to delight in confusing and confounding the conspirators. In February 1941, for example, he visited Kaiser's office and confessed that he was depressed, lonely, and unable to confide in anyone. "Maybe he has some higher calling . . . ," wrote Kaiser with typical cynicism, "or he just felt like drinking Champagne."[10] Whether or not Fromm suddenly craved one of the high-quality beverages that Kaiser could supply, he kept playing his double game.[11] Several months later, showing the "arrogance and aloofness of a [Turkish] Pasha," he told his officers that "Germany has never been in better shape."[12] Until the very end, the conspirators found his contradictory signals unfathomable.

Nevertheless, they had to continue planning. Schlabrendorff, whose role as a broker was as important as Kaiser's, had met Hassell in October 1941. He reported on the development of the conspiracy in the east and prepared the ground for future cooperation. At the end of 1941, Tresckow traveled to Berlin, where he first met Olbricht, as well as Beck and Goerdeler. Oster, who, according to Schlabrendorff, held in his hands "the threads of the entire plot," served as a go-between behind the scenes but avoided meeting Tresckow in person out of caution. There was no point in putting the conspiracy at risk just when it was beginning to reawaken.[13]

At the same time, Field Marshal Witzleben, then in Paris, was reconsidering the possibility of a coup. Oster assured Schlabrendorff, the tireless broker, that Witzleben was prepared to move his forces as soon as Tresckow had liquidated Hitler. Hans Crome later related to his Soviet interrogators that armored forces in Paris were in fact prepared to carry out the coup. Hassell suggested that Witzleben commence action independently in the west, but the latter refused. The field marshal maintained that an anti-Nazi revolt could not be accomplished on one front alone. To make an isolated move in the west would be a futile fantasy. In fact, Witzleben was extremely pessimistic about the chances of bringing down the regime. In private conversations, he warned against separate and uncoordinated initiatives by the various resistance cells. He placed what hopes he had on a coup centered in Berlin, in the style of the 1938 plot.[14]

The preliminary planning took an entire year. Tresckow continued to live a double life. He did his duty as an officer serving the regime, while planning to overthrow it at the same time. A few more officers in his army group joined the conspiracy. In the summer of 1941, Tresckow conducted a long nighttime exchange "on the riverbank, in the starlight," with Maj. Carl-Hans von Hardenberg, adjutant to Field Marshal Kluge. Tresckow complained bitterly about the cowardice of the generals, who could not summon enough courage to speak out against Hitler's war crimes and military folly. The time had come, he told Hardenberg, to rebel: "One has to resort to active revolutionary means. To take this path, we have to throw away everything we learned from our forefathers about the honor of the Prussian-German soldier, as well as our property, families, our personal honor and the honor of our class."[15] Tresckow's argument convinced Hardenberg, and he joined the conspiracy.

Tresckow's close associate Capt. Alexander Stahlberg was sent to Army Group South, where he became adjutant to the force commander, Field Marshal Erich von Manstein, whom Tresckow also hoped to enlist. But Manstein refused to even consider the matter. When Stahlberg sought to inform him, in Tresckow's name, about the murder of one hundred thousand Jews, Manstein fiercely denied the reports. "Such a number of people," he countered, "could have filled the Olympic stadium in Berlin. It is difficult to murder [so many people]." Stahlberg needed to bring tangible evidence if he expected Manstein to report these "findings" to the higher echelons. Besides, asked the field marshal, exposing his true sentiments, "is it really so negative that Jewry, so dangerous for Germany, is being decimated?"[16]

Tresckow did better with his immediate superior, Field Marshal Günther von Kluge, whose nickname was "Clever [*kluger*] Hans." In December 1941, Kluge replaced Bock as commander of Army Group Center. He was cynical, cautious, and apprehensive in the extreme. He had refused to cooperate with the conspirators of 1938 and sent Gisevius back to Berlin empty-handed. But Tresckow was not Gisevius. He had the charisma to bring Kluge slowly around to the resistance, largely by frightening him with grim reports of the ever-worsening military situation. Tresckow had long since realized that there was no point in talking about Nazi crimes committed in the rear to anyone outside his immediate circle. Such moral arguments would not have persuaded Kluge to join the conspirators. Only his personal ties to Tresckow and their discussions about the war could have any effect on him.[17]

Schlabrendorff later compared Kluge to a watch that had to be wound every day. It took months of persuading, but Kluge finally recognized that the conspirators were right. He told Tresckow that he was prepared to support a military coup, but only after the resistance had eliminated Hitler. Yet he categorically refused to cooperate in the planning or execution of an assassination attempt. Tresckow and Schlabrendorff understood that they had to take matters into their own hands.

Very little is known about the military activity of the conspirators during 1942, but one surviving fragment from Kaiser's diary indicates that March, at least, was busy with preparations. The energetic broker hurried from city to city, met the various leaders, and coordinated their activity. The fragment, dated March 3, 1942, documents a frantic, almost breathless schedule of meetings and discussions, under the ever-threatening shadow of the Gestapo:

> O [Olbricht] is on vacation. If there are specific questions—speak with Beck.

> An urgent conversation between O [Olbricht] to G [Gisevius] through O [Oster].

> There is an agreement with W [Witzleben]. Articles 1 and 2 above suggest that it is required to first take the initiative in order to make it easier for W.

> Messer [Goerdeler] in a private trip to Paris.

> According to M [Goerdeler] there is no more time to lose.

> Arrest.

> O [Olbricht] Telegraph. Trial.[18]

The military situation worsened at the end of 1942. The German Sixth Army, under the command of Gen. Friedrich Paulus, failed to take the southern city of Stalingrad, and during the course of the autumn it became surrounded by the Red Army. Hitler, stubborn and rash, refused to permit Paulus to retreat from the city, instead demanding that he fight to the last bullet. In doing so, he doomed three hundred thousand Germans and their allies to death or imprisonment.

At this point, Tresckow began planning the coup itself. Schlabrendorff met with Olbricht in Berlin, and the latter asked for two months to organize his forces. Capt. Ludwig Gehre, an officer seconded from the Abwehr for this purpose, served as Oster's eyes in headquarters and stayed in contact with Tresckow and the eastern clique. It seems that as far as the assassination itself was concerned, Oster was reluctant to rely on the communication network of Kaiser and Schlabrendorff; he preferred to personally monitor the preparations. Tresckow was assigned the part of sparking the flame: eliminating Hitler. Afterward, Olbricht was supposed to mobilize the Home Army. Gehre was assigned the critical task of leading the Abwehr commando squads, the shock troops of the revolt.[19] Witzleben, who was fired by Hitler in 1942 because of ill health, agreed to lead the Wehrmacht after the coup, "but only if Beck agrees."[20]

Tresckow exploited for his purposes a strange event that took place at the end of October 1942. The occasion was Field Marshal Kluge's sixtieth birthday. Count Philipp von Boeselager, Kluge's personal assistant, listened in on a telephone call between the field marshal and Hitler. "Herr Field Marshal," Hitler said, "I have heard that you wish to build a barn at Böhne [Kluge's wife's estate]. As a sign of gratitude for your services to the German people, I am giving you a gift of 250,000 Reichsmarks in ration cards for construction materials. Goodbye." The Führer ended the conversation, leaving Kluge confounded. "Boeselager," he called to his attaché, "you heard what the Führer said at the end of the conversation. What do you think of it, that is, the gift?" Philipp Boeselager, a young officer, patriot, and anti-Nazi, had been one of Tresckow's close associates for some time but knew nothing of his plans. "Sir," he replied, "to the best of my memory I have never heard of a Prussian field marshal or general accepting money when a war is in progress . . . In your position I would donate the money to the Red Cross." Boeselager later related that "I quickly went to Tresckow . . . and told him about the conversation between Kluge and Hitler . . . 'The field marshal should not be dependent on the Führer,' he said. 'We need him for the war against Hitler.'" Tresckow displayed his cards. "From that moment on," wrote Boeselager, "I was a member of Tresckow's resistance group."[21]

At this point, the break that the conspirators had been waiting for came. Kluge's avarice overcame him. He accepted the gift from Hitler and used it to renovate his manor house. In the days that followed, he could not look Tresckow in the eye. Tresckow seized the opportunity. He told his commanding officer that he (Kluge) had acted shamefully. He could redeem his reputation in the history books only by resolving to join the resistance.[22] Kluge finally agreed.

During the summer and autumn of 1942, Tresckow and Schlabrendorff had trouble deciding how best to assassinate Hitler. Tresckow first thought of shooting him himself, but he knew that Hitler wore a bulletproof vest when visiting the fronts and that his fearsome bodyguards were the quickest draws in Germany. A single bullet, fired under great pressure, was likely to miss and to risk uncovering the entire conspiracy.[23] A second option was massive gunfire. For several months, Tresckow had been in touch with Count Georg von Boeselager, brother of Philipp and commander of a cavalry battalion at the front. At Tresckow's initiative and with Kluge's sanction, Boeselager put together an elite cavalry force that was meant to open fire on Hitler, or alternatively to arrest him, as soon as he arrived at Army Group Center.[24]

The Sixth Army, surrounded at Stalingrad, surrendered in January 1943. Hundreds of thousands of German soldiers were killed or taken prisoner, and the army's commander, Field Marshal Paulus, was brought to Moscow, where he commenced anti-Hitler broadcasts. The fall of the Sixth Army shocked all Germany. Impassioned speeches by Göring and Goebbels did not help, nor did the declaration of the Wehrmacht high command that "they died so that Germany could continue to live."[25] The German people, who had until then believed in the invincibility of the Wehrmacht, tasted bitter defeat. From here on in, the Red Army would push the Germans back on all fronts.

A few months beforehand, in summer 1942, Tresckow had decided to bring Gersdorff, his intelligence officer, into the plan to assassinate Hitler. First, he had tested his subordinate's loyalty. "Please, don't ask me why," he said, "but I need some particularly effective explosives." The sharp-witted Gersdorff understood very well what he was being asked for. He visited the chief of the sabotage unit and asked him for a thorough report on his work. The chief, according to Gersdorff, "was very pleased with my sudden interest and presented me with a program for a visit to his entire unit . . . There I saw a huge amount of explosive material, fuses, and other devices needed by sappers."

Gersdorff quickly realized that German bombs could not kill Hitler, because they operated on loudly ticking timers and emitted a sharp whistle ten seconds before exploding. He thus took an interest in quieter British bombs: "I was shown a large number of British bombs, which had been parachuted by the British for underground French and Dutch fighters in the occupied territories . . . I asked him to place before me a selection of [explosive] devices, so that I could show the field marshal the newest ones."

The chief agreed, of course, but demanded, as military procedure required, that Gersdorff sign a receipt. The intelligence officer was concerned that if he signed and the plan failed, it would be easy to discover who had ordered the bomb. Yet he took the risk and signed. "I wondered," he wrote in his memoirs, "whether I was signing my own death warrant."[26] Gersdorff returned to Colonel Tresckow with a container full of bombs. Tresckow took him to an isolated area near the army group headquarters. The two walked down a secluded path. "Tresckow spoke with me with utter frankness about the need to eliminate Hitler and release mankind from this horrible criminal. He said that after much thought he decided to kill the Führer with a bomb, the method that seemed to have the best chance. This was a condition for the success of the entire plan for a military coup. We had to be sure that Hitler would die and not just be wounded."[27]

From January through February 1943, Tresckow stayed in Berlin and led intensive discussions with Olbricht, Beck, Goerdeler, and Kaiser. He reported that the eastern front was on the verge of collapse. Maybe it could still be saved through rapid action, provided that the conspirators took over the government and negotiated for a separate peace with the Western Allies. As if the atmosphere was not tense enough, the members of the inner circle began to squabble with each other. "There is nothing but contempt," wrote Kaiser in his diary. Olbricht went back on his promises and insisted that he couldn't do anything without Fromm's consent: "Goerdeler spoke on January 19 with Olbricht, Gisevius and Beck. Olbricht is unable to move without

Fromm. Even Beck turned pale. Goerdeler: 'I lost all the esteem I ever had for Olbricht.'"

Kaiser noted, cynically, that Olbricht and Fromm shared a kind of symbiotic incompetence: "One is ready to act only when commanded, but the other is ready to command only when others act first."[28]

Just like the others, Tresckow stood aghast at the sight of Olbricht's excessive caution, and implored Kaiser "to do everything possible to reinforce his resolution."[29] And indeed, after the defeat in Stalingrad, Beck, Tresckow, and Goerdeler were desperate for action and seriously doubted Olbricht's resolution to move forward. "Not to lose even one day," said Goerdeler, "to move as soon as possible. We cannot expect the field marshals to take the initiative. They are waiting for orders, just like O [Olbricht] here." Meanwhile, Kaiser heard from his sources that Hitler was aware of the conspiracy. Military policemen might knock on his door at any moment.[30]

The conspirators overcame their remaining doubts. "Is it not horrifying," Tresckow asked Gersdorff, "that two German General Staff officers are discussing the best way of eliminating their supreme commander? Yet we have to do it because this is the last opportunity to save Germany from the abyss. The world must be freed from the greatest villain in history. We will eradicate him as if he were a mad dog endangering humanity." To another officer he said simply, "No matter how you look at it and talk about it, our catastrophe is the doing of a single man. He must perish. We have no choice."[31]

With some effort, Tresckow managed to persuade Beck, the commander of the resistance movement, that assassinating Hitler was a precondition for the success of the coup. Beck, frustrated by the opportunism of the generals and enraged by the regime's crimes, gave his consent. The assassination was set for March 13, when Hitler was scheduled to visit Army Group Center. Tresckow's first plan, spraying the Führer with gunfire from the cavalry during a meal or a military consultation, was quickly rejected. Tresckow had to tell Field Marshal Kluge about the plan, to ensure that he would not be hit during the barrage. Kluge refused to hear of it. It was not honorable, he insisted, to kill a man while he was dining. And in any case, he continued, "there is no point, as Himmler will not be there."[32] Tresckow would have to kill Hitler in some other, more discreet way. To their annoyance, the conspirators discovered that Kluge restrained them with one hand, only to spur them on with the other. On March 3, he sent a message to Olbricht, urging him to "speed up" because of the situation at the front.[33]

The only option remaining was a bomb. In the winter of 1943, Gersdorff and Tresckow went out to the snowy fields of Smolensk, near the army group's headquarters, to see whether a bomb would explode at low temperatures. Gersdorff had managed to obtain some British plastic explosives. The two set off dozens of controlled explosions and found that the material worked only between zero and forty degrees centigrade. They were apprehensive at first that the temperature would drop below freezing at the critical moment, which would wreck their carefully laid plans, but they devised a number of technical fixes to overcome the problem. The British bomb was based on an acid-activated fuse: setting the bomb broke a glass capsule; acid then leaked out and ate through a spring wire, driving a firing pin onto a detonator cap, and the bomb exploded. The conspirators tried out bombs in a number of abandoned buildings near the front, all of which were demolished completely.

Schlabrendorff shaped the deadly plastic into two rolls and wrapped them sumptuously, so that they looked like two bottles of Cointreau liqueur. March 13 finally arrived. Hitler landed at Army Group Center headquarters, accompanied by a large number of SS guards, his driver, his cook, and his personal physician. At first, Tresckow planned to plant the bomb in the Führer's car, but he saw that the SS kept the vehicle under constant surveillance, and he had to find another solution. In the meantime, Kluge hosted the Führer at a lunch to which all the senior staff officers were invited. Schlabrendorff had a chance to see his quarry up close:

> Hitler was served a special meal, every part of which had been prepared by his personal cook. It was tasted before his eyes by his physician, Professor Morell. The entire procedure was reminiscent of an Oriental despot of a bygone age. Watching Hitler eat was a most revolting spectacle. His left hand was placed firmly on his thigh, with his right hand he shoveled his food, which con-

sisted of various vegetables, into his mouth. He did this without lifting his right arm, which he kept flat on the table throughout the entire meal. Instead he brought his mouth down to the food.[34]

During the lunch, Tresckow approached Lt. Col. Heinz Brandt, one of Hitler's staff officers, and asked him whether he could take two bottles of liqueur to Col. Helmuth Stieff, one of his friends in the high command. Stieff was an anti-Nazi officer who had turned against the regime in the wake of the slaughter of Poland's Jews, but he knew nothing about the conspiracy. Brandt agreed. Schlabrendorff went to the telephone and gave Captain Gehre, his contact in Berlin, the code word "flash." The countdown had begun. Schlabrendorff later wrote,

> I waited until Hitler had dismissed the officers of the Army Group Center and was about to board his plane. Looking at Tresckow, I read in his eyes the order to go ahead. With the help of a key, I pressed down hard on the fuse, thus triggering the bomb, and handed the parcel to Colonel Brandt who boarded the plane shortly after Hitler. A few minutes later both Hitler's plane and that carrying the other members of his party, escorted by a number of fighter planes, started back to East Prussia. Fate now had to take its course. Tresckow and I returned to our quarters, from where I again called Gehre in Berlin, and gave him the second code word, indicating that Operation Flash was actually underway.[35]

Hitler sat in an armor-plated compartment inside the airplane. On the strength of their experiments, the conspirators knew that the explosion would be strong enough to tear this cubicle apart, along with the rest of the plane. Tresckow and Schlabrendorff sat by the radio and waited for the news of a plane crash somewhere above Minsk.

As they waited tensely, they were troubled by moral qualms. Tresckow and Schlabrendorff knew that they had to kill a single criminal in order to save potentially millions of people, but what about the innocent officers who would die with Hitler in the crash? The two had come to the conclusion that, given the horrifying crimes that had been committed in the east, no German officer was innocent. All those who had kept silent as Jews, Russians, and Poles were being slaughtered, and even those who had protested but continued to serve, bore responsibility and thus deserved death. And even if these men were not guilty, their deaths were necessary. As Tresckow put it, "In order to free Germany and the world from the greatest criminal in history, it is permissible to kill a few innocent people."[36] But nothing happened, Schlabrendorff recounted:

> After waiting more than two hours, we received the shattering news that Hitler's plane had landed without incident at the airstrip at Rastenburg, in East Prussia, and that Hitler himself had safely reached Headquarters. We could not imagine what had gone wrong. I called Gehre in Berlin immediately, and gave him the code word for the failure of the assassination. Afterward, Tresckow and I, stunned and shaken by the blow, conferred about what our next move should be. We were in a state of indescribable agitation; the failure of our attempt was bad enough, but the thought of what discovery of the bomb would mean to us and our fellow conspirators, friends, and families, was infinitely worse.[37]

Despite this setback, Tresckow did not sink into depression. He quickly took action. He called Lieutenant Colonel Brandt, who had already arrived at the headquarters, and told him that a mistake had been made and that the wrong bottles of liqueur had been sent. He asked the lieutenant colonel to keep the package until they could deliver the real Cointreau. Tresckow had to prevent the bomb from being delivered to Stieff, who knew nothing about the assassination plot. Schlabrendorff set off for the high command headquarters, gave Brandt two real bottles of Cointreau, and reclaimed the original package. Brandt, who was oblivious to the deadly content of the package, juggled it back and forth. Schlabrendorff, who did everything possible to conceal his dread and nervousness, seriously feared a belated explosion. He took the package to the railway station, where a Berlin-bound military night express stood waiting.[38] There, Schlabrendorff entered the sleeping car, locked the door, and opened the package with a razor blade. He removed the wrapping and made an amazing discovery: "I could see that the condition of the explosive was unchanged. Carefully dismantling the bomb, I took out the fuse and examined it. The reason for the failure immediately became clear: Everything but one small part had worked as expected. The bottle with the corrosive fluid had been broken, the chemical had eaten through the wire, the firing pin had been released and had struck forward—but the detonator had not ignited."[39]

The malfunction seems to have been due to a defect in the manufacture of the explosive and to the low temperature inside the plane. Gersdorff, Tresckow, and Schlabrendorff had done the best they could, but, as in earlier resistance efforts, fortune intervened to save the Führer. Soon they decided to try again.

On March 21, Hitler was scheduled to make a speech at the official commemoration of Heroes' Memorial Day in Berlin. Following the speech, he was to visit the armory (*Zeughaus*), where he would view an exhibition of captured Russian war materiel. Gersdorff's intelligence department had organized the exhibition, and he was supposed to guide Hitler through the display and explain it to him. Tresckow asked Gersdorff whether he was willing to take the opportunity to strike Hitler along with Himmler, Göring, and Goebbels. Apparently, he would need to blow himself up along with Hitler.[40]

Gersdorff agreed to do it, even though he understood that it probably meant sacrificing his own life. With a huge effort, Tresckow managed to convince Field Marshal Kluge not to attend, as he was supposed to be a critical figure in the anti-Nazi coup that would follow the assassination.

Gersdorff traveled to Berlin with Field Marshal Walter Model, one of Hitler's most ardent loyalists. A day before the event, the two of them met with Schmundt, Hitler's adjutant. Model asked about the precise hour set for the visit to the museum, because he wanted to visit his wife before returning to the front. At first, Schmundt refused to say, on the grounds that security procedures forbade letting anyone know. He, Schmundt, would be subject to the death penalty if he leaked the secret, he said. Model persisted, and Schmundt finally gave in. Gersdorff listened alertly. Afterward, Schmundt said that he had checked the list of invitees and that Gersdorff did not appear there. Luck was once again with the conspirators; Model protested vehemently and said that he was not versed in Russian armaments. What if Hitler were to ask him a question he could not answer? He demanded that Gersdorff accompany him and respond to all of the Führer's technical questions. Schmundt gave in and added Gersdorff to the guest list. Gersdorff later wrote, "I spent March 20 at the Armory to examine the possibilities for an assassination attempt. Laborers were at work everywhere, in the yard of the museum, where the ceremony was to take place, and in the exhibition halls themselves. A speakers' stand had been set up, and a stage for the philharmonic orchestra. The entire area had been festooned with wreaths of flowers. SS and SD troops roamed ceaselessly among the workers . . . guarding the place day and night."[41]

Gersdorff realized that he could not conceal the bomb in the exhibition hall. The security procedures were too thorough, the room was too large, and there was no way of knowing exactly where Hitler would stand. Alternatively, he could plant the bomb in the speaker's podium outside, but that, he saw, was guarded day and night by the SS. Gersdorff concluded that he would have to carry the bomb on his person and detonate it when he stood next to Hitler, killing himself along with the dictator. At 10:00 p.m., as he sat in his room in the Eden Hotel, deep in thought, Schlabrendorff knocked on the door and delivered a bomb with a ten-minute delay. Gersdorff recalled,

> I arrived at the Armory on the late morning of March 21 . . . At 11 a.m., officers and party officials began to gather, but they had no idea that the ceremony would begin only at 1 p.m. A few acquaintances tried to speak to me, and I must have given them the impression of being a distracted, dreamy man . . . After Bruckner's 7th Symphony, Hitler began to speak. I heard him only intermittently . . . I remember that, despite all the optimistic forecasts about the military situation, he spoke in mystical terms about "the twilight of the gods." I did not know how long he would speak for, so I could not activate the fuse during the speech.[42]

After concluding his address, Hitler entered the armory with Gersdorff, Göring, Himmler, Keitel, Field Marshal Bock, and several other officers. Gersdorff tried to start explaining the exhibits to the Führer, but Hitler did not listen and began instead to walk frantically toward the door. Fifty seconds later, the radio announced, to a drumroll, that Hitler had left the armory and had begun inspecting the honor guard at the Tomb of the Unknown Soldier.[43] Gersdorff later told a historian,

So the window of opportunity for the assassination closed, because the fuse needed at least ten minutes, even if the temperature were normal [and longer if it was cold]. Hitler's life was saved by a last-minute change, a typical stratagem of his sophisticated security system. Tresckow listened to the broadcast of the ceremony in Smolensk with a stopwatch in his hand. When he heard . . . the announcer declaring that he [Hitler] had left the Armory, he understood that the plan could not have been completed.[44]

Gersdorff remained active in the resistance movement to the end, but he did not again dare to try to assassinate Hitler himself. Tresckow also vowed to carry on, but the conspirators continued to be plagued by bad luck. At the beginning of March, shortly before the failure of the assassination attempt in Smolensk, Beck was hospitalized and diagnosed with cancer of the stomach. He became a shadow of himself, pale and depressed. Members of the inner circle were distressed by his condition. "Only now his importance becomes clear," Kaiser told another conspirator, agreeing with him that "people are ready to take only [Beck] in consideration. No one can replace him. Witzleben must step forward, but he is not a statesman . . . May God watch over Beck."[45]

A month later, Fritz-Dietlof von der Schulenburg, one of the most active conspirators in the army, was arrested and interrogated on suspicion of treason. He was released only at the intervention of high-ranking officers. Beck, Goerdeler, and Hassell felt that they, too, were under Gestapo surveillance. The room for maneuvering was diminishing quickly.[46]

Tresckow, who observed strict rules of caution, was not yet a suspect, but he knew that he wouldn't be safe forever. Everyone sensed that a terrible catastrophe was at hand. On April 5, 1943, it happened. Tresckow heard, at his headquarters in Smolensk, that the Gestapo had raided the Abwehr offices in Berlin, where they arrested Hans von Dohnanyi and seized many incriminating documents. Worst of all, Maj. Gen. Hans Oster, the heart and soul of the anti-Nazi military conspiracy, was relieved of his command and placed under house arrest. The resistance's nerve center in Berlin was collapsing.

# 14

# CODE NAME U-7:
# RESCUE AND ABYSS

THE HEADQUARTERS OF the German military intelligence service (Abwehr), in Tirpitz-Ufer, Berlin, was a dull, gray office building. In this spartan, unassuming environment, the directorate of the anti-Nazi military resistance also operated, enjoying the direct support of the chief, Adm. Wilhelm Canaris. Both busy with their official military duties and underground tasks, Hans Oster and his right-hand man, Dr. Hans von Dohnanyi, found the time and energy to stage sophisticated operations to rescue Jews, converted Jews, and their relatives.

None of these operations could be arranged without the consent and active support of Admiral Canaris. The "little admiral," as he was known, was a controversial figure. A short, soft-spoken, white-haired spymaster, he kept excellent working relationships with most National Socialist leaders. His extraordinary ability to play double and triple games led even fanatical Nazis to believe that it was impossible that he would cooperate with traitors and conspirators.[1] Inside the Abwehr, he was known as a strict and highly distrustful chief, neither gregarious nor friendly. Even his relationship with his own family was cold. Generally, he was a misanthrope who preferred the company of Seppl and Sabine, his beloved dachshunds. Every day, he brought them to his office, and he would sometimes lock the door and play with them for hours. His biographer Heinz Höhne relates that anyone who was not fond of dogs could never expect to win his grace. Another sensitive spot was officers who were too tall. Such people tended to be shooed away, marginalized, and discriminated against.[2]

Very few people doubted Canaris's loyalty to Hitler and the Nazi regime. During the Weimar period, he was known as a monarchist and staunch antidemocrat. As a member of several subversive cells of the radical right, he was involved in the activities of the terror organization Consul. It is unknown whether Canaris was directly involved in assassinations of Weimar politicians committed by this group, but he helped the terrorists to obtain funds and maybe even ammunition. He was also notorious for helping another good friend, Spanish dictator Francisco Franco, to overthrow the young Second Spanish Republic in a bloody civil war. His contribution to the Fascist cause in Spain was crucial, and he was later remembered as "one of the people to whom Franco owed his power."[3] In 1937, he still refused to listen to his friend and deputy commander Hans Oster, who tried to open his eyes to the real nature of the Nazi regime. Back then, he was still a convinced National Socialist. "I require you to stand foursquare by the National Socialist state," he told his officers. "Adolf Hitler's ideas are imbedded with the following soldierly spirit: honor and a sense of duty, courage, military preparedness, a readiness for commitment and self-sacrifice, leadership, comradeship and a sense of responsibility."[4] For him, Hitler was a conservative, nationalist leader set to restore Germany's glorious past.

But apart from his nationalist worldview, Canaris could never share some of the more brutal aspects of Nazi ideology. Surprisingly for a man with a past such as his, he was sensitive to the travails of innocent people and found it hard to stand idle while they suffered. He had helped German Jews before the war and was never a Jew hater, even when loyally serving the Nazi regime. The notorious anti-Semitic newspaper *Der Stürmer* denounced him and his wife, Erica, for consistently shopping in Jewish-owned shops.[5]

Slowly, as with many other future conspirators, the accumulating force of events moved Canaris to change his mind about Hitler. The Fritsch affair, especially, along with the outbreak of war, opened him up to the influence of Oster and Dohnanyi, who were working with him on a daily basis. Another turning point was the Polish campaign, marred as it was by German atrocities. Canaris was busy then in a frenzy of intelligence and sabotage operations, and he took special pains to dispatch spies to foreign countries, including British colonies. He often left Berlin for the field and witnessed the conditions in occupied Warsaw, which horrified him. According to Heinz Höhne,

> The scenes of devastation in Poland left an indelible mark on Canaris. Land warfare was something new to him. His knowledge of war was based on memories of cruisers dueling at long range and colored by the rites traditional among gentlemen of the sea. This was another kind of war, an orgy of mass slaughter and total destruction, a battle between fanatical beliefs and ideologies waged amid burning cities and the ruins of a national culture. What he saw evoked a sense of personal and national guilt which soon became condensed into the realization that was to plague him more and more as time went by: "God will pass judgment on us."[6]

"Canaris was a pure intellect," testified his close associate Erwin Lahousen, "an interesting, highly individual and complicated personality, who hated violence as such and therefore hated and abominated war, Hitler, his system and particularly his methods. In whatever way one may look at him, Canaris was a human being."[7] Knowing full well that he was serving the side responsible for the atrocities, he found a way to live with his conscience. In addition to his formal military duties and the support he gave to the resistance, he made increasing efforts to save individual victims. He did so at the request of an old acquaintance, the wife of the former Polish military attaché in Berlin:

> While visiting Poznan, Canaris was accosted and asked for help by a pale, bewildered-looking Polish woman. The admiral stared at her in dismay as recognition slowly dawned. It was Madame Czimanska, wife of the Polish military attaché and a popular hostess in prewar Berlin . . . She had no idea of her husband's whereabouts . . . Sobbing, Madame Czimanska told Canaris the story of her escape and expressed shame at the Polish forces' apparent lack of determination. Canaris consoled her. "Don't distress yourself . . . The Polish armies have fought well and bravely." When she asked permission to join her mother in Warsaw, however, he shook his head. "I wouldn't go to Warsaw," he said. He walked over to a big map and ran his finger across it. "Switzerland," he told her,

"that's the best place." Canaris produced papers which enabled Madame Czimanska and her children to settle in the neighborhood of Bern, where she found an apartment which he sometimes visited in his subsequent trips to Switzerland. He also acted as a staging-post for correspondence between her and her mother in Warsaw. Having discovered that the latter was living in Ulonska Street, he enlisted Horaczek [the Abwehr commander in Warsaw] to drive him there. "We'll go to the old lady and pass on the news that all's well with her daughter and the children."[8]

Canaris also strove to rescue Jews. One of them was Rabbi Joseph Yitzchak Schneersohn, the spiritual leader of Chabad, more commonly known as the Lubavitcher Rebbe. Very few people, then and now, have known that Canaris himself stood behind this operation.[9]

Like many other Jewish communities, Chabad congregations in Europe were surprised by and unprepared for the Nazi onslaught. When it became clear that Poland was soon to be overrun by the Nazis, Rabbi Schneersohn ordered emergency measures to be taken. He instructed all yeshiva students with American citizenship who studied in Warsaw to return at once, and traveled to the Polish capital himself to save his precious library. Unfortunately, a few days after his arrival, the Wehrmacht occupied Warsaw. Rumors circulated among his Hasidim that the old rabbi, a Latvian citizen, was trapped in occupied Warsaw and even seriously injured. The Chabad lobby in the United States sprang into action. Some of the Hasidic Jews, who had contacts in the administration, urged the State Department to pressure the Germans to save the rabbi. The efforts took a long time but finally paid off, and at a certain stage even the secretary of state, Cordell Hull, became personally involved.

The Americans made contact with a man named Helmuth Wohlthat, a senior German diplomat who was opposed to the war. Wohlthat immediately concluded that the rescue of such a prominent personality might motivate the Americans to mediate between Germany and Britain. Like many Germans, he seriously overestimated the power of the Jewish lobby in the United States. Wohlthat, of course, could not do such a thing by himself, and therefore he made contact with Canaris to ask for help.

Canaris, who supported Wohlthat's peace initiative, threw himself into the mission with zeal. He entrusted the operation to a pair of Abwehr agents, Ernst Bloch, of Jewish descent, and Johannes Horaczek, a fluent Polish speaker. The chief ordered Bloch and Horaczek to go to Warsaw, find the rabbi, and take care of his safe transfer to Riga, which was still free from German occupation at the time. The two made their way to the rabbi's hideout in a military car escorted by armed soldiers. To calm the frightened Jews, who would think the soldiers came with murderous intent, Bloch introduced himself to the rabbi as a Jew. Chaim Liebermann, Rabbi Schneersohn's secretary, testified later that Canaris's agent carried his Great War medal to keep the convoy safe from wandering German soldiers.[10] Thus, in a smooth Abwehr operation, the rabbi was smuggled to Berlin, then to Riga, and finally to a ship bound for the United States. He never knew that he owed his life to the commander of the German Abwehr.

By 1940, Canaris's reputation as somebody who was ready to help had been established in the eyes of his friends and neighbors, and he was constantly burdened with requests. Annemarie Conzen, a converted Jew, asked him to help her mother, who had disappeared into one of the concentration camps. Annemarie herself was defined by the government as fully Jewish, and had to live under the constant threat of deportation to the east. After the death of her Aryan husband, nothing could protect her anymore. She had to leave her own home and move with her two daughters, Irmgard and Gabriele, to a small apartment next to Canaris's. Irmgard was a classmate of Brigitte, Canaris's daughter, and the two girls' mothers also shared a friendship. In 1940, Annemarie tried her luck, and pleaded to the admiral directly about her mother.

Canaris could not refuse. Through his personal courier, Wilhelm Schmidhuber, he located the woman in the concentration camp of Gurs, in southern France. Under orders from his chief, Schmidhuber supplied Annemarie's mother and other Jewish inmates with clothes, food, and money. A little later, the Abwehr chief was able to obtain for Annemarie's mother a permit to leave Gurs and immigrate to Argentina. (That was not as unlikely as it may sound. Two thousand inmates received permits to emigrate from Gurs, through various channels.)

Unfortunately, the old lady declined, as she did not want to leave her fellow inmates. Her decision was fatal: beginning on August 6,

1942, Gurs was evacuated, and most of its Jewish inmates were sent to Auschwitz and other extermination camps. The tragedy affected Canaris deeply, and he decided to save Annemarie and her daughters by any means possible. At the end of 1942, an opportunity presented itself. Hans von Dohnanyi proposed an ambitious rescue operation of Jews and converted Jews, under the cover of a legitimate espionage mission. Canaris agreed right away and asked to also include in the list Annemarie Conzen and her daughters. Some say that he did so partly at the request of his wife, Erica.[11]

In addition to supporting rescue operations, Canaris spoke out against German crimes in the occupied territories, such as the atrocities in Poland, especially those perpetrated by the SS Totenkopf Division. Later, he also raised his voice, almost alone, against the murder of Soviet commissars and the starvation of Russian POWs.[12] Among all the section heads of the Supreme Command of the Armed Forces, Canaris was the only one who did so.

And still, Canaris knew that most of his soldiers and officers were loyal Nazis. As is shown in Winfried Meyer's thorough study on the Abwehr and the Jews, Abwehr agents in Russia were deeply implicated in extermination operations, the most notorious example probably being a force called the Secret Field Police (Geheime Feldpolizei), a counterintelligence force formally under Abwehr command. The official duty of this unit was to purge the front of traitors, spies, and other "hostile elements." But during Operation Barbarossa, Jews were increasingly associated with all of the above, and were exterminated en masse by army, police, and SS alike. The Secret Field Police was so active in these operations that it practically became an Einsatzgruppe. Its commander was very close to SD chief Heydrich. Formally, he was under Canaris, but in fact he answered to the SS security service.[13]

As the mass murder continued, so did attempts to rescue a fortunate few. In March 1941, another rescue operation was brewing in the Abwehr high command. It was ambitious in its scale, and, interestingly enough, its original impetus was not humanitarian but commercial. For quite a few months, Harry Hamacher, the director of Brasch & Rothenstein in occupied Amsterdam, smuggled Jews across the border for a hefty fee. Initially, Hamacher was able to secure border permits using contacts and generous payments, but, as time went by, the smuggling trade became increasingly difficult. Adolf Eichmann's Jewish Affairs department became stricter and stricter in such matters. Quickly, Hamacher discovered that it was almost impossible to obtain visas for his customers. To overcome this problem, he appealed in early March 1941 to Maj. Walter Schulze-Bernett, the commander of Abwehr I (espionage) in occupied Holland. For the latter, Hamacher's plea constituted an excellent opportunity to help Jews and, at the same time, to smuggle spies abroad. His motives were therefore both humanitarian and military. Knowing that such a large-scale operation would require support from the higher echelons, he turned to Canaris and asked for his blessing.

The Abwehr chief quickly sent Schulze-Bernett a coded reply. "Thank you for the cigars you've sent me," he wrote. "They made me very happy." Schulze-Bernett understood the subtext: Canaris had agreed and would offer protection, "owing to his known humanitarian concerns and his opposition to the persecution of the Jews."[14] The operation was code-named Aquilar.

Once Canaris gave his consent, Aquilar developed at breathtaking speed; the list of Jewish refugees grew by the day. Most of them had nothing to do with spying and intelligence operations. Schulze-Bernett included some Jewish friends and acquaintances in the list, and even Gen. Friedrich Christiansen from the occupation government (a man deeply implicated in war crimes) added one or two people "whose personal stories moved him." Another rescuer was Albrecht Fischer, an employee of Bosch and member of the conspiracy. He secured a place on the train for his Jewish friend the banker Rudolf Kahn. Helmuth Wohlthat, already involved in the Schneersohn operation, expanded the list further with eleven additional Jews.

Operation Aquilar began on May 11, 1941. Walter Schulze-Bernett and his subordinates personally watched over the first refugee train leaving Amsterdam on its way to Spain. The second one left the station four days later, and the third on May 18. Many of the refugees traveled further, to Lisbon, and from there on to the United States or South America. The impending invasion of the USSR made it difficult to get emigration permits for a while, but the operation was revived on August 4, 1941, with the fourth Madrid-bound train, again under the watchful eyes of three Abwehr officers. Yet another train leading Jewish refugees to freedom left Amsterdam on August 11, and the last one reached its destination in late January 1942. All in all, almost four

hundred Jews were saved in this rescue operation, the largest one ever
to be staged by the Abwehr.

The official reason for the operation was the growing need to install spies abroad. In reality, the intelligence obtained by Aquilar was
close to zero. Schulze-Bernett himself confessed that the operation
had no success as far as intelligence was concerned, because the Jewish refugees could not be expected to cooperate with the Abwehr.[15]
Indeed, the number of actual spies implanted abroad was very small,
indicating that most passengers were innocent refugees sent for their
rescue alone. The spying mission was mostly (though not exclusively)
a cover story to fool Eichmann and his bureau. The list of refugees
grew as the operation went on—another indication of its humanitarian nature.

It is indeed surprising that just when Eichmann was allowing fewer
and fewer exceptions, Canaris and Schulze-Bernett were able to smuggle out so many Jews. To achieve this end, they obtained fraudulent
visas for the refugees, thereby endangering their own lives. It is also
important to note that the last train left the station three months after Himmler had forbidden further Jewish emigration from the Reich.
Eichmann was no fool, and his suspicions grew by the day. In late
1941, he began to look for ways to expose Canaris's real intentions.
This was well expressed in a letter he sent to the Düsseldorf Gestapo
station on December 2, 1941, around the end of Operation Aquilar:

> Recently, during deportation transports, there has been a suspi-
> cious intervention of Wehrmacht authorities or officers on be-
> half of Jews. Among the excuses for doing this is the notion that
> [these Jews] are to be used for Abwehr interests abroad . . . Un-
> der these circumstances, the possibility is not to be ignored that
> in most cases these requests are motivated by personal interests.
> In the future, Jews should not be allowed to be excluded from
> the transport . . . unless OKW [the Supreme Command of the
> Armed Forces] produces a well-reasoned letter confirming that
> these Jews will actually be used for intelligence operations.[16]

The only person in the Abwehr authorized to sign for the Supreme Command of the Armed Forces was Canaris. The letter was
likely a ploy on Eichmann's part to make the Abwehr chief personally

responsible for the operation. Now, with his personal signature, he would have to answer for any suspicions raised over individual Jewish agents.[17] Canaris, one must assume, was well aware of the trap, but he still would not stop his efforts to rescue Jews.

In late 1942, Canaris approved another large-scale operation, known retrospectively as Unternehmen Sieben (Operation 7), or "U-7" for short. Hans von Dohnanyi turned to Canaris and proposed to smuggle Jews abroad as "intelligence agents." The chief agreed and even asked to include his neighbor, Annemarie Conzen, and her two daughters. As usual, his involvement was crucial. Without Canaris, such a rescue operation could never take place.

However, the key figure in U-7 was not Canaris but his "special adviser" Dr. Hans von Dohnanyi.[18] His office was located in the most important wing at the Abwehr headquarters, close to the rooms of the chief and his deputy. At thirty-seven, Dohnanyi looked young for his age. He wore suits and ties, almost never uniforms, and had round glasses. It was easy to mistake him for a nondescript government functionary. However, he was no faceless bureaucrat but one of the kingmakers in German military intelligence, a personal confidant of Hans Oster and Wilhelm Canaris. A sworn enemy of the Nazi regime since its inception, Dohnanyi later testified that he had begun his struggle against the regime not only because of its lawlessness but also because of the "Nazi treatment of the Jews and the church."[19] After 1933, he decided to remain inside the system to fight it from within. His biographer Marikje Smid wrote that, as a resistance fighter and a "better German," he decided to use his power to slow down the slide to evil as much as he could.[20] He did that through his energetic activity in the German resistance and through saving victims.

During the 1930s, Dohnanyi was called upon by countless Berlin Jews, dissident clergy, Freemasons, and other persecuted people. They came to him for advice, and he used his connections, know-how, and financial resources for their sake. "His office," testified his wife, Christine, "turned into a haven for people of all kinds who needed help." He assisted with emigration procedures, gave friendly support, and sometimes even obtained concessions from Justice Minister Gürtner, his direct superior until 1938.

By the end of the 1930s, Dohnanyi had become one of the key

members of the German resistance, a connector between civilian and military groups. When he was removed from the justice ministry because of his politically incorrect views, Oster got him a post as a special civilian adviser (*Sonderführer*) in the Abwehr. During his Abwehr tenure, Dohnanyi was involved in assassination attempts, and Oster entrusted him with day-to-day maintenance of the networks. "My husband decided not to fight for his country," Christine said after the war, "but for those who will safeguard the eternal values of Europe." For the same purpose, Dohnanyi also helped to record the crimes of the Nazi government, and he collected a large file of incriminating documents to be used for the prosecution of the Nazi leaders following the overthrow of the regime.[21]

The event that finally led to Operation U-7 took place in mid-November 1941, when an unusual guest came to Abwehr headquarters in Tirpitz-Ufer: a gray-haired man in his fifties limped to the gate on a wooden leg. He was admitted and taken to Dohnanyi's office. His name was Fritz Arnold.[22]

Arnold was a lawyer of Jewish descent, a Lutheran Christian by confession, who had served as the representative of the Jewish lawyers in Berlin. He was worried nearly to the point of despair. So far, he and his good friend the Jewish lawyer Julius Fliess had been able to avoid deportation to the east. But now, they felt the noose tightening around their necks. Arnold and Fliess both earned medals in the Great War, but in 1941 past achievements meant little. The Jewish Council of Berlin advised Fliess that his name had been added to the Gestapo's deportation list. In a few days, they told him, he must board the transport with his wife, Hildegard. Their nineteen-year-old daughter, Dorothee, was allowed to remain, since she worked in an ammunition factory. Fliess and Arnold knew that the journey to the east would be one-way.

Arnold and Fliess turned to several high-ranking officials for help, but no one was ready to fight with Eichmann and his bureau on their behalf. Eichmann was ordered to make Germany *Judenrein*, free of Jews, and he intended to finish his job to the last. In his despair, Fritz Arnold remembered Dohnanyi, with whom he had been in touch in his (Arnold's) capacity as the representative of Jewish lawyers. At that point, Dohnanyi worked at the bureau of Justice Minister Gürtner. With the passing years, this contact was forgotten. Dohnanyi left his job in 1938, and for many months Arnold heard nothing about him. Now, he heard that Dohnanyi had a new job in the Abwehr. He asked for a meeting, which he was granted.

Arnold told his former colleague about the deportation order for Fliess and his wife. "We must save them!" replied Dohnanyi, and he promised to do everything to have the order withdrawn. That was not his first attempt to help Arnold and Fliess. In 1938, he tried to protect them from the discriminating bylaws that prevented Jewish jurists from practicing law. "These two will be harmed only over my dead body," he had said. Now, in late 1941, the situation had become a matter of life and death. Dohnanyi, like most of his coconspirators, knew well that the Nazis were exterminating Jews in the east. His wife, Christine, testified that during spring 1942, she had long nocturnal conversations with him about the options for rescuing the two Jewish lawyers. Around that time, probably, he made up his mind to save them using the resources of German military intelligence.[23]

Dohnanyi turned to his commander, Admiral Canaris, for help and advice. First, he asked for a recommendation letter for Julius Fliess, stressing his bravery during the Great War. After Canaris agreed, Dohnanyi quickly sent the letter. He hoped that Canaris's power and influence could save his friend. Eichmann gave in this one time and agreed to postpone the deportation, but Dohnanyi was certain that the sword was in its sheath only temporarily. Soon, Eichmann would strike again. In summer 1942, Dohnanyi found out that Eichmann had decided to end outside interventions in his affairs. SD headquarters sent the following letter to the Jewish Council in Berlin: "The Reich Main Security Office has found out that Jews subject to deportation have attempted to thwart this by appeals to other authorities. We clearly announce that such pleas are proscribed. If a Jew subject to deportation attempts to apply for such interventions, his entire family will be deported as well."[24]

Dohnanyi had to change his strategy. The time for pleas to Nazi authorities was over. Again he had a long, private discussion with Canaris, and he proposed to smuggle Arnold, Fliess, and their families to a neutral country as German intelligence agents. Canaris said yes.[25] At that moment, Operation U-7 was born.

Unlike Operation Aquilar, which had been carried out a year earlier in a semilegal fashion, Operation U-7 was illegal from the start. In late 1942, it was already strictly forbidden for Jews to leave the Reich, and anyone who helped them was considered a traitor, subject to the death penalty. Therefore, unlike in previous operations, the risk for the Abwehr officers involved was concrete and acute. Furthermore, it put the entire conspiracy at risk. Canaris and his men all knew this, but it did not change their decision.

Immediately after confirming the basic idea with Canaris and Oster, Dohnanyi informed Fritz Arnold of the plan. He, Julius Fliess, and their families would be smuggled abroad as German spies. Arnold was skeptical at first and stressed that he would never agree to spy for the Third Reich. Dohnanyi calmed him down and told him that he, Oster, and Canaris did not expect the refugees to work as spies but that this cover story must be used as a concealment measure. Dohnanyi even asked Arnold to help with the organization of the operation.[26]

U-7 was managed as an intelligence operation. Canaris, as was his habit, stayed away from the details and entrusted Dohnanyi with the planning. Maj. Gen. Hans Oster secured Abwehr funds and negotiated with Swiss authorities. That wasn't easy, as the Swiss were usually unwilling to accept Jewish refugees. Fritz Arnold was appointed the "leader of the refugees" and received an office in Abwehr headquarters. There, he busied himself with countless small details necessary for the planning and execution of the operation. First, a final list of refugees had to be made. Who, exactly, would be sent to Switzerland? The initial plan was modest: to save only Fritz Arnold, his wife, Ursula, and their daughter Irmingard, as well as Julius Fliess, his wife, Hildegard, and their daughter Dorothee. But the list kept growing. Canaris asked to add his neighbor, Annemarie Conzen, and her daughters, Irmgard and Gabriele. Afterward, Pastor Dietrich Bonhoeffer, a noted theologian and one of the resistance fighters in the Abwehr, heard of the operation and petitioned to include a converted Jewish woman, the church activist Charlotte Friedenthal. Like Annemarie Conzen, she had been defenseless since her Aryan husband's death. When Bonhoeffer asked Dohnanyi to save her as well, he agreed without hesitation.

The list continued to grow. At a certain stage, Dohnanyi also added Christof and Friederike, Arnold's children from his previous marriage. And Canaris asked Dohnanyi to open the list once more, for the sake of the Jewish doctor Ilse Rennefeld.

Rennefeld's route to Operation U-7 was long and winding. As a young physician, she emigrated from Germany in the 1930s and settled in the Netherlands. But the German invasion cut her plans short. She had to wear the yellow star and, according to the occupation government's regulations, could not practice her profession or take part in professional or cultural activities. When her name appeared on the deportation list, she turned to a German friend, who promised to help. The friend called on the physician who had treated Canaris's sick daughter, and mediated between her and Otto, Ilse Rennefeld's blind Aryan husband. The German physician, who agreed to help the Jewish family, spoke with Erica Canaris, and she brought the matter to her husband.

In mid-June 1942, Otto Rennefeld visited Canaris to personally ask for help. The Abwehr chief greeted him with warmth (which he rarely expressed in his professional or even personal life). "Admiral Canaris, with whom I spoke only twice for about fifteen minutes," related Rennefeld after the war, "was a good man and a martyr. I understood it immediately when he started speaking with me with kindness and understanding, and showed himself ready to help me."[27] Rennefeld did not know that at the same time Dohnanyi was already working on the planning of U-7. Otto and Ilse Rennefeld were added to the list, which finally included fourteen men, women, and children. Accepting new people was never easy, as Canaris had to negotiate with the Gestapo for each and every refugee. Still, he could not refuse a person in distress whenever one came calling.

The organizers faced much bigger difficulties than they had for Operation Aquilar, and not only because of the ban on Jewish emigration. (As has been mentioned, the Abwehr was not allowed to employ Jewish agents without the explicit approval of the Reich main security office.) Eichmann and his superior, Gestapo chief Heinrich Müller, were very suspicious of Canaris and tended to be unresponsive. For long, tiring months, Canaris and Dohnanyi held negotiations with Eichmann, who was engaged in a pitched battle against their intentions "to employ Jewish agents in Switzerland."[28] For a while, it seemed that Operation U-7 had reached a dead end.

A breakthrough finally came from unexpected quarters. In January 1942, Hitler ordered Canaris to organize a large-scale sabotage operation in the United States. To do that, the Abwehr chief had to smuggle agents in a submarine to the East Coast and entrust them to local German spies. The mission was to hit strategic industrial facilities, especially those related to the aluminum industry. Canaris and Erwin Lahousen, a coconspirator and the chief of his sabotage section, chose ten to twenty agents, all of them loyal Nazis. Surprisingly, a short while before the operation, the American consulate in Bern received an accurate report on its details, allegedly based on an interception of a conversation between a submarine commanding officer and his family. In June 1942, the agents arrived in the United States and were arrested immediately by the FBI. Most ended their lives in the electric chair.

As expected, Hitler summoned Canaris and Lahousen to severely reprimand them. They had to choose their men more carefully, he said, so as not to have a traitor among them. Canaris, cunning as always, said that all the agents had been loyal National Socialists chosen from the ranks of the party. Hitler fell into the trap. He lamented the fate of the loyal patriots, now subject to the death penalty. It cannot be right, he said, that good Nazis should fall victim to amateurish intelligence work. "If that's the quality of your work," the Führer yelled, "employ Jews or criminals!" Canaris saluted and left the office. Later, when he and Lahousen were in the airplane, the Abwehr chief was beaming. "Did you hear, Langer?"—he used Lahousen's nickname—"employ Jews or criminals."[29] Unwittingly, Hitler had authorized Operation U-7.

After another round of fruitless negotiations with Eichmann and Müller, the green light was finally given in a summit meeting between Canaris and Himmler. Through his persuasive arguments, experience, and ingenuity, Canaris was able to convince the SS chief of the dire need to send Jewish agents to Switzerland. Afterward, he promised, they would be transferred to the United States and South America. The operation was urgent, because the espionage network in North America had disintegrated after the latest debacle. Himmler had to agree.

No less complicated were the negotiations with the Swiss authorities. Dr. Heinrich Rothmund, the commander of the Swiss Foreigners' Police, enforced a restrictive immigration policy, especially as far as Jewish refugees were concerned. Gisevius led the talks with Rothmund and his immigration officers, who demanded a large sum for each refugee. Gisevius had to agree, and he also promised that the Abwehr would finance the refugees until their departure from Switzerland. Hans Oster was responsible for the financial side of the operation, and he gave the refugees one million goldmarks in dollars and Swiss francs.[30]

By September 1942, Dohnanyi, Oster, and Gisevius had finally secured immigration permits for all fourteen refugees. Operation U-7 was moving toward its last, crucial stage. In mid-September, the whole group met Dohnanyi one last time and thanked him for his efforts on their behalf. There is no need to thank me, Dohnanyi replied. "I am only doing my duty, my duty toward Germany." He instructed the refugees to turn to Gisevius with any problem they might face during their stay in Switzerland. At the same time, Admiral Canaris asked for a private meeting with Fritz Arnold, the leader of the group, to say farewell.

The first to travel was Charlotte Friedenthal, who already held a Swiss immigration permit. For the sake of security, Dohnanyi instructed her to wear the yellow star until her arrival on Swiss soil. Gisevius greeted her at the train station, to guide and orient her through the new environment. On September 29, 1942, it was the turn of the main group to depart. Yet Dorothee Fliess refused to leave her friends, fellow slave laborers at the ammunition factory. Years later, she admitted that Arnold had to make a real effort to take her away. Five months after she left, Gestapo agents sent all Jewish workers in the factory to the east.[31]

On the evening of September 29, Julius, Hildegard, and Dorothee Fliess; Fritz, Ursula, Friederike, and Christof Arnold; Annemarie, Irmgard, and Gabriele Conzen; and, finally, Otto and Ilse Rennefeld embarked on a Basel-bound train. Under Canaris's orders, an Abwehr agent traveled with them to ensure their safe passage at the border. At noon on September 30, the train finally stopped at Basel's main station. Encouraged by the Swiss officials, the Jewish refugees removed the yellow star from their clothes. Irmingard, the adult daughter of Fritz Arnold, joined them on December 15, and with that, U-7 came to an end. Fourteen people had been saved from death by the efforts of Hans Oster, the provider of funds; Adm. Wilhelm Canaris, who gave protection and support; and, above all, Dr. Hans von Dohnanyi, the initiator and organizer of the entire operation.

Satisfied with the result of U-7, Oster, Canaris, and Dohnanyi were determined to organize similar operations. They even considered reviving Operation Aquilar to smuggle more Jewish refugees into Spain. Dohnanyi kept in touch with Arnold and asked him to test the ground for the reception of more refugees in Switzerland. Then, catastrophe struck.

In autumn 1942, Nazi authorities discovered the illegal monetary transfer that underlay the operation. Suspicions arose that high officials were embezzling Abwehr funds. Agents of the German resistance were warned by their sources in the police. They, in turn, warned Oster that Canaris's personal emissary, Wilhelm Schmidhuber, was being followed by the Gestapo in Italy. Josef Müller, the representative of the Abwehr and the resistance in the Vatican, met Schmidhuber, offered him money, and ordered him to leave immediately for Portugal. Schmidhuber hesitated. When he decided to depart, it was too late. Italian policemen arrested him in the Tyrol and handed him over to the Gestapo.[32]

Schmidhuber was interrogated, and soon he revealed details about resistance activities within the Abwehr. The SS intelligence service, for years a rival of the Abwehr, was quick to seize the chance, and it formed an alliance with Nazi elements inside the Abwehr legal department. Even on Oster's home turf, where the resistance network was supposed to be strongest, it was still small and isolated. Though Oster and Dohnanyi enjoyed strong support from the Abwehr chief, they were still hated by many, if not most, of the officers, who were loyal Nazis. While the investigation went on, the Gestapo officials were reminded of old letters of complaint against Dohnanyi, sent by a lawyer in the legal department.

The first stone fell in Rome. The Gestapo caught Josef Müller, Canaris's emissary to the Vatican, and placed him under house arrest. On April 3, 1943, the investigating magistrate, Manfred Roeder, ordered the Abwehr headquarters to be searched for incriminating evidence. Dohnanyi tried to resist arrest and called Oster for help. The latter came in, accompanied by Canaris. In a moment of reckless panic, he grabbed a piece of paper and hid it beneath his jacket. That was a fatal mistake. The officials, who were so far oblivious to Oster's role, forced him to hand back the document, on which names of conspirators were written. Manfred Roeder ordered him taken away, along with Dohnanyi and Bonhoeffer. The last two were arrested, and Oster was confined to his home. Keitel had him expelled from the Abwehr.[33]

The arrest of Bonhoeffer and Dohnanyi led to the rapid disintegration of the resistance movement at the Abwehr. Many incriminating documents were discovered, including lists of conspirators. The real nature of Operation U-7 had been exposed.[34] Oster's confidants were arrested or fired one by one, and Himmler practically placed the Abwehr under his own control. The Jewish agents employed by Canaris were demoted, and many of them were sent to Auschwitz. Even the parents of the U-7 survivors, who had enjoyed Abwehr protection thus far, were promptly deported to extermination camps in Poland. The chief of the sabotage section, Gen. Erwin Lahousen, was fired as well. Canaris stayed, for now, but lost all power. For all practical purposes, he was a puppet.

A final blow came several months later. On September 10, a Gestapo agent infiltrated a tea party of an anti-Nazi social circle, leading to the arrest of several conspirators, including Helmuth James von Moltke.[35] Two anti-Nazi Abwehr agents, a married couple, were connected with one of the arrested women. Anxious for their own safety, they made contact with the British secret service and escaped to Cairo. Himmler was furious. This time, Canaris could not escape responsibility, and he was promptly discharged by Hitler. The Abwehr, excepting some departments, was dissolved and integrated into the SS.[36]

In Russia, Colonel Tresckow understood the full implications of events and hurried to Berlin, ostensibly to "convalesce" but in fact to replace Oster as the main connector and hub of the network. He would be transferred back to the front a short while later. After a few months, though, a fresh young officer was recruited. Transferred to Berlin, he was ready to take charge from Tresckow and to dramatically transform the resistance. More than anyone else, he would become associated with German opposition to Hitler in the popular imagination. His name was Claus von Stauffenberg.

# 15

# COUNT STAUFFENBERG:
# THE CHARISMATIC TURN

AROUND SPRING 1943, a severely injured young German officer was visited in his hospital room. He received a very unusual offer: "Would you agree, by chance, to lead a military conspiracy to overthrow Hitler and the Nazi regime?" He had just lost an eye, an arm, and two fingers. The new job could lead to the loss of his head. It took the young officer, Count Claus von Stauffenberg, several days to reply. The answer was yes.

What led this man, with a brilliant career ahead of him, to accept such a dangerous proposition? Why was he chosen over others? How could a newcomer take control of a dense network, brimming with rivalries and jealousies, and become its de facto leader, admired by many almost as a demigod? To understand how this young man, physically ravaged by the war, became such an extraordinary leader, we must first examine his background, military career, and intellectual development.

First, a word of caution. Stauffenberg left very few writings. Almost everything we know about his early life comes from testimonies of friends, acquaintances, and former class- and army mates, most of them given during the postwar era. By then, Stauffenberg had become the quintessential hero of the German resistance. As with those of other resistance fighters, testimonies, including those this chapter is based on, tend to be glowing, even hagiographic, and, most of all, tend to project the future resistance fighter onto his earlier incarnations—

child, teenager, and young officer — as if all his life were a preparation for the plot of July 20, 1944.

Of course, most witnesses were not lying, only overemphasizing Stauffenberg's extraordinary qualities while passing over or trivializing less flattering aspects. It is indeed the case that some of the qualities that Stauffenberg developed early on, such as his charisma and romantic bent, marked his style of leadership in the resistance. However, he might have steered his life on a different course if it weren't for a unique combination of circumstances, some related to other people's decisions, some sheer coincidence. The account of Stauffenberg's life in this chapter, shaped as it is by ex post facto testimonies, must be read with this warning in mind.

Claus von Stauffenberg was born in November 1907 at Jettingen, a small village in Swabia, in southwestern Germany. His family was well established in the ranks of the southern German aristocracy. Claus's father, Count Alfred, was for years a close vassal of the king of Württemberg, and the family had a long tradition of service to the royal house. In his childhood, Claus moved between his family's country estate, situated amid the breathtaking scenery of the Swabian Alps, and the royal castle in Stuttgart. Count Alfred was a die-hard German conservative, monarchist, and devout Catholic, but his wife belonged to the Lutheran Church. According to the custom in those days, the children were educated according to the father's denomination and were therefore baptized as Roman Catholics. Nevertheless, their mother, Countess Caroline, was the most significant figure in their early life. Count Alfred's duties required him to be absent for long periods of time, and Claus and his older brothers, the twins Alexander and Berthold, usually stayed with their mother. They often traveled for vacation to the North Sea or the Alps, visited other aristocrats, and even attended tea parties with the royal family itself.

Caroline educated her children toward Christian piety, on the one hand, and to the love of poetry, art, and music, on the other. Berthold, later one of Claus's closest collaborators in the struggle against Hitler, was particularly sharp intellectually, with blue, penetrating eyes. Claus and Berthold were also gifted cello and piano players, respectively, and admirers of German romantic poetry. Claus, especially, was preoccupied with dreams of personal and national grandeur. As a teenager, he despised the cynical, materialistic worldview of many adults around him, and he firmly believed that money should be abolished. Only then would all men be brothers, regardless of faith or social class. Money, after all, was the source of all evil. Wasn't that proved by the destructive power of the ring in the German epic myth *The Nibelungenlied*?[1]

As a child, Claus often expressed his wish to be a hero. Yet he was weak in physical terms. His schoolmates remembered him as a pale, sickly boy who was frequently sent home on long sick leaves. He made incredible efforts to improve his physical fitness, never giving up on his heroic dreams. For a while, he considered becoming a professional cello player, but he ditched the idea after understanding that he would never be a virtuoso. The essence of human life is not in the immortal soul, he told a friend who was about to be ordained into the priesthood, but in achievements in this world. Even as a child, he said that he wanted not to go to heaven after death but to stay "here" forever, amid the Swabian Alps.[2] Architecture was another early love. After giving up his dream of a professional music career, Claus considered for a while becoming an architect, as he wrote in one of his childhood poems:

> *I often feel I must draw plans*
> *Of high vast palaces*[3]

His personal charisma was apparent from at least the age of seventeen. As one of his schoolmates related, somewhat hagiographically, "His glowing eyes clearly expressed his cheerfulness . . . and generosity. Their color was dark blue . . . His hair was shining black . . . always cut short. His development from youth to adulthood . . . was rapid. He was tall and flexible, with a slender, powerful body . . . The three brothers were blessed with the very rare advantage of a good heart. With Claus, it was expressed in everything he did, and every word he said."[4]

Claus's best friend was his older brother Berthold. Both of them were intelligent, with a spiritual bent toward German romanticism, even mysticism.

The Great War, which broke out in August 1914, changed the life of the Stauffenberg family, though not dramatically at first. The boys were too young to be drafted and were still in school, but their mood, like everyone else's, shifted violently between hope and fear, for every letter from the front might herald the death of a loved one. The Great War changed Europe utterly. Millions of soldiers—entire generations of Frenchmen, Englishmen, and Germans—lived for years in trenches, mud, maggots, and blood all around them. A large contingent did not make it home. The nightmare seemed unending.

One morning, Claus came to his mother in tears. His older brothers had told him that in ten years' time they would be allowed to join the war, but not he. His mother soothed him by saying that she would be "heroic" and let all her boys go. Like most Germans, the brothers Stauffenberg were shocked when their country parleyed for armistice on October 3, 1918. The writing on the wall was clear: the Reich was losing the war. "My Germany cannot perish," Claus said with tears. "If she goes down now, she will rise again strong and great. After all, there is still a God."[5]

Following the surrender, Germany was swept up in a revolutionary maelstrom. The leaders of the Social Democratic Party took over Berlin and declared a republic from the balcony of the Reichstag. The kaiser abdicated, clearing the way for struggles between left and right. Finally, right-wing "free battalions" (*Freikorps*) joined the Social Democratic government against the Communist revolutionaries in a campaign of bloody repression. The kings of the German states were deposed one after another. Germany was in chaos.

Many German aristocrats, seeing themselves as the natural elite, far superior to the "rabble" and common folk, were, of course, afraid of the revolutions and their aftermath. Countess Stauffenberg feared that the revolutionaries would soon reach Württemberg. On November 9, two days before the armistice was signed, an angry mob of demonstrators tried to break into the royal palace but was blocked by Count Alfred and his loyal group of noblemen and servants. The revolutionaries dispersed, but not before replacing the royal standard with a red flag and installing their own guard outside. Claus, Berthold, and Alexander, who were still in school, heard the thunder of drums and saw the demonstrators crowding in front of the palace. The king decided to resign. "I will not let blood spill only for my own sake," he told the Stauffenbergs with tears in his eyes. Claus, only eleven years old, was furious and unforgiving. "When he says that, what does he mean?

The king is not the issue here. The monarchy is." From that moment on, Claus admitted later, he ceased being a monarchist. The Treaty of Versailles only made things worse for German aristocrats such as the Stauffenbergs, and for many other patriots as well. In that year, Claus refused to celebrate his birthday, "the saddest day in my entire life."[6]

The economic situation in the new republic was not encouraging. The war reparations burdened the defeated country, and from 1921 to 1923, it was hit by hyperinflation. Savings disappeared, and the quality of people's lives sank precipitously. Many suffered from malnutrition or shivered in the winter cold. The Reich government had to face daunting political challenges. In 1920, a right-wing militia attempted to overthrow the government in the Kapp Putsch, followed by Hitler's Beer Hall Putsch in 1923. In the same year, France invaded the Ruhr area to help itself in the wake of unpaid war reparations.

What were Stauffenberg's political opinions in these stormy years? His friends related later that, in spite of his reservations, he was against all violent insurgencies, irrespective of political orientation. Christian Müller, one of his early biographers, wrote that Claus and Berthold had agreed to serve the democracy and did not support the Hitler putsch, though they were never among the supporters of the republic.[7]

Maybe as a reaction to the gloomy reality, the brothers increasingly turned to spiritualism and metaphor. If it was impossible to achieve greatness in this world, maybe it could be achieved in the world of letters. They joined a literary circle led by the notable poet Stefan George. This man, a romanticist with mystical ideas, assembled a group of young admirers, who referred to him reverently as "the Master" (der Meister). Alexander and Berthold joined the circle in the early 1920s. George's ideas, associated with the New Right ideology of "people's community" (Volksgemeinschaft), stressed the role of an aristocratic avant-garde as the carrier of sublime spiritual values, love of fatherland, and patriotic service. His disciples, both Christians and Jews, saw themselves as the secret elite of the worthy, designated to bring salvation one day to the fatherland under the genial leadership of der Meister.

The group's meetings, as noted by Peter Hoffmann, were "bathed in a mystic, luminous haze."[8] The members read poetry and discussed art, music, literature, and philosophy. Young, educated aristocrats ventured to escape the misery of the real Germany for an imaginary "Secret Germany" led by Master George. Berthold and Claus quickly became favorites and were lauded by the Master as perfect, sublime beings. Berthold was praised for his determination, sincerity, natural charisma, and beauty. Claus, who joined a little later, was no less admired. He won a great honor when George decided to carry his poems wherever he went, which he would do for years to come.[9]

In the ideal world imagined by George, power of spirit and greatness of soul alone determined one's social status, not money or political cunning. Classical culture, well known and admired by educated Germans of the time, served as a model for George and his circle. When some of them, Berthold included, visited Italy, they knelt before Roman statues, and placed a wreath at the sarcophagus of an ancient German emperor "in the name of Secret Germany."[10]

George's most lasting and most important lesson for Stauffenberg was that one must have a purpose in life, some higher calling or heroic mission to be fulfilled regardless of circumstances. That purpose has to naturally grow out of romantic attachment to ancient history and must be in the service of people and nation. Claus had internalized this message by 1924, as he wrote in a poem that the sublime deeds of ancient heroes and their "glory-crowned blood" moved him to transcend day-to-day limitations. "How can I orient my life," he wrote, "if not in the highest sense?"[11]

In 1924, Claus needed a mission. Exactly what mission, he had yet to determine. He could have chosen a nonpolitical, a Nazi, or an anti-Nazi one. He had already thought about the leadership of high-minded, noble people. Later on, in 1944, he clearly expressed this idea in his "oath," written for his closest confidants as a unifying common pledge in their fight against Hitler. In that important document is a crystallized version of the Secret Germany ideology: a sense of calling, elitism, belief in natural leadership, and the importance of secret comradeship:

We believe in the future of the Germans.
    We know that the German has powers which designate him to lead the community of the occidental nations toward a more beautiful life.

We acknowledge in spirit and in deed the great traditions of our nation which, through amalgamation of Hellenic and Christian origins in the Germanic character, created Western man.

We want a new order which makes all Germans supporters of the state and guarantees them law and justice, but we scorn the lie of equality and we bow before the hierarchies established by nature . . .

We want leaders who, coming from all classes of the nation, in harmony with the divine powers, high-minded, lead others high-mindedly, with discipline and sacrifice . . .

We pledge to live blamelessly, to serve in obedience, to keep silent unswervingly, and to stand for each other.[12]

In 1925, Claus had perhaps not decided yet what his sublime calling was, but he had come to a decision about where to begin. To the astonishment of many of his friends, who were certain that he would study architecture, Claus declared that he was going into the army.

The Reichswehr of the Weimar Republic was not the venue of Stauffenberg's heroic dreams, but it was at least a starting point. During a hike in the hills near Lautlingen, he spoke with a friend about the "painful birth of a new Germany," about the duties of the state and the possibility of influencing it, and about his personal career aspirations in the army.[13]

Stauffenberg, still a sickly youth in 1925, did not pass the physical entrance exams easily. The Reichswehr authorities were not eager to accept the pale young man who frequently suffered from head- and stomachaches. A well-connected relative, however, eased his passage into the army, and he was finally admitted to the cavalry. The first year he spent in intensive cavalry training in Bamberg, a small picturesque town in Franconia. On July 28, he wrote a friend from the George circle about four nerve-racking weeks of sickness, but he insisted that he still felt committed to his profession of choice.[14] In October 1927, he qualified and was admitted as a cadet to the Dresden Infantry School, where he began three years of officer training.

All the while, society was changing fast. In 1924, hyperinflation was reversed by means of a currency reform, the economic crisis was subsiding, and the political situation stabilizing. With higher standards of living than before, the public was losing its taste for radical parties of both right and left. Germany made several unprecedented scientific and cultural achievements. In the thriving universities, luminaries such as Albert Einstein, Erich Fromm, Theodor Adorno, and Edmund Husserl, to name just a few, paved new ways in physics, psychology, philosophy, and other fields of learning. The high tide of art, science, and high culture was followed by a new, modern popular culture. The big cities of Germany were brimming with cabarets, circuses, and other forms of light, affordable entertainment. Most people learned to live in peace with the Weimar Republic.

The republic did impressively in foreign policy, too. The Treaty of Locarno was signed in 1925, beginning a new honeymoon in European politics. Under the leadership of Foreign Minister Gustav Stresemann, the greatest statesman the republic ever had, Germany recognized its new western border. The French and Belgians finally left the Ruhr. In 1926, Germany joined the League of Nations, and two years later it signed the Kellogg-Briand Pact outlawing war as a means of solving interstate conflicts. Many Europeans stopped seeing Germany as a menace to world peace, and its prominence in the continent grew economically, scientifically, and culturally.

Stauffenberg, isolated in his military bubble, did not experience the full extent of these political and social transformations. He had spent the good years of the Weimar Republic doing backbreaking field training, playing cello, reading, and riding his beloved horse, Jagd ("Hunt"). On January 1, 1930, he passed the qualifying exams with special honors, and one year later he received his first command post as an officer. Elitist though he was, he nevertheless enjoyed working with soldiers. "I manage well with subordinates, farmers and soldiers . . . ," he wrote. "And not with people on my own education level, whose friendship is nothing but egoism, and their pride no more than foolish arrogance."[15] Still, he was a strict, uncompromising commanding officer who expected a lot from his men. Orders had to be obeyed efficiently, precisely, and without delay. In his command posts, as well as in other things, Stauffenberg always strove to be better than others.

In 1929, when Stauffenberg was still training in the cavalry school, dark clouds moved in over the Weimar Republic. The good years would soon be over. October 3, 1929, witnessed the death of Foreign Minister Gustav Stresemann, the person who symbolized the stability of the republican regime. None of his successors had sufficient prudence, talent, or international standing to lead Germany through the challenges ahead.

Three weeks after Stresemann's death, on a day retrospectively called Black Thursday, the New York stock market crashed. The American economy plunged, taking most European states with it. The crisis was especially potent in Germany, which was still dependent on American loans. Suddenly, the "rich uncle" across the Atlantic had no more money to spend, and the Weimar bubble burst. The middle class, having barely recovered from the hyperinflation, was especially hard hit. The number of unemployed rose quickly, and by January 1930, more than three million men, 14 percent of the workforce, were registered as jobless. Hopeless millions all over the country were easy prey for Adolf Hitler and his propagandists. Their success was enormous. In the elections of 1930, the Nazi Party turned, almost abruptly, from a marginalized group at the edge of the radical right to the second-biggest party in Germany. Hitler, the obscure demagogue mocked and abused by many, became one of the most important figures in national politics.

Stauffenberg later said that he followed the rise of the new movement "with interest" and was impressed by its rapid political success. In 1933, when President Hindenburg appointed Hitler chancellor, the young officer was quite happy with the result, believing Hitler's take-over to be what Germany needed most at the moment. As a soldier, Stauffenberg could not vote, but even a year before, in 1932, he preferred Hitler for president over Hindenburg.[16] Just like many other German conservatives, he believed that the new leader would moderate his views after taking power. Moreover, National Socialist promises to strengthen and expand the army were certainly welcome, as was the Nazi commitment to breaking the "shackles of Versailles." Stauffenberg, who believed in national unity, also hoped that the new government would forge the nation into a truly unified community (*Volksgemeinschaft*).

It is less clear whether Stauffenberg was influenced by the anti-Semitic wave that swept through Germany after 1933. His brother Berthold told the Gestapo, more than ten years later, that he and his younger brother "accepted National Socialist principles of race" but believed that they were "exaggerated."[17] According to other testimo-

nies from Stauffenberg's friends, he deplored the persecution of the
Jews, especially the boycott of 1933, which he and his friends saw as
"shameful." Some attested that he supported a restriction on the number of Jews in journalism and public service but opposed violent anti-
Semitism. A testimony from 1936 is also very instructive: "Do you
mind that I'm Jewish?" a British officer asked him during a short visit
to London. "No," replied Stauffenberg, explaining that it was enough
that he was a British officer, just as Stauffenberg himself was a German officer.[18] Hence, Stauffenberg's initial National Socialist inclina-
tions did not necessarily mean that he shared the regime's anti-Semitic
ideology, at least not in full.

In November 1933, Stauffenberg married Nina von Lerchenfeld,
the daughter of an old diplomat, whom he first met at a ballet soirée.
The dashing young officer was popular at such aristocratic events. At
first, Nina kept her distance from Claus, unlike other women, who fell
for him at first sight. Only later, when Nina came to know him, did her
initial reserved attitude turn to love, which was to last till death.[19] In
December 1933, the couple married at the Gothic cathedral of Bamberg. Claus came to his wedding wearing his helmet, telling his bride
with all seriousness that "to marry is to be on duty."[20]

His married life was guided by traditional notions. His wife bore
five children, three boys and two girls. As a father and husband, he
was strict and uncompromising—military-style—and required clean-
liness, order, and discipline. When he returned home from work, he
expected the food to be ready on the table. The children were ordered
to put their belongings, including their shoes, in the right place. Furthermore, Nina was not allowed to participate in all aspects of his life.
The George circle, for example, was an exclusively male club. When
his friends from the circle visited, he always asked Nina to stay in their
bedroom or to leave the house altogether.

Still, he loved his family and never showed violence, verbal or physical. He took every opportunity he could to play at home with his children and spend quality time with his wife, entertaining her with his
cello playing or sitting beside her on the floor reading English novels
for hours. Years later, Nina became privy to her husband's secret war
against Hitler.

In early December 1933, when Nina and Claus returned from their
honeymoon in Italy, bad tidings greeted them. *Der Meister,* Stefan

George, had passed away in Switzerland. Only the inner members of Secret Germany attended the funeral; among them were Claus and Berthold. Berthold, who had been appointed by George as his heir, said that the "best part" of his life ended with the Master's death.[21] Claus grieved similarly.

Stauffenberg's military career progressed quickly. In 1934, his regiment was dissolved as part of the military expansion plans, and he was appointed a riding instructor in the Hannover Cavalry School. His evaluations were outstanding. Stauffenberg's commanding officer wrote in a formal report that he recognized in him an "iron will, discretion, extraordinary spiritual qualities and high tactical and technical abilities. [Stauffenberg] is an example in his treatment of NCOs and enlisted men, taking pains to educate his subordinates. Besides he is an excellent rider, with true love and understanding for the horse." The commanding officer had some criticism, too. "Claus is very much aware of his military abilities and intellectual superiority, and sometimes speaks arrogantly, but never with an intention to insult."[22] In 1936, Stauffenberg won a promotion and was admitted to the military academy in Berlin, in the course reserved for prospective General Staff officers.

His classmates in Berlin noted that Stauffenberg already had some doubts about National Socialist policy. "He hated German nationalist arrogance," wrote one of his colleagues later, "but above all he was an aristocrat who kept trying to bridge, at least on the soldierly level, his personal views and formal Reich policy."[23] He was still impressed by Hitler's foreign-policy achievements, especially because they had not yet led to war. Unlike General Beck, then chief of the General Staff, Stauffenberg was certain that Hitler would not provoke a world war. He told one of his friends that a man like Hitler, who served in the Great War and was well familiar with its horrors, would never open a conflict between Germany and the entire world.[24] In June 1938, during a study tour in the Rhine Valley, he expressed his unorthodox views clearly: Franco-German relations would have to be improved. The two nations must find a way to overcome past difficulties, putting an end to aggressive, hegemonic thinking. "If the Western world did not disintegrate in the Great War," he said, "that was only because the crucial battle on the Rhine was averted."[25]

Stauffenberg had no contact with the resistance in 1938, and, contrary to later legends, he was not involved in the September 1938 conspiracy. But he, too, had become afraid of a European conflict. "That lunatic will make war," he said furiously after the occupation of all of Czechoslovakia in 1939.[26] After Kristallnacht, he started to ponder the possibility of a violent coup. But his misgivings faded away after the German victory in the Polish campaign, and for a few months he turned back into a Hitler supporter.

Like most Germans, Stauffenberg heartily disliked Poland and held it responsible for Germany's humiliation after the Great War. He wanted to teach the Poles a lesson and to bring Danzig and the corridor back to the fatherland. And if England and France declared war, Germany would defeat them as well. The war had the "high aim of self-preservation" and could be won only "in a good, long fight."[27]

Charlotte, the wife of Fritz von der Schulenburg, recalled how Stauffenberg lectured her enthusiastically on the sweeping victory at the front.[28] Hitler won admiration as man and leader alike. To his bookseller, Stauffenberg said that whatever he had opined about the Führer before was no longer relevant. Now, Hitler was fighting for Germany's survival. He stimulated creative thinking, and one must help him win the war. "This man's father was not a petty bourgeois," he concluded admiringly. "This man's father is war."[29] From Poland, he wrote his wife letters burning with patriotism and clear racist, imperialist overtones: "The inhabitants are an unbelievable rabble, very many Jews and very much mixed population. A people which surely is only comfortable under the knout. The thousands of prisoners-of-war will be good for our agriculture. In Germany they will surely be useful, industrious, willing and frugal."[30]

This letter reiterates accepted Nazi clichés. Was Stauffenberg yet another loyal German officer? In some sense, he was. His near intoxication with military triumph went hand in hand with dehumanization of the enemy. Still, Stauffenberg never went past a certain point. He was, for example, very much opposed to the atrocities committed during the Polish campaign, even if he believed them to be SS excesses rather than formal, organized policy. When one of his friends, an officer, shot to death two Polish women out of suspicion that they had made a signal to Polish artillery, Stauffenberg used all of his influence to remove the officer from the army. After witnessing atrocities, Stauffenberg told some friends that in principle he was not against removing the regime but that it could not be done then, when Hitler was at the peak of his success.[31]

In November 1939, Stauffenberg was promoted again, formally admitted to the General Staff, and appointed quartermaster of an armored division. An official report commended his "great organizational talent." The division commander glowingly praised him in front of the troops and raised the hope that he "would never leave us." As long as Stauffenberg was with the commander, the latter "never had to worry about supplies," because "under Stauffenberg they worked superbly."[32] One of the officers, who knew him from staff meetings, described him as follows:

> Stauffenberg, tall, slender, agile and with extraordinary charm, greeted us in truly beaming kindness. He took care that everyone had something to drink, a cigar or tobacco for his pipe, updated us, asked questions . . . and so time went by, without any of our problems being solved . . . Until suddenly, in an unofficial, unassuming manner he began to speak: "Well, I believe that what we should do is as follows . . ." His left hand in his pocket and the right holding a glass of wine, he passed thoughtfully across the room, stopped here and there, took maps and gave perfectly detailed orders for [the organization of] supplies.[33]

In 1940, Stauffenberg was transferred to the General Staff, and from there he observed the final victory over France. "There is no greater pleasure," he said, "than winning a war along with friends." Stauffenberg's biographer Peter Hoffmann notes that his patriotic zeal was out of place in the cool atmosphere that prevailed in the corridors of the General Staff. When one officer predicted that Germany would ultimately lose the war, Stauffenberg reprimanded him for his defeatism. He wanted to work hard, to advance his career, and even to conduct some reforms in the General Staff. "The entire existing organization would have to be examined," he wrote Nina.[34]

Yet irritating doubts came back to haunt him at an unexpected time: the final occupation of France. Stauffenberg, as we have seen, was thrilled to settle old scores from the Great War, but right after the capitulation of France, he sat with other officers, some of them future conspirators, and thought aloud. A victory, he said, must be capitalized on politically. If Hitler used the victory to achieve final peace, then all would be well. If not, he must be forced to do otherwise, and if that was not possible, he must be removed.[35] However, that fleeting thought by no means marked Stauffenberg as a future conspirator. He even blamed Hitler for giving up the invasion of England, which he saw as promising.[36] Had he known of the conspiracy of Voss and Schwerin to take Hitler down with a squad of sharpshooters, he would probably have disapproved.

In June 1941, when Germany declared war on the Soviet Union, Stauffenberg was already known and esteemed in the General Staff. As part of his duties, he traveled to different fronts; met officers, including generals and field marshals; and was generally appreciated by most. Even after the invasion had started, he continued to serve his homeland with great dedication and zeal, eager to fight against the "Bolshevik enemy."

Only later in 1941 did his mind gradually turn. Stauffenberg was well aware of the activity of the Einsatzgruppen, the murder squads that slaughtered entire Russian Jewish communities. He felt unhappy about their activities but couldn't draw conclusions for practical action from his feelings.

Count Helmuth James von Moltke, who believed that such a young, talented officer would be a blessing for the resistance, checked, through a middleman, whether Stauffenberg was ready to join the conspiracy. Stauffenberg, then a major, declined the request. He was well aware that the Nazi regime must go, he said, but no such measure could be taken during a war against Bolshevism. Soon enough, he predicted, the officers and soldiers would come home from the front. Then, he said, "we will purge the brown plague [i.e., the Nazis]."[37] Indeed, during the first months of the war, Stauffenberg looked hopefully on the advance of the three army groups—north to Leningrad, centrally to Moscow, and south to Ukraine—and believed that Russia could be defeated. However, he emphasized, such a thing must be done with—not against—the local population.

The official position of the Wehrmacht, let alone the Nazi government, was very different. Russians and Ukrainians, who had initially welcomed the Germans as liberators come to throw off the Soviet yoke, quickly realized their error. Hitler, Himmler, and their ilk saw the locals as *Untermenschen*, slaves whose purpose in life was serving the Germans. This was the policy of large parts of the army as well. National Socialist field marshal Walther von Reichenau, for example, issued an order that fires started by withdrawing Soviet troops should not be put out. The destruction, in his mind, was an inseparable part of the fight against Bolshevism.[38] The SS Einsatzgruppen, police battalions, and army units destroyed entire villages, massacred inhabitants on the pretext that they were partisans, and sent many more off to slave labor in Germany. Orders issued by Keitel practically allowed soldiers to commit atrocities at their discretion, without fear of punishment.[39]

Stauffenberg was angry and disappointed at the policy of his army and government in the east. For him, the local villagers, Russians and Ukrainians, were not enemies but potential allies in the fight against Bolshevism. He warned, again and again, that the war couldn't be won without such cooperation.[40] He tried to establish local anti-Bolshevik units to fight Russia along with the Wehrmacht. He really hoped that such units might form the basis for a future Russian-German partnership. Indeed, the official statistics indicate that in the first months, before Soviet soldiers understood that POW camps were more or less starvation cells, the rate of desertions from the Red Army was relatively high.[41] The National Socialist policy in the east was therefore not only immoral but also impractical. Stauffenberg knew it well.

In spring 1942, Stauffenberg still believed that his country could win the war in the east, as long as the German abuse of the local population abated. In April, in a conversation with an Abwehr officer, he "expressed outrage at the brutal treatment of the civilian population in the German-occupied Soviet Union, the mass murder of 'racially inferior' persons, especially Jews, and the mass starvation of Soviet prisoners of war."[42] In May, he met an officer fresh from the front, who told him about a massacre committed by the SS in a Ukrainian Jewish town. "They led them [the Jews] to a field, made them dig their own mass grave, and then shot them." Stauffenberg replied, "Hitler must be removed." As he heard more about the escalating atrocities, he became increasingly convinced that the Nazi regime must be removed by force without any further delay. He believed that doing so was the duty of the high command. The Wehrmacht leaders would surely not be indifferent to such horrors for long. He was still unhappy at the idea of isolated assassination attempts. When told that Schulenburg was planning something, for example, he advised his counterpart to ignore the "little bomb throwers." A revolt must be done not by individuals but by the army as a whole.[43]

Stauffenberg was ripening for conspiracy, but he still had to lose his belief in the generals and field marshals. More importantly, circumstances needed to change. As we saw in chapter 3, people usually become conspirators when legitimate social connections mutate into revolutionary ones. This mutation presumes an internal change in outlook and opinions, but it is also dependent on being socially connected to people in the resistance. Stauffenberg knew some such people in 1942, but these connections were still not solid enough to draw him toward their cause.

Yet his resistant ideas continued to develop quickly. In August 1942, he even tried, quite awkwardly, to form an oppositional network of his own. "You seem to believe that I am engaged in conspiracy here," he told an officer half jokingly. When broaching the subject in a conversation with a friend, he maintained that after Hitler's overthrow, neither the Weimar Republic nor the empire should be reestablished, but, rather, "something new" must come into being.[44] Not for a moment did he stop dreaming about the ideal Secret Germany imagined by *der Meister*, Stefan George, and his circle.

Meanwhile, the German war effort faced mounting difficulties. Army Group North failed to occupy Leningrad, and Army Group Center could not reach Moscow. Hitler ordered his army to turn to the south, simultaneously occupying Stalingrad and the oil-rich Caucasus. The Sixth Army, led by Gen. Friedrich Paulus, was getting close to Stalingrad. While it is true that many postwar accounts have exaggerated Hitler's personal responsibility for the debacle, it is certain that his incessant meddling in operational affairs precluded clear, organized strategic thinking. Stauffenberg was very bitter over the way the war was being fought, and his hatred of Hitler was growing by the day. In August, he explained to his close friend Maj. Joachim Kuhn what had precipitated his dramatic change of mind. The amateurish management of the armed conflict was bad enough, but the main problem lay elsewhere. A few years later, Kuhn recounted this conversation to Red Army intelligence officers: "The daily staff reports on the treatment of locals by the civil administration, lack of political direction in the occupied countries, and the treatment of Jews—all of these prove that Hitler lied to us when saying that his intention is to fight for a new European order. Therefore, this war is monstrous."[45]

Stauffenberg told other officers that "they are shooting Jews in masses. These crimes must not be allowed to continue." The young major was so indignant that tyrannicide began to seem justifiable. Germany could not and should not win the war, he emphasized, because that would allow Hitler to continue murdering Jews and committing other horrors.[46] From that moment on, his remarks about the legitimacy of tyrannicide grew in frequency and intensity "in nearly every outing." "It is time," he said bitterly, "that an officer went over there with a pistol and shot the dirty fink." During a conversation with another embittered officer after Halder's removal, in 1942, he said that there was no point in telling Hitler the truth. "No fundamental change is possible unless he is removed. I am ready to do it." That remark expressed yet another dramatic shift in his mode of thinking. Now, Stauffenberg was placing himself—and not only the generals and field marshals—at the heart of the equation. He was taking responsibility.[47]

At this time, Stauffenberg was working as a lone wolf, without a support network. He warned yet more colleagues that Hitler's military folly would bring disaster upon Germany and that his crimes would sully its name for generations. "We are sowing hatred that will visit our children one day," he told a senior officer in despair.[48] All was for nothing. Many officers in the high command agreed with him in principle, but then there were so many practical difficulties: the time was not ripe, one should not betray one's country during war, the front might collapse, civil war might break out, and—crucially—the officers had made the oath of allegiance, attaching each of them to the Führer in a personal bond of loyalty.[49]

Stauffenberg did not know, and actually could not know, that the main network of the resistance was at work all around him. Tresckow and others watched him from a distance but did not acquaint him with their plans.[50] In a police state like Nazi Germany, one had to be extremely careful with whom one spoke. Here, the absolute importance of network structure is apparent. Had Stauffenberg joined the conspiracy in 1942, he would have probably reached the margins of Tresckow's clique in the east. Gradually, he could have become an important conspirator. Certainly, he could not have been a leader in 1942, as the center was still occupied by strong wire-pullers such as Oster. For Stauffenberg to assume the central role he eventually would, the center had to be cleared. This was not to happen until almost a year later.

Resentful and tired, Stauffenberg understood that he had failed. He could not convince senior officers to join him, nor could he build a network of his own. The danger was acute, and he knew he was putting his family at risk. In one instance, when he was trying to win over an officer, he got a cold and angry response. The officer who reprimanded him asked that the conversation be written down "for further examination."[51] In December 1942, Stauffenberg asked to be transferred from the General Staff to find refuge at the front for a while.

In February 1943, freshly promoted to lieutenant colonel, he assumed his new role, divisional chief of staff in North Africa. At the end of the month, he arrived at the Tunis headquarters of Major General Broich, likewise a critic of the regime. Stauffenberg enjoyed being at the front, then as always. "How refreshing it is to visit [the front]," he wrote hapless General Paulus, commander of the Sixth Army, several months before his troops fell into captivity, "a place where one dares without hesitation and sacrifices without complaints . . . while the leaders, or the people who should serve as an example squabble over prestige and fail to rise to the level suitable to their responsibility over the lives of thousands."[52] Stauffenberg escaped from the center to the margins. Had he not done so, or had he transferred later to Italy, the Balkans, or Greece, he would probably never have met the conspirators again. Chance, no less than his talents or the internal development of his ideas, played a crucial role in igniting his conspiratorial career.

"Stauffenberg's uniform had not yet been bleached by the African sun," writes Peter Hoffmann. "And he looked very much the newcomer, but this impression faded more quickly than the color of his uniform."[53] In autumn 1942, military conditions in North Africa were difficult, as the Axis forces were already on the defensive. The German and Italian armies, led by Field Marshal Erwin Rommel, were defeated in El Alamein and pushed back to Libya. In November that year, combined British and American forces landed in North Africa to surround the Germans in a pincer movement. The Allies, led by General

Eisenhower, were set to destroy Rommel's Africa Corps, occupy North Africa, and form a naval base for a landing in Italy. For the Axis powers, that posed an existential danger.

To thwart Eisenhower's plans, Rommel decided to occupy the ports of northern Tunisia before the Americans did, thus taking control of vital supply routes. But Rommel could not push the Allies back into the sea, and his forces were diminishing. The RAF controlled the sky, its planes pulverizing the ammunition, tanks, and other vehicles of the Africa Corps. Reinforcements from Germany arrived, but too late, and the days of the Axis in North Africa were numbered.

From his limited capacity as a divisional chief of staff, Stauffenberg did everything possible to avert catastrophe. For two months, from February to April, he became known as a daring combat officer able to make quick decisions and keep his composure under fire. In early April 1943, he helped to orchestrate, along with his commander, Major General Broich, the German retreat from Tunis. But on April 7, his life changed again. Misfortune brought him back to Berlin, and to the conspiracy.

Late that morning, Stauffenberg took leave from Broich in order to direct the division's retreat to the new command post, near Mezzouna. Broich warned Stauffenberg that there was a high danger of fighter bombers attacking, and indeed, Stauffenberg's force found itself locked in an inferno of enemy fire. The fighter bombers shot again and again into the burning vehicles, and wounded men were abandoned amid exploding ammunition rounds. As Stauffenberg was driving around in a desperate attempt to control the troops, the enemy airplanes targeted his car. The lieutenant colonel threw himself to the ground and covered his head with his hands. And then the bullets pierced his body.[54]

The young officer was badly wounded, and when his soldiers rushed him to the military hospital, it seemed that hope was lost. But the local medical officers were able to stabilize his condition, albeit at a cost: they had to amputate his right hand and two fingers of the left. During the attack, he had lost an eye, too. When he regained consciousness, it became possible to evacuate him back to Germany. His high-ranking friends took care to bring him to the Charité Hospital in Munich to be treated by the best surgeons.

An endless stream of officers came to visit him. His mother and wife were always by his side, and, so that he could visit, his brother Berthold was granted a special leave from the naval court where he served. Many acquaintances, friends, and colleagues from all over the Wehrmacht came to pay their respects, including Chief of Staff Zeitzler, who brought with him a golden medal and a bottle of good liqueur.

One of the visitors was Stauffenberg's uncle Count Nikolaus von Üxküll, known in family circles simply as Uncle Nux. A German aristocrat from the older generation, Nux was leading a battalion of Azeri volunteers in Russia. At the time, Stauffenberg didn't know that his uncle was a member of the anti-Nazi conspiracy, or that his involvement went back to 1938. Üxküll, like many others, had supported Hitler in 1933, but his eyes had since been opened by military crimes and military folly. To save Germany's good name in the world, he believed, Hitler must be removed. And that was the real reason for his visit to the hospital. He came to see Claus not only as his uncle but also to represent the conspirators.

Like his coconspirators, Üxküll was deeply anxious. After Oster's demise, the resistance cell in the Abwehr had been broken. But because it was organized in a structure of connected cliques (see chapter 11), the network had not been fully destroyed. Tresckow's group in the east, for example, was still functioning, but the temporary arrests of Kaiser and Schulenburg indicated that one small mistake could lead to Oster's fate being shared by Tresckow and everyone else. The structure of connected cliques was especially vulnerable: one lethal strike on the brokers, Kaiser and Schlabrendorff, and the whole network could collapse.

The biggest immediate concern, though, was the center. Beck was old, tired, and unhealthy. He could lead discussions, advise, and help, but could not serve as a military planner and connector between the center and the periphery. A younger officer with greater energy was required for that. Indeed, once Oster could no longer fulfill that role, Tresckow came to Berlin to take charge. But his presence at the center was likely to be only temporary, as he could be recalled to the front at any moment. Thus, a hole opened at the center of the network.[55] Üxküll tried to convince his fellow conspirators that his nephew Stauffenberg was the right man to fill it. This plan verged on the foolhardy and was probably accepted only because the group had no other good options.

Stauffenberg listened attentively to Uncle Nux. At first, he refused to commit himself and told his uncle he needed more time to think about it. But by Üxküll's second visit, a few days later, his mind was made up. "If the generals have not achieved anything," he told his uncle, "it is time for the colonels to get involved." Nina was also notified. "It is time for me to save the German Reich," he said to her, adding that, as an officer of the General Staff, he had to take responsibility.[56] He understood that radical measures must be taken. "The struggle against National Socialism, with its fanatical goals and theories," he told his confidant Joachim Kuhn, "could be done only one way: by eliminating Hitler and the men around him."[57]

First, though, Stauffenberg had to recover. He spent a few quiet months convalescing with his family in Bamberg, during which time he learned to dress using his remaining hand and teeth and practiced writing with his left hand every day. He could not take up his most cherished hobby again: the cello was beyond him. Uncle Nux took upon himself a new duty. From now on, he would take care of Stauffenberg: "Any chance, be it the slightest, that our conspiracy still has, opened only with Claus's arrival. He is our life and soul. He gave form to our efforts all throughout these years. Now he is the finger on the trigger. I am an old man, and see my main duty in taking care of Claus . . . I believe I can do something useful by taking care of his physical needs, helping him, for example, in the bathroom, or to get dressed. It is unbelievable that one person can carry such a heavy weight."[58]

And indeed, "finger on the trigger" and "one person" are the key phrases here. As the new leader, the compelling Stauffenberg changed the resistance beyond recognition. The time had come for the last major shift in the conspiracy: the charismatic turn.

# 16

# THOU SHALT KILL:
# THE PROBLEM OF TYRANNICIDE

*It must be by his death, and, for my part,*
*I know no personal cause to spurn at him . . .*
*And therefore think him as a serpent's egg*
*Which hatch'd would as his kind grow mischievous,*
*And kill him in the shell.*
— WILLIAM SHAKESPEARE, *Julius Caesar,* Act 2, Scene 1

W HEN STAUFFENBERG TOOK charge of the German resistance, in late 1943, it had become clear to most members of the inner circle that Hitler must die. Yet the decision to assassinate him—the sovereign leader to whom an oath had been sworn—was difficult for most, tortuous for some, and almost impossible for others.[1] This decision, as we shall see, was not only a consequence of inner developments of this or that conspirator but also a group decision and, as such, was subject to the influence of network dynamics and structural constraints.

Even in 1943, consensus had not yet been reached on the assassination attempt. Dr. Carl Goerdeler; Count Helmuth James von Moltke; many members of the Kreisau Circle; and even Lt. Werner von Haeften, Stauffenberg's right-hand man in the July 20 assassination plot, all strongly opposed assassination on moral or practical grounds, or both. Goerdeler's position, as the civilian leader of the movement and prospective chancellor, was especially influential. He rejected assassination mainly on moral grounds, and proposed instead the so-called western solution: a joint action of the Wehrmacht leaders in the west against Hitler, leading prospectively to his arrest and trial.[2]

Even as late as 1942, Ulrich von Hassell continued to prefer Goerdeler's western solution over assassination.[3] Beck presumably held the same view for a relatively long time, as he did not want to make Hitler a martyr, but he changed his mind around January 1942. His reasons were practical: as long as Hitler was alive, all commanders would be bound by his charisma. Nicholas Reynolds has also suggested that the war crimes of the regime were one of Beck's motives. His observation is supported by a document written in 1944, coauthored by Beck, stating that the "crimes taking place behind the army's back" constituted the "most important" motive for the coup, and presumably also for the assassination.[4]

In January 1942, though, Beck's endorsement of the assassination was still equivocal. Instead, he chose a typical solution of compromise. The plan, he told the members of the inner circle, was still to arrest Hitler, as before, but "in case of failure" the Führer would "fall victim to a terrorist act." This decision was originally a part of an unrealistic plot employing a retired "panzer general," most probably Hoepner, to storm Hitler's headquarters with tanks.[5] Beck's basic decision, though, was much more important than the abortive plan to which it was related. By deciding to kill Hitler "if all else fails," Beck was trying to have it both ways: supporting the killing of Hitler, on the one hand, and giving due respect to the opposing voices, on the other. As it was all but impossible to arrest Hitler in early 1942, the logical implications of the plan were clear to everyone. Col. Hans Crome testified about the meeting to his Soviet interrogators. At the end of January 1942, he said, there was a conspiratorial meeting in Dr. Jessen's abode. Oster was appointed by Beck to plot the assassination, because his position in the Abwehr gave him access to explosives and knowledge of Hitler's security arrangements.[6]

According to Beck's biographers Klaus-Jürgen Müller and Nicholas Reynolds, a year later, in February 1943, the leader of the resistance was already past any moral or ethical qualms about assassination.[7] Kaiser's diary also indicates that Beck fully supported Tresckow's attempt to kill Hitler.[8]

It was even clearer to the younger officers of the resistance that Hitler must die. As has been mentioned, Stauffenberg had expressed his wish that someone would "shoot the dirty fink" in late 1942. Tresckow and Gersdorff likened it to an act of self-defense—a slaying of a mad dog. "Hitler is the source of all misery," Tresckow told Kaiser, according to the latter's diary.[9] Therefore, he had to be removed. It is notable that these three young officers—Tresckow, Gersdorff, and Stauffenberg—advocated assassination with the simultaneous resolution to participate in a coup d'état. For them, killing Hitler was an integral, self-evident part of the revolt. The assassination plan, accepted by only a small minority in 1938 and pushed, by Beck, through the back door in January 1942, had become the appropriate course of action in the view of most leaders by winter 1943.

This sea change was related not only to the inner convictions of the conspirators but also to their dynamics as a group and to the shifting structure of their networks. In 1938, only a few conspirators had endorsed assassination. The reason was clear: at that time, they still had a chance to win over Halder, and maybe even Brauchitsch. The possibility, however theoretical, of having the entire armed forces at their disposal was favorably received by the majority of the resistance members. Why not arrest Hitler and try him before a German court? At that time, only a few had seen assassination as necessary.

Once the war had begun, however, the chance to win over Halder and Brauchitsch to the conspiracy became ever smaller. Thus, around 1942, the basic strategy had undergone a dramatic shift: now it was to confront the senior generals with an assassination planned and carried out independently, without the assistance of high-ranking officers. That decision was part of the strategy underlying the "connected cliques" of Tresckow, Kaiser, Oster, and Schlabrendorff.

The fact that young officers such as Tresckow, Gersdorff, and Stauffenberg, who had begun to resist Hitler around 1942, became enthusiastic supporters of assassination makes sense when perceived within the context of the networks in which they worked. To arrest Hitler, one needed ample power right at the center: members of the high command with constant access to Hitler and enough troops to arrest him. The conspirators had no such men, and, as Tresckow observed, under the frantic conditions of the war, the chances to arrest Hitler and hold him captive were nearly nonexistent.[10] However, the connected cliques had the ability to plan assassinations. They had access to bombs through contacts in the Abwehr, willing assassins at the eastern front, and, once in a while, access to the Führer during his visits to the front line. The 1938 Berlin clique, concentrated near Hitler at the center, theoretically could either arrest the dictator (through Halder) or assassinate him (using Heinz's shock troops). The scattered cliques of 1942, however, could not arrest Hitler—only kill him. Given that fact, opting for assassination made sense. Ringleaders who continued to oppose the assassination were veterans of the resistance—people stuck in the bygone world of 1938; the possibility of getting rid of Hitler bloodlessly, through a "legal revolution," lingered in their minds.

Still, the changing external conditions affected even the staunchest opponents of assassination; one by one, they were carried with the stream of dominant opinion. Take, for example, Dr. Carl Goerdeler. This highly moralistic man, who could never separate ethics from realpolitik, formally remained opposed to assassination up to the attempted coup of July 20, 1944. A coup destined to bring about a moral regeneration of Germany should not begin with the violation of the divine commandment "Thou shalt not kill."[11] The alternative espoused by Goerdeler was usually the western solution, and he kept on proposing it until almost 1944, well after it became clear that it was a pipe dream. This "solution," no doubt, was nothing more than an anachronistic attempt to enliven the plan of September 1938, which Goerdeler still remembered. And yet, Goerdeler's position was much more ambiguous than is usually recognized, as the National Socialist People's Court later observed: "Goerdeler countered time and again with the argument that one had to give him the opportunity to challenge Hitler openly on the radio, instead of treading the path of murder. Even if it was so, he could not distance himself from the murderous conspiracy . . . The political fruit of murder—power—he still wanted to pick and enjoy."[12]

The People's Court was right on the mark. Kaiser wrote of Goerdeler in his diary on January 18, 1943, that he "does not want to wait any longer. Not to lose even one day. But to move as soon as possible. We cannot expect the field marshals to take the initiative. They are waiting for orders."[13] The former lord mayor of Leipzig might have opposed the assassination, but when his arguments were rejected, he kept on working with the conspirators and even urged them to move faster, knowing full well the direction the movement had taken. His opposition to the assassination was therefore more formal than real, an attempt to keep the moral high ground while allowing reality to take its course. Goerdeler's position could be likened to that of a legislator who votes against an unpopular but necessary plan, knowing that his or her vote will not change the outcome. In Goerdeler's role as a civilian leader, his opposition to the assassination was meaningless unless he left the conspiracy altogether. Lt. Werner von Haeften, no less opposed to assassination than Goerdeler, had to abandon his qualms and actively support it, because his position in the network (as Stauffenberg's adjutant) did not allow him to do otherwise.

The shift from unrelenting, conscious rejection of murder to tacit support also occurred in the Kreisau Circle. Some of the members, such as Leber and Schulenburg, were consistent supporters of the assassination from the outset. Others, such as Yorck, began to support it at around the same time as Beck. Some never gave their support.[14] More interesting, and more ambiguous, was the position of the circle's founder, Count Helmuth James von Moltke. He initially opposed not only the assassination but also the coup d'état. "You do not have anyone who could do it right," he wrote, "and it won't help anyway. Everything's too far gone, and so horrendous. You can't change anything. We have to leave it to the Allies, whether you want to or not."[15] The only solution, according to Moltke's view, was to help the persecuted and the Allies ("We are ready to help you to win both the war and the peace," he wrote to one of his British friends) and, most importantly, to carefully plan the future of post-Nazi Germany, as the Kreisau Circle had done. Stauffenberg, practical to the core, became furious with this high-handed approach. "I can't stand that fellow Helmuth Moltke," he snapped after an especially irritating meeting with the leader of the Kreisau Circle.[16]

Still, just like Goerdeler, Moltke kept on working with the conspirators, though he despised the practical political work of the conspiracy —"Goerdeler's trash," as he disdainfully called it. Deeply involved in practice, and not only in drafting plans for postwar Germany, Moltke was very active in the negotiations between the conspirators and the British. His letters indicate that he also became involved in the preparations for the coup, a course of action that distressed him greatly.

Moltke abhorred violence, even conspiratorial political violence, throughout his life. In the last days before his arrest, in late 1943, he felt that he was being dragged forward reluctantly. In a way, his arrest "saved" him. "I was and am still uninvolved in violence of any sort," he wrote to his wife; but that was not a disavowal of the coup, as it is usually interpreted, only an expression of personal relief that he had been saved from involvement.[17] The stories of both Moltke and Goerdeler show that when the circumstances and the structure of networks dictate a strategy of assassination, those who oppose it may continue to do so as long as their network position allows them not to become involved. As circumstances change, they find themselves dragged in sooner or later.

Although people are greatly influenced by external circumstances, constraints, and group dynamics, personal views still determine, to some extent, whether somebody wavers in supporting the group decision or commits to it entirely. The strong religious faith of many conspirators pushed them into endless struggles with ethical and religious dilemmas involved in the attempted assassination of Hitler. In this regard, the dialogue between Dietrich Bonhoeffer, a Lutheran pastor and spiritual authority in the resistance circles, and Stauffenberg's adjutant Lt. Werner von Haeften is particularly enlightening. Bonhoeffer, who wrote extensively, using veiled language, on the question of violent opposition in his book *Ethics*, believed that political assassination counted as murder. Thus, the assassins had to accept the guilt for taking the tyrant's life. But in situations such as in Nazi Germany, when Hitler's government not only killed millions but also threatened the survival of the nation and the core of its Christian values, the conspirators might have to take guilt upon themselves for the sake of others. By responsibly taking guilt upon himself, Bonhoeffer argues, the Christian does not betray Christ but emulates him. Christ, after all, was sinless yet nevertheless consented to take all the guilt of humanity upon himself.[18]

This is indeed a paradox, as Bonhoeffer himself was the first to recognize. In the complexities of reality, we do not have an objective, universally accepted set of rules. Assassins have to make their own choice, and all options are problematic. "Responsible action," wrote Bonhoeffer, "takes place in the sphere of relativity, completely shrouded in the twilight that the historical situation casts upon good and evil. It takes place in the midst of the countless perspectives from which every phenomenon is seen. Responsible action must decide not simply between right and wrong, good and evil, but between right and right, wrong and wrong."[19]

Around November 1942, Lt. Werner von Haeften visited Bonhoeffer at his home to ask about the legitimacy of tyrannicide. Bonhoeffer gave him a very unusual answer, which may have left the young lieutenant more confused than before. A friend of his later recounted the scene:

"The shooting itself would have no significance," said Bonhoeffer, "unless it brings about a change in the circumstances. The elimination of Hitler alone will not suffice—things can turn out to be much worse. The role of the resistance fighter is so difficult because he must meticulously prepare for the aftermath. After the assassination there must be a group ready to take power immediately." Haeften was not satisfied yet. For him [the discussion] was too theoretical ... "Should I? May I?" he asked. Bonhoeffer explained that he could not decide for him. While it is true that he would have to bear the guilt for not using the opportunity, he may also be guilty in acting recklessly. No one can escape such a situation without guilt. But, and this was Bonhoeffer's comfort, guilt is always the guilt born by Christ.[20]

Tyrannicide, then, is legitimate under the conditions of Nazi Germany, but it must be done only if one could be quite certain that it would improve things. At the end of the day, it was the responsible action of the assassins, and, as they would have to bear the guilt, it was also their duty to decide (and here I requote) "in the sphere of relativity, completely shrouded in the twilight that the historical situation casts upon good and evil." Seen through Bonhoeffer's lens, then, Stauffenberg, Haeften, and the others had to make an almost impossible moral decision. They had to dare to jump into the unknown. And they were ready.

# 17

# A WHEEL CONSPIRACY: THE STAUFFENBERG ERA

EVEN WHILE RECUPERATING from his extensive injuries in the summer and autumn of 1943, Stauffenberg started playing his new role. He visited Berlin a couple of times and met his fellow ringleaders Beck, Olbricht, and Tresckow. Another meeting, in which Goerdeler was also present, convened in the office of the broker Hermann Kaiser. At that gathering, Stauffenberg confirmed his commitment to "joint, violent action against the Führer," and accepted the overall leadership of Beck.[1] The general, as Stauffenberg later told his confidant Joachim Kuhn, had given him full powers to plan the operation: "Although the two of us, General Olbricht and myself, are fully competent to deal with all of the technical aspects of the organization, I report weekly to General [Beck] . . . Every time I am astounded by his clear judgment and far-sighted political observations. His basic views fully correspond to our own."[2]

Tresckow, while convalescing in Berlin, was quick to establish a good working relationship with Stauffenberg, who was an old acquaintance of his. Now, Stauffenberg was finally informed of the abortive assassination attempts of spring 1943, as well as the prospective military plans and contacts in other resistance cells, such as the Kreisau Circle and the Social Democratic group. From the outset, Stauffenberg endorsed a policy of cooperation with all opposition groupings. His working relationship with both the remnants of the Kreisau Circle, formed through his relative Peter Yorck von Wartenburg, and the Social Democrats was especially warm. As part of his new responsibilities, Stauffenberg was very active in drafting cabinet lists, and he consistently lobbied to give key positions to the Social Democrats in order to build a basis for cooperation between right and left.[3]

He focused his main efforts, however, on extending the resistance movement's military reach. During the end of 1943 and early 1944, Stauffenberg met dozens of officers, shared his plans, and tried to convince them that eliminating Hitler was unavoidable and that Germany's survival was now on the line. His new mansion, in the quiet suburb of Wannsee, partially shrouded by shrubs, quickly became (along with Olbricht's house) the unofficial headquarters of the resistance.

Meanwhile, Hermann Kaiser kept up day-to-day communication between the various civilian and military groups. "Kaiser was a confidant and mediator," wrote historian Ger van Roon.

> He enjoyed the trust of the resistance leaders. Goerdeler, Beck, Tresckow, Olbricht, and many others stayed in constant touch with him. Meetings were often held in his office. Kaiser also tried to smooth over differences of opinion, which were minor in his view. Tresckow discussed with him the general state of affairs, as well as the possibilities and the details of the operation: Goerdeler shared with him plans and memoranda and asked for advice. Besides, [Kaiser] was the point of liaison between him [Goerdeler] and the army. Olbricht treated him with great confidence, entrusted him with secret files, assigned him important tasks and covered up his activity.[4]

Kaiser's centrality, however, was as dangerous as it was vital. At the end of August 1943, the conspirators learned that networks dependent on a small number of brokers and connectors could be seriously compromised, even eliminated altogether, if these actors were neutralized. A few months after Oster's downfall, the Gestapo opened criminal proceedings against Kaiser because of some reckless anti-Nazi remarks he had made that hinted at his membership in a "resistance movement." Given that Kaiser, the Berlin broker of the German resistance, was in personal touch with most groupings, his arrest could have compromised the entire conspiracy. Finally, Olbricht was able to have the pro-ceedings dismissed with the help of powerful contacts, but he, like the others, knew that the resistance was now on the brink.

In that instance, the negligence of the Gestapo is almost unbe-lievable. Even if one does not believe the unfounded theories that Himmler wanted the coup to succeed so that he could take Hitler's place, it is a fact that the Gestapo could have done much more to crush the resistance.[5] In fact, in 1939, the Gestapo had been very close to uncovering Oster's attempt to warn the Belgians about the western offensive, as well as Josef Müller's negotiations in Rome. Over time, much information was gathered on the civilian resistance, and rumors of a planned coup d'état were widespread. The conspirators made mis-takes that could have given everything away. For example, Prof. Jo-hannes Popitz, a prominent member of Goerdeler's circle, recklessly tried to win over Himmler, of all people, to the movement. Yet, in Nazi Germany, strange rumors of all kinds were common, and the Gestapo found it hard to separate the wheat from the chaff. Nonetheless, the failure of the secret police to adequately follow Kaiser, despite the se-rious suspicions against him, was one of the gravest blunders of the National Socialist security apparatus, a blunder without which July 20, 1944, would not have been possible.[6]

How long, however, could the conspirators count on their enemies' negligence? As the abortive proceedings against Kaiser showed, one tactless remark was enough to push the resistance to the edge of the abyss. In order to forestall such disaster, the leaders of the military re-sistance set strict rules of secrecy. "Never mention names," Tresckow warned the resistance secretary, Margarethe von Oven, "and above all never mention Stauffenberg's name. The group must be kept as small as possible, otherwise it will get out." He further instructed her to wear gloves while typing in order not to leave incriminating finger-prints.[7]

Already in 1943, well before Stauffenberg's rise to leadership, there had been strict rules of compartmentalization in the military wing of the resistance. Tresckow insisted that every conspirator should know "only the necessary minimum to carry out his duties." When dispatch-ing couriers with messages for other ringleaders, he did not inform them about the content of the letters they carried. Hans Crome, a key liaison in Paris and then at the eastern front, was never updated

*"There is no going back for me anymore."*

Colonel (later, Major General) Hans Oster was the key military leader of the German resistance in its early years. A cunning and resolute intelligence officer, he was constantly watching for opportunities to win over allies in the regime's higher echelons.

© Gedenkstätte Deutscher Widerstand

*"God knows that I risked everything only to save the youth, the men and the women of all countries from further misery."*

Dr. Carl Friedrich Goerdeler was one of the founding fathers of the German resistance movement and the most important leader of its civilian wing. Deeply committed to strict rules of legality and morality, he crossed the line to illegality due to his opposition to the persecution of the Jews. Had the coup on July 20, 1944, succeeded, Goerdeler would have become the chancellor of Germany.   © Bundesarchiv, Bild 183-1987-1223-501

*"Witzleben was a refreshingly uncomplicated man . . . who had his heart in the right place . . . a man firmly rooted in the chivalric traditions of the old Prussian officer corps."—Hans Bernd Gisevius,* To the Bitter End

Field Marshal Erwin von Witzleben was one of the earliest conspirators in the German army and the commander-in-chief of the Wehrmacht in the resistance's shadow government.

© Reproduktion Gedenkstätte Deutscher Widerstand

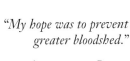

*"My hope was to prevent greater bloodshed."*

An introverted carpenter, Georg Elser initiated a sophisticated attempt to assassinate Hitler by planting a bomb set to explode during a Nazi ceremony. Alone and without help, he came the closest to killing the dictator.

Schweizerisches Bundesarchiv Bern, E. 4320 (B) 1970/25, CH-BAR#E4320B#1970/25#2*, Az. C.02-102, Strasser, Otto, Dr., 1897, 1934–1939

*"I can with a clear conscience stand by all I have done in the battle against Hitler."*

Colonel (later, Major General) Henning von Tresckow was a key leader in the German resistance and the mastermind of several attempts to kill Hitler. In his schemes, Tresckow used exploding liquor bottles, sharpshooters, and suicide bombers. Known as one of the most hard-line anti-Nazis in the resistance, he believed that Hitler had to be killed "like a mad dog."

*"If the generals have not achieved anything, it is time for the colonels to get involved."*

Colonel Claus Schenk Graf von Stauffenberg, a dashing, aristocratic officer with a romantic bent, became the symbol of the German resistance to Hitler. As the last military leader of the conspiracy, he smuggled a bomb into Hitler's briefing room in a bold attempt to kill the dictator, lead a coup d'état, and take over the government of the Reich.

Hitler's briefing room after the explosion of Stauffenberg's bomb, July 20, 1944. Mussolini, who visited the Führer the same day, was astounded that someone dared to launch an assassination attempt inside the regime's supreme headquarters.

*"All great men in history had to face the decision, whether to be denounced by history or be remembered as saviors in times of emergency."*

Colonel Rudolf-Christoph Freiherr von Gersdorff, an intelligence officer on the eastern front, was Henning von Tresckow's confidant and assistant. He took part in several attempts to kill the Führer, and finally volunteered to blow himself up with the dictator during a tour in the Berlin armory.

The courtyard in the former compound of the Wehrmacht high command, on Bendlerstrasse in Berlin. Here, Stauffenberg and three of his coconspirators were shot on the night of July 20, 1944, after the failure of the coup d'état. In 1955 the street was renamed Stauffenbergstrasse to commemorate the leader of the coup. Today it is part of the German Resistance Memorial Center and the venue for induction ceremonies in the Bundeswehr, Germany's federal army.

on Tresckow's assassination attempts. Even the omnipotent broker Hermann Kaiser discovered some things very late. For example, only around February 1943 was he informed that an assassination attempt was being planned. Then, he ordered Captain Gehre, the leader of the Abwehr shock troops, not to brief his officers until the very last moment.[8] Olbricht took care to hide his clandestine work even from his closest confidants.

Stauffenberg considerably tightened the existing regulations for his coconspirators. As he suspected that Oster, who by the end of 1943 was under house arrest, was being constantly monitored by the Gestapo, Stauffenberg forbade all members of the resistance to meet or speak with him. Indeed, the mere existence of the military resistance was a closely guarded secret, all but unknown outside certain restricted military and (to a lesser extent) civilian circles. Though Stauffenberg tried to win over many officers, he guarded his secrets well from people he deemed unreliable.[9] A Nazi lieutenant who worked with him on a daily basis, for example, was completely oblivious not only to his anti-Nazi activities but even to his oppositional sentiments. In spring 1944, Tresckow was defined in an official report as having a "spotless National Socialist worldview," indicating that his direct superiors were either completely in the dark about his nocturnal activities or very keen to cover up for him.[10] Even a sharp observer such as the Finnish ambassador to Berlin, Toivo M. Kivimäki, who monitored the activity of the civilian resistance and reported what he saw to Helsinki, knew nothing about the military wing of the resistance.[11]

These stricter rules of compartmentalization were part of Stauffenberg's unique style of leadership, marking the last dramatic shift in the network structure of the resistance. Under his command, the movement hardly resembled the cozy, dense clique founded by Oster and Gisevius in 1938, or even the model of connected cliques gradually developed in 1942 by Oster, Tresckow, Kaiser, and Olbricht. The fall of Oster and the disintegration of the resistance clique in the Abwehr, as well as Tresckow's gradual loss of power after his transfer from Army Group Center, removed competing sources of power and marked Stauffenberg as the undisputed military leader of the movement and its supreme broker and connector.

To use terminology taken from criminal-law theory, Stauffenberg's style of leadership would turn the movement into a "wheel conspir-

acy." That model has one commander (the hub) and many subordinates (spokes) who receive their respective missions directly from the
commander. Unlike in a clique, in a wheel conspiracy "each member knows some of the other members, but not all of them," while
everybody knows and obeys the person at the center.[12] As we have
seen in chapter 3, Oster's clique was dense enough to allow almost
every conspirator to know most of his confederates. Above all, it was
a circle of friends. The connected cliques of 1942–1943 were dependent on a small number of brokers, such as Schlabrendorff and Kaiser,
and did not have one distinct leader. In Stauffenberg's wheel conspiracy, by contrast, he himself stood at the center and demanded that all
coup-related information pass solely through him. When later refer-
ring to the conspiratorial methods of Stauffenberg, Gestapo investigators rightly observed, "Stauffenberg was considered the person who
was updated on all of the individuals and the discussions in the circle
of the conspirators. He orchestrated them as such, striving to murder the Führer and taking upon himself the management of the coup
d'état. Goerdeler reports that Stauffenberg demanded to be informed
also of the political measures and about the people who were supposed
to [fulfill political functions] after the revolt."[13]

Thus, Stauffenberg held firmly in his hands the roles of leader, connector, and broker, which had in the past been assigned to different
people; as a result, the new leader had unprecedented power. Still,
even under his leadership, the movement was not entirely identical
to the ideal model of a wheel conspiracy. The count, who was subject,
at least nominally, to Beck's supervision, did not know every individual in the movement and often had to rely on subconnectors such as
Goerdeler, who led the civilian wing, or on the brokerage services of
Kaiser and Stauffenberg's cousin, Lt. Col. Caesar von Hofacker.[14] Nevertheless, even though some old brokers and connectors kept their
prominence, they were subject more and more to the influence of
Stauffenberg, the hub of the clandestine wheel. The superstructure
was maintained by Stauffenberg's charismatic personality, and it integrated people usually ignorant of each other, who knew only the necessary minimum about the conspiracy.

The achievements of Stauffenberg and his associates—and in particular, his aspirations to centralize power in the superstructure of a
wheel conspiracy—outraged several veteran conspirators. Many of

them, embittered and marginalized, remembered fondly the cozy, small clique of 1938 and resisted Stauffenberg's new system. Most bitter, perhaps, was Hans Gisevius, who quickly returned from Switzerland to take part in the expected coup. After his return, in early July 1944, he heard from his old friends, especially Count Helldorff, of serious grievances concerning Stauffenberg's behavior. Both Helldorff and Gisevius heartily disliked the new leader. They were shocked to see how he was filling the movement with new members loyal to him alone, all the while marginalizing seasoned veterans of proven loyalty. Especially outrageous for them were Stauffenberg's proclaimed intentions to replace Goerdeler with his Social Democratic friend Julius Leber as the future chancellor of the conspiracy. It cannot be, they protested, that a man as dedicated as Goerdeler would be humiliated by an opportunistic officer who had served Hitler loyally for years, only to abandon him now, when the war was evidently lost.

The dislike was mutual. Stauffenberg distrusted Gisevius and Helldorff and despised Goerdeler, who was, in his eyes, an obsolete relic of Weimar politics. He even remarked once that he was not planning "a geriatric revolt." Only at Beck's insistence did he accept Goerdeler's leading role, at least temporarily.[15]

Intramural rivalries were merely a nuisance for Stauffenberg, as more serious troubles were at hand. On September 15, 1943, he took up his new position at the Home Army and began a highly stressful daily routine. His formal military duties, feeding the collapsing fronts with ever more reserve troops, were loathsome to him, and enough to bring a normal man to the brink of a nervous breakdown. "I must . . . send tens of thousands to their senseless deaths," he told a relative.[16]

Stauffenberg devoted as much time, if not more, to his nocturnal duties, however. His office was buried in the German War Ministry, a gray, dull cluster of buildings on Bendlerstrasse, in Berlin. There, he organized his daily routine as an officer and as a conspirator. Thus, for example, he looked for secretaries whom he could trust to type the plans of the coup. As usual in the German resistance, family ties were utilized for the job. Through Tresckow, Stauffenberg got in touch with three female volunteers: Erika von Tresckow (Henning's wife), Ehrengard von der Schulenburg (Fritz's relative), and Margarethe von Oven, a close friend of the Tresckows' and a former military secretary. "I was nervous, nervous as a puppy," she later related. "I prayed that I would break my hand so that I could get out without disgrace."[17] But, in the end, she took the job on.

"The Führer Adolf Hitler is dead." Upon encountering this sentence in the draft plan, Oven realized that she was privy to more than high treason; this was a plan to assassinate the supreme leader of the German Reich. In his Stauffenberg biography, Peter Hoffmann notes that Tresckow told her about the "tens of thousands" of murdered Jews, who were his and his friends' main motive for joining the conspiracy.[18] Stauffenberg knew, too, that masses of people were being exterminated in the gas chambers. In response to Yorck's report about the killing of tens of thousands of Hungarian Jews in Auschwitz, Stauffenberg told him that this was yet another good reason to quickly assassinate the "mass murderer."[19] Oven reported that Stauffenberg was "businesslike yet radiating an inner fire." When asked, he gave her an explanation similar to Tresckow's, but in his usual style, accompanied with a poem written by his spiritual mentor, Stefan George, emphasizing the calling of heroic aristocrats to fight on behalf of the nation's honor and its moral and spiritual standing.[20]

Berthold, Claus's brother, who was, as always, his closest confidant, told an acquaintance that "those responsible in Germany must be punished for their crimes, such as concentration camps, persecution of the Jews, before Germany's total military defeat, and . . . no sacrifice was too great to achieve this."[21]

Apart from the technical details, Claus von Stauffenberg had to tackle the most sensitive and difficult task at hand: finding a volunteer to assassinate Adolf Hitler. Stauffenberg was able to win over dozens of officers, some of them in Hitler's own headquarters, but none of them would agree to carry out the assassination. Stauffenberg's right-hand man, Fritz von der Schulenburg, was roaming the fronts, under official pretexts, searching in vain for volunteers. As for Stauffenberg himself, his coconspirators agreed that he was not the right man for the job, mainly because of his severe disabilities.

In November 1943, Schulenburg finally located a volunteer: Capt. Axel von dem Bussche, a highly decorated front officer. A year beforehand, on October 5, 1942, Bussche had witnessed a life-changing spectacle at an abandoned airport in Ukraine:

In our Dubno garrison, a former Tzarist army base, the prefectural governor asked us to help in an operation, which Führer orders explained as an "anti-Jewish measure." To refuse — that is all we could do. After a few days the residents of the Jewish quarter, 2,000 to 3,000 people, were made to stand in long lines in front of mass graves, to be killed one by one by shots to the base of the neck. On the following day, I was in the Ghetto. They began a manhunt after the few who had managed to hide. A woman literally kneeled in front of me and begged for her life, but there was nothing I could do for her.[22]

At Dubno, Bussche had witnessed for the first time a massacre committed by the government to which he was duty bound. His sense of impotence in the face of such evil engendered a conversion, a religious-like change of heart; and a vision, a higher calling, crystallized in his mind. Unlike other conspirators, he volunteered not only to aid and abet but also to be the cutting edge. The only thing he felt he could do to atone for his guilt was assassinate Hitler himself. In autumn 1943, Schulenburg arranged a meeting between Bussche and Stauffenberg, who promptly asked the young man whether he was ready to kill the Führer. "Yes," he said simply.[23]

Stauffenberg, Schulenburg, and Bussche began to plan the operation. First, they ruled out assassination by firearm. The Führer was known to wear an armored vest and was surrounded by elite bodyguards. As in the past, the conspirators feared that one bullet shot under great mental stress would likely miss its target. Worse, the assassin might well be caught alive, and Bussche knew Stauffenberg; if Bussche could not endure torture, the entire conspiracy would be done for. The sole alternative was to dispatch Hitler with explosives, preferably via a suicide bomber. In December 1943, Hitler was set to watch a military demonstration of newly designed winter uniforms. Bussche, who had perfect "Aryan" looks and proven combat experience, was the ideal man to model the uniforms and answer the Führer's questions about their benefits and drawbacks in battlefield conditions. Bussche waited in East Prussia and reflected on his imminent death. "These days," he later wrote, "were illuminated in that shining clarity that soldiers learn to recognize in the hour before they charge."[24]

Until that fateful day, Stauffenberg and his coconspirators had been preparing, down to its last detail, the coup d'état's operational plan. They treated it—as they were trained to—as staff work, and applied careful concealment procedures. When Beck, for example, visited Olbricht for consultations, he took pains to shake off Gestapo agents on his trail. First, he went to the train station and waited on the platform as if he were going to take the express train. When the train came, he sneaked into the tunnel between the platforms and took an exit to a side street, where Olbricht's son-in-law, Friedrich Georgi, was waiting in a military vehicle. Likewise, Olbricht followed strict procedures when meeting Gisevius. No conspirator, under any circumstances, was allowed to visit Olbricht without notice, lest he draw unwanted attention.[25]

From the summer of 1943 onward, Olbricht had collaborated with Stauffenberg on the reworking of his old plans from 1942. Once a week, Stauffenberg visited Beck in his house at Goethestrasse in order to take advice on the drafts. The operational code name was Valkyrie. In the ancient legends of northern Europe, the Valkyries were war fairies, hovering above battlefields to decide the fate of the combatants and to carry the fallen mighty to the seat of the gods, Valhalla. It was the fate of Adolf Hitler that the modern Valkyries of the resistance were about to decide.

Originally, the Valkyrie orders were designed to reinforce the eastern front in case of a sudden military collapse. Valkyrie II, a revision drafted by Olbricht's office in spring 1942, authorized the Home Army to promptly deploy its units locally in case of a paratrooper attack, an uprising of foreign workers, or another emergency inside the Reich.[26] On July 31, 1943, Olbricht dramatically revised the orders for the purpose of the coup d'état. According to the revision, which was duly authorized by General Fromm, the commander of the home front had the authority to deploy not only his own troops but all detachments and soldiers within reach, including military schools, personnel on leave, and units in training and reorganization. They were to be organized within six hours into combat detachments and to be moved as quickly as possible, using all available means, wherever they were needed. All other existing security measures and plans were to be carried out exclusively in accordance with Valkyrie.

By carefully redrawing the plan along these lines, the conspirators, whose bastion was the Home Army, secured for themselves almost un-limited control over the Wehrmacht in Germany, most importantly in the Greater Berlin area. They also took care to practice, drill, and re-hearse the plan multiple times in different military districts to improve performance and, above all, the reaction time of the troops. Wisely, it was decided that "the preparations must be carried through as secretly as possible. By no means should authorities or individuals outside the Wehrmacht be informed about the intentions or the preparations."[27] The idea was, of course, to keep the prying eyes of the SS, Gestapo, and SD away from the plans.[28]

The leaders of the resistance decided that immediately upon the Führer's death, the Valkyrie orders would be sent to all Wehrmacht district commanders.[29] The first communiqué would disclose that Hit-ler was dead and that an irresponsible clique of Nazi leaders had plot-ted to take over the country. In addition, the order would note that, as a preventive measure, the army had taken the government into its own hands. Military forces would arrest the SS leaders, Reich ministers, governors, and other top-echelon officials, and take hold of electricity, water, and gas, as well as communication and radio facilities. Incrimi-nating documents, carefully prepared by Hans von Dohnanyi and oth-ers, would be utilized as evidence in special military tribunals orches-trated by Stauffenberg to condemn the Nazi leaders to death in the first days after the coup. According to the plan, Field Marshal Erwin von Witzleben, who had long urged the conspirators to do away with Hitler, would take over the Wehrmacht, and Major General Tresckow would lead the police. In Greater Berlin, four key individuals had de-clared unconditional loyalty to Beck and Stauffenberg: Maj. Gen. Paul von Hase, the commander of the Berlin garrison and Dietrich Bon-hoeffer's uncle; Maj. Hans-Ulrich von Oertzen from the *Wehrkreis* (re-gional) headquarters; Col. Wolfgang Müller, a left-leaning officer re-sponsible for infantry training in the Home Army; and Berlin police chief Count Wolf von Helldorff. The conspirators expected that the officers of the armored school at Krampnitz and the commander of the guard battalion in Berlin, Maj. Otto Remer, would follow orders from Olbricht and Stauffenberg even though they were not privy to the conspiracy.[30]

In the west, the conspirators could rely on an important force led by the military governor of France, Gen. Karl-Heinrich von Stülpnagel, and on Lt. Gen. Hans Speidel, the chief of staff of Army Group B. There were also other seasoned, loyal veterans of the conspiracy occupying key posts in France. The broker connecting Stauffenberg to the western front was his cousin Caesar von Hofacker, who was deployed in the Wehrmacht headquarters in Paris.

Another important component of the plan was the takeover of the Führer's headquarters in Rastenburg, East Prussia. By autumn 1943, Stauffenberg and Tresckow had worked on detailed operational plans to take control of the compound, under the heading "Calendar: Measures." This plan, the details of which were only recently discovered in the archive of the Russian secret service, included complex joint actions of the Berlin conspirators and units in Lithuania and at the eastern front. Immediately after the assassination, the conspirators were supposed to submit the code names Swallow and Seagull to loyal commanders. These commanders, in turn, would issue orders to take over the headquarters of Hitler, Himmler, Göring, Ribbentrop, and all SS garrisons in the region under the pretext that "traitorous elements in the party and the SS plan to abuse the grim situation at the Eastern Front and stab the army in the back." Documents, prepared in advance, denounced both terror in Germany and Hitler's lust for foreign conquest, and promised soldiers that from then on, only sacrifices required for the protection of their homes and families would be demanded. Tresckow and his confidants were supposed to orchestrate this operation.[31]

Once the conspirators had seized control of Berlin, the provisional government of Ludwig Beck would take over. After lengthy, stormy debates, it was decided that Beck would become head of state, Goerdeler would be his prime minister, and the Social Democrat Wilhelm Leuschner would be deputy prime minister. Ulrich von Hassell would serve as foreign minister, and the powerful Ministry of the Interior (including control of the police) would be granted to another Social Democrat, Dr. Julius Leber. Olbricht would serve as minister of war, with Stauffenberg as his deputy. Once the radio stations were under anti-Nazi control, Goerdeler would broadcast to the German people in the name of the new administration. We can learn something of the plans and intentions of the conspirators from "An Appeal to the German People," a document that was supposed to be signed by Beck, the prospective head of state. According to available evidence, it was probably written by Stauffenberg, with the assistance of other conspirators:[32]

> Germans!
>
> The tyranny of Hitler is broken!
>
> In the last years frightful things have taken place in front of our very eyes. Hitler, never entrusted with power by the German people, usurped the chancellorship using the worst kind of manipulations . . . To keep power in his own hands, Hitler established a reign of terror. In the past, our compatriots were able to take pride in their honesty and integrity, but Hitler despised the word of God, undermined the law, destroyed integrity and devastated the happiness of millions. He ignored honor and magnanimity, the liberty and lives of others. Countless Germans, as well as people from foreign nations, have been languishing for years in concentration camps, where they suffer agony and are subjected to horrifying tortures. Many of them have died. Our good name has been stained by cruel massacres. With bloodstained hands, Hitler continues to walk the path of madness, leaving behind him a trail of tears, grief and agony . . . while his phony military ingenuity has brought disaster upon our brave soldiers . . . The brave sacrifices of the nation have all been squandered in vain. Ignoring expert advice, Hitler has sacrificed entire armies to satisfy his craving for glory and his megalomania.

The authors of the document knew that only Hitler's death would liberate the multitude of officers of all echelons from their oath of allegiance, and therefore they attributed great importance to the assassination itself. Beck and Stauffenberg also believed that they had to explain the radical path they had chosen—the utter violation of their own oaths. They wrote,

> Hitler has broken countless times his oath of allegiance to the nation . . . violating divine and human laws. Therefore soldiers, public servants and even ordinary citizens are not bound to him by oath any longer. In this time of emergency I rose up and took action, along with others from all classes and regions of the motherland. Temporarily, I accepted the responsibility of leading the

German Reich, and formed a government under the leadership of the Reich chancellor. The government began its duties. [Field Marshal Witzleben] is the supreme commander of the Wehrmacht, and on all of the fronts, the commanders in chief have submitted to his command.

Here follows a general, nonbinding declaration of the government:

The principles and plans of the government will be published. They will be binding, until the German people have the opportunity to decide ... We would like to replace power and terror with law and liberty ... we would like to restore our standing and honor in the community of nations ... With our best efforts we would like to stretch out our hand and heal the wounds caused by this war to all nations, and rehabilitate the mutual trust between them. The guilty men, who have brought disgrace on our good name, and caused so great a suffering to our people and other nations, will be punished.[33]

These proclamations reflect the conspirators' attempts to explain their acts, prove their patriotism, and give some hope to the German masses, who were languishing under air raids and economic deprivation. The same tendency can be found in Field Marshal Witzleben's proclamation to the Wehrmacht (coauthored by Beck, Tresckow, Kaiser, and Stauffenberg). It emphasized Hitler's military folly and responsibility for the loss of the Sixth Army in Stalingrad, in order to contrast it with Beck's farsightedness in his opposition to the war. Furthermore, it made clear to the soldiers that "above all we have to act because of the crimes committed behind your backs."[34]

The leaders of the Social Democratic resistance group promised their coconspirators in the army that in case of a civil war, they would be able to agitate the workers, organize strikes, and disrupt the movement of National Socialist forces. According to the memoirs of Emil Henk, the charismatic leader Carlo Mierendorff had renewed contact with his old Social Democratic comrades at the end of 1942. Under his auspices, related Henk, they had carefully built a network of activists throughout urban and rural Germany. The network was well compartmentalized, and Mierendorff was supposed to trigger it by command as soon as the generals took over Berlin.[35] Mierendorff's death, in an air raid in December 1943, was a significant blow, but the network continued to work under the supervision of Wilhelm Leuschner and Julius Leber. It is not known how large the network was, and in any case Henk's self-celebratory account must be read with extreme caution. Even if such a network did exist, one has to doubt the extent of its influence on the large masses of German workers, taking into account the frequent reports on their weakness and apathy recounted by SOPADE, the central committee of the Social Democratic Party in exile.[36]

After taking over the government, the conspirators hoped to reach a truce with the Western Allies as quickly as possible. Most of them hoped, almost until the very end, to keep fighting at the eastern front in order to prevent the Bolsheviks from occupying Germany. Between 1942 and 1944, both Moltke and Goerdeler held talks with American diplomats and neutral intermediaries in Istanbul and Stockholm. At the same time, Gisevius had formed a strong contact with Allen Welsh Dulles, the commander of the U.S. intelligence service's Office of Strategic Services in Bern, and frequently updated him on the development of the conspiracy.[37] But the Western counterparts in these talks, both diplomats and intelligence operatives, were not qualified to give any concessions to the conspirators, and the talks failed to impress the decision makers in London and Washington. By and large, Great Britain and the United States insisted on an unconditional surrender of the German Reich, in accordance with what had been decided at the Casablanca Conference, in January 1943. This, as one may guess, did not give the conspirators much room for maneuvering. Even the attempts of Allen Dulles to convince Washington to grant something to Gisevius and Goerdeler did not bear significant fruit.[38]

In the opening months of 1944, the conspirators realized that they could expect very little from the Western Allies. A ray of hope, however, came from the western front. Through Caesar von Hofacker, Stauffenberg had been able to get in touch with his old commanding officer Field Marshal Erwin Rommel, the celebrated "Desert Fox" and now the man in charge of Army Group B in occupied France. After the ignoble failure of the African campaign, Rommel's relations with Hitler had steadily deteriorated, and by summer 1944, he began to seriously tilt toward the conspirators.[39] He staunchly opposed an assassination, for fear of civil war and internal unrest, yet, according to Hofacker's testimony, he promised to cooperate nevertheless. The prospect of an alliance with one of the most popular generals in Germany was a great boon for Stauffenberg and his associates. They knew that his cooperation could give them access to immense military forces on the western front.

The good news, though, came with a wide array of operational difficulties. Stauffenberg, Olbricht, and Tresckow were able to revise the Valkyrie plans as a covert operation for a coup d'état, but they did not have the authority to set them in motion. According to the operational procedure, only Gen. Friedrich Fromm, the commander in chief of the Home Army, was authorized to sign these orders.[40] As we have seen in chapter 13, Fromm played a sophisticated double game for many years, neither giving the conspirators away nor joining their cause. The general continued to play that game almost to the last moment. When Olbricht lectured him on the urgency of a coup d'état, for example, he merely thanked him and led him to the door.[41] On another occasion, he told Olbricht and Stauffenberg "not to forget that fellow Keitel when you do your putsch."[42] The conspirators, as usual, could not understand his message. Was he promising to cooperate with the coup, or merely expressing his well-known animosity to Field Marshal Keitel? No one could tell or predict what his response would be when the time came.

If Fromm refused to cooperate, the conspirators had planned to arrest him and bring in Gen. Erich Hoepner, an esteemed panzer leader, as his replacement. Hoepner, denounced by Gisevius as an "opportunist," had indeed been privy to the plans of the conspirators in both 1938 and 1939. At the same time, though, he was a highly enthusiastic supporter of Hitler's war of extermination in the east. During the first months of the operation, he published virulently anti-Semitic orders of the day and enjoyed a "cordial relationship" with Einsatzgruppen murder squads.[43] After the collapse of the Moscow offensive, when he was sacked because of his failure to obey the Führer's "no withdrawal" orders, he resumed cooperation with the conspirators. In winter 1941–1942, he was even mentioned as part of the unrealistic plan to storm Hitler's headquarters with an armored unit.[44] From the conspirators' point of view, the main problem was that Hoepner had been forbidden, through a personal order from Hitler, to wear a uniform. Many officers were likely to disobey the orders of a sacked general. In short, Hoepner was a far from reassuring alternative to Fromm.[45]

Anyway, the coup was still a way off. The demonstration of the new winter uniforms to the Führer had been delayed and rescheduled for the beginning of 1944. Then, a few days before the planned assassination, Bussche was notified by telephone that the design for the uniforms had been destroyed in an air raid. Subsequently, he had to return to the front, where he was seriously wounded.[46] Nevertheless, the conspirators were quick to find a new volunteer: Ewald-Heinrich von Kleist. A scion of a noble family, this young lieutenant was the son of Ewald von Kleist-Schmenzin, one of the founders of the German resistance movement. Many decades later, the younger Kleist recalled how he had been drafted:

> It was January 1944. I was on leave at the time when I received an urgent telegram from Schulenburg telling me to report back for duty with my regiment—the 9th Infantry. I met him in his apartment. He got straight to the point by telling me: "Look, we're ready. Everything is in place. But we need a volunteer to assassinate Hitler. Are you willing to do it?" He explained to me that it would have to be a suicide attempt in which I would blow myself up with Hitler. Schulenburg took me to see Stauffenberg in Berlin who proceeded to brief me further. Stauffenberg greeted me in his usual warm-hearted manner and offered me a cognac. We discussed the plan until I said, "Okay, give me 24 hours to think it over." I went home to brief my father about it.[47]

The young officer traveled from Berlin to Pomerania to seek his father's advice. Ewald von Kleist-Schmenzin, a veteran of the conspiracy, had once put his life on the line by traveling to London as the resistance's emissary, but would he agree to sacrifice his son for the cause? According to the young man's testimony, his father paced to the window, paused for a moment, and then advised him to go ahead. "Anyone who fails to respond in such a moment would never be happy again." Kleist accordingly returned to Potsdam and informed Stauffenberg that he was ready.[48]

Stauffenberg gave Kleist British plastic explosives and installed him as Bussche's replacement in the winter uniform demonstration. Once again, fate intervened: Hitler canceled the demonstration at the last minute, and Kleist had to return to his unit. Before he did, he told Stauffenberg that he was ready to take part in a coup d'état. Counting the failures of Gersdorff and Bussche, Kleist's had been the third failure of an officer who had volunteered as a suicide bomber. Nothing seemed to work.

The conspirators never stopped hatching plots. This time, it was Tresckow's turn, and Capt. Eberhard von Breitenbuch was the prospective assassin. Breitenbuch was the adjutant of Field Marshal Ernst Busch, Kluge's successor at Army Group Center. "Tresckow took me to my private room . . . ," he later related, "and asked me whether I was aware of my responsibility . . . I could end this war, with all of its horrors, all by myself . . . He spoke like a priest, with a persuasive power that did not allow you to contradict or to say 'but . . .'"[49]

Just like Bussche and Kleist, Breitenbuch was ready to sacrifice his own life, but he was loath to use explosives. Instead, he offered Tresckow his skills as a seasoned sniper; he would take Hitler down with a precise pistol shot. The plan seemed reasonable, as officers were allowed to carry guns in the Führer's presence. Tresckow warned that, because of Hitler's vest, the shot must be aimed at his head or neck. Now, the conspirators only had to arrange a suitable pretext for Breitenbuch to take part in Hitler's staff meetings.[50]

The moment came in March 1944. Breitenbuch was supposed to accompany his commander, Field Marshal Busch, to a meeting with the supreme leader. His duty was to carry the maps and documents and to assist Busch during his military briefing. The two men entered Hitler's palatial chalet in Berchtesgaden in the Bavarian Alps, with Breitenbuch carrying a Browning in his trouser pocket. However, when they were about to enter the meeting, a stern SS guard stopped the junior officer at the door. "No," he said. "Today no entry for adjutants." Breitenbuch waited for several hours in the anteroom, anxious that the assassination plot had been discovered. Every moment, he expected the SS guards to arrest him, but nothing happened. Breitenbuch swore that he would never go through such a nerve-racking experience again. Another plot had failed.[51]

Spring 1944 passed, and the German military situation was becoming worse by the day. On June 6, the Western Allies invaded Normandy in the largest amphibious strike in history, and breached the defense of Fortress Europe. Numerous officers gathered that the war was lost. On the eastern front, the news was even worse. Summer 1943 had seen the Russians advancing westward toward Poland, threatening the eastern borders of the Reich. By July, the last German offensive, in Kursk, had failed to meet its goals. The conspirators, urged on by these developments, increased the pace of their preparations. Some, however, were moved by the Normandy invasion to rethink their plans. Would it be best to let the war run its course, so Hitler alone could bear the responsibility for the final collapse? What was the use of a coup d'état, when the Western Allies would demand the Reich surrender unconditionally on all fronts?[52] Stauffenberg, who had no ready answer, turned to Tresckow for advice. The leader of the eastern clique was quick to respond and left no doubts about the required course of action: "The assassination of Hitler must take place *coûte que coûte* [cost what it may]. Even if it does not succeed, the coup d'état must be attempted. The point now is not the practical purpose, but to prove to the world and before history that the German resistance have staked their all and put their lives on the line. Beside that, nothing has any weight."[53]

So the die was cast. Stauffenberg, Tresckow, and their friends agreed that the "practical purpose" did not have "any weight." Germany would probably be defeated and would have to surrender and even suffer occupation, though the conspirators still hoped to keep the Bolsheviks at bay. Maybe, they hoped, the coup would save the lives of millions: soldiers at the fronts, citizens in bombed-out German cities, and prisoners, both Jewish and Christian, in the camps. Stauffenberg himself confided to Nina, his wife, that though the occupation of Germany could no longer be prevented, the coup must still take place. "The decisive question is not the fate of this or that individual," said General Beck, "and not even the consequences for the nation. The decisive, intolerable fact is that for years crimes have been committed in the name of the German people, and we have to put an end to it using all the means at our disposal." Goerdeler had expressed similar thoughts in a draft letter written to an unidentified general: the German resistance had to destroy the regime not necessarily as a response to the military defeats but mainly because "during and preceding this war, more than one million POWs and civilians from the different nations, men, women and children, were murdered under orders."[54]

The psychological tension involved in the planning left its mark on the ringleaders. "The few survivors," wrote Hardenberg, "will never forget these weeks of waiting that racked our nerves to breaking point." Stauffenberg himself was hardly unaffected. In summer 1943, when he had taken it upon himself to lead the conspiracy, he was described as a young, energetic officer, "radiating an inner fire." A year later, he had become a tired, irascible, and bitter man. He did not rate the chances of success, but he still agreed with Tresckow that the coup must take place. "The most terrible thing," said his brother Berthold von Stauffenberg on July 14, "is knowing that we cannot succeed and yet that we have to do it, for our country and our children."[55]

After the failure of the previous assassination attempts, Stauffenberg decided to kill Hitler himself. Back in 1942, he had wondered whether there was an officer ready to do it. Now, it seemed, he was the man.[56] The other conspirators insisted that he was invaluable for the coup, but they had to acknowledge that there was no alternative. Major General Stieff, the only other conspirator with access to the Führer, could not pull together enough courage for the job.[57] On July 1, 1944, the commander of the Home Army, General Fromm, appointed Stauffenberg his chief of staff and promoted him to the rank of colonel. As part of his new duties, Colonel Stauffenberg had to participate in routine staff meetings with the Führer.

By July 1944, the precarious situation of the resistance had deteriorated still further. The civilian leaders felt that they were being followed, and many feared that informers had infiltrated the movement. Furthermore, many civilian leaders were ignoring the strict rules of secrecy and compartmentalization observed in the military wing. In his diary, Hermann Kaiser used clumsy code names that could be deciphered by a five-year-old. For example, Count Helldorff, whose last name can be translated as "bright village," appeared under the code name Dunkelstadt (dark town). Goerdeler was endlessly chattering about the coup d'état and "tried to win over anyone who came in touch with him for personal or professional reasons." Even Tresckow, who usually held Goerdeler in high esteem, complained about his "exaggerated" behavior. The civilian wing was now fully exposed to the security service, which could eliminate it at its discretion.[58] Notwithstanding the strict secrecy rules in the military wing, reckless behavior on the part of the civilians could lead the whole movement to ruin. In June 1944, the conspirators learned this lesson yet again.

It all began with a well-intentioned initiative. Adolf Reichwein, an activist in the Social Democratic group and the Kreisau Circle, had long striven to form a contact with the Communist underground in Germany. Stauffenberg, who had no love for Bolsheviks, hesitated at first but then agreed to let Reichwein speak with them.[59] Apparently, Stauffenberg was ready to initiate the representatives of the Communist Party into his plans, provided that they would not attempt to bolshevize Germany. His decision, as expected, evoked much resentment not only among die-hard conservatives, such as Goerdeler and Gisevius, but also among some of the Social Democrats. But Stauffenberg remained firm.

On June 22, a first meeting took place. Reichwein and his colleague Julius Leber represented Stauffenberg. The Communists accepted, in principle, Stauffenberg's conditions, and asked to meet the military leaders.[60] One of the Communists was actually an undercover Gestapo agent. He filed a report on the meeting and brought about the immediate arrest of Reichwein and Leber. Stauffenberg, who refused to attend the second meeting, for security reasons, was saved from arrest. Fortunately for him, Reichwein and Leber withstood the interrogation without mentioning his name. However, he knew that two of his best friends might be facing execution, and that was painful. Schulenburg sent a short message to Leber's wife, probably in the name of his commander: "We are aware of our duty."[61]

Stauffenberg knew that he could be arrested at any moment. Even walking down the street became traumatic, as he imagined undercover policemen lurking in every shadow. One day, as he walked along with Tresckow and Margarethe von Oven, he stumbled upon a group of SS men. Oven was carrying the operational plan of the coup under her arm.[62] How long could Reichwein and Leber put up with such torment? Sooner or later they would succumb, and Stauffenberg would be promptly arrested. He had to act, and quickly.

On July 11, Stauffenberg tried his luck for the first time. He entered the Führer's staff meeting with a bomb, but upon discovering that Himmler was not present, decided not to carry out the plan. He and Beck had agreed in advance that in order to prevent civil war,

Himmler had to be killed along with Hitler.[63] The next day, the conspirators were dealt a heavy blow. Gen. Alexander von Falkenhausen, the military governor of Belgium and a conspiracy collaborator, was unexpectedly relieved of his command. The failure to act on July 11 had cost them dearly—in retrospect, it was a tragic mistake—as they lost a key ally with a substantial military following.

On July 15, Stauffenberg tried again. In order to save precious time, General Olbricht had activated the Valkyrie orders in the morning and instructed the panzer forces from Krampnitz to move toward Berlin. At noon, Stauffenberg entered Hitler's cabin with a bomb in his briefcase, but could not find the time to activate the fuse. As he was supposed to give a presentation to the Führer, he could not leave the room either. Once more, an assassination attempt had come to naught.[64]

Meanwhile, armor and infantry units left Döberitz and Krampnitz and moved to their positions in Berlin. After a frantic phone call from Stauffenberg, Olbricht understood that the Führer was alive, canceled the orders, and told Fromm that they had been only a drill. He knew that the same excuse would not work twice. Keitel and Fromm, he reported, were already suspicious. Next time, Olbricht said, he would activate the orders only when he was certain that the assassination had taken place.[65] This seemingly reasonable decision was to have heavy consequences on July 20, 1944.

On July 16, the leaders of the conspiracy held a meeting in Stauffenberg's flat. The count argued that in the best-case scenario, the western front would hold for six weeks longer. Time was up. Adam von Trott zu Solz, a member of the Kreisau Circle and one of the diplomats of the resistance, reported that he had some basis to believe that the Allies would open negotiations with an anti-Nazi German government.[66]

On July 17, a disaster occurred in the west. A low-flying Allied plane strafed the staff car of Field Marshal Rommel. The commander of Army Group B was seriously wounded, and the conspirators lost the most powerful of their potential allies.[67] On July 18, they were dealt another devastating blow. Arthur Nebe, the informant of the conspirators in the criminal police, gave them a tip that an arrest warrant for Goerdeler would be issued at any moment. Kaiser and Stauffenberg advised him that he was being hunted, and ordered him to go into hiding at once.[68]

This chain of setbacks nearly stalled the conspiracy. However, on the same day that Goerdeler was going into hiding, a new ray of hope appeared. Stauffenberg was ordered to attend a Führer briefing on July 20. He decided to make another attempt on Hitler's life.

On July 18, while the conspirators were busy making final preparations, Fritz von der Schulenburg decided to leave Berlin for a day in order to celebrate the birthday of his wife, Charlotte. After a "jolly party" with his family, Schulenburg shared with her his fears, hopes, and expectations. "The chances are fifty-fifty," he finally said.[69] Tresckow told his friend Margarethe von Oven, "I won't have you in Berlin when it happens. The assassination is a job for men. I want you to be out of it. If we need you, I'll send a plane." On July 19, alerts were sent to as many conspirators as possible. Stauffenberg was engaged in preparations of his own. In the evening, he asked his driver to stop in front of a Catholic church, where he prayed for a few minutes. A chance visitor in the Bendlerstrasse later recalled that the count was peaceful and kind. He was ready for the most difficult trial of his life.[70]

On the morning of July 20, 1944, Count Claus von Stauffenberg left his home in Wannsee, to be driven to the airport en route to Hitler's headquarters in East Prussia. His briefcase held a bomb designed to change the course of history. The moment of truth had finally come.

## 18

# THE FINAL SHOWDOWN:
# JULY 20, 1944

What I will never forget about July 20, 1944, was the sensation
that we all felt of being part of a moment in which history was balancing on the edge of a knife.

— LT. EWALD-HEINRICH VON KLEIST

THE SUN ROSE on yet another day of hardships for Berlin's inhabitants. The town, heavily bruised, had suffered mightily from bom-
bardments by the Americans and the British, and the casualties were
increasing by the day. Hitler's war, enthusiastically applauded at first
by the majority of Germans, had reached their own homes. Bombers
were constantly in the air, and many Germans predicted darkly that
soon enough they would be joined by hostile ground troops. The eastern front was collapsing, allowing the Russians to move quickly westward. In France, too, the Western Allies were overpowering the Wehrmacht, advancing apace toward Germany's western borders.

Stauffenberg rose at 6:00 a.m. to dress with his teeth and remaining arm. Soon after, he picked up his black briefcase and departed
into a side street of the quiet lakeside suburb of Wannsee. A staff car
was waiting for him with his personal driver and Dr. Hans-Bernd von
Haeften, a veteran of the Kreisau Circle and one of the remaining
conspirators in the Ministry of Foreign Affairs. Stauffenberg eased
into the backseat, his briefcase resting by his feet. Inside the briefcase,
he and Haeften both knew, lay a standard British bomb.

Stauffenberg and Haeften, adhering to security regulations, kept their silence during the trip. After forty-five minutes, the car stopped near Rangsdorf Airport, in the suburbs of Berlin. There, Stauffenberg was joined by his adjutant, Lt. Werner von Haeften. This young officer, Hans-Bernd's cousin, was personally loyal to the colonel and was ready to risk everything for him. True, in the preceding weeks he had had misgivings about the cause, and serious moral qualms about the planned assassination. Now, however, he was ready to follow his commander through fire and water, even into the Führer's own abode. In his briefcase, he carried a second bomb. The two officers took their leave from Hans-Bernd and boarded a military plane bound for Wolf's Lair, Hitler's gloomy headquarters in the forests of East Prussia. The Führer held Stauffenberg in high esteem and had summoned him to discuss the recruitment of new divisions—more fodder for the hungry front.

Around 10:30, the officers disembarked at Rastenburg Airport. A staff car was waiting to take them to the military base. Before they left the airport, Haeften ordered the pilot to stand ready in his plane from 12 p.m. onward. After the explosion, they would have to escape with all haste.

En route to Wolf's Lair, the two officers were driven across a narrow, winding road in the middle of the forest. The compound was among the world's most secure, surrounded by minefields and guarded by elite troops, trained dogs, and antiaircraft guns—"an impregnable lair of reinforced concrete," as described later by Soviet intelligence. Visitors were greeted by ominous signs that threatened trespassers with death.[1] The officers had to go through three different roadblocks until they reached the last, most secure "Compound A" or "Third Ring," home to the bunkers of Hitler, Göring, and other leaders of the Reich. SS guards patrolled the area constantly.

After Stauffenberg and Haeften had passed through the last checkpoint, they were greeted by the commandant of the base and his adjutant, who invited them for breakfast under the large oak tree at mid-camp. The day was very hot and humid, under a cloudless blue sky. The commandant told them that because of the oppressive heat, all windows in the briefing hut had been opened. Stauffenberg probably knew that this was bad news, as the open windows could release some of the blast waves of pressure, diminishing the bomb's effectiveness.[2]

After breakfast, Stauffenberg left the junior officers and spent a few minutes aside with Gen. Erich Fellgiebel, the resistance's insider in Führer headquarters. This career officer, praised by his friends as a "humanistic, philosophically inclined soldier, and an expert in the natural sciences," had been an enemy of the regime from the outbreak of the war. His duties as the commander of the Signal Corps involved frequent trips to headquarters throughout the Reich, including Berlin, and thus he could easily connect his group with the central network in the capital. According to Hans Crome's testimony, Fellgiebel became involved in the conspiracy no later than February 1943, and probably before.[3]

Between 1943 and 1944, Fellgiebel persevered to create a network of resistance in the Signal Corps—a highly dangerous task, given the fact that the communication lines were partly supervised by internal security organizations such as the Secret Field Police. He and Stauffenberg were aware of the importance of controlling the communication facilities in order to cut off Hitler's men from the outside world in the hours following the assassination. Using trusted men at the respective switchboards, Fellgiebel was ready to block communication between Wolf's Lair and the army and yet permit the conspirators to use the system for their own needs. Contrary to some later accounts, Fellgiebel was unable to "blow up" the facilities. They were scattered in too many buildings, most of them made of reinforced concrete. In the circumstances, he could use his authority as a commander only to block hostile communication. In addition, the conspirators knew that Fellgiebel could do so only until Keitel or another senior leader interfered. At best, the conspirators would have one or two hours of unhindered communication.

After briefing Fellgiebel one last time,[4] Stauffenberg daringly showed some of the documents in his briefcase to a member of Hitler's entourage. The senior commander did not see the bomb, which was (according to one account) wrapped up in a shirt. Stauffenberg believed that the meeting with Hitler would start at 1:00 p.m., as had been scheduled in advance. However, because of Mussolini's planned visit on the same day, the Führer ordered Keitel to reschedule the meeting for 12:30, half an hour earlier. Stauffenberg, met by the field marshal near his office, was notified accordingly.[5] While they were on their way to the briefing hut, Stauffenberg suddenly asked for permission to change into a fresh shirt. Keitel reluctantly agreed, and directed the colonel to a changing room near his office. Stauffenberg was disabled, and therefore it was only natural that his adjutant, Haeften, should accompany him and help him inside.[6]

While Stauffenberg was "changing," the meeting at the briefing hut got under way. Hitler was not known for his patience, so Keitel ordered one of the sergeants to hurry Stauffenberg up. Peeping through the half-opened door, the sergeant saw Stauffenberg and Haeften putting a wrapped object inside the briefcase, but he did not suspect foul play.[7] The two conspirators, however, were probably panicked by the event. They couldn't order the sergeant to leave. Sheer luck alone had kept them from being caught red-handed.

Then, Stauffenberg made a crucial decision. He took his briefcase, where the first bomb was already ticking, and left the room. He and Haeften were running out of time. They decided to neither trigger the second bomb nor bring it to the briefing hut. It's possible they knew that if they used two kilograms of explosives instead of just one, everyone in the room would perish. The decision not to use the extra kilogram was wrong: the two officers did not know, or forgot in the heat of the moment, that there was no need to trigger the second bomb, as the first would activate it automatically in its explosion. Now, the whole operation depended on a single device. Stauffenberg joined Keitel in the briefing hut, knowing that nothing could prevent the detonation of the bomb in ten minutes' time.

When he entered the meeting, General Heusinger, head of operations and acting chief of the General Staff, was reporting on the eastern front. He stood to the right of Hitler. All officers present, representing the Wehrmacht, Luftwaffe, and Waffen SS, were studying maps set upon a thick oak table. In front of the Führer, at the other side of the table, stenographer Heinrich Berger was typing the minutes of the meeting. At Heusinger's right side stood General Korten, chief of the General Staff of the Luftwaffe, and next to him Colonel Brandt, the unsuspecting officer who had carried Tresckow's bomb in 1943. Göring and Himmler were not present.

Hitler nodded in response to Stauffenberg's salute, warmly shaking the colonel's hand. Keitel cut Heusinger short, took his usual spot to the left of the boss, and presented Stauffenberg's report in brief.[8] Standing between Brandt and Korten, the colonel put his briefcase under the table, all the while trying to push it as close as possible to Hitler's feet. The clock showed 12:35, and Heusinger went on speaking.

Stauffenberg left the room quietly, leaving behind his briefcase, hat, and belt. That was not uncommon, as all those present at the meeting were used to seeing officers going out to contact their units. The colonel lit a cigarette, passed through the corridor, and left the briefing hut. One of the guards spotted him, walking and smoking without his black briefcase. Stauffenberg turned to Fellgiebel's office to await the explosion. Haeften was waiting near one of the staff cars, ready to speed his commander out of the camp. A few minutes later, Keitel left the conference to summon Stauffenberg, who was scheduled to be the next speaker, failed to find him, and turned back to the meeting. Colonel Brandt, keen to take a better look at the map, leaned over the table and unwittingly kicked Stauffenberg's briefcase away from the Führer.

Heusinger was still speaking. "The Russian," he said, "is strongly advancing to the northwest of the river Duna. His spearheads are already southwest of Dunaburg . . ." Hitler listened and leaned on the map to take a better look. "If the army group around Lake Peipus does not withdraw immediately, a catastrophe —"[9]

Stauffenberg's briefcase exploded in a deafening blast. Those present were hurled to the walls, their vision blurred. Everything went up in green and yellow flames. From Fellgiebel's office, Stauffenberg witnessed the explosion and saw the hut burning "as if it was hit by a shell." He was sure that Hitler and the others were dead or dying. Soon after, he nodded to Fellgiebel and entered his staff car. The operation had finally begun.

Stauffenberg ordered the driver to head to the airport. Quickly, they reached the camp gate, only to be blocked by armed, nervous guards. The alarm had not yet been raised, but they had seen the blast and blocked the entrance and exit. Stauffenberg, using his trademark authoritative tone, told them to open the gate immediately, and was obeyed. "Forward!" the colonel urged the driver. "Show us your skills! Every minute is decisive!" En route, Haeften tossed the briefcase with the second bomb out of the window.[10] It was imperative to get rid of such "smoking guns" as quickly as possible.

The second checkpoint proved to be a greater challenge. Now, alarms were ringing throughout the compound, and the guards refused to let the officers through. This time, they had explicit orders, and Stauffenberg's commanding voice was not enough to impress them. Keeping his composure—in a way he had not managed to in the changing room before the assassination attempt—the colonel left his car, picked up the phone at the checkpoint, and promptly called the commandant of the camp. On the other end of the line, he was greeted by the commandant's adjutant, with whom he had had breakfast that morning. Stauffenberg complained that he had been summoned on urgent business in Berlin but was now being detained by the guards. The adjutant, stepping beyond the bounds of his authority, ordered the guards to let the colonel through. A few minutes later, he and Haeften reached the airport. "Thank you very much, and wish us luck," Stauffenberg told the driver before taking off to Berlin.[11]

Inside the Third Ring, in Hitler's briefing hut, chaos reigned. The legs of the stenographer had been blown off, and his dying body was gushing blood beneath the table. Korten, Schmundt, and Brandt were severely injured, and many others had suffered bruises, burns, and other light injuries. The chandelier fell on General Jodl's head. "Where is the Führer? Where is the Führer?" rang the panicked voice of Keitel, who was miraculously unharmed.[12]

Hitler was certainly shocked. A heavy beam had fallen on his back, his right arm was wounded and temporarily paralyzed, his right ear was deafened for good, and his trousers were torn. But he remained stubbornly alive. Trembling with excitement, he praised "Providence" for saving his life. "I always knew," he murmured while being examined by his physicians, "that I am surrounded by traitors. Now is the time to uproot this conspiracy once and for all."[13]

General Fellgiebel, the conspirators' agent in headquarters, observed the mayhem from his office. A few minutes later, he saw to his horror that Hitler was alive and walking. Still, he decided to proceed with the plan, understanding that all the bridges had now been burned and that there was no way back. He entered his office and called the two chiefs of staff subordinate to him, General Thiele and Colonel Hahn. The former was the commander of the Signals Corps in Berlin; the latter was responsible for "Anna" switchboard, the center of communications in East Prussia. Both were members of the conspiracy. Thiele received the call while sitting with Olbricht in the Bendlerstrasse, Berlin. The line was bad, and Fellgiebel's voice was unclear. Probably, he tried to tell him that the bomb had exploded but the assassination attempt had failed. Immediately afterward, he called Colonel Hahn. "Something terrible happened," he said. "The Führer is alive. Block everything."[14] Fellgiebel hung up, blocked a large part of the communication between Wolf's Lair and the outside world for two hours, and gave his friends in Berlin time to act.

Thiele, who heard the news from Fellgiebel, informed Olbricht about the ambiguous situation. The two men were dumbfounded. During the long months of preparation, the conspirators had made themselves ready for only two scenarios. Either the bomb would not explode (as had happened many times before) or Hitler would be killed. That the bomb would explode and Hitler survive never seemed to cross their minds. Accordingly, Olbricht did not activate Valkyrie, having learned his lesson from the blunder of July 15. It was difficult for him to begin the coup in this new, uncertain situation he was not prepared for. This time, there was no chance of covering everyone's back if there was a misunderstanding.

In Hitler's headquarters, there was still great confusion, as no one yet knew who was responsible for the assassination attempt. Members of Hitler's entourage raised several possibilities, with the main suspicion falling on laborers working in an adjacent construction site. The pit that opened in the floor of the hut led some to believe that a bomb had been hidden beneath the floorboards. Then, the guard who noticed Stauffenberg leaving without his briefcase reported to Martin Bormann, head of the chancellery of the Nazi Party. From there, it wasn't hard to put two and two together and identify the assassin. Subsequently, Keitel called Berlin and ordered Stauffenberg's immediate arrest. Himmler, who had been appointed by the Führer to lead the Home Army, was sent to Berlin to take countermeasures against a possible insurgency.[15]

Two and a half hours later, Mussolini arrived as planned, and Hitler took him to see the shattered briefing hut. Dr. Paul Schmidt, Hitler's personal interpreter, testified:

> Mussolini was absolutely horrified. He could not understand how such a thing could happen at Headquarters; his face expressed utter dismay . . . some time elapsed before he pulled himself together enough to congratulate Hitler on his escape. Hitler's reaction was completely indifferent. "I was standing here by the table. The bomb went off just in front of my feet. Over there in the corner of the room colleagues of mine were severely injured; just opposite me an officer was literally blown through the window . . . Look at my uniform! Look at my burns! When I reflect on all this I must say that to me it is obvious that nothing is going to happen to me. Undoubtedly it is my fate to continue on my way and to bring my task to completion."[16]

During dinner, the Nazi leaders were still busy with internal fights. Dönitz, the grand admiral of the navy, was outraged by the "army's betrayal" and criticized Göring over the "failure of the Luftwaffe." Göring ignored him and attacked instead his usual nemesis, Foreign Minister Ribbentrop, over the "bankruptcy of German foreign policy," calling him a "dirty Champagne seller" and almost attacking him with his marshal staff. Ribbentrop defended himself noisily, while Hitler sucked a sedative candy and stared at the table. When someone mentioned the so-called Röhm Putsch, the rumors of which had triggered the Night of the Long Knives in 1934, the Führer angrily broke his silence. "Röhm and his fellow traitors were treated gently!" he yelled, hinting that the current conspirators should receive crueler treatment. He seethed with even more fury when informed about an insurgency in Berlin and perhaps in some provincial towns. "I will uproot and destroy them! I will throw their wives and children into a concentration camp! No mercy will be shown."[17]

The conspirators were still waiting for an order to activate Valkyrie. Until 4:00 p.m., more and more of them were assembling at the main hub, the war ministry complex at the Bendlerstrasse, Berlin. Among those present were the veteran Kreisauer Peter Yorck von Wartenburg and Pastor Eugen Gerstenmaier (who carried with him both gun and Bible), Count Schwerin von Schwanenfeld, Stauffenberg's brother Berthold, and his adjutant Capt. Friedrich von Klausing. In the second anti-Nazi hub, the Berlin police headquarters, Berlin police commandant Helldorff was waiting for orders with his friend and confidant Hans Bernd Gisevius. At noon, a short time before the assassination attempt, an emissary from Olbricht had called in and told Helldorff that the coup was about to begin and that he must be prepared. His job was to arrest the Nazi leaders in Berlin when orders from the Bendlerstrasse arrived. In response, Helldorff demanded soldiers be posted all around the government buildings, and was answered positively. Seconds afterward, he burst into the room where Gisevius waited. "It begins!" he announced. "I have heard from Olbricht ... An important message should come from the Bendlerstrasse in half an hour." At the third hub, Berlin city headquarters, Lieutenant General Hase was waiting as well.[18] At 4:30 p.m. he appointed a conspirator, Major Hayessen, as his chief of staff.

The rumors about the blast in Wolf's Lair had quickly reached the center of the conspiracy in Paris, too. In Zossen, the home of the Wehrmacht's supreme headquarters, the news reached another conspirator, Qm. Gen. Eduard Wagner. He accordingly informed his contact in Paris, Col. Eberhard Finckh, that time was up and that the Western conspirators had to be on high alert.[19] Ludwig Beck and Erwin von Witzleben, prospective head of state and commander in chief, were also notified, but they failed to hurry to take control of the Bendlerstrasse, just at the moment when the conspirators needed an authoritative figure to push them on.

At 3:45 p.m., Stauffenberg disembarked at Rangsdorf, Berlin, and Haeften updated the Bendlerstrasse that he had arrived. A few minutes later, he called Olbricht and was astounded when asked what had happened to Hitler. Stauffenberg said explicitly that the Führer was dead, and he was furious that Valkyrie was not yet activated. "The orders have to be sent right away!" he said, and raced through empty streets with Haeften to the Bendlerstrasse. Stauffenberg hoped to see tanks and troop trucks, but by 4:00 p.m., they were still far away in their respective camps.[20]

After the conversation with Stauffenberg, the Bendlerstrasse came to life. Olbricht believed Stauffenberg and expressed his readiness

to act without further delay. General Hoepner reached the Bendlerstrasse to take over the Home Army in case Fromm refused to collabo-
rate. He wore the uniform of a general, violating Hitler's prohibition.
The conspirators also called Witzleben in Zossen and told him that
his presence was required in Berlin. Olbricht, meanwhile, stepped into
Fromm's office to convince him to cooperate with the coup. For the
cautious commander of the Home Army, the moment of truth had finally come.

Fromm was meeting another officer at the time, but Olbricht insisted that the matter could not be delayed. Hitler had perished in
an explosion, according to Fellgiebel's update from East Prussia, and
therefore Valkyrie must be activated immediately to counter impending disturbances. Fromm, however, demanded concrete proof before
approving Valkyrie. Olbricht, encouraged by Stauffenberg's telephone
call from the airport, advised his commander to verify the rumors.
Fromm picked up the phone and asked to be put through urgently to
Keitel in East Prussia.

Keitel was almost immediately on the line. To Fromm's question he
responded that the rumors about Hitler's death were nonsense. "There
was an assassination attempt," he said, "but fortunately it failed. The
Führer is alive and was only slightly injured. By the way, where exactly is your chief of staff, Colonel von Stauffenberg?" Fromm replied,
"Stauffenberg still hasn't reported for duty." For Fromm, the matter
was closed.[21] Keitel's last question indicated that the Nazi leaders still
did not know where (or even whether) the coup was taking place.

Olbricht was confused by Keitel's confidence, but the coup was already under way. In fact, Col. Albrecht Mertz von Quirnheim, Olbricht's chief of staff and Stauffenberg's confidant, had already sent
the Valkyrie orders to the commanders of the *Wehrkreise* (military districts). In the Berlin *Wehrkreis*, the conspirators' man, Major Oertzen, bypassed his Nazi commander, Gen. Joachim Kortzfleisch, and
dispatched the order to the units through a reliable courier. Oertzen,
as was mentioned in chapter 17, was one of four key players in Berlin
known for their unconditional loyalty to Beck and Stauffenberg. Following Mertz's request, Lieutenant General Hase ordered the guard
battalion Grossdeutschland to mobilize with haste to the city center.[22]
The battalion commander, Maj. Otto Remer, was to report to Hase as
soon as possible for detailed orders. Meanwhile, Helldorff, the com-

mandant of the Berlin police, and Kortzfleisch, chief of the military district, were summoned to the Bendlerstrasse. The former was called to be briefed, and the latter—a dyed-in-the-wool Nazi—to be neutralized.

Olbricht was hardly out of Fromm's office when Beck and Stauffenberg finally arrived at the Bendlerstrasse. The former chief of the General Staff was dressed in a dark civilian suit to mark his intention to lead a civil government rather than a military dictatorship. Stauffenberg ran up the stairs, panting heavily and wet with perspiration. Everything he had seen in Wolf's Lair was quickly related to Beck and the others: the flames, the enormous explosion, the doctors hurrying to help the wounded. The others told him that, according to Keitel, Hitler was alive. "Field Marshal Keitel is lying, as usual," said Stauffenberg. "Hitler is dead. I saw him being taken out."[23]

Here, the conspirators entered a dangerous mental loop. They were unable to contemplate a scenario in which the bomb exploded but Hitler survived. During that afternoon of July 20, the conspirators, Stauffenberg in particular, did not consciously mislead their fellow officers; they really believed that Hitler had perished.[24]

Beck, however, was doubtful. His cautious words since his arrival at the Bendlerstrasse indicate that he understood, much earlier than the others, that something terrible had happened and that the Führer was alive. Still, he was determined to go on with the coup, fully realizing that this was perhaps the last chance to overthrow the regime. Even if Hitler spoke over the radio, Beck must speak before him. In that case, he said, it would be "a trial of strength."[25]

Stauffenberg's next move was to widen the insurgency to Paris, where the conspirators had a dense network of like-minded officers. As was dictated by the structure of the network, he first called his cousin Caesar von Hofacker, the broker connecting Berlin to the western front. Stauffenberg told him that the action in the capital had begun and that success in the west was the key to the whole operation.[26] Only there, and not in Berlin, did Stauffenberg have a chance to lay his hands on a considerable army led by loyal officers.

A little more than two hours beforehand, at 2:00 p.m., the phone rang in the office of Col. Eberhard Finckh, the quartermaster of Army Group West and a loyal ally of the conspirators. The colonel, Stauffenberg's former classmate in the military academy, was an old enemy of the Nazi regime. He picked up the phone. "Hier ischt Finckh" (Here is Finckh), he said in his thick Swabian accent. The other side was silent. One second, two, three passed, and then Finckh heard the code words "Übung abgelaufen" (Exercise finished). The conversation was over.

Finckh did not lose a moment. He quickly left his office, stepped into the car, and ordered the driver to take him to Field Marshal Kluge's headquarters in Boulevard Saint Germain. Kluge was not there, and Finckh was greeted by his close colleague General Blumentritt, a pragmatic officer not associated with the conspirators. Like most German military leaders, he knew that the final defeat at the western front was soon to follow, but it was hard to foresee his reaction to the new situation. Finckh tried his luck and told him the usual cover story. "General," he said in a formal tone, "the Gestapo is trying to stage a coup in Berlin. The Führer was assassinated and is no longer alive. Witzleben, Beck, and Goerdeler have formed an emergency cabinet."[27] After a moment of silence, Blumentritt reacted favorably. "It should be welcomed," he said, "that the people you have mentioned are at the helm. They will probably quickly begin preliminary peace talks."[28] Blumentritt called Lt. Gen. Hans Speidel, Rommel's chief of staff and a member of the resistance, and the three men decided to work for the new government.

At around 4:30 p.m., Hofacker picked up Stauffenberg's call from Berlin and promptly updated the young conspirators who were waiting in the Majestic Hotel, the headquarters of the German army in Paris. They were still in high spirits. One of them, Walter Bargatzky, later related,

I sat in my office in Majestic. At 4 p.m., a German radio concert was on air. Every moment the radio station might be occupied by the insurgents. Every sound brought the explosion ever nearer, bursting in the prison-like silence of eleven long years. My friend G. entered the room, tormented with expectation and looking almost crestfallen. I grabbed his arm. "Always think on this moment," I told him. "It is the most important in the whole war." G. himself did not know what was happening, but I guessed it dawned on him and I was grateful for his silence ... Now Stauffenberg, back in Berlin ... spoke with Hofacker on the military radio. "Hitler is dead," he told him.[29]

Soon afterward, Hofacker rushed to see General Stülpnagel, the military governor of occupied France, and updated him on the coup in Berlin. Stülpnagel was exultant when he heard that Hitler was dead and the operation in the capital was in full swing. At that very moment, Hofacker told him, armed troops were surrounding the government quarter in Wilhelmstrasse. Stülpnagel immediately summoned his chief of staff, Colonel Linstow, along with Paris commandant Boineburg-Lengsfeld and his chief of staff. The three officers found the governor standing behind his table. His commands were unequivocal: "The SS and SD are staging a coup against Hitler. You must arrest right away the members of the SS, SD, Colonel Knochen, the police commandant of France, and all the rest of the people whose names you know very well. In case of resistance, open fire. Is everything clear?"[30] The officers saluted, clicked their heels, and left the room.

The conspiracy headquarters in Berlin were bristling with activity. After Stauffenberg updated Hofacker in Paris, he tried, one last time, to win over his superior Gen. Friedrich Fromm. Olbricht and Stauffenberg entered the office together, and the former reported on the issue of Valkyrie. The commander of the Home Army was furious. "Who issued the Valkyrie orders?" he snapped. "You both know that only I am authorized to do so!"

"My chief of staff, Colonel Mertz von Quirnheim," replied Olbricht.

Fromm summoned Mertz at once and told him he was under arrest. "No one is leaving this room," he said.

Now Stauffenberg could contain himself no longer. "Sir, General," he said, "you are wrong. Hitler is dead. I placed the bomb myself. A moment ago I returned from supreme headquarters, and with my own eyes have seen that no one in the briefing hut remained alive."

"This is a revolution!" yelled Fromm. "This is treason ... punishable by death. You will all face a firing squad." Then he snapped at Stauffenberg, "The assassination has failed. You must shoot yourself at once."

"You cannot arrest us," said Olbricht in reply. "You do not understand the real power relations. We are arresting you."

Fromm, his face red, waved his fists at Stauffenberg. At that moment, the door opened, and Haeften and Kleist entered with pistols drawn. The two men aimed their guns at Fromm. "Armed officers are guarding your door," Stauffenberg told him briskly. "If you force us, we will resort to arms. Lieutenant von Haeften, cut his telephone lines."

Five minutes later, General Hoepner entered the room, clad in his uniform. After apologizing to Fromm, an old friend, for the inconvenience, he asked him whether he would nevertheless be ready to cooperate. The commander of the Home Army shook his head sadly. "I think that the Führer is alive, and that you are all making a mistake. I am sorry," he said, "but I cannot do otherwise. I cannot sign the Valkyrie orders for you."[31] Fromm preferred to be arrested than to cooperate with the conspirators.

Where were the Valkyrie orders, anyway? Two hours earlier, Mertz had sent them to Major Oertzen in the Berlin military district headquarters. Now, he handed them over to Captain Klausing, Stauffenberg's other confidant, and ordered him to personally go to the switchboard and distribute the commands among all headquarters throughout the Reich. Upon reaching the control room, Klausing ordered the technicians to urgently submit the orders through the teleprinter. The head technician asked whether to classify them as top secret, and Klausing instinctively answered in the affirmative.[32] Later, the conspirators would suffer as a result of this mistake. The procedure to hand over top-secret commands was cumbersome, and Klausing's decision delayed their transmission to some of the units by two to three hours, causing significant disturbances to the operation.

The first message opened with the ominous words "The Führer Adolf Hitler is dead." It declared that a "conscienceless clique of party leaders has tried to take over the government for their own selfish ends. Therefore, the army is taking over the government of the Reich." The order was to occupy all institutions of the National Socialist Party, to disarm the SD, SS, and Waffen-SS, and to take control of all communication facilities. It was signed by Witzleben, as commander in chief of the Wehrmacht. This was followed at 6:00 p.m. by

another, more radical message. Officers from all over the Reich read it
with astonishment as it slid out of their teleprinters:

> The following will be relieved of their offices forthwith and placed
> in secure solitary confinement:
>
> All Gauleiter, Reichsstatthalter, Ministers, Governors [*Ober-
> presidenten*], Police Presidents, Senior SS and Police Commanders
> [HSSPF], heads of Gestapo and SD offices, heads of propaganda
> offices, Kreisleiter. Exceptions only by my special order.
>
> CONCENTRATION CAMPS:
> Concentration camps will be occupied at once, camp comman-
> dants arrested, guard personnel disarmed and confined to bar-
> racks. Political prisoners are to be instructed that, pending their
> liberation, they should refrain from demonstrations or indepen-
> dent action.
>
> WAFFEN-SS:
> If compliance by commanders of Waffen-SS formations or by the
> senior Waffen-SS officers appears doubtful or if they seem unsuit-
> able, they will be taken into protective custody and replaced by
> Army officers. Waffen-SS formations whose unquestioned com-
> pliance appears doubtful will be ruthlessly disarmed. Firm action
> with superior forces will be taken to avoid further bloodshed.
>
> POLICE:
> Gestapo and SD headquarters will be occupied. Otherwise the
> regular police will be used as far as possible to relieve the Wehr-
> macht. Orders will be issued by the Chief of German Police
> through police channels . . .
>
> To deal with all political questions, I attach to each Wehrkreis
> Commander a political representative. Until further orders he
> will be responsible for administration. He will advise the Wehr-
> kreis Commander on all political matters.
> The headquarters of the Commander in Chief of the Home
> Army is the executive agency for all matters concerning the ex-
> ercise of executive power. It will dispatch a liaison officer to
> Wehrkreis Commanders for the exchange of information and
> views.
> In the exercise of executive power no arbitrary acts or acts of

revenge will be tolerated. The people must be made aware of the difference from the arbitrary methods of their former rulers.

Commander in Chief of the Home Army[33]

"The arbitrary methods of their former rulers"? Stauffenberg, who signed this order in Fromm's name, was surely aware of the recklessness of that last sentence: it gave away the revolutionary logic of the order, thus depriving the conspirators of their legal cover. Soon after, additional orders were sent, calling to confiscate the documents of the Nazi Party and to establish courts-martial. Here, legal cover was completely abandoned, but these orders reached the commanders of the military districts relatively late, only at 8:00 or 9:00 p.m.

At 4:30 p.m., after arresting Fromm, the conspirators still ruled over only their own building. Colonel Mertz and General Hoepner briefed the section heads. Mertz informed them that the Führer had been murdered and that the army was quelling a traitorous revolt by party elements. Hoepner maintained that Beck and Witzleben had therefore taken over leadership of the Reich and army, respectively. Hoepner himself was appointed commander in chief of the Home Army. They should understand the importance of the moment and perform their respective duties.[34] Stauffenberg sent one of his men to arrange a guard for the Bendlerstrasse. Shortly afterward, a unit from the guard battalion Grossdeutschland reached the compound and guarded all entries. No one was allowed to enter or exit without a permit signed by Stauffenberg or the personal consent of one of the commanders.[35] In that manner, just after 5:00 p.m., Stauffenberg took control of the building. Along with Beck, Olbricht, and Hoepner, he began a marathon of telephone calls to the district commanders to ensure their full cooperation.

At around 4:15 p.m., a short while after Beck's arrival at the Bendlerstrasse, the conspirators had other prominent visitors. Following Olbricht's request, Count Helldorff and Gisevius came to report. Their limousine stopped at the gates of the Bendlerstrasse, and soon they were meeting Beck, Stauffenberg, and Olbricht. Olbricht briefed Helldorff on his duty: to arrest the Nazi leaders after the occupation of the government quarter by the guard battalion. Beck, ever careful, told Helldorff that Hitler might have survived the blast. Helldorff was unmoved and once again declared his unconditional loyalty. Soon after, he left the building to join his forces. Now, it was certain: the corrupt member of the SA, an enthusiastic supporter of the Nazi Party from its early days, had finally bound his fate to the conspirators.[36]

A few minutes after 5:00 p.m., the conspirators had to cope with a half-baked attempt at a countercoup. An SS officer named Pfiffrather ("a butcher-type," in Gisevius's view) arrived with a few soldiers. In the name of the Reich main security office, he asked to question Stauffenberg about his unusual behavior in Wolf's Lair that day. The colonel, of course, had him arrested forthwith. The rest of Pfiffrather's entourage was seized at the gate by the guards. The Nazi general Kortzfleisch, who also ventured into the conspirators' den, was arrested in the same manner. To Beck's fury, he recited over and over again his oath of loyalty to the Führer.[37]

The main problem was now in Berlin. The conspirators had to have troops, and preferably tanks, to occupy the radio stations, to take over the government quarter, and, as importantly, to arrest and neutralize Propaganda Minister Josef Goebbels, the key Nazi leader in the capital. Orders to this effect were dispatched by Lieutenant General Hase to the guard battalion Grossdeutschland, the armored school at Krampnitz, and the infantry school at Döberitz. Similar commands were sent also to the eastern front, where Philipp von Boeselager, Kluge's former adjutant, was waiting with a company of soldiers. Taking measures to reinforce the conspirators in Berlin, he ordered his troops to march west to the airport.[38]

In Döberitz, the officers of the infantry school were dumbfounded by the unusual orders. They formed a "war council" of sorts but could not reach a decision, especially given that the unsuspecting commandant, Lt. Gen. Otto Hitzfeld, was away at a funeral. A senior conspirator, Col. Wolfgang Müller from the Home Army, was stationed at the base, but he returned from a tour of duty relatively late, at around 8:30 p.m., and even then could not convince all officers to act.[39] Still, some of the junior commanders did decide to move, and several small units were successfully dispatched to take control of a radio station and several communication facilities in Greater Berlin. Major Jacob, who led the unit, was ready to follow orders from the Bendlerstrasse, even though he had never been a conspirator. He and his men entered the station with drawn pistols, declared that the SS guards were subject to their command, and ordered the technicians to stop all broadcasts.

The problem was that Jacob, a highly decorated tactics instructor, was ignorant of the correct communication procedures. He did not know that the broadcasts were not running from the studio but, rather, from an adjacent bunker camouflaged as an air-raid shelter. He was easily fooled, and the broadcasts did not stop.[40] The other radio stations, occupied only briefly, were also not being used. The occupying officers were not conspirators. Most of them were confused, and they stopped all cooperation when they heard that Hitler was alive. Had a resolute anti-Nazi conspirator been sent to each station, things might have developed differently.

Colonel Müller, the only conspirator at Döberitz, was ineffective even when he came back to his office, at 8:30 p.m. He tried to do his best to urge the officers to act, and they finally decided to contact the commander of the school, General Hitzfeld. The latter at first demanded a written order, but then was convinced and ordered "a relentless attack on the SS."[41] Müller's response was awkward. Instead of capitalizing on Hitzfeld's order and sending the units at once, he drove to the Bendlerstrasse to receive written orders from Olbricht. From a strictly military point of view, that made sense, because Müller belonged to the Home Army, not the command staff of the school, and written authority over the school was formally required. Yet, in continuing to act as an officer rather than a revolutionary, he rendered Döberitz useless for the entire evening. Also here, the physical presence of a senior, authoritative conspirator, preferably a general, could have brought about a very different result.

It is one of the many unsolved riddles of the coup that even at this critical hour, Stauffenberg and Beck failed to dispatch trusted conspirators to the key points in Greater Berlin, such as the infantry school and the radio stations. There was no lack of available manpower. Fritz von der Schulenburg and other conspirators were unemployed. The leaders were mainly busy with telephone calls, almost oblivious to how events were unfolding around them. Stauffenberg, for example, was certain that his orders were being followed in Berlin and that the real drama was actually taking place in the provinces—a grave mistake.

Gisevius, though, was uneasy. He pressured Stauffenberg to radicalize the putsch by executing senior Nazis, starting with the SS officer Pfiffrather. Stauffenberg snapped that "his turn will come," but he refused to let Gisevius lead an arrest squad of officers. However, Stauffenberg promised to form such a unit under the leadership of Col. Fritz Jaeger, veteran of the 1943 conspiracy. Jaeger saluted, commandeered some troops from the guard battalion Grossdeutschland, and tried to get even more from Hase. But the latter had sent most of his available troops for other tasks, forcing Jaeger to wait for reinforcements.[42] The clock showed 5:30 p.m., and time was running out.

Ironically, Jaeger did not need that much manpower, as strategic sites were nearly unprotected. In Berlin, for example, there was an almost unguarded conference where many Reich ministers were in attendance. The SS and Gestapo headquarters were likewise in disarray and could easily have been taken over.

The situation was difficult for the conspirators in other military districts, too. Most local commanders refused to accept the authority of the conspirators and chose instead to believe Goebbels, who broadcast at 6:00 p.m. that Hitler had escaped an assassination attempt. Many obeyed the counterorders sent by Keitel through the teleprinter.[43] Some conspirators in East Prussia did try to convince their superiors to act, and maybe even to occupy the Führer headquarters, but their efforts were mainly improvised and uncoordinated. The conspirators did not have time to update the old plans drafted by Tresckow and Stauffenberg to occupy Wolf's Lair, and the plans were still hidden deep belowground. No one even bothered to unearth them, and they remained in the dark until the Soviets discovered them after the war.

Only in three cities, Prague, Vienna, and Paris, did the conspirators enjoy temporary success. In the Czechoslovakian capital, the local district commander arrested the Nazi deputy governor, and in Vienna, officers sympathetic to the conspirators confined the local SS leader. One of the deputies of General Esebeck, the acting commander, spoke with Stauffenberg on the phone and obtained his chief's consent to follow the Bendlerstrasse.[44] In Paris, the leading figure was the military governor of France, Gen. Karl-Heinrich von Stülpnagel, the sole conspirator who fulfilled his duty as planned. Far from repeating the mistakes made in Berlin, Stülpnagel personally ordered his officers to arrest all SS men in Paris. Every arrest squad was accompanied by an anti-Nazi officer who reported directly to the governor.

At nightfall, the squads went out and the arrests began. Major General Brehmer, deputy commandant of Greater Paris, led the occupation of the Gestapo headquarters in Boulevard Lannes. The soldiers stormed into the building brandishing their weapons and overpowered the guards. Brehmer himself arrested Lt. Gen. Carl Oberg, the commander of the SS in France. Oberg was frightened and did not resist. Brehmer locked him in his room and told him he was under arrest until further notice.[45] Meanwhile, Boineburg-Lengsfeld was standing on the corner of Avenue Foch and Boulevard Lannes to orchestrate the operation.

Soldiers from the security regiment took control of the SD headquarters at Avenue Foch. Boineburg-Lengsfeld spoke with them personally, and, according to some testimonies (which, perhaps, have to be taken with a grain of salt), they received the mission with enthusiasm. The SD commander in France, Col. Helmut Knochen, was recalled from a nightclub and arrested as well. The officers were detained in a hotel, while the soldiers were loaded into trucks and confined in a Wehrmacht prison, evacuated especially for the purpose. The operation was not without its faults and loopholes. Some SS soldiers, for example, were able to escape and notify the SS division Hitlerjugend about the insurgency. The troops also missed one SS communication facility, which meant the Reich main security office was also informed about the uprising. Still, the central authorities were very slow to react. Until midnight, twelve hundred of Hitler's supporters in France were under lock and key. Under Stülpnagel's directive, courts-martial were organized, and sandbags were piled in the yard of the École Militaire for the convenience of the firing squads. The "guilty"—presumably Oberg, Knochen, and their like—were set to be shot as quickly as possible. Indeed, jurists in Boineburg-Lengsfeld's office had already begun to collect material on the SS commanders, incriminating them for deporting Jews, burning synagogues, and plundering abandoned property.[46]

After the war, one of Stülpnagel's men related that in the summer of 1944, secret negotiations were conducted between the military governor's bureau and Free France, in order to reach an understanding with the French resistance and maybe even mediate between the Allies and the new regime in Berlin. Gen. Henri Navarre, a senior French intelligence officer, confirmed this in his memoirs. According to Navarre, he met several times with a German general, "a very moral man, staunch German patriot but anti-Hitler." The Wehrmacht general asked him whether he could guarantee that the Allies would permit the Germans to withdraw from France in good order and concentrate their efforts on checking the Russian advance in the east. Navarre passed the request on to Gen. Marie-Pierre Koenig, the commander of Free France on the Normandy front and de Gaulle's senior military adviser. Koenig briskly refused, without really saying why. Yet his response was predictable, considering the deep suspicion of both French and Americans toward the German resistance and de Gaulle's own hatred of "Prussian militarism." The fact is that the French resistance did not respond to the arrest of the SS men in Paris.[47] The operation itself was conducted smoothly and bloodlessly, and after its conclusion most soldiers were released to head back to their barracks.

For a while, it seemed as though the conspirators were making some headway in Berlin, too. Major Remer, the commander of the Guard Battalion, was fulfilling his duty with great energy. Until 5:00 p.m., the government quarter in Wilhelmstrasse was sealed. Remer asked for and received reinforcements from Major Hayessen and Lieutenant General Hase to block the entrance to the Reich main security office. At around 5:30 p.m., the putsch had reached its zenith, with Berlin partially controlled by Stauffenberg and his men. In Bendlerstrasse, the conspirators kept on trying to summon more troops. Colonel Mertz dispatched urgent orders to the armored school at Krampnitz, and won at first a favorable response. "Orderly, a bottle of Champagne! The pig's dead!" exclaimed Col. Harald Momm, commander of the Riding and Driving School, at first hearing the news. Momm sent one of his officers, Lieutenant Colonel Glaesemer, to Berlin with an armored unit, which advanced up to the golden Victory Column in the center of the Reich capital.[48]

Major Remer now turned to the most important task at hand: arresting Goebbels. The propaganda minister asked according to whose commands he was being apprehended, and Remer replied that since the Führer was dead, he must obey his commander, Lieutenant General Hase. Goebbels, of course, insisted that Hitler was alive, and, to Remer's surprise, he then picked up the phone. Goebbels asked to be put through to supreme headquarters in East Prussia and gave the phone to Remer. Upon hearing Hitler's voice, the young major stood to attention:

"Major Remer, do you recognize my voice?"

"Yes, my Führer."

"Major Remer, they tried to assassinate me, but I am alive. I am speaking with you as the commander-in-chief of the Wehrmacht. You must safeguard Berlin for me. Use all necessary force; shoot anyone refusing to follow your orders."

"Yes, my Führer."[49]

Hitler ordered Remer to suppress the uprising, and raised him to the rank of colonel. The battalion commander, for his part, put himself under Goebbels's command and directed his troops to lift the siege on the government quarter. As he had still failed to grasp the importance of the Bendlerstrasse and did not know where the epicenter of the coup was, he sent an emissary to find out. At about the same time, the secret agent Otto Skorzeny arrived in Berlin to organize the Gestapo troops, though he did nothing tangible against the putsch. Then Lieutenant General Hase went to check on Remer in the propaganda ministry. He found Goebbels instead and was promptly arrested. In one moment, the hub of the Berlin headquarters had been destroyed.

This was perhaps the worst blunder the conspirators made on the afternoon of July 20, 1944. Why did one of the higher-ranking conspirators not accompany Remer on his mission? In Paris, even young officers trusted by Stülpnagel were personally escorted by his closest collaborators. Remer was then a person deeply sensitive to immediate authority, and not the fearless Nazi warrior he portrayed himself to be after the war. A stronger anti-Nazi general would have scarcely permitted Goebbels to call Hitler in East Prussia. Goebbels could have easily been arrested by Jaeger or some other loyal officer. Moreover, were his telephone line cut, he would have had no way of calling the Führer.

Around 7:00 p.m., Field Marshal Witzleben finally arrived at the Bendlerstrasse and saluted General Beck as his commander in chief. "Reporting for duty, sir," he said. When he saw Stauffenberg, however, his mood changed abruptly. "A fine mess, this is!" he muttered angrily. Witzleben, tired and embittered, severely reprimanded Stauffenberg on his negligent behavior. Gisevius, who never lost an opportunity to shame Stauffenberg, wrote that the count stood like a "drenched poodle" while Witzleben showered him with abuse. The exact details of the conversation are unclear, but it seems that the field marshal believed that everything was lost and there was no more reason to go on. Beck refused to surrender, and Witzleben left the Bendlerstrasse in fury. He went to Zossen and reported on the outcome of the conversation to Wagner, the quartermaster general who was already out of the conspiracy. "Well," said Wagner, "let's go home." And so they did: Wagner to end his own life, Witzleben to wait for the Gestapo.[50]

And still, generals from all over Europe were calling Hoepner and Stauffenberg to ask for explanations. Gisevius later testified about these telephone conversations:

> Everyone listened to every conversation. Sooner or later there would have to be important messages from the provinces, and we could really do with a little good news. At our end of the wire Stauffenberg incessantly repeated the same refrain: "Keitel is lying . . . Don't believe Keitel . . . Hitler is dead . . . Yes, he is definitely dead . . . Yes, here the action is in full swing."
>
> The questions he was being asked can easily be imagined. What is interesting is the variety of tones in which Stauffenberg responded. One moment his voice was firm and commanding, the next friendly and persuasive, the next imploring. "You must hold firm . . . See to it that your chief doesn't weaken . . . Hayessen, I'm depending on you . . . Please, don't disappoint me . . . We must hold firm . . . We must hold firm . . ." Stauffenberg was the only one in control of the situation, the only one who knew what he wanted.[51]

But, enthusiastic and charismatic as he may have been, he was already working beyond his powers. Worst, the Führer was alive, and no amount of charisma could persuade the majority of officers to turn against his orders.

The hesitancy, even timidity, of Hoepner did not help. Upon hearing that Hitler was alive, the general, whose voice was "close to tears," told his coconspirators that there was no reason to continue. Only Beck's persuasion urged him to keep on going. Still, the panzer general was no match for Keitel and Hitler's headquarters. He could not convince the commanders of the military districts or their chiefs of staff, and when a serious argument began, he was usually quick to end the conversation altogether.[52]

Only in one place did the tide really turn in favor of Stauffenberg, Beck, and their friends. In the west, seated in his La Roche-Guyon headquarters, Field Marshal Kluge was optimistic, even enthusiastic. At 6:45 p.m., he and Blumentritt agreed that first they should stop the missile attacks on London and discuss conditions for an honorable surrender to the Western Allies. But when, during the discussion, Kluge was notified that Hitler was alive, his new resolve weakened immediately. Next, he phoned several people and concluded, to his surprise, that Hitler was in fact dead.

Shortly afterward, Beck called Kluge and urged him to support the new government. Kluge still hesitated, explaining that he couldn't commit himself and his officers before clarifying the political situation. He promised to call back after consulting his men.[53] This did not seem an ill omen, as among his men were the conspirators Hofacker, Speidel, and Stülpnagel. In fact, the military governor of France traveled to La Roche-Guyon in order to use his personal influence on Kluge.

In a last attempt to find out the truth, Kluge called Maj. Gen. Helmuth Stieff, the head of the Organization Section of the General Staff. This senior officer, who became anti-Nazi because of the murder of Jews in Poland, was a member of the inner circle of the conspiracy. Still, he chose to betray his friends and told Kluge the truth: Hitler was alive.[54] Even before this phone conversation, he had recommended to officers who called him that they follow Keitel's orders. Like so many others, Stieff was sure that everything was lost, and he wanted only to save his own skin. Later, he was to discover that the Nazis did not favor those conspirators who switched sides at the last moment.

The conspiracy in the west was crumbling. Hofacker, Stülpnagel, and Speidel tried to convince Kluge to act even though Hitler was alive. "Sir, Field Marshal," said Stülpnagel, "I was under the impression that you knew all about it."

"No," said Kluge. "I had no idea whatsoever."

"The honor of the army is in your hands," implored Hofacker. "Do not give it away to the National Socialists. Through resistance, we can still create a fait accompli and reach our goal."

Kluge hesitated for a moment, then said, "My hands are tied because that swine [Hitler] is alive. I have my orders to follow."[55] Constantine FitzGibbon, one of the early historians of the conspiracy, interviewed some of the survivors and re-created a description of the atmosphere in the room: "This denial, Stülpnagel knew, was untrue: he also knew what it meant. Kluge was abandoning them. He was abandoning Beck and the others in Berlin, Tresckow and his friends in Russia, his country and the future. Kluge's moral courage had failed him, and he had sought refuge in his soldier's oath. Stülpnagel stepped through the open window and for a few minutes walked up and down between the beds of roses outside."[56]

Speidel, Rommel's chief of staff, later related that the officers sat at a silent candlelit dinner, in an atmosphere that reminded him of a "morgue."[57] The desperate Stülpnagel, now using his last card, told Kluge that he had already ordered that the SS be arrested; there was no way back. "Release them immediately!" yelled Kluge. "Do you hear me? If not, I cannot take responsibility. I cannot answer for what will happen." Kluge relieved Stülpnagel from duty and advised him to doff his uniform and hide somewhere in Paris in civilian clothes. Stülpnagel refused to shake Kluge's hand, saluted, and left the castle.[58]

Among the Paris conspirators, the atmosphere was not yet as gloomy. From 6:00 p.m. onward, the resistance officers in the Hotel Majestic started to realize that something was amiss, but still they kept on following Stülpnagel's orders. At that moment, they believed that the war could still be brought to an end, and Germany saved. As Walter Bargatzky recalled many years later,

> We climbed the stairs to room 405, so closely bound to the story of the insurgency. Here, in this room . . . we had drafted only a week before the prospective surrender note of Rommel to Montgomery. We moved the armchairs to the open balcony, letting the dusk sun shine upon us. The radio was now incessantly broadcasting Wagner operas. I cannot stand Wagner, though Teuchert [one of the conspirators] liked him. At that moment, though, even he was annoyed by Wagner. Every second we expected to hear the first sentences of Goerdeler's address [to the nation]. Instead

the radio message on the failure of the coup repeated itself tor-
turously. Around 9:30 p.m. the door was gently opened. Linstow
brought in the latest news from Berlin. "Everything is going according to plan," he said. "What they say on the radio is false."[59]

Even then, Stülpnagel briefly considered continuing alone, although
he could not fail to notice that the chances of success were already
slim to none. The Nazis were no longer paralyzed and confused, and
navy, Luftwaffe, and SS units were closing in on him. At 10:00 p.m.,
Stauffenberg called from Berlin and reported that the Bendlerstrasse
was under attack. "The hangmen are racing down the corridor," he
said in despair. Stülpnagel, the last man standing, finally decided to resign. His fate was sealed; he was just too deeply involved. Yet, as a commander, he still had to ensure the safety of his loyal troops.[60]

Around midnight, Stülpnagel finally surrendered. He ordered the
release of the detained SS troops and had a long talk with their commander, Lieutenant General Oberg. Using the good offices of Otto
Abetz, the German ambassador, the two reached an agreement that
the rank-and-file soldiers would remain unharmed. Abetz and Oberg
created the impression that everything might still be portrayed as a
misunderstanding. All night long, the SS officers and their Wehrmacht
counterparts drank themselves into oblivion. In the morning, General
Stülpnagel was summoned to Berlin to answer for his actions. The
conspiracy in the west was over.[61]

The insurgency in Berlin had been extinguished two hours before. Remer's soldiers, reinforced by SS troops, surrounded the Bendlerstrasse
in a tight ring, yet the leaders of the conspiracy ignored this sure sign
that the end was nigh. The telephone, wrote Gisevius, still worked, and
the "phantom putsch" dragged on.[62] Even at the last moment, an eyewitness saw Stauffenberg speaking clearly and resolutely on the telephone in a hopeless attempt to enliven the dying insurgency. Ironically,
Colonel Müller from Döberitz showed up at the last moment at the
Bendlerstrasse. He was ready to fight the SS, dispatch a security detail
for the Bendlerstrasse, and occupy the radio facilities and concentration camps near Berlin. Only, he asked, might he have written permission to lead the Döberitz troops? Olbricht signed the order—the last
one ever produced by the one-day government of Ludwig Beck.[63]

Most of the guards at the Bendlerstrasse belonged to Remer's battalion and were ordered to leave the place without further ado. The
Wehrmacht authorities established firm control over the armored
school in Krampnitz, and the tanks stationed in Berlin were ordered
to turn back to base. The conspiracy hub in the Berlin headquarters
was, anyway, done for after Hase's arrest. Helldorff was not ready to
employ his police without Wehrmacht support, and upon hearing that
Hitler was alive and the putsch over, even Philipp von Boeselager surrendered. He understood that there was no point in moving his troops
to Berlin. The "wheel conspiracy" of Stauffenberg, that cross-Europe
network which seemed only hours ago so dense and formidable, had
disintegrated, the spokes sheared off. Only the hub of the wheel remained: sad, lonely brokers, connectors without connections, generals
and colonels without troops.[64]

The clock struck eleven, and the last hopes were fading into the
night. The junior officers in the compound, who were so far more or
less cooperative, renounced Olbricht's authority, running amok in the
corridors armed with pistols, submachine guns, and even hand grenades. They stopped anyone they saw, asking if he was "for or against
the Führer" and arresting those who failed to produce the right answer. Olbricht himself was disarmed and led with Mertz to Fromm's
office, where he was detained along with Beck, Hoepner, and Haeften.
The rest of the conspirators were held in Mertz's room. Hoepner, pa-
thetically enough, tried to deny any involvement and told his guards
that he was merely an innocent bystander. Meanwhile, Nazi officers
spotted Stauffenberg running through the corridor. "This is the traitor!" they shouted. The colonel, clearly at his wits' end, opened fire,
and was fired at in return. He retreated to Beck's office, bleeding heavily, to be arrested along with the others.[65]

General Fromm, the commander of the Home Army, finally released from his confinement, faced the conspirators in a vengeful
mood. "Ah," he said. "Here are the gentlemen who arrested me at
noon. You are all my prisoners. I have caught you in the act, committing treason, and according to existing legislation, you will all
face a firing squad." His sentiments were more than mere vengeance.
Fromm was worried for himself and wanted to get rid of all witnesses
who knew about his own silent involvement in the conspiracy. Lieu-

tenant Haeften, somehow still armed, drew his pistol and threatened to shoot Fromm, but Stauffenberg stopped him. There was no use in further bloodshed. Fromm asked whether they wanted to write something. Olbricht asked for an envelope and scribbled a farewell letter to his wife. Hoepner, too, was writing his wife, adding something in his own defense. Fromm asked them to be quick, "so that it will not be too hard for the others."[66]

Beck asked for permission to draw a pistol "for his own use." Fromm consented, but asked him to "do that at once." "Now I remember bygone days," said Beck, but Fromm was in no mood for sentimentality. "We do not have time for that now," he snapped. "Please go ahead." A shot was heard, but Beck had managed only to injure himself. The former chief of the General Staff sat on his chair, bleeding and still holding the smoking pistol. "Help the old gentleman," Fromm ordered one of the officers, who could not bring himself to follow orders.[67] Beck was taken to an empty office and finished off there by an NCO.

With Beck out of the way, Fromm was ready for his next move. He declared that he had summoned a court-martial "in the name of the Führer," and sentenced four of the accused to death: "Colonel of the General Staff Mertz, Infantry General Olbricht, this colonel whose name I will not mention [Stauffenberg], and this Lieutenant [Haeften]." The four were duly led to the courtyard to face a firing squad, led by one of Remer's junior commanders.[68]

The countdown began a few minutes later, illuminated by the lights of a military car. Eyewitnesses said that the four stood calmly in front of the muzzles. Olbricht and Mertz died first, in silence. Then, the guns were aimed at Stauffenberg. In a last act of bravery and loyalty, Lieutenant Haeften jumped in front of his commandant to die first. Count Stauffenberg stood alone, surrounded by the bodies of his friends. The command to fire was broken by his last cry: "Long live our sacred Germany!"[69]

A short while later, SD chief Ernst Kaltenbrunner, Otto Skorzeny, and their SS men arrived at the Bendlerstrasse. They did not help Remer and his soldiers to suppress the revolt. Probably, Skorzeny saw the conspiracy as an internal affair of the Wehrmacht and believed the army was responsible for clearing its own ranks. He and his men fettered the remaining conspirators to each other. Having done that,

Skorzeny left the building and overheard Fromm saying, "I am going home. You know how to reach me by phone." Then, he shook Kaltenbrunner's hand and left.[70]

At 1:00 a.m. on July 21, the citizens of the German Reich heard the voice of Adolf Hitler on all radio stations:

> For the third time an attempt on my life has been planned and carried out. If I speak to you today, it is first in order that you should hear my voice and that you should know that I myself am unhurt and well. Second, in order that you should know about a crime unparalleled in German history. A very small clique of ambitious, irresponsible, and at the same time senseless and criminally stupid officers have formed a plot to eliminate me and the German Wehrmacht command.
>
> The bomb was placed by Colonel Graf von Stauffenberg. It exploded two meters to my right. One of those with me has died. A number of collaborators very dear to me were very severely injured. I myself sustained only some very minor scratches, bruises and burns. I regard it as a confirmation of the task imposed on me by Providence to continue on the road of my life as I have done hitherto . . . Suddenly, at a moment when the German army is engaged in a bitter struggle, a small group emerged in Germany, just as in Italy, in the belief that they could repeat the 1918 stab in the back. But this time they have made a bad mistake . . .
>
> The circle of the conspirators is very small, and has nothing in common with the spirit of the German Wehrmacht, and above all none with the German people. It is a miniature group of criminal elements which would be ruthlessly exterminated . . . This time we shall get quits with them in the way that National Socialists are accustomed.[71]

Why did the coup d'état fail? Israeli historian Frank Stern, an unrelenting critic of the military resistance and the men of July 20, 1944, has doubted not only the moral integrity of the conspirators and their motives but their military skill as well. The assassination attempt, he writes, "failed due to amateurish dilettantism."[72] Although Stern is not exactly an expert in military history, his views nevertheless merit some consideration. Did the conspirators really fail because they were "dilettantes," amateurs clueless about military matters? Goebbels made the same insinuation. Even his little daughter, he said, would not have made silly mistakes like failing to cut his telephone line.

An important clue for a different interpretation can be found, though, in the postmortem research of the Gestapo. The investigators who studied the dynamics of July 20, 1944, were astounded by the stiff, inflexible, nonrevolutionary behavior of many military conspirators:

> [Maj. Bernhard] Klamroth said: "I put the blame for the blunder first and foremost . . . on my insufficient determination. Most officers are helpless when encountering sudden problems outside their field of military expertise, and tend to try and solve them by orders." What the direct superior orders is done, and what he does not order—is not done. Colonel Jaeger confirmed it, when answering for his failure to take measures for the revolt. "I did not do it because I was awaiting orders, as the big picture was still unclear to me."[73]

Contrary to the criticism of Frank Stern and others, the testimonies of Klamroth and Jaeger do not at all indicate that they were dilettantes or strangers to the military arts. In fact, the question of why such experienced officers failed so miserably is misplaced. The military profession is structured on a hierarchy of ranks, established channels of commands, and unconditional obedience to orders. Military professionalism usually requires cooperation, patience, and an ability to wait for the decisions of superiors, presuming that they have more knowledge of the "big picture," just as Jaeger explained. True, sometimes the military profession also requires improvisation and quick decision making from junior officers, and cases of justified disobedience during war are not unheard of. But in most armies, such improvisation can be tolerated only in tactical questions—not in strategic, let alone political, ones.

Operation Valkyrie was planned methodically over more than two years, and the effort, talent, and even imagination put into its planning were indeed remarkable. But there was a sting in the tail: the ringleaders adhered too tightly to the original plan, failing to act spontaneously as revolutionaries must. Stauffenberg was an exception, perhaps, but he was exhausted from playing the impossible double role of assassin and coup leader, even without considering the fact that he was seriously disabled.

Indeed, sticking to the original plan, following accepted procedures of command, and being utterly unable to adjust to changing circumstances characterized most of the officers involved in the conspiracy. The best example is perhaps Klausing's disastrous decision to dispatch the Valkyrie orders as top secret. This was not done out of stupidity or dilettantism; in fact, secrecy was an essential part of the Valkyrie orders from their earliest formulations, in 1942. Yet, in the staging (as opposed to the planning) phase of revolts, coups d'état, and revolutionary conspiracies of all kinds, secrecy becomes inconsequential. Speed is everything.[74]

Klausing was not the only one who misstepped. Jaeger, too, failed to show enough initiative and creativity in commandeering troops. Colonel Müller, from the infantry school in Döberitz, went to Berlin to ask for written orders, causing a crucial delay. Stauffenberg relied on cooperation with outsiders, such as Remer, being certain that they would follow orders given by a superior. Indeed, sticking to accepted procedure, usually considered a military virtue, can be very harmful for conspirators and revolutionaries. In that sense, the events in Paris on July 20 are an exception that proves the rule. No one there asked for written orders to arrest the SS. A verbal command by Stülpnagel was enough. The governor also took care to send a trusted confidant with every arrest squad, in order to ensure that each one did its job.

Hence, the conspirators of July 20, 1944, failed not because they were dilettantes but rather because they were excessively professional. A military revolt has some elements in common with military operations, and it presumes a certain kind of ordered, methodical work; but, at the end of the day, it is very different from a military operation. More than order, it requires improvisation, even wildness—an ability to ignore good caution and to leap into the unknown. The conspirators were educated soldiers, not revolutionaries. No one had any training in the art of coup d'état. Nor could they take advantage of an oral lore of military revolutions, such as is the case in Middle Eastern, African, and South American armies. Professionals they were—just not at the right profession.

# 19

# THE SHIRT OF NESSUS

A ship may sink, but does not have to strike its flag.
— COUNT NIKOLAUS VON HALEM,
*when sentenced to death by the People's Court in Berlin*

A VERY SMALL CLIQUE ... of criminally stupid officers ... will be ruthlessly exterminated ..." Hitler's hoarse voice came out of Fabian von Schlabrendorff's radio in the Second Army. The veteran conspirator, a crucial broker and Tresckow's right-hand man, was deeply shocked. He understood that the coup had ended in failure.

The news was devastating. The fact that Hitler named Stauffenberg probably meant that the admired leader of the conspirators had been arrested and executed; the Gestapo was destroying the resistance movement that very moment, and he and Tresckow were in immediate mortal danger.

The hour was 1:00 a.m. on July 21, 1944. Schlabrendorff rushed to Tresckow's room and woke him up with the bad news. Tresckow's response was quick: "In the interrogation they will squeeze names out of me, and therefore I intend to shoot myself." The man whose resolution served as the ideological compass of the resistance ship felt obliged to stay on board and sink with it. But, as Nikolaus von Halem would later say, even a sinking ship does not have to strike its flag—nor did Tresckow. He implored Schlabrendorff to not give out names of conspirators, and to go on living. He went on:

Now they will all fall upon us and cover us with abuse. But I am convinced, now as much as ever, that we have done the right thing. I believe Hitler to be the archenemy not only of Germany, but indeed of the entire world. In a few hours' time, I shall stand before God and answer for both my actions and the things I neglected to do. I think I can with a clear conscience stand by all I have done in the battle against Hitler. Just as God once promised Abraham that He would spare Sodom if only ten just men could be found in the city, I also have reason to hope that, for our sake, He will not destroy Germany. No one among us can complain about his death, for whoever joined our ranks put on the poisoned shirt of Nessus. A man's moral worth is established only at the point where he is prepared to give his life for his convictions.[1]

In the early hours of July 21, 1944, shortly before his death, Tresckow invoked an ancient Greek myth. The legend tells of Nessus the centaur, who cursed his shirt moments before his death. Subsequently, it brought a horrible end to everyone who wore it. There was no better metaphor for the enormous risk the conspirators had taken upon themselves, nor for the fate they would suffer after their defeat. "You know," confided Tresckow to another friend, Maj. Joachim Kuhn, "as Beck's subordinate I was the spiritual leader of the event that took place yesterday, even before Stauffenberg. I know the organization inside out, and feel, like Beck and Stauffenberg, responsible for the outcome. Therefore, my hour, too, has come."[2]

Tresckow took his leave from Kuhn on July 21, at first light. He went to his office, answered routine phone calls, and took care of some military matters. Even at this hour, his biographer Bodo Scheurig maintains, he felt responsible for his soldiers, who were being pressed hard by the Russians.[3] He summoned Captain Breitenbuch, the conspirator who attempted to kill Hitler with a pistol in spring 1944, and opened his heart one last time. "I do not wish to give our enemy the pleasure of taking me alive," he said. "I intend to go alone to the no-man's land in the district of the 28th Division, to stage a battle . . . and end my own life. The impression will be that I died fighting partisans." Finally, he said, "Goodbye until a better world."[4]

Tresckow entered a staff car and ordered his driver to move toward the front. En route, he stopped at the divisional headquarters, called Schlabrendorff, and asked, one last time, whether the terrible news was true or whether, perhaps, there were encouraging developments. Schlabrendorff's response was negative. Tresckow spoke cheerfully with the driver, but as the car neared no-man's land, he became silent, sank deep in his seat, and turned his face to the sun. Finally, the car stopped at an abandoned field near the front line. The general told his driver to wait in the car, and then he disappeared into the woods. A few seconds later, the driver heard a barrage followed by the explosion of a hand grenade. Running through the trees, he saw Tresckow dead, his pistol resting by his side.[5]

Thus, Henning von Tresckow escaped the fate in store for many of his comrades. Most of the conspirators present in the Bendlerstrasse had been arrested on the night of July 20. General Fromm, keen to cover his own involvement, executed four of them and "helped" one, General Beck, to end his own life. Others, such as Captain Klausing and Captain Hammerstein, escaped the building. The latter, who once played in the compound as a child, when his father was commander in chief of the army, knew the complicated building inside out and was able to find his way onto the street. Nevertheless, both he and Klausing were later found and arrested.

After the execution of Beck, Stauffenberg, Mertz, Olbricht, and Haeften, the Bendlerstrasse was combed by SS teams led by Skorzeny and Kaltenbrunner. They had the conspirators chained to each other, and brought them to the notorious Gestapo headquarters at Prinz Albrecht Strasse. Many were greeted there with beatings.[6] On the same night the authorities arrested Gen. Erich Fellgiebel, one of the most important actors of July 20. During the evening, the general understood the implications of the failure, and yet he did not try to avoid his impending arrest. He and his closest colleagues, all of them conspirators, sat around the table and discussed the existence of the netherworld. "Had we believed in eternity," he told his deputy, "we could have bid each other farewell."[7]

In Paris, Gen. Karl-Heinrich von Stülpnagel, the military governor of occupied France, knew that his hour, too, had come. Field Marshal Kluge, eager to save his own skin, reported to the General Staff about Stülpnagel's part in the conspiracy. En route to Berlin and the Gestapo, the former governor asked his driver to stop near the old battle-field of Verdun, where he had fought as a young officer in the Great War. The driver parked the car, and Stülpnagel walked a little in the field to "stretch his legs." When he believed he was out of sight, Stülp-nagel entered the river, put the pistol to his temple, and pressed the trigger. But his fatigue was stronger than his hand. Instead of hitting the temple, he shot himself in the eyes. The driver found him in the river, bleeding and blind. A wreck of himself, Stülpnagel was led to the Gestapo on a hospital bed.[8]

Hermann Kaiser, the relentless broker of the German resistance, whose work made it possible for the various cells to function as a movement, was arrested on July 21 in his sister's apartment. Unfor-tunately for the conspirators, the Gestapo discovered his diary and used it as an inexhaustible source of information on the movement. A network, it seemed, is best exposed and dissolved through its normal channels of communication, in this case by squeezing information out of the main broker, who stood in contact with most groups. Ironically, the Gestapo's failure to capitalize on Kaiser's arrest in 1943 had saved the German resistance movement from destruction. Now, National Socialist security authorities made amends for this mistake. Hitler was determined to eliminate the organization root and branch. Under his orders, Himmler established the Special Committee 20 July, led by SS officer Dr. Georg Kiessel and supervised by the respective chiefs of the SD and the Gestapo, Kaltenbrunner and Müller.[9]

The conspirators were not left in peace even after death. The bod-ies of Beck, Stauffenberg, Olbricht, Haeften, and Mertz were exhumed and burned. In a sweeping wave of arrests, National Socialist authorities seized most members of both the civilian and the military resistance. Erwin von Witzleben was found by the Gestapo in the country estate of one of his friends. Old and tired, he had gone there to wait for them. The other commanders, Berthold von Stauffenberg, Erich Hoep-ner, Peter Yorck von Wartenburg, and Fritz von der Schulenburg, were arrested in the Bendlerstrasse that same night. The Gestapo offi-cials soon began a marathon of interrogations to learn as much as pos-sible about the members and leaders of the resistance.

At first, the conspirators tried to save their friends by playing down their actions. Berthold von Stauffenberg, for example, said that this was merely an assassination attempt that had been planned a few months before by a small group of pessimistic officers. To save Germany, they had decided to kill Hitler and take over the government. Berthold used a well-known strategy of the interrogated: minimizing the time span of the offense so the interrogator would have as little as possible to ask about. Fabian von Schlabrendorff later used the same tactic by arguing that when he came to Army Group Center, Tresckow was still "one hundred and fifty percent" Nazi; later, he gradually became "pessimistic" and finally decided to assassinate Hitler to save the military situation. Hoepner and Witzleben created the impression that they had acted out of their own unbridled lust for power.[10]

Yet the conspirators were broken one by one. Torture was probably used, though it isn't explicitly mentioned in the official documents. Many could not stand the pressure and began confessing to their interrogators. Hayessen and Oertzen were arrested in Berlin. Qm. Gen. Eduard Wagner understood that the Gestapo would soon come, and he ended his own life with a pistol shot. Major Oertzen somehow stole a hand grenade while arrested and blew himself up in the corridor. But most conspirators remained alive, at least for a time.[11]

A few weeks after July 20, the Gestapo had been able to extract a great deal of information from interrogations and confiscated documents. A key discovery was the exposure of Tresckow's resistance group at the eastern front. He had not died in a battle with partisans, it was discovered, but by his own hand. A wave of arrests swept Germany and the remaining occupied territories: hundreds of conspirators were taken, almost every member of the civilian and military resistance. A few went undetected because of brave detainees such as Fellgiebel, who took care not to mention the other conspirators in his headquarters. Even some of the people who confessed tried to incriminate only themselves or people who were already dead, thus saving at least some of their friends.

Life in the Gestapo prison was hard. Col. Wolfgang Müller later related that he and his friends were held in small cells at the mercy of incessantly abusive guards. According to Müller's account, the prison authorities constantly invented new regulations to make their life as miserable as possible. They were forbidden to read, write, or cover themselves in the cold nights. Lieutenant Kleist recalled that at night they were dazzled by bright spotlights and forced to stand for long hours. Another witness said that the heat was set high enough to make the prisoners unbearably hot. Some, like Dohnanyi, begged for water but were often refused. The interrogations were long and exhausting. "It was as if I was in a trance," recalled Margarethe von Oven. "I have no idea what I answered."[12]

At the beginning of August, the Gestapo reached the conclusion that some of their subjects were exhausted, and they passed on eight prominent conspirators to the People's Court, the platform for National Socialist political justice. Unsurprisingly, Hitler did not want the accused to be tried in military courts. "This time," he said, "the trials will be quickly concluded. These criminals will not be tried in a military court by their partners in crime, who will be able to delay judgment, but rather expelled from the Wehrmacht and brought to the People's Court. No honorable death by a firing squad for them—they will be hanged like common criminals . . . The verdict will be executed in two hours, by hanging, without mercy. Most importantly, they are not to be allowed to deliver long speeches."[13]

Through "Courts of Honor," chaired by Field Marshal Keitel, Field Marshal Rundstedt, and General Guderian, the hapless conspirators were duly expelled from the Wehrmacht. All achievements were derecognized, decorations annulled, and, in Tresckow's case, at least, personal files burned to ashes. On one surviving page, a large red $X$ covered the paragraphs describing his prior military appointments, with the remark "committed suicide, expelled from the army." Guderian recalled later that the meetings of the court were "gloomy" and involved "very difficult questions of conscience."[14] But it was the same Guderian, as well as his colleagues, who had handed former friends over to the mercy of the People's Court.

The show began on August 7, when the People's Court convened for its first session. The president of the tribunal was Dr. Roland Freisler, the notorious Nazi judge who had ruled over the execution of countless "political criminals" and "traitors" of all kinds. More than just the straightforward bully he is portrayed as in much of the resistance literature, Freisler was also a National Socialist legal theorist who really believed that the justice he administered represented pure principles of leadership, struggle, and, most importantly, the essence of the Führer's will. To Hitler he had written, immediately after taking office, that the "People's Court will try to sentence [defendants] just as you, my leader, would do [had you presided over the court]." "The judges should not hide meekly behind the law . . . ," wrote Freisler's direct superior, Justice Minister Otto Thierack. "They have to adjust themselves [to the conditions of the war]. This is possible only when they know the intentions and the goals of the leadership, with which they had to be constantly and closely attuned."[15] With such a judicial system, the conspirators could expect only the worst.

The defendants at the first trial were Field Marshal Erwin von Witzleben, the conspirators' commander in chief; Gen. Erich Hoepner, their leader of the Home Army; Capt. Albrecht von Hagen, who had helped to procure Stauffenberg's bomb; Capt. Friedrich von Klausing, Stauffenberg's adjutant; Berlin commandant Lt. Gen. Paul von Hase; and Count Peter Yorck von Wartenburg. Next to them stood Maj. Gen. Helmuth Stieff, whose desertion at the last moment did not save his neck; and Col. Robert Bernardis, one of Stauffenberg's men in Berlin. All were exhausted from their lengthy interrogations. The worst was still to come.

Justice Roland Freisler, clad in a cap and crimson gown, has often been stereotyped as a hysterical brute. Indeed, he yelled and screamed, cut the defendants off in mid-sentence, and didn't allow them to explain their motives. The fact that he was not used to a microphone and yelled right into one amplified the effect of his unique "style." He was not always noisy, though. Whenever he noticed that a certain conspirator was humiliating himself or getting entangled in lies, he questioned him softly and encouraged him to go ahead and speak at length. Rules of decorum were not observed. Freisler, who served as both prosecutor and judge (the real prosecutor was relatively silent), used again and again terms like *coward, swine, ass, traitor,* and *criminal.* Take as an example the following "dialogue" with Hoepner:

FREISLER: If you deny [that you're a swine,] how should we zoologically classify you?

HOEPNER: An ass.

FREISLER: No! Because being an ass is an intellectual disability. In our dictionary, however, "swine" signifies a defective character.[16]

It is all too easy to denounce this specific judge, but one must understand the theoretical framework he adhered to, and the judicial context he worked within.

Freisler was not an independent judge, even when Hitler did not decide the verdicts, as was the case here. National Socialist judicial theory expected the court to rule "as Hitler would have done," or, to borrow Ian Kershaw's apt phrase, to "work toward the Führer."[17] Unlike jurists in liberal democracies, National Socialists (and Bolsheviks) abhorred the idea of impartiality, which underlies the liberal notion of an independent judiciary. Just like any other arm of the state, the court system is a tool to further and protect national ends. In National Socialist Germany, these ends were intimately tied to the person of the Führer.[18] Trying to assassinate him was therefore the worst crime of all. The accused was an enemy who should be destroyed, rather than a defendant who had the right to be heard and judged impartially.

As in many other totalitarian regimes, the Nazis perceived themselves to be constantly threatened by conspirators, spies, and enemy agents. The events of July 20, 1944, not to mention the world war, amplified these threats dramatically. One way to destroy the enemies of the state was by using propaganda, and this was the most important reason for humiliating the defendants. Freisler wanted to show all Germans how miserable and degenerate "traitors" were, even—and especially—if they were previously decorated officers.

In any case, Freisler's one-man show almost leads one to forget that there were other judges on the bench. They, like the prosecutor, were almost completely silent. The court-appointed attorneys, with one important exception, competed with Freisler in tirades against their own clients, and some of them even demanded the death penalty. Dr. Arno Weissmann, Witzleben's attorney, admitted in his concluding speech that "the court has only one duty: to confirm and execute the sentence verbatim."[19] With such attorneys, there was hardly a need for a prosecutor.

"Witzleben," wrote SD Chief Kaltenbrunner in a report to the party chancellery, "was revealed in the trial as a decrepit, miserable old man, who had lost the last remnants of his self-respect. Furthermore, it was clearly established that he had agreed to take part in the assassination mainly because he resented his transfer to the reserves."[20] This sentence perfectly reflects the line taken by Kaltenbrunner and Freisler, who did their best to degrade the conspirators as much as possible. The prison guards had given Witzleben, the former field marshal, oversized beltless trousers, forcing him to hold them until even Freisler decided that was too much. His false teeth were also taken away. Sick, a shadow of himself, he stood broken before the judge and answered mainly in monosyllables. It was clear that Witzleben found it hard to face the flow of accusations and abuse being hurled at him.

Some of the conspirators tried vainly to save their necks. Captain Hagen claimed he knew nothing about the assassination plot and had procured the bomb only at the request of his superiors. He had not given them away, he added, out of personal loyalty. "He pushed back the thought," wrote Kaltenbrunner sardonically, "that loyalty to Führer and nation is more important than any personal tie."[21] Others, like Hase, Hoepner, Bernardis, and Klausing, stood repentantly before the judge, trembling in fear.

The only exception was Count Peter Yorck, who represented the Kreisau spirit at its best. When asked by Freisler why he failed to join the Nazi Party, he answered that he "is not and never could be a Nazi." President Freisler, knowing full well that Yorck had denounced the murder of the Jews in his interrogation, asked him if the reason was "opposition to the National Socialist concept of justice, that the Jews have to be uprooted." "The vital point running through all of these questions," answered Yorck, "is the totalitarian claim of the state over the citizen to the exclusion of his religious and moral obligations toward God."[22] Freisler cut him short immediately. The trial was being filmed for educational purposes, and the show must not be spoiled by "long speeches." The verdict was obviously predetermined: all defendants were found guilty of treason and sentenced to death by hanging:

In the name of the German People! The honorless, ambitious, oath breakers, Erwin von Witzleben, Erich Hoepner, Helmuth Stieff, Paul von Hase, Robert Bernardis, Peter Yorck von Wartenburg, Albrecht von Hagen and Friedrich Karl Klausing, betrayed the fallen soldiers, the people, the Führer and the Reich. Their betrayal is without precedent in German history. Instead of fighting in a manly way, adhering to the Führer until victory like the rest of the German people, they tried to murder the Führer in an abominable, traitorous act, thus putting our nation at the mercy of its enemies, only to enslave it in the dark fetters of reaction. These traitors, who betrayed everything we live and fight for, are sentenced to death. Their property is confiscated by the Reich.[23]

The next morning, August 8, Field Marshal Erwin von Witzleben was led to the gallows in Plötzensee Prison, Berlin, along with Hoepner, Stieff, Bernardis, Klausing, Hase, Yorck, and Hagen. The conspirators were hanged slowly with piano wires dangling from meat hooks. During the war, the hangman, a tough named Roettger, earned a bonus of eighty marks and extra cigarette rations for every head he chopped by guillotine and neck he hanged by rope. He always had a cigarette in his mouth.[24]

The horror scene was duly filmed and sent the same day to Hitler for his personal enjoyment. A few days later, the Führer received additional photos during one of the daily meetings. "Hitler put on his spectacles," recalled one of those present, "eagerly grabbed up the macabre images, and gazed at them for an eternity, with a look of ghoulish delight." They were then passed around. General Guderian was there but did not protest the humiliation of his former colleagues.[25]

This was only the first trial of many. Fritz von der Schulenburg, one of the main defendants in the second trial, behaved very differently from Hoepner, Bernardis, Hase, and Klausing, who tried to excuse themselves or to repent during the trial. "We took this deed upon ourselves," he said to Freisler, "to save Germany from untold misery. It is clear to me that I'll be hanged, but I do not regret the act [of the assassination attempt], and hope that another will accomplish it at the right moment." Likewise, Count Schwerin von Schwanenfeld said clearly, before being cut short by Freisler, that he had turned against Hitler "because of the murders within and without Germany."[26] "Soon you will be in hell," the judge told another conspirator, the Catholic lawyer Dr. Josef Wirmer. "Gladly," he replied, "if you will join me there, Mr. President."[27]

In a subsequent trial, Helmuth James von Moltke was also sentenced to death. Moltke wrote, a short while before his execution, that he stood before Freisler not as a nobleman, Protestant, Prussian, or even German, but only "as a Christian"; and furthermore, he referred thus to himself and to two other prominent Kreisauers who shared the dock with him: "The thoughts of three lonely people were enough to frighten National Socialism . . . Isn't that a compliment? We are being hanged because we thought together. Freisler is right, 100 per cent right. If die we must, better to do so under this charge."[28]

Moltke was executed along with the once-omnipotent broker Hermann Kaiser and many military resistance fighters arrested at the end of July and the beginning of August. The former governor of France, General Stülpnagel, was led to the hangman in a hospital bed. Among the executed were also Fritz von der Schulenburg, Berthold von Stauffenberg, Count Schwerin von Schwanenfeld, and General Fellgiebel. By the end of August, almost thirty key conspirators had been hanged. Until the end of the war, the number of the resistance fighters executed or murdered without trial grew to more than one hundred.

Often, family members of conspirators were also arrested. "You should look at the Germanic Sagas," Himmler told the Nazi governors. "When they declare a family as fair game, they say, 'This person committed treason, his blood is a traitor's blood which has to be destroyed.' As part of the vendetta, his family is uprooted, eliminated to the last person. The family of Count von Stauffenberg will be uprooted."[29]

The Nazis never went as far as that rhetoric implied. Wholesale extermination was reserved for Jews and other "inferior races," not for Germans, dangerous as they might have been. Nina von Stauffenberg was arrested a few days after the failure of the coup, even though she was heavily pregnant. Later, she recalled that Claus had ordered her to denounce him so that one of them, at least, could survive to take care of the children. Therefore, she said, "I passed myself off to the Gestapo as a stupid little housewife taken up with children and nappies and dirty laundry." Moreover, Nina hid the full truth from her children, telling them only that "Daddy made a mistake, and was therefore shot." She was held in solitary confinement in Ravensbrück, a notorious concentration camp for women, not only because she was pregnant but also because it was thought (or so she assumed) that her influence on other prisoners might be politically dangerous. Her cell was tiny and "infested by cockroaches," as her daughter recalled many years later, but she did not have to do forced labor.

From the window of her cell, Nina witnessed every day the crimes of the regime her husband had fought. "By the fence in front of my window, women were punished," she recalled, "[and] some of them wailed heartbreakingly. Once in a while, SS women came from their barracks and beat them with leather belts. I saw pitiful female slaves, barefoot, clad in thin prisoner clothes in the cold winter." During her arrest, Nina heard that her elderly mother was held at the same camp, but the two were not allowed to communicate.[30]

Nina was not the only one to be arrested. The Gestapo detained dozens of people named Stauffenberg, Mertz, Olbricht, and Goerdeler. The wives of many conspirators were kept, like Nina, in concentration camps and other detention facilities. Many children, Stauffenberg's included, were ordered to "forget" their parents and move to National Socialist boardinghouses under new names. "They took our identity from us," remembered Uta von Aretin, the daughter of Henning von Tresckow.[31]

The wave of arrests swept through almost all groupings, military and civilian alike. They were not restricted to the conspirators of July 20, to the external circles, or to people involved with them directly or indirectly. Of the thousands who were arrested, many had nothing to do with the conspiracy. In fact, the Gestapo had been planning for a long time to arrest potential subversives, including activists in illegal parties (that is, all political parties apart from the Nazi Party), in an action known as Operation Thunderstorm, and they took advantage of the July 20 events to do so, as well as to execute hundreds.[32]

The storm raged all around him, but Hans Gisevius, cunning as always, was still fooling the Gestapo. On the evening of July 20, he was sent away from the Bendlerstrasse on an assignment, and upon hearing about the failure of the assassination, he took refuge with friends. On July 23, while trying to escape the city, he bumped into an old acquaintance at the train station:

> I suddenly saw Ambassador Ulrich von Hassell. He seemed to be hurrying like someone who wants to catch a train, and yet I could tell that in reality he was in no rush; but his head was bent in such a curious fashion. It was as if he were trying to hide from some terrible danger that was pursuing him. I involuntarily felt: There goes someone who has death at his heels. I called out to him in a low voice. He was startled in fright, then we walked up and down

for a while, so that I could tell him about the details of the putsch
—the uprising for which he had longed all these many years. He,
too, had heard about its failure only over the radio.

As we talked, his posture changed; he stood upright again,
and showed once more the same impressive bearing and inner
strength I had always known him to possess. But the picture of
Hassell as he walked, brooding and trying to escape from himself,
will always remain with me as one of my most vivid impressions of
the days after July 20 . . . His was the tragic situation of hundreds
of thousands (and not only after July 20!); his was the fate of famous and unknown men, of Jews and Christians.[33]

In early August 1944, soon after his meeting with Gisevius, Hassell
heard a knock on his door. Sitting behind his desk, he calmly received
the Gestapo, and, like so many others, he did not survive the consequences. Meanwhile, Gisevius did not intend to meet his pursuers,
calmly or otherwise. Along with Theodor and Elisabeth Strünck and
SS general Arthur Nebe, he gambled on leaving Berlin and hiding in
the countryside. A friend gave him the address of a rural pastor who
might give him shelter. The party knocked on the pastor's door after
midnight, but it seems that their luck had run out. The pastor made
it clear that no one in his parish could risk sheltering famous fugitives
on the run. In any case, the village was brimming with bombed-out
refugees, who were very suspicious of one another. Whenever dubious strangers were spotted, every prefect and village policeman was
required to report. "I implore you for the sake of my wife and children
not to come here again," the pastor told Gisevius and his friends as
they were leaving. The pastor was already under watch, as he had had
"more than one run-in with the Gestapo." However, he advised the
group to hurry to another, more remote hamlet. His colleague there
might help them; recently, he had hidden a number of Jews.[34]

The whole group traveled by deserted village roads, finally reaching the remote hamlet. The pastor took them for lunch. Yes, he was
hiding Jews, he said, and naturally he could not put them at risk for
the sake of wanted conspirators. Admitting an SS general, in uniform,
to a house where Jews were hidden seemed unwise. The fact that Arthur Nebe, an Einsatzgruppe leader who shared direct responsibility

for implementing the Holocaust, had sought refuge with Jews in their hiding place was probably one of the bitterest ironies in the history of the Third Reich.

Finally, the four escapees decided to split up. The SS uniform of Nebe would no longer protect him from arrest. The Strüncks gave up, returned to their home, and were swiftly arrested. Nebe halfheartedly attempted suicide, failed, and was arrested as well. Himmler declared him a "traitor, who shamelessly violated his oath as an SS man," demoted him to the rank of private, and expelled him from the organization.[35] Nebe and Theodor Strünck were sentenced to death and hanged. Only Elisabeth survived, miraculously.

Gisevius was still roaming around Germany. As creative as he was daring, he tried to hide in the most improbable place: Berlin. It seems, though, that for all his resourcefulness, what really helped him was the fact that, unlike those of the others, his personal networks went far beyond the conspiracy.[36] Temporarily, he took refuge with friends while trying to contact the most useful, but also the remotest, part of his network: contacts in the American OSS.[37]

Dr. Carl Goerdeler, the civilian leader of the German resistance, moved from one acquaintance to another in an attempt to escape his Gestapo pursuers. Many brave friends sheltered him, but his hope of seeking refuge in the Swedish community in Berlin ended in failure. He decided to travel to East Prussia, to see the grave of his parents for the last time. His dangerous journey was made, ironically, in a police car. Upon reaching his old hometown, Goerdeler moved around as a refugee. At the entrance to the cemetery, he sensed he was being followed, and he left without seeing the tomb. He spent a few nights in the forest, until finally, on August 8, he entered a village inn to get some breakfast.[38] He was one of the most wanted criminals in Germany. The Nazi press promised one million marks to anyone contributing to his arrest.[39]

While Goerdeler was waiting for his meal at the inn, a middle-aged woman recognized him. The lady immediately handed a note to some Luftwaffe officers who were dining nearby. Goerdeler recognized her, too. She was Helene Schwarzel, a worker who used to live near his home in Königsberg. Sensing the danger, he gave up breakfast and sneaked outside, but it was too late. "Don't let this man run away!" Schwarzel implored the officers. Finally, one of them took his bicycle, chased Goerdeler down the street, and turned him over to the police. Helene Schwarzel won her blood money, one million marks, from Hitler personally.[40]

After Keiser, Goerdeler was the last remaining connector, the sole missing piece. In a series of lengthy confessions, he told the story of the German resistance from beginning to end, giving the authorities, for the first time, a more or less full picture of it. Although he certainly tried to incriminate only himself and people who were already implicated or dead, his confessions harmed many.[41] That cannot be explained away by fatigue, and even less by fear of torture (for which we have no evidence). According to his biographer and admirer Gerhard Ritter, who was held at the same prison, Goerdeler wanted to show the Nazis, and through them the entire world, that the members of the resistance were not "a small clique" of stupid and ambitious officers but an expression of the true will of the German people. He believed that through his confessions, the truth about himself, his friends, and their real motives would be recorded in history for generations to come: "In his eyes it was not a coup d'état of officers . . . but an uprising of an entire people, represented by its crème de la crème: the most noble, righteous people from all walks of life, the parties from right and left, and both Christian denominations."[42]

As with the other trials, Goerdeler's was run by Freisler as a one-man show. The veteran anti-Nazi, throughout his adult life used to public speaking, could not stand being silenced by the judge every time he attempted to explain his motives. More than anything, Goerdeler wanted to be heard. Yet not even his own attorney would allow that. "His [the attorney's] defense was a disgrace," he wrote. "He came in the evening before the trial for 45 minutes to accuse me, but did not make the slightest effort to defend me from the espionage charge brought by the prosecution . . . None of us, the defendants, were permitted to finish even three whole sentences. The judge was almost speaking alone. We could not explain our motives. It was fixed ahead that we should be portrayed as stupid criminals devoid of honor."[43]

Until the last moment, Goerdeler was thinking of the future of the German people. His anxiety for the fatherland knew no bounds: no longer could it be saved by conspiracy and revolt. In his despair, he wrote imaginary peace terms to the Western Allies, which he hoped to smuggle from prison and pass on through the Swedes. He put his

hopes in people who were long dead. He even asked for a personal interview with Hitler, feeling that there might be the slightest chance
that he could divert him, even a bit, from his insane course. Indeed,
Goerdeler's adherence to enlightenment ideology was extreme. His
belief in the power of reason and rationality was carried to thoroughly
irrational lengths. As observed by Klemens von Klemperer, "All that
he had striven for in the past decades had now, at the threshold of a
cruel death, come to naught. An outcast in his own country, he could
no longer expect even to be heard abroad. From his utter loneliness he
kept sending out into the void what were in effect appeals and incan-
tations."[44]

Some of these desperate appeals were indeed intended for the
world. "God knows," he wrote, "that I risked everything only to save
the youth, the men and the women of all countries from further misery. Oh, God, where is the answer to the riddle? The criminals win."[45]
Other appeals were for his family. The ghost of his beloved son, who
fell in the war, came to haunt him yet again. Now he was tormented
that he had failed to spend enough time with him, and with Anneliese,
his wife. "How much pain did I cause my beloved wife in 25 years!"
he wrote. "Anneliese, my dear Anneliese, do you hear me? Yes, now I
understand why you were jealous and angry at times. I deprived you
of the daily happiness of our great and passionate love, and yet—[this
love] was the power keeping me going."[46]

There was yet another problem—that perennial, bleeding "Jewish
question." Few Germans spoke up against the Holocaust, or stood up
for their persecuted countrymen, as loudly and clearly as Goerdeler
had. Even fewer tried to stop it by a coup d'état, as Goerdeler had,
with fatal consequences for himself. Still, he felt that all his efforts had
been ignored, unregistered—and that tormented him. His irrational
belief in rationality and reason was even more glaring here. Yes, he felt,
there was enormous hate. True, millions had been exterminated. But
could people not try, at least try, to use reason and arguments to bridge
the gap between both sides? In a way deemed extremely insensitive to
Jews after the Holocaust, he tried to convince each side to recognize
its own mistakes, called for the Jews and the Western leaders to forgo
revenge, and denounced the Holocaust one last time, hoping to form
the basis for future reconciliation:

I hereby implore the statesmen and the nations to accept as atonement our death, the death of our women and children, the death of hundreds of thousands of noble Germans whose love of fatherland was abused, the destruction of our cultural assets and our towns, and to give up vengefulness and revenge . . . Jews, do not fan the flames. If someone respects you and your history, as the only nation centered around the alliance with God and his laws —I am the one. You, too, deserve an independent state, where every Jew will have citizenship. The farsighted people among you warned many years ago, that you should keep away from the internal problems of other nations. Now give a hand to reconciliation . . . you will see, that I, inside Germany, have done my best to protect you. It was painful for me, this inhumanity in which Hitler persecuted and exterminated you. These [crimes], as well as my pain over the misuse of my people, moved me to do what I have done . . . Let my people atone for the wrong it committed with the terrible wrong it has suffered. If you think and behave in such a noble way, you will be blessed with the fruits of your labor.[47]

Subsequently, he reckoned one more time with the abhorrent Führer:

This war was criminal . . . Hitler wanted it, seized by megalomania and lust for glory. His hands are red with the blood of innocent Jews, Poles, Russians and Germans who were murdered and starved. The blood of millions of soldiers from all nations is on his conscience. So God will justify us in judgment and grace for trying to rid the world of a vampire, a defiler of humanity . . . They [the Nazis] scarified the homeland to Moloch, and tried to dethrone God for their racial madness . . . The world has never seen such ruthless, inhuman atrocities. Hundreds of thousands of Jews were murdered by [Hitler], some shot, others poisoned and strangled in gas, and yet others starved to death: husbands in front of their wives, wives in front of their husbands, children in front of their parents, and parents in the desperate gaze of their children . . . German men, young Germans, were forced to perform these orgies of horror. Hundreds of thousands of Jews, Ruthenians, Ukrainians and Slovenians were expelled from their homes, their property looted while they were murdered or left to starve. Hundreds of thousands of Russians were starved to death on Hitler's orders ... I myself love my homeland with all of my heart, and for that very reason I feel the entire ignominy of its shame, which was—like never before—brought upon a people by its own citizens.[48]

This memorandum, like many others by Goerdeler, was smuggled from prison by a sympathetic guard. It was published only after the war.

Goerdeler was finally condemned to death in early 1945, along with Popitz and other conspirators. For a few weeks, Himmler delayed his execution and toyed with the idea of sending him as a peace feeler to the Western Allies. Goerdeler, who wanted to save his life and perhaps even do something for the fatherland, was ready to cooperate. But he wanted to do it as a free man, and Himmler would not hear of it. In February 1945, Goerdeler was hanged. A short time earlier, the Social Democratic leaders Adolf Reichwein, Julius Leber, and Wilhelm Leuschner were hanged as well. "Tomorrow I go to the hangman," said Leuschner to his Social Democratic and conservative friends. "Unite!" This was a fitting epitaph to a life devoted to cooperation between anti-Nazi left and right.[49]

Even some of those who had turned against the conspiracy were not spared. Gen. Friedrich Fromm, the man responsible for the execution of Stauffenberg, Beck, and three of their colleagues, was arrested on the same night. He was tried and found guilty of cowardice. The court recognized that there were some mitigating circumstances and therefore spared Fromm from the hangman's noose. Instead, he faced a firing squad. To the soldiers who shot him he said, "I fought for Germany, I worked for Germany. Long live Germany! Fire!"[50]

In the west, the noose had tightened around Rommel and Kluge. Colonel Hofacker, Stauffenberg's broker in Paris, was probably tortured and mentioned Rommel's name. From Hitler's point of view, that was enough. He decided that it was dangerous to let Germany's most famous war hero face the People's Court, and preferred to get rid of him quietly. In early October 1944, the field marshal was convalescing from his injuries at home when there was a knock on the door. Two generals who were close to Hitler had come to give his terms to Rommel, once his most beloved military leader. The three went together to a private room, and there the two told Rommel that the Führer knew everything about his involvement in the conspiracy. Now, he had two choices: either to end his life by poison and win a hero's funeral and pension for his family, or to face the People's Court with all the consequences that entailed. Rommel chose the first option.

"I have come to say goodbye," he told his wife Lucie-Maria.

In a quarter of an hour I shall be dead . . . They suspect me of having taken part in the attempt to kill Hitler. It seems my name was on Goerdeler's list to be president of the Reich . . . I have never seen Goerdeler in my life . . . They say that von Stülpnagel, General Speidel, and Colonel von Hofacker have denounced me. This is the usual trick . . . The Führer has given me the choice of taking poison or being dragged before the People's Court. They have brought the poison. They say it will take only three seconds to act.

His wife tried to convince him to argue for his innocence in a public trial. "No," said Rommel. "I would not be afraid to be tried in public, for I can defend everything I have done. But I know that I should never reach Berlin alive."[51]

Rommel donned the old coat of the Africa Corps, took the field marshal staff, and climbed into the car. It stopped in a clearing, and the two generals gave Rommel a vial of poison. The driver later said, "I saw Rommel in the back seat. He was obviously dying, sunk in himself, without consciousness, and sobbing; not groaning or rattling, but sobbing. His cap had fallen. I straightened him up, and put the cap on him again."[52]

Even before Rommel's suicide, Field Marshal Kluge understood that his time was also running out. On July 21, he tried, in panic, to loudly denounce the conspirators, and wrote Hitler that "a vicious hand, my Führer, was sent to assassinate you, but it failed by the blessing of Providence . . . I promise you, my Führer, absolute loyalty, whatever will happen." In an appeal to his soldiers, he heaped abuse upon the conspirators and called them "criminals" and "a small clique of ex-pelled officers." But Fromm's fate showed that turncoats were not to be spared, and Kluge was incriminated by too much evidence.[53]

If that were not distressing enough for Kluge, a few days after July 20, a ghost from the past came to haunt him. Colonel Gersdorff, of all people, turned up at the headquarters and tried to convince Kluge to do something by himself. All was not yet lost. Kluge could surrender now to the Western Allies and overthrow Hitler. In a second conversation, Gersdorff tried his luck again with a similar proposal. "But if it fails," protested the field marshal, "Field Marshal von Kluge will go down in history as the biggest swine." Gersdorff countered that "all great men in history had to face the decision, whether to be denounced by history or be remembered as saviors in times of emergency." Kluge, sad and resigned, put his hand on Gersdorff's shoulder. "Gersdorff," he said, "Field Marshal von Kluge is no great man."[54]

All his fears came true. A short while afterward, Kluge received a brief telegram from headquarters: he was relieved from duty, to be replaced by Field Marshal Model, an ardent National Socialist. Kluge drove to a quiet country road in France and took poison. For Hitler he left a last letter, expressing and explaining the ambiguity of his behavior throughout the war, from the bribe he received in 1942, through his limited cooperation with the resistance in 1943, up to his final betrayal on July 20, 1944:

> Both of us, Rommel and I, predicted the current development. Our advice went unheeded ... Field Marshal Model has varied experience, but I do not know if he is able to cope with the situation. I hope with all my heart that he can. But if things develop differently, and your new weapons do not work, please consider, my leader, ending the war. The German people have suffered so terribly, and the time has come to put an end to this horror ... I have always admired your greatness ... If fate is stronger than your genius and power of will, Providence is stronger too ... Be great enough now, to end a hopeless struggle when necessary.[55]

At the Nuremberg Trials, General Jodl recalled that Hitler read Kluge's letter in silence. A few days afterward, on August 31, he remarked that but for his suicide, there would have been no choice but to arrest him.[56]

On July 27, the National Socialists "took care" of the scattered remnants of Tresckow's group. Joachim Kuhn, the right-hand man of both Tresckow and Stauffenberg, was advised by his division commander that a warrant had been issued for his arrest. Unlike Tresckow, he did not commit suicide, nor did he wait for his hangman as Witzleben had. Instead, he crossed the front lines and gave himself up to the Red Army. Margarethe von Oven, Tresckow's loyal friend, was arrested by Gestapo agents in Berlin. Fabian von Schlabrendorff was picked up from his bed on August 17. As Tresckow had committed suicide, Kuhn had deserted, and Gersdorff's involvement had not been discovered, Schlabrendorff—the eastern broker—was the only link through which the Nazis could get to the others. He was led to a Gestapo cell in Berlin and there met many of his coconspirators, including Canaris, Oster, Dohnanyi, Goerdeler, Bonhoeffer, and Popitz. Subsequently, he was handcuffed and led to be interrogated, where he was told that his activities were already known and he had better confess. Schlabrendorff denied any involvement in the conspiracy and said emphatically that he knew nothing about Tresckow and his plans. A few days later, he was led to the crematorium of Sachsenhausen to witness the cremation of Tresckow's remains. But the psychological trick failed. He still refused to confess, and his interrogators turned to violence. Schlabrendorff's hands were chained behind his back and he was told he had one last chance to confess. When he refused, he was tortured by a device that forced pointed pins into his fingers. Then his legs were pierced with nails.[57]

Schlabrendorff kept his silence, even when his interrogators resorted to medieval tortures such as the rack. In the end, he was severely beaten and then splashed with cold water to wake him up. One day later, he had a heart attack but was tortured again after a short while. Finally, he confessed but took pains to incriminate only himself and others who were already dead. The interrogators then decided to hand him over to the People's Court.

The trial opened on February 3, 1945, chaired again by Dr. Roland Freisler. Schlabrendorff stood at the dock along with his old friend Ewald von Kleist-Schmenzin. Kleist, the fearless aristocrat who had fought against Nazism since before 1933, stood calmly in the dock. When Freisler accused him of treason, he answered, "I have committed treason since January 30, 1933, always and by all means. I never denied my struggle against Hitler and Nazism. I see this struggle as the will of God. Only He will be my judge."[58] When Schlabrendorff's turn came, air-raid sirens began to wail. Thousands of American bombers were pulverizing Berlin in the heaviest bombardment since the outbreak of the war. The court moved to a shelter. Freisler, undaunted, began to read the indictment against Schlabrendorff. Then a bomber scored a direct hit on the court building. A heavy beam fell on Freisler's head; he died on the spot. One of the lawyers turned to his bloody carcass on the floor and saw the indictment still held tightly in his fist.[59]

Another session of the court, chaired by Freisler's vice president, Dr. Wilhelm Crohne, continued Schlabrendorff and Kleist's trial. Kleist was sentenced to death, but Schlabrendorff was spared. The judge was afraid that the description of the tortures, given by the defendant in chilling detail, would leak out. "After I finished speaking," recalled Schlabrendorff, "silence reigned in the courtroom. My true statement made such an impression, that I noticed it even on the judge's face." Crohne said, "I forbid all present, without exception, to speak about what they heard here." He was probably worried for the public image of the Nazi justice system. "That includes written descriptions and formal addresses to the authorities." Crohne decided to acquit Schlabrendorff and ordered him released.[60]

Still, after Schlabrendorff was led back to the Gestapo prison, officials explained to him that the "People's Court was wrong," but out of "respect for the court" they would only shoot him, not hang him. In a cynical bureaucratic gesture, he was even forced to "acknowledge this information with his signature."[61] Subsequently, he was transferred to Flossenbürg, a notorious concentration camp, along with Canaris, Oster, Bonhoeffer, Thomas, Schacht, and others. When they passed inside the electric fence, it seemed to many that all hope was lost. "No one gets out of here alive," Schacht whispered to Thomas.[62]

Gisevius, as usual, had been luckier than others. While he was hiding in a Berlin safe house, his friends from the American OSS worked to save his life: "Good news came from Switzerland for me personally. Help was on the way. I had friends there—and friends helped.

A 'book' given to intermediaries was to serve as a confirmation to me that I could trust the messenger. A week passed—two, three, four. Then at last it came."[63]

In addition, Gisevius was informed that help would arrive "shortly." After months of nerve-racking anticipation, a mysterious woman came into the hideout and asked him if "everything was all right." A few moments later, the doorbell rang again. Gisevius rushed out, only to see a blacked-out car racing away. A package was waiting for him in the mailbox. There, he found a Gestapo ID and a forged passport under the name Dr. Hoffmann, complete with a top-secret document from the Gestapo in Berlin. Gisevius must have been astonished: Dr. Hoffmann, it was written there, was an agent going to perform a confidential and important duty in Switzerland. All officials of the government and the party were required to help him as much as they could. Gisevius left for the train station immediately. Resourceful and ruthless as ever, he showed the ID, declared himself a Gestapo agent, and secured a comfortable seat. A few hours elapsed, and he arrived at the Swiss border.

The atmosphere at the border was calm. According to Gisevius, "The two officials, the Gestapo man and the customs officers, rubbed their eyes sleepily" as he came for inspection. When presented with Gisevius's faked credentials, they might have wondered about his shabby appearance. In fact, Gisevius was worried that his cover story might blow up, as his dirty clothes and overgrown hair did not fit the strict standards of the SS. He had worn the same crumpled suit since July 20, and his hat, "borrowed" from another passenger on the train, was also ill fitting. Yet the officials did not ask too many questions. Maybe, he surmised, they believed his strange appearance was tailored for a particular spying mission. When they opened the gate, Gisevius later recalled, he raised his arm "limply in response to their greeting, for the two of them stood stiffly to see me out of the Gestapo's Germany. And then I was free."[64]

But Gisevius's friends and superiors, the members of that old resistance cell in the Abwehr, were not so lucky. In spring 1945, Canaris was still fighting a pitched battle with his interrogators to refute their evidence and prove to them that everything he had done was part and parcel of his military duties. He never knew of Müller's talks with enemy agents about the information leaked by Oster, or about the conspiracy and treason lurking all around him.[65] But in April, the Gestapo commissioners searched the Wehrmacht high command at Zossen and came back with a big fish in their net. They had found Canaris's diary, full of incriminating evidence about his involvement starting from 1938 and 1939, the protection he had granted to the conspirators in his service, and, even worse, attempts by his closest confidants to give secret information to the Allies and sabotage the German war effort.[66] The fate of Adm. Wilhelm Canaris, the man who combined the "purity of a dove with the guile of a snake," was sealed. During the war, he had saved hundreds, both Jews and Christians, but he could do nothing for himself. Once, as the commander of the Abwehr, he had had at his disposal thousands of agents, troops, and an enormous budget. Now, the SS faced an old, depressed man, beaten and abused by guards. "I was not a traitor," he told a Danish officer held next to him. "I only fulfilled my duty as a German. If you survive, let my wife know."[67]

Hans von Dohnanyi was no longer the energetic jurist of bygone days, the heart and soul behind the rescue and resistance operations at the Abwehr. In a futile attempt to delay his trial, he swallowed poisoned food sent by his wife and contracted diphtheria, which paralyzed half of his body.[68] The Nazis had no mercy. A special SS court convened at Sachsenhausen and sentenced him to death. Canaris, Oster, and others were condemned to death as well by a similar court.

Canaris's Danish neighbor later testified that on April 9, 1945, the admiral was dragged naked from his cell to the gallows. He was killed with Oster and Bonhoeffer, and his body was found two days later by U.S. forces. Hans Oster, the first conspirator in the German army, was one of the last to be hanged—the first to rise up, the last to fall. Ewald von Kleist-Schmenzin was executed in Berlin that same day.[69]

Schlabrendorff was supposed to die with them, but again a coincidence saved his life. He was transferred to Dachau and then to the south Tyrol. There, he was interned with other prominent survivors from the resistance movement and beyond: Gens. Franz Halder, Georg Thomas, and Alexander von Falkenhausen; former minister Hjalmar Schacht; Dr. Josef Müller of the Abwehr; and the families of Goerdeler and Hassell. Along with them were prisoners from abroad: Best and Stevens, the two British officers kidnapped at Venlo in 1939; the French former premier Léon Blum; and Kurt von Schuschnigg, the last chancellor of Austria. Finally, the whole group, conspirators and foreign prisoners alike, was released by Wehrmacht soldiers and delivered unharmed to the U.S. army.[70]

Under the orders of the local commander of the Allied forces, the former conspirators were transferred to Naples and from there to a hotel on Capri, the picture-postcard island in the Bay of Naples. U.S. intelligence agent Gero von Gaevernitz, a German American who had been in contact with the conspirators before, went at once to see them. As he entered the hotel, he was immediately surrounded by an agitated group of former political prisoners, some of them barely saved from SS execution squads. "My family does not know that I'm alive," said one of the prisoners. "The Gestapo has announced my execution." "Never mind my clothes," said a woman next to him. "I was dragged through twelve concentration camps." One man, however, stood out among the others. He was calm, cool-headed, and less eager to speak about his experience. And then it dawned on Gaevernitz: in front of him was Fabian von Schlabrendorff, the man who planted a bomb in Hitler's plane in 1943."[71] Subsequently, Schlabrendorff was allowed to repatriate to Germany. His memoir *The Secret War Against Hitler* became one of the major firsthand accounts of the German resistance.

Because of the fortitude and silence of Schlabrendorff and other conspirators, some of the men of July 20 lived to witness the end of the war. Col. Rudolf von Gersdorff, Capt. Axel von dem Bussche, Capt. Eberhard von Breitenbuch, and Lt. Ewald-Heinrich von Kleist, all suicide-bomb volunteers, were saved from the noose. Margarethe von Oven managed to hide the extent of her involvement from the Gestapo and was released from arrest after two weeks of questioning. Other survivors included Capt. Philipp von Boeselager, Lt. Gen. Hans Speidel, Gen. Georg Thomas, and a handful of members from the Kreisau Circle and from the Social Democratic and conservative resistance.

Maj. Joachim Kuhn was released from Soviet captivity in 1955 in body, but not in soul. He had suffered severe torture and came back a deeply disturbed shadow of his former self. He spent the rest of his life in delirium. A lost German prince in his own mind, he sent countless letters to West German authorities claiming imaginary inheritance rights. Stauffenberg, his former friend, became an object of hatred to him, as did all the other conspirators. When Axel von dem Bussche came to see him, the visitor was kicked out of the house. In Kuhn's clouded inner world, perhaps, the resistance had come to be associated only with personal misfortune.[72]

Countess Nina von Stauffenberg gave birth in prison to her fifth child, Constanze. Nina was released a few days before the Third Reich surrendered, and she located her children relatively quickly, but only after going through some dangerous adventures (including an encounter with an angry, drunk American soldier who threatened to kill her as revenge for his fallen brother, before softening up and showing her pictures of his family). Her excellent English helped her to communicate with U.S. occupation troops and mediate between them and the local German population.[73]

So ended the story of the German resistance movement; honorably, perhaps, but in utter failure. Its members were able neither to prevent the outbreak of the war nor to bring it to an early end. Notwithstanding all of their efforts and sacrifice, most Germans still followed Hitler to the bitter end.

# 20

# MOTIVES IN THE TWILIGHT

What good are our tactical and other capabilities when the critical questions remain open?

— HENNING VON TRESCKOW

THE LONG DEBATE in the resistance literature about whether the conspirators had "moral" or "patriotic" motives has usually been oblivious to the ambiguity of the basic definitions. What is a motive? What does *morality* actually mean? Are morality and nationalism mutually exclusive? What happens when there is a clash between two moral considerations, or between moral purism and the practical interests of a conspiracy? These questions were painfully relevant for the conspirators, especially the military ones. We have to confront them, too, if we want to understand the motives of these men and women; just as we must try to overcome the temptation to project our categories, in the twenty-first century, onto the bygone world of the Second World War.

However, before we start our discussion, it is important to counter three obstinate myths prevalent in German resistance historiography. Many observers and scholars have argued, first, that the conspirators were fighting Hitler only to save themselves or to "restore their past careers."[1] Yet conspiring against the Nazi regime was not the best way to preserve one's life, and the danger certainly outweighed the slight chance of getting a lucrative job after the planned coup. If personal security or professional frustration had been the conspirators' primary concern, they would not have jeopardized their own lives and those of their families. Most likely, they would have bowed to the regime and later kowtowed to the occupiers, aiming to safely restore their past careers in East or West Germany. The lethality of any anti-Nazi activity in the Third Reich, let alone attempting to assassinate Hitler, surely precludes such selfish motives.

Others contend, second, that the most important motive for joining the conspiracy was to save Germany from an overall military defeat. This argument carries some weight, and it certainly holds for officers like Rommel, who seemed to "jump on the bandwagon" at the eleventh hour in summer 1944. In other cases, we just don't know. The scarcity of sources does not allow us, for example, to assess the motives of conspirators such as Jaeger or Klausing; even the motives of Witzleben, a key figure, aren't completely clear. However, the source material does help us assess the motives of some leading conspirators. We know that many, if not most, were active when Germany's defeat was not yet on the horizon, which is hard to reconcile with the theory that the conspiracy was attempted only to save Germany from defeat.

Yet it was certainly part of the motivation for others besides Rommel. This concern about the impact of defeat to Germany often morphed into a concern for the impact of the war more generally. Ulrich von Hassell wrote in his diary that it was still imperative to oppose the Nazi regime even after the conquest of France. Dr. Carl Goerdeler had similarly written in one of his last memoranda:

> During the war's first two years, Hitler proceeded from triumph to triumph. My colleagues and I were not fooled. After the sad scene [of the French surrender] in Compiègne Forest, . . . we knew that each new victory would whet [Hitler's] appetite for power, as well as feed his lack of proportion . . . and we sought with all our might to do everything to minimize the disaster, to save precious human lives from all nations, and to halt as quickly as possible the destruction of the last reserves [of Europe's peoples] and the desolation of priceless cultural assets.[2]

Recall that Stauffenberg was certain of a German victory at the start of Operation Barbarossa. Then remember his remark that the conspirators should use the momentum of the victory over the Russians to put an end to the Nazi regime. As the massacres proliferated, he decided that the regime had to be overthrown immediately, without waiting for the ultimate victory. "It is true that [the defeat at] Stalingrad had a significant psychological effect on many, but, contrary to the common wisdom, this was not the driving force behind the July 20 conspirators," wrote Rudolf von Gersdorff, Henning von Tresckow's right-hand man. "The decision was made because of the [conspirators'] confrontation with the brutality in Russia, the persecution of the Jews, the atrocities in the concentration camps, and the other crimes of the Nazi policy of force." Similar sentiments were voiced by Axel von dem Bussche, who began to oppose the regime after witnessing the massacre of Jews in Ukraine.[3]

A third common argument holds that individuals, especially Tresckow and his friends, joined the resistance because of their objection to Hitler's military strategy in late 1941.[4] This argument is likewise difficult to credit. It is hard to find examples of men and women who betrayed their countries, risked their lives, and even put their families at risk simply because they disagreed with some of the government's political or military decisions, which they otherwise perceived as legitimate. In 1940, many British officers and high officials opposed Churchill's decision to keep on fighting, and some of them were certain that he was leading their country into disaster. Yet none of them conspired against His Majesty's government. Likewise, in the United States, more than a few officers thought that certain decisions made by the top generals were bad, but none of them suggested assassinating President Roosevelt. Military motives alone cannot explain why the German conspirators, officers who grew up in a tradition of strict obedience, risked their lives in armed opposition to the government. The evidence shows clearly that they were motivated by moral concerns, according to their own definition of the term, and that they saw Hitler's internal, foreign, and war policies as deeply immoral.

In fact, the decisive question is not whether the conspirators' motives were moral but, rather, what *morality* meant for them. As was noted long ago by Quentin Skinner, it is a serious mistake to assume that the meaning of a given term is identical across generations, social circles, and even within the lifetime of an individual.[5] Indeed, what the German resistance fighters understood by the word *morality* was very different from its generally accepted meaning in Germany today.

Some of them, for example, believed that several of the principles of National Socialism, for instance, the *Volksgemeinschaft*, were essentially moral and that it was only in the way they were executed that they became immoral.[6] At the time, hardly any of them could imagine morality as separate from patriotism. In their view, nothing could be more moral than saving German civilians and soldiers, German territory, and even German power. The conspirators saw themselves as loyal soldiers truly serving their fatherland by fighting the government. As the final downfall drew near, they became even more anxious to save their country and accelerated the preparations for their coup d'état.

Gersdorff argued that the primary impetus for him and his associates was the horror they felt witnessing the crimes committed by the regime. Yet he also wrote, on the next page, that the rebels could not have risked the collapse of the eastern front. If that were to happen, Germany would be conquered by the Russians and Europe overrun by "millions of Slavs and Asiatics."[7] The morality he and his associates understood, then, was inseparable from their feelings about their country, their existential fears, and even the racial prejudices so typical of their time. Certainly acts that seem, in retrospect, purely moral were also bound up with the conspirators' views about what was best for Germany. Resistance fighters like Hans von Dohnanyi who worked to save Jews sincerely believed that they had to perform these compassionate labors in the service of Germany. Goerdeler and Hassell, as we have seen, spoke out passionately against the massacres of civilians not only out of sympathy with the victims but also because they wished to prevent Germany from being forever blemished by these crimes.[8]

In other words, contrary to the simplistic dichotomy prevalent in the resistance literature, the conspirators made no distinction between patriotic and military motives on the one hand, and moral imperatives on the other.[9] Most did not view saving the German people as any less a moral duty than halting the slaughter in the concentration camps. They acted not according to "pure morality" but, rather, in the name of a system of political and military values and goals. These internal forces of conscience were cemented by their real-life experiences. As the historian Klaus-Jürgen Müller has observed,

> The morality that motivated the resistance fighters was not an abstract, theoretical morality detached from actual life experience.

These were moral impulses that grew out of concrete experiences and visceral judgment. Anyone who seeks to ascribe to them only pure and abstract moral motives ... detracts from the magnitude of their inner struggle and the inner development they went through before deciding in principle to resist the regime. It would not be realistic to argue that they, from the start, planned only a "revolt of conscience," disconnected from the facts and from the circumstances in the field. Such an argument does not do justice to their historical distinction.[10]

Evidence for the overlap between patriotism and morality can be found in the writings of almost all major conspirators who left documentation. However, in most cases, patriotism was merely one component of their moral system. Most conspirators were not exclusively patriots who cared only about their own people. Indeed, several also empathized with the non-German victims of Hitler: Poles, Russians, French, Jews, and others.[11]

Dr. Carl Goerdeler wrote how tormented he was, almost in the physical sense of the word, by the suffering of starving POWs, exterminated Jews, and Slovenians cruelly expelled from their homes. Already in 1938, he viewed Kristallnacht as a good enough reason to rule out reconciliation with the Nazi regime.[12] In the diary of Ulrich von Hassell, who expressed strong sympathy with the Warsaw Ghetto uprising, there is similar evidence attesting to the same concerns.[13] Stauffenberg indicated that the "treatment of the Jews," in addition to Hitler's military folly, moved him to join the conspiracy. The extermination of Jews was "yet another good reason to get rid of the mass murderer [Hitler]."[14]

Tresckow and his friends, particularly Gersdorff, served at the eastern front while genocide and mass murder raged around them. That's why Tresckow called Hitler not only "the archenemy of Germany but the archenemy of all humanity." Hans Oster, Dietrich Bonhoeffer, Wilhelm Canaris, Hans von Dohnanyi, and others risked their lives to save Jews. Axel von dem Bussche was ready to sacrifice his life upon his encounter with the murder of the Jews in Dubno, Ukraine. From the relatively little information we have on Beck and Olbricht, it seems that their cases were similar. The very concept of national interest was thus linked, for most of the conspirators, with questions of morality. A government that slaughtered innocent civilians and ruled cruelly and tyrannically struck at the national interest in the most fundamental sense, even if, for the time being, it was victorious in war.

A somewhat different example, disturbing but thought-provoking, can be found in the diary of Hermann Kaiser. His anti-Semitism and racism are evident throughout the diary, but he never endorsed murder or violent persecution. He valued morality no less than Goerdeler, Hassell, or Tresckow. "Morality," he wrote, "is the most profound basis for the work of the statesman."[15] Generally, it is not easy to reconstruct his thoughts or motives from the diary, because his way of reporting was so cryptic. He often wrote about the state of affairs at the front, and was truly distressed by the military developments. Sick and anxious, Kaiser poured his heart into the diary, confessing his misery and long, sleepless nights. "Dead tired, but I did not sleep all night," he wrote in 1943. "The fate of the fatherland is depressing me."[16] The suffering of his German brethren in the air raids moved him deeply.

Atrocities against Russians, Poles, French hostages, and of course Jews are frequently mentioned in the diary. In one case, Kaiser wrote that Goerdeler had reported on the killing of Jews by poisonous gas and, in another, on a massacre of Romanian Jews.[17] As far as Kaiser's telegraphic style can be understood, it is obvious that he disapproved of these atrocities. In general, they strengthen the feeling of misery pervading his journal.[18] However, Kaiser's journal sometimes displays his set of moral priorities and his definition of morality. When reporting that Nazi ruffians were desecrating crucifixes in rural areas throughout the Reich, he poured forth his rage:

> I could not overcome my humiliation and outrage, and said in a loud voice: this is not a spiritual struggle, just criminal violence ... Cowardice rules here, and lack of courage and fear to speak the truth. I would have hunted the fellows who desecrated these crucifixes in pairs [*zu paaren treiben*]. It is so sad that there are Germans able to sin against the Christian religion, going back for centuries in our tradition ... There is nothing in their hearts ... only crude violence and viciousness. In my opinion, the basis of every government is justice and freedom of conscience. Whoever

violates these principles pushes his nation into the abyss. Whoever challenges them, destroys himself.[19]

Other conspirators, to be sure, were also extremely distressed by the Nazi struggle against Christianity. But for Goerdeler, Hassell, and Bonhoeffer, to take only three prominent examples, murder of unarmed civilians was an integral part of Germany's dechristianization. Kaiser was no less devout, and no less anxious about moral degradation, but an attack on the external symbols of religion outraged him more than the massacre of people.

Yet another example—that of Ewald von Kleist-Schmenzin—demonstrates the same kind of complexity. Kleist, as we have seen in chapter 3, was perhaps unique among conservative conspirators in his unrelenting opposition to National Socialism from even before 1933. He refused to donate so much as one mark to the Nazi Party or to fly the swastika flag over his castle. Even when sentenced to death after July 20, 1944, he took pride in his "betrayal," proclaiming it "the will of God." Furthermore, Kleist's opposition to the regime, more than that of other conspirators, was formulated in clearly moralistic terms. He defined the Nazis as worshippers of Ba'al and Ashera, and the resistance fighters as biblical heroes. In short, his was a textbook example of resistance based on moral grounds.

And yet, considering the usual equation between moral resistance and determination to stop the Holocaust, one may be surprised that the latter was not so high on Kleist's agenda. "I believe that Kleist did not know too much about the extermination of the Jews," testified Schlabrendorff after the war. "He was generally familiar with the facts, but not with the details. In addition, this question was not as prominent for him as it has become for us nowadays. For him, the moral and political momentum always took precedence."[20] That is an interesting point: the Holocaust seemed to play a much larger part in the motives of resistance fighters such as Goerdeler or Stauffenberg, who cooperated with the regime up to a point, or for people, such as Tresckow, Gersdorff, and Bussche, who witnessed the genocide firsthand. In such cases, it is only natural to highlight the crimes as a justification for moral indignation and resistance against the regime. But for a man like Kleist, who had always seen Nazism, root and branch, as absolute evil, there was no need to get into the details of its crimes. Obviously, absolute evil will perform abominations. Only the big picture, the "moral and political momentum," matters. We can therefore see how different people invoked morality as something that underlay their resistance, but attached very different meanings to it.

We can also see how differing moral considerations clashed within the conspiracy itself. A typical example is the internal debate in the conspiracy on the efforts of Dohnanyi, Oster, and Canaris to save Jews in operations such as U-7. Dohnanyi, who viewed these rescue operations as a "duty to Germany," convinced Oster and Canaris to finance and cover them. Oster gave the order to move funds, but the actual transactions were made by Hans Gisevius, who lived in Switzerland and functioned as the banker of the conspiracy. Did Gisevius feel that he was fulfilling a moral duty by abetting rescue operations? In fact he opposed them, not because he was anti-Semitic but because he felt that such large transactions might expose the conspiracy to Nazi authorities.[21] It is easy to condemn Gisevius, but he was essentially right. U-7 led to the exposure of the Abwehr cell and nearly to the complete obliteration of the resistance. Still, fourteen men, women, and children were saved from death. Was the price worth it? Gisevius and Fritz Arnold, the leader of the group of survivors, passionately debated the issue years after the event. In any case, it is clear that the conflict here was not between morality and opportunism but, rather, between different sets of moral values.

It is even more difficult to explain the resistance activities of officers whose behavior during the war was outright criminal. How shall we decipher the story of Count Wolf von Helldorff, the police commandant of Berlin? Virulently anti-Semitic, violent, and corrupt to the bone, this SA officer was directly responsible for a pogrom before 1933 and extorted money from German Jews long afterward.[22] Helldorff told the Gestapo that he agreed with the principles of National Socialism but not with their implementation, especially not with the judicial arbitrariness and the struggle against the church.[23] There is no additional reliable information on his motives.

It is also difficult to explain the motives of Arthur Nebe, a commander of a murder squad (Einsatzgruppe) on the eastern front, for joining the conspiracy against Hitler. His friends from the resistance, above all Gisevius, argued after the war that he had joined the Einsatzgruppen only to feed the resistance with inside information, and that he helped the conspirators save as many people as he could. The evidence does not support this claim, indicating that Nebe was as cruel and murderous as his SS associates. It is tempting to agree with Nebe's biographer Ronald Rathert that this SS officer was nothing but an opportunist who joined the conspiracy in order to "safeguard his life by a double game."[24] After all, how can conventional logic explain the involvement of a mass murderer in the German resistance to Hitler except as an opportunist?

Still, we should eschew the easy answer. As has been noted, joining the conspiracy was extremely dangerous, hardly the best way to save oneself. True, unlike regular army commanders, a mass murderer like Nebe could realistically expect a British or American death sentence. If he had joined the conspiracy in 1944, when the war was already lost, one could just about explain his choice as an attempt to avoid the American scaffold by taking the risk of stepping onto a Nazi one. However, Nebe joined the conspiracy in 1938, well before the war, and remained committed throughout. Why? One can assume that patriotic considerations were involved, but the truth is that we have no reliable evidence. Until more documents are found, Arthur Nebe will have to remain a riddle.

It was not only the SS that was implicated in Nazi crimes; the Wehrmacht was, too. Therefore, conspirators who served in the east had to deal with daily moral dilemmas. They weren't professional murderers like Nebe, yet many could not escape responsibility.

"The military obedience," Gen. Ludwig Beck wrote, "finds its limits when . . . knowledge, conscience, and responsibility forbid following an order."[25] "What good are our tactical and other capabilities," asked Henning von Tresckow, "when the critical questions remain open? . . . We remain resolute in our claim that our fight is for the very existence of the fatherland, but are we permitted to ignore the fact that we are doing this in the service of a criminal?"[26] Tresckow indeed disobeyed the Commissar Order and spared a Russian prisoner who, under its terms, should have been executed.[27] He and others realized that insubordination became a duty when the orders were unconscionable. But their disobedience was selective rather than comprehensive. According to Gersdorff, Tresckow believed that the army must be kept intact after the coup and, in addition, felt a strong responsibility for the safety of his troops: bad military leadership costs lives. "The German Resistance Movement was not a profession to which one could devote oneself exclusively," remarked Fabian von Schlabrendorff. "We were Germans. We were in the middle of a war. We had to protect our country against the enemy by force of arms."[28] He and his comrades lived double lives: they served in the Wehrmacht and at the same time in an anti-Nazi shadow army.

But at what cost? Tresckow and his associates took an active part in antipartisan warfare, which was often used as a cover for German atrocities. We have already seen that Gersdorff and Tresckow protested against Nazi war crimes. Gersdorff came out publicly against anti-Semitic propaganda and the murder of Jews. Tresckow denounced the Commissar Order and the massacre in Borisov. At least in one case, he tried to thin out the number of the SS units in his theater of operations. But, contrary to the story told by Count Boeselager after the war, these efforts were ineffective and hardly saved anyone.[29] Criminal orders passed through Tresckow, and he often had to pass them on or even sign off on them with his initials. On June 28, 1944, for example, only three weeks before July 20, Tresckow signed, in his capacity as the chief of staff of the Second Army, one of the orders of Operation Hay (Aktion Heu). This operation set out to collect orphaned Russian children from the front and send them to forced labor in Germany. Although the operation was neither initiated by Tresckow nor controlled by him, he was still responsible for the command he signed. The story of Operation Hay shows that even the most resolute conspirator was inevitably implicated in the war of extermination in the east.

The only way for Tresckow to keep his conscience clear was to resign. But could he then orchestrate the attempts to assassinate Hitler? If an attempt had been successful, the rescue of all victims would have been well within reach, and Tresckow would probably have been considered one of the greatest heroes of the Second World War. Dietrich Bonhoeffer noted that doing one's duty in a time of moral twilight often requires taking guilt upon oneself. Tresckow did just that.

An even more morally complicated case is that of Gen. Karl-Heinrich von Stülpnagel, the commander of the Seventeenth Army in Russia and afterward the military governor of France. His responsibility for war crimes in both Russia and France was more grave and direct than Tresckow's. Even if there is disagreement over the extent and gravity of Stülpnagel's personal culpability, he indisputably took part in war crimes. He passed on to the Seventeenth Army every one of Hitler's criminal orders, and himself issued racist and anti-Semitic orders of the day. Stülpnagel's army marched through Galicia, a province with a large Jewish population, and the SS's Einsatzgruppen committed mass murders in the territory under his control. But even historians who judge Stülpnagel severely acknowledge that tens of thousands of Jews were murdered in zones controlled by other armies, for example, those of Reichenau and Manstein, on an order of magnitude greater than in the zone under Stülpnagel's command. Even more importantly, most of the Jews murdered in the Seventeenth Army's territory were killed after Stülpnagel had given up this command. The slaughter of Jews increased dramatically under his replacement, Gen. Hermann Hoth.

Some conclude from this that, although Stülpnagel had command responsibility for war crimes, he, unlike most other commanders in his position, did not willingly cooperate with the murderers of the SS. Others argue, with a paucity of clear evidence, that Stülpnagel resigned his post because he was fed up with and disgusted by the war crimes he was compelled to take part in.[30] Whatever the case, it's clear that, on the one hand, in his capacity as military governor of France, Stülpnagel ruled harshly and, among other things, ordered the execution of hostages. As in Russia, he viewed his country's military requirements as trumping all moral considerations. On the other hand, it seems that at the same time he tried, through back channels, to disrupt the deportation of the country's Jews, or at least to slow it down. Evidence on that count can be found in an official document that Heinrich Himmler wrote when the blind Stülpnagel was sent off to the hangman in his hospital bed. The SS chief wrote that "the military governor's hostile attitude [to the SS] hindered the deportation of France's Jews." Stülpnagel's children claim that their father sharply opposed both the deportations and the genocide policy as a whole.[31]

Did Stülpnagel really have no choice but to commit war crimes? If he loathed doing so, why did he not resign his commission when he saw what it required of him? There is no conclusive answer to that question, but we do know that had he resigned, he could not have worked to topple the regime. We also know that he remained a loyal member of the conspiracy throughout, and that he acted bravely in Paris at the price of his life.

Nearly all the members of the German resistance chose to remain in the army and to oppose Hitler as best they could instead of standing aside or voicing their outrage, as the German exiles in London and Washington did. Many of them, unlike Stülpnagel and others, managed to avoid involvement in war crimes. However, they, too, felt torn at having to cooperate with a regime they detested, and the psychological conflicts they confronted daily took a heavy toll. Axel von dem Bussche, for example, didn't think that his resistance activity atoned for his service in a criminal army. After the war, every time he encountered a Jew or an Israeli, he felt a profound sense of shame for having served in the Wehrmacht.[32] Dietrich Bonhoeffer, the clergyman who worked in the Abwehr, expressed similar feelings. The powerful Christian image of Pilate washing his hands as an act of shedding responsibility for the crucifixion of Jesus profoundly affected these men. It helps explain Bonhoeffer's sense of personal guilt: "We became silent witnesses to iniquitous acts. We have washed our hands in much water. We learned the art of dissimulation and ambiguous speech . . . We were worn down and even grew cynical as a result of excruciating conflicts. Are we of any use anymore?"[33]

Until now, this chapter has focused on the conspirators' sense of morality, the link between morality and patriotism, and the dilemma of "opposition from within." Now, we must ponder the meaning of the second word in the phrase "moral motives." *Motives* is a word often used so casually that we hardly even think about its meaning. This question, rarely asked in the resistance literature, is the key to understanding who, among the multitude of people in the Wehrmacht and beyond, was most likely to become a conspirator in the first place.

Scholars have suggested a number of factors, among them the Prussian military tradition, religious faith, and humanistic education. But were these elements sufficient unto themselves to form a motive for resistance? Can, for example, the Prussian ethos be taken as the ideological platform of the German resistance movement? Was it the antithesis of Nazism? True, Tresckow, a proud scion of a Prussian noble family that had provided the Prussian army with twenty-one generals over three centuries, became an indomitable foe of the Nazis.[34] Still, many German officers felt a powerful allegiance to the values of this tradition and yet remained loyal to the regime. Moreover, many of the conspirators had no stake in this warrior heritage.

What about religious faith? It is true that nearly all of the resistance fighters were religious—almost all the July 20 plotters, including many of the left-wingers among them, as well as Elser and the members of the Kreisau Circle. All were Christians and felt themselves bound by Christian values. Some nonreligious conspirators actually became believers during their years of fighting the Nazi regime. Reverence for God could thus be seen as the most powerful engine of the resisters. Faith in what they saw as higher values and the possibility of a better world pushed them through their day-to-day travails. When it was time to sacrifice their lives, their faith helped them hold up heroically under interrogation and torture, and face the People's Court and the gallows. "I stood before [People's Court president] Freisler as a Christian, a Christian and no more," said Count Moltke, giving religion its rightful place in the chronicles of the German resistance.[35] As he stood before the Nazi judge, Moltke saw himself not as a member of the German underground arraigned before a tyrant's emissary but, rather, as a believing Christian surrendering his life to Satan's legions, one more link in a long chain of Christian martyrs.

But even religion does not satisfy the motive question. Germany was home, as Klaus von Dohnanyi wrote about his father's involvement in the U-7 rescue operation, "to plenty of believing Christians who never did for their neighbors what my father did for the 'seven.'"[36] The German churches, Catholic and Protestant, were by and large loyal to Hitler. As a God-fearing Christian, Henning von Tresckow was stunned time and time again by the abject cowardice of most religious Germans, both Protestants and Catholics. "I don't understand," Tresckow told his wife, "how people who are not fierce opponents of this regime can be considered Christians. A truly devout Christian must also be a devout resister."[37] In other words, although most of the conspirators had in common an intense faith in God, religion was certainly not sufficient by itself to make a German stand up to the Nazis.

This leaves no definitive answer to what led these people to oppose Hitler. Perhaps it comes down to the elements composing the motive, the aggregate of psychological processes and factors pushing one across the Rubicon into the shadowy world of revolutionary conspiracy. It may well be difficult to define the elusive mix that constitutes such an imperative. The best I can do is to suggest three necessary components: its foundation, substance, and impetus.

The foundation upon which the conspirators' morality was built was empathy. These were men and women who profoundly felt and cared about other people's feelings and lives. Their empathy rendered them unable to disregard the atrocities they witnessed and their country's plunge into defeat. Built around this foundation was a system of values—what I call substance—whether Christian faith, patriotism, socialism, Prussian military tradition, humanism, or some other set of principles. Finally, the impetus was provided by exceptional courage.

Each of these components was a necessary condition for making resistance possible. A person emotionally indifferent to the fate of others would never risk his or her life to save them, even if he or she claimed to subscribe to a moral code of one sort or another. The value system itself is no less important than the framework within which it operates, because each conspirator's set of values, whatever its origin, provided him or her with the inner justification needed to act. Tresckow underlined this when he wrote in his diary, "Every ideal, whether or not based on reality, gives a person a purpose, strength to go on living and to move forward."[38] No less vital was the impetus; only exceptional bravery could move him to act on his values, even at the risk of death. These three necessary conditions seem to have been met in almost all of the conspirators, no matter what their other differences were.

# 21
# NETWORKS OF RESISTANCE

To UNDERSTAND THE German resistance to Hitler, it is hardly enough to discuss its most prominent individuals and their motives. Apart from the unusual case of Georg Elser, military resistance to Hitler was a group rather than an individual activity. Groups have dynamics all their own, which are based on the connectivity and interaction between their members.

In this book, the network structure of the German resistance movement, guided by the rule of revolutionary mutation, has been discussed at length. We witnessed the birth of the network in 1938, based on the interaction between salesmen, connectors, and brokers. In its lifetime, the movement went through three main phases: the dense little clique of 1938, the connected cliques of Tresckow (1942–43), and finally Stauffenberg's centralized "wheel conspiracy" (1943–44). Now, we turn to discussing the influence of each of these phases on the functioning of the resistance, its initial achievements, and its ultimate failure.

Many historians and others contend that this failure was inevitable. If that is so, they might ask, why bother discussing the movement's strengths and weaknesses? Hitler was not assassinated, Germany kept on following him, and the Second World War raged till the bitter end. The conspirators' failure was inevitable, and its methodology is moot.

Obviously, this book is founded on the premise that, their failure notwithstanding, we have much to learn from the conspirators' thoughts and actions, their triumphs and errors. The cliché learned by every student of history that "historians do not ask counterfactual questions" is inaccurate at best. It would be more right to say that historians, generally speaking, don't ask counterfactual questions explicitly. But counterfactual scenarios trail every explanation like a shadow. If, for example, we blame the result of the July 20, 1944, assassination attempt on Stauffenberg's failure to activate the second bomb, we imply that if he had done it, the result would have been different. Counterfactual scenarios are therefore merely attempts to openly discuss what is more commonly just hinted at.

Not a few historians assume that everything that comes into being has to happen because of "long-range" processes: cultural, demographic, economic, and so on. Evan Mawdsley, for example, argues that all events after September 1939 were inevitable: Hitler had to fail to invade Britain, then he had to invade Russia, and from that moment his defeat was inexorable.[1] Mawdsley consistently rules out every alternative option in order to prove that events had to unfold just as they did. These attempts, interesting and brilliant as they may be, smack of intellectual indolence: no matter how reality plays out, someone will always explain that it just had to be that way. Ironically, convincing deterministic explanations can always be found to explain opposite outcomes. Yet reality is not a straight highway; it is a convoluted, narrow road, full of junctions and contingencies. At any given moment, a different choice could bring about an altogether different outcome.

Historians tend to ignore luck and randomness, but they are crucial influences whenever we reach a junction or historical contingency. Hitler left a speech early in 1939 and thus escaped Georg Elser's attempt; Tresckow's bomb malfunctioned in March 1943; a sergeant peeped into Stauffenberg's dressing room and prevented him from activating the second bomb; and, most famously, Colonel Brandt decided to move Stauffenberg's briefcase to the other side of the table. In every one of these examples, Hitler was saved by sheer luck.

Nevertheless, history is more interesting than this, because even when luck or randomness does influence the outcome of events, structural factors and short- and long-range processes might affect the probabilities and odds of each outcome.

In trying to understand the strong and weak points of the network structure of the German resistance movement, we should examine the advantages and disadvantages of each phase, its prospects and dangers.

To do this, we must take into account three main measures: the security of the network (namely, its ability to remain hidden from the security services); its revolutionary autarky (in other words, its ability to rely on insiders rather than outsiders); and, finally, control (how well the leaders could govern the network). I would argue that revolutionary autarky is inversely proportional to security and control. That is, as networks become more powerful and self-sufficient, they become less secure and harder to control. In this chapter, we shall see how these parameters affected the resistance in 1938, 1942–43, and 1944, respectively.[2]

## The Berlin Clique: 1938

The Berlin clique, created around 1938 by Oster, Gisevius, and Goerdeler, had several substantial advantages over the subsequent configurations of the conspiracy. First of all, it was very safe. Most of its members knew each other well and had strong ties of solidarity. These dense ties created a cozy, warm atmosphere, which eased somewhat the emotional and mental pressure of resisting. The surviving testimonies show that questions over whether a certain clique member could be trusted were hardly raised at all. The group's small scale significantly increased control: three charismatic, resourceful connectors were enough to effectively manage communication throughout the network. Problems of communication with remote actors were also minimal, because most members were concentrated in Berlin.

Even with all these advantages, the Berlin clique had a serious problem in revolutionary autarky, and this problem significantly decreased the probability of its success. In order to reach its goal—namely, a coup d'état—it couldn't count on clique members alone. The minuscule size of the network, which gave rise to increased security and control, was the main obstacle here: the clique members were not numerous enough to organize a coup all by themselves. True, they still had commanders with troops, such as Witzleben, Liedig, and Heinz, but, except for Hoepner, no loyal allies were deployed in the provinces. In case of a coup, therefore, Berlin could have been quickly isolated by loyalist forces. The only solution to this problem was winning the cooperation of Halder and Brauchitsch, who could presumably mobilize the entire army. However, these senior commanders were not clique members, and their commitment was either limited (Halder) or nonexistent (Brauchitsch).

In any case, dependence on top-brass officers was highly problematic from the revolutionary point of view. Such officers, as the history of the resistance clearly shows, were very hard to win over to rebellious schemes. Among the top commanders of the Wehrmacht, the conspirators won consistent support only from Canaris and Witzleben, and were never able to obtain support from the powerful armygroup leaders in the east. Halder, as we have seen, supported the conspiracy in principle but was not really committed to its success. Again and again, he backed off at the last moment and left the conspirators in the lurch.

Many historians see Halder's "cowardice" as the root of the issue, but the reality is not so simple. Halder was certainly not a resolute man, but the problem might have been more structural than personal. Consider, for example, the interaction between Halder and Beck. When the latter was chief of staff, Halder tried to persuade him to do something against the regime, and failed. Later, Beck, then a retired civilian, tried to push, and Halder applied the brakes. More than the character of the person, the requirements of the job were the root of the problem. Top commanders, field marshals, chiefs of staff, and commanders of big units such as army groups tended to be more circumspect, less adventurous, and more conscious of the burden of their responsibility.[3] For that reason, the leaders of the resistance were usually junior commanders and staff officers, whose burden of responsibility was relatively lighter.

The most effective strategy for winning cooperation from senior commanders was to surround them with conspirators, to pressure them, and, finally, if all else failed, to confront them with a fait accompli.[4] The resistance leaders tried several times to win over influential generals—Kluge in particular—in that manner. For that to happen, however, the network had to be dependent on cooperation with dubious allies such as Halder and, even worse, Brauchitsch. The political and military responsibility of Halder led him to demand cooperation from the British. Hence, the conspirators were dependent on internal politics in Zossen and London alike. Needless to say, these factors were completely outside of their control. To succeed, therefore, the clique had to enjoy an extremely fortuitous coincidence: good work in Berlin, and cooperation with Zossen and London. The probability of such multiple coincidences was low.

In conclusion, the smaller a network is, the lower its revolutionary autarky and the more it depends on outsiders, events, and decisions beyond its control. The case of Georg Elser is an even more extreme example of that pattern. Elser, an exceptionally talented assassin who operated without a network at all, had no ability to correct mistakes, because he was completely dependent on coincidences, chance, and the decisions of others (for instance, Hitler's unusual vulnerability in the beer-hall ceremony). One unfortunate coincidence was enough to compromise his well-prepared plan. To increase autarky, the network had to grow. From 1938 to 1942, through four years of bitter disappointments, the conspirators gradually learned that lesson and changed their strategy accordingly.

## Connected Cliques: 1942

For reasons discussed in chapter 11, the structural transition the conspiracy went through from the end of 1941 to the closing months of 1943 was related to a shift in its basic strategy. As the Berlin clique's dependence on nonmembers such as Halder failed the movement again and again, the obvious response was to increase its revolutionary autarky. This strategy had been developed by Oster in 1938 and enthusiastically adopted by Tresckow in 1942. The resistance ought to assassinate Hitler independently, without asking the generals for permission. Then, when confronted with a fait accompli, the high-ranking military commanders would cooperate. However, the stringent wartime security regulations meant Hitler could be assassinated only when he was visiting one of the fronts.

The vast area of the eastern front, its isolation, and the difficulty of monitoring subversive activities created better conditions for such an assassination attempt. Nonetheless, in order to prepare a simultaneous coup in Berlin, the resistance fighters had to establish two distinct, geographically separate cliques and had to constantly coordinate their activity. Hence, the role of brokers such as Kaiser and Schlabrendorff became crucial, much more so than had been necessary in 1938. Stra-

tegically speaking, this structural shift was for the better: revolutionary autarky was bolstered (Tresckow was able to plan the assassination
attempt without dependence on outsiders), and the resistance, for the
first time, developed an infrastructure that enabled it to methodically
plan assassination attempts that would occur simultaneously with a
Berlin coup.

The cost, as the conspirators learned to their dismay, was that their
security was seriously compromised. The increase in revolutionary autarky required separate cliques and significant expansion of the networks. As the number of participants grew, the danger of reckless
remarks, leaks, and treachery became significantly higher, which undermined mutual trust. Despite the potential structural weakness of
treachery, the chance of its taking place was still low, because the charismatic clique leaders, especially Tresckow, had a high degree of control over their respective groups. However, the relative independence
of the cliques could potentially lead to careless acts that would expose the brokers to danger. And the brokers, as we have seen, were
the Achilles' heel of the structure. The proceedings against Hermann
Kaiser, along with the downfall of Oster and Dohnanyi, proved that.
Reckless remarks (Schulenburg and Kaiser) or noble but dangerous
rescue operations (Oster and Dohnanyi) could lead to the downfall of
the entire conspiracy. Only luck prevented the arrest of Schulenburg
and Kaiser and the demotion of Oster from becoming irrevocable dis-
asters.

An equally pressing problem was control, which was also seriously
eroded after 1938. The model of connected cliques required strong
brokers, but a broker was not necessarily a leader. At the end of the
day, strong ties existed inside the cliques (especially Tresckow's), but
not necessarily between them. Erika von Tresckow related that up to
autumn 1943, her husband had been worried that the cliques were not
coordinated enough, that there was no one military leader to hold all
the strings.[5] According to Gerhard Ringshausen, even the decisions of
Tresckow and Witzleben to assassinate Hitler at the end of 1941 were
made at first separately, and only later as part of a coordinated effort.[6]
This state of affairs necessitated daily, tedious negotiations that racked
the ringleaders' nerves. The early 1943 entries in Kaiser's diary reflect
this: endless squabbling ("there is only contempt"), depression, and,
most of all, uncertainty.[7] Would Olbricht act? Would Tresckow use

the opportunity to assassinate Hitler? What would happen if Goerdeler were to give his usual anti-Nazi speech to the wrong person? And what about Fromm? Interacting variables led to deep uncertainty and severe mental tension.

In conclusion, the model of connected cliques substantially increased the chance of assassinating Hitler and putting a coup d'état in motion. However, despite the continuous efforts of talented brokers like Schlabrendorff and Kaiser, the chronic problems of coordination decreased the likelihood of success, even if Hitler was successfully knocked offstage. An improvement in one aspect increased the risk in others.

# The Wheel Conspiracy: 1944

Stauffenberg's wheel conspiracy was an attempt to increase both revolutionary autarky and control without damaging overall security. According to the pattern mentioned earlier, the task was difficult, if not impossible. On the one hand, to bolster autarky, there was a need for more confidants and partners. On the other, when the conspiracy expanded, control and security suffered.

Stauffenberg tried to square the circle through a unique, charismatic style of leadership and ability to command. The demise of a competing center of power in the Abwehr and the decline in Tresckow's power because of his transfer to the Second Army left the ground open for Stauffenberg. The new cells were mainly dependent on him and his associates, and thus he became the hub of the wheel, a "superconnector" dominating the flow of information throughout the entire structure. However, he did not fulfill that function alone. Contact with the cell in Paris, for example, was maintained through Stauffenberg's cousin Caesar von Hofacker, the broker for the western front. The connections and brokerage of Goerdeler and Kaiser were still very important. Nonetheless, there is no doubt that Stauffenberg held unprecedented power. A less energetic charismatic hub could never have maintained such a structure and the level of control he had over it. Stauffenberg set strict laws of secrecy and compartmentalization to ensure that the arrest of one member would not expose the whole network.

The results were mixed. As regards revolutionary autarky, Stauffenberg's achievements were certainly impressive. The resistance movement became much more extensive. (This was also due to the deteriorating situation at the fronts.) The troops under the control of trusted allies, such as Stülpnagel's forces in Paris, became more numerous than ever. Stauffenberg and his associates at the hub, who dominated resistance cells in many fronts and provincial towns, hoped that Hitler's death might ignite a general rebellion all over the Reich and the occupied territories. It's important to note that since the autarky was still partial, the conspirators had to obtain the cooperation of fickle allies such as Field Marshal Kluge.

As far as security was concerned, Stauffenberg's stringent compartmentalization rules lessened the danger but failed to extinguish it altogether. At the hub, any reckless decision of Stauffenberg was far more dangerous than a similar blunder made by a rank-and-file member. Adolf Reichwein's talks with the Communists, for example, exposed him to a Gestapo agent and threatened to dismantle the entire conspiracy. Stauffenberg, who was usually very careful, behaved recklessly in authorizing talks with civilians unknown to him. The expansion of the networks inevitably increased the danger of a security breach, and, in fairness, all the precautions in the world could not have eliminated this danger altogether.

Control, presumably the greatest advantage of Stauffenberg's wheel conspiracy, became its Achilles' heel. In this respect, Stauffenberg's talent did more harm than good. So many people fell for his charms and admired him like a demigod that he doubted that anyone would betray him. However, on July 20, 1944, the spokes of the wheel disintegrated one by one. Some generals refused to cooperate, and others "disappeared" when they heard that Hitler was alive: Stieff betrayed Stauffenberg, Hoepner was unenthusiastic and ineffectual, and Kluge's promises evaporated into thin air. Stauffenberg's last-minute telephone pleas to officers "not to let him down" only highlight these failures.

Trusting Maj. Otto Remer was perhaps Stauffenberg's oddest blunder. He placed the most important mission — the siege of the government quarter and Goebbels's arrest — in the hands of an unknown officer, fully confident that Remer would follow orders. Stauffenberg didn't even bother to send a conspirator to watch him, so confident was he that people would not disobey his commands.

The expansion of the conspiracy decreased control, as expected, but Stauffenberg's charisma created an illusion of increased control. So great was the illusion that the conspirators believed, as was ironically noted by one of their rivals in the Bendlerstrasse, that "both the Wehrmacht and the civilian population would cheer them along. It never crossed their minds that they might encounter resistance."[8] The illusion blinded Stauffenberg to the disloyalty of some officers. When it became clear that Hitler was alive, his power dissolved completely.

# EPILOGUE

## Knights in Dirty Armor:
## Heroes of the Resistance and Us

TERMS LIKE *heroes* and *heroism* tend to make contemporary historians suspicious. In our age, they sound pompous and smack of discredited ideologies like fascism or Stalinism. Scholars of history are trained not to believe everything they read and to fearlessly criticize even the most celebrated "heroes" of the past. For every historical hero, there is a new historian—usually more than one—eager to bust the myth and add another slaughtered sacred cow to his or her résumé. Yet because the phrase "heroes of the resistance" is still in common use, it makes sense, just as we did with motives and morality, to revisit the basic definition. What does *hero* mean? Do the German resistance fighters, with all of their flaws, mistakes, and failures, suit the definition? Most importantly, what does the story mean for us, as readers of history and citizens of the twenty-first century?

A tough question, indeed. As I was writing this book, over ten years, I never stopped grappling with it. To start looking for a solution, it may be worth taking a step back from the resistance literature, and even from the story altogether. I have found my first hint in *Jews for Sale?*, Yehuda Bauer's classic study of the efforts to save Jews in Hungary. Here is what he wrote on the Jewish activists who worked to save their brethren in the dark years of the Holocaust:

> The Jewish heroes were not knights in shining armor. Weissmandel was a fanatic, ultraorthodox opponent of Zionism; Brand was

an adventurer, a drinker, and a person whose devotion to the truth was not the most prominent mark of his character. Kasztner was an ambitious, overweening and authoritarian personality, guilty of rescuing Nazis from post-war justice to satisfy his sense of honor and power . . . Mayer was a pedantic philanthropist—and so on. Yet heroes they all are. Their attempt to save Jews involved tremendous self-sacrifice, courage and devotion.[1]

The German resistance fighters, too, were not "knights in shining armor" as they were portrayed by some early historians. In fact, they were a relatively random group of people, taken from all walks of life and barely distinguishable from others before they joined the conspiracy. An opponent of the Nazi regime could be an educated, sophisticated colonel from the nobility, a craggy combat officer at the front, a button-down conservative mayor or intellectual, a labor-union activist, a diligent schoolteacher, or an unassuming carpenter. True, as we have seen, most of them had some special mental attributes that left an imprint on the minds of their associates: strong religious beliefs, bravery, and empathy for others. These attributes, though, were not always evident before the time of emergency.

Prone to human failings, they were not saints, and at certain junctures they were inclined to be aggressive and manipulative, at times even cruel. Oster, for example, was described by some of his colleagues in the Abwehr as a scheming and slippery officer who flirted with the secretaries in his office. Dohnanyi forbade his wife to complete her dissertation because, he asserted, academic studies would conflict with her wifely duties.[2] Goerdeler was, in the minds of many, a conservative, antagonistic, and narrow-minded bureaucrat.[3] Tresckow was implicated in antipartisan warfare (which may well have entailed atrocities). And Hase, in his role as the Greater Berlin commandant, condemned deserters to death even while trying to help other political "criminals."[4] Human beings are always complex and often conflicted; the conspirators were no different. However, given the difficult circumstances they found themselves in, the great majority consented to risk their lives for others. In that sense, and only in that sense, they were true heroes.

Once we have understood that their armor is not shining but rather tarnished and scratched, we can see "heroes" for what they are in the real world: people able, perhaps only briefly, to transcend ideology and selfishness and even existential dangers for the sake of a greater good. Any other interpretation makes life much too easy for us, the readers of history. If Stauffenberg, Tresckow, and Goerdeler were perfect, larger than life, "heroic" in the mythical sense, while we are not, their lessons would not be useful to us. Ordinary people cannot follow the example of demigods. If, by contrast, the German resisters are seen as pure opportunists, we again receive a soothing message. It is reassuring to measure oneself against wicked criminals, embodiments of evil. When new historians in Germany go out of their way to show how evil Tresckow was (using late-twentieth-century moral standards), the underlying message is "I am a new German. I am not like him. See how righteous I am?"

But what if one were to find oneself in circumstances such as Stauffenberg's, Tresckow's, or Goerdeler's? Fallible, imperfect individuals as we are, susceptible to stereotyping and other failings, what would we do when moral dilemmas abounded: in the midst of a propaganda storm, receiving news of the death of loved ones, not to mention colossal genocide? The terrible history of the twentieth century has proved more than once that such nightmares are never too far away. "Responsible action," wrote Dietrich Bonhoeffer, "takes place in the sphere of relativity, completely shrouded in the twilight that the historical situation casts upon good and evil. It takes place in the midst of the countless perspectives from which every phenomenon is seen. Responsible action must decide not simply between right and wrong, good and evil, but between right and right, wrong and wrong."[5]

Under such circumstances, the complex type known as a "hero" perpetually challenges everyone and everyone's definition. You, the senior civil servant—would you be ready to sacrifice your career in order to protect the persecuted, as Goerdeler did? You, the officer—would you refuse "one out of ninety-nine commands," as Olbricht declared he was ready to do, or put the lives of your friends, loved ones, and family at risk, as Tresckow, Oster, and Stauffenberg did? How would you cope with a whirling array of moral dilemmas in a "sphere of relativity, completely shrouded in the twilight"? If these questions make you ponder, then I have done the job I set out to do.

**ACKNOWLEDGMENTS**

**NOTES**

**SELECT BIBLIOGRAPHY**

**INDEX**

# ACKNOWLEDGMENTS

*The Plots Against Hitler* could not have been published but for the generous help of a dense network of family members, friends, teachers, and colleagues to whom I owe endless gratitude.

Andrew Lownie, my dedicated agent, cleverly navigated in the stormy water of the international literary market in order to publish this book in English and in translation. I also thank Jemma McDonough from the March Agency for her help in negotiating the Italian edition of this book. My dear mother, Lily Orbach, invested considerable time and effort in reading the first drafts of the manuscript and giving valuable comments. Ned Pennant-Rea, one of the best language editors I've ever encountered, worked very hard to make this book readable. Kristen Hamilton ("Kristen Corrects") also helped during the editing process.

I am also deeply indebted to the wonderful publishing team of Eamon Dolan Books, Houghton Mifflin Harcourt. Eamon Dolan, my editor, believed in this project and made an enormous effort to bring it into print. Rosemary McGuinness showed incredible patience with my nagging on an endless array of administrative issues, and Tammy Zambo did an excellent job with the copyediting.

Prof. Niall Ferguson from Harvard University, through his sharp and pointed criticism, directed the way to the rewriting of this book while I worked under him as a teaching fellow—a truly unforgettable experience. Prof. Moshe Zuckermann, my most esteemed teacher from Tel Aviv University and an expert in German intellectual history, stood by this project since its inception, when I was only an (overly) ambitious high school student with no experience in research. Prof. Moshe Zimmermann from the Hebrew University of Jerusalem gave me valuable insights. Prof. Peter Hoffmann from McGill University, an eminent historian of the German resistance movement, graciously supported me through many barren years of research with kind help and advice, even when he deeply disagreed with my conclusions and methodology. Dr. Maximilian Schich (Zurich Technical University), along with two of my Harvard friends, Anshul Kumar and Mazen Elfakhani, first inaugurated me into the fascinating world of social-networks analysis and tirelessly answered even my most uninformed questions. Linda von Keyserlingk, a curator from the Military History Museum in Dresden and a PhD candidate at Potsdam University, graciously shared some of her findings about social networks in the German resistance. I have benefited in the same way from the free instruction given by Prof. Lada Adamic, a renowned expert in social networks, through the academic internet site Coursera; and from the instruction of the network analyst Smadar Porat. Prof. Winfried Meyer, a historian of German military intelligence, gave me precious advice and documents from his personal collection. I am also grateful to my adviser at Harvard, Prof. Andrew Gordon, who was always willing to listen and showed remarkable tolerance toward the time I invested in the research for this book, at the expense of my yet-to-be-finished dissertation project.

Furthermore, I owe special gratitude to the German resistance fighters and their family members who consented to speak with me or to be interviewed for this book. The lamented Count Philipp von Boeselager, a confidant of the resistance leader Gen. Henning von Tresckow, graciously agreed to meet me in his handsome castle at the village of Kreuzberg, near Bonn, and to answer many questions. Similarly, the late Dr. Marianne Meyer-Krahmer, the daughter of the civilian leader of the resistance, Dr. Carl Goerdeler, gave me a lengthy and highly useful interview during her stay in Tel Aviv. I received useful advice also from the sons of Col. Claus von Stauffenberg, Heimerann von Stauffenberg and Franz-Ludwig von Stauffenberg. Christina Blumenberg-Lampe from the Stiftung 20 Juli 1944 helped me to arrange some of these interviews. Nicholas Netteau, an American creator of documentaries, allowed me to use his own interviews with key conspirators and their relatives. Dr. Mordechai Paldiel, the former head of the Department of the Righteous, Yad Vashem, gave me access to useful documents from the Hans von Dohnanyi file.

During my research trip to Russia, I was tremendously helped by Prof. Aleksandr Bezborodov, chair of the Department of History and Archives at RGGU University; his colleague Prof. Boris Chavkin; Valentina Apresjan from the Russian Language Institute; and the research staff of Memorial, a brave and dedicated human rights organization based in Moscow. In Aberdeen, Scotland, the family of the late British diplomat Sir George Ogilvie-Forbes was generous enough to give me access to his private papers. I was also helped by the following archivists and research-library officials: Petra Moertl from the

Institut für Zeitgeschichte (Munich), Andreas Grunwald from the Bundesarchiv (Berlin), Achim Koch from the Bundesarchiv-Militärarchiv (Freiburg), Michelle Gait (Aberdeen University Archive), Steven Bye (U.S. Army Heritage Center), Elton-John Torres (Special Collections, University of Pennsylvania), and the staffs of the Wiener Collection at Tel Aviv University and the Goethe Institute in Tel Aviv. I am also deeply grateful to the German Resistance Memorial Center in Berlin; its director, Prof. Johannes Tuchel; and the Bundesarchiv in Bern, Switzerland, for the gracious permission to reproduce some of their photos. Laura Tuomi generously helped me to translate documents from Finnish.

The early drafts of this book could not have been written without generous scholarships from the Bosch Foundation (Germany) and the Bloomfield Science Museum (Jerusalem). I also thank the following friends, teachers, and colleagues who read the manuscript, in part or in whole, and/or gave me precious advice: Michael Olinger, Florin Stefan-Morar, Cian Power, Dr. Konrad Lawson, Prof. Sven Saaler, Prof. Harald Kleinschmidt, Prof. Ishida Yuji, Prof. Moshe Zimmermann, Prof. Aviad Kleinberg, Dr. Igal Halfin, Dr. Shulamit Volkov, and Prof. Shlomo Sand. Rabbi Yosef Kaminetski from the Jewish Orthodox movement Chabad shared with me invaluable information on the rescue of the Lubavitcher Rebbe from Warsaw. Iris Nachum and the German reading group at Tel Aviv University gave useful comments on a key Goerdeler document. My dear friends from Tel Aviv University Dikla Doitch and Clara Shikhleman gave sharp and intelligent feedback.

The following people were kind enough to host me during my frequent research trips. In Carlisle, Pennsylvania, Alison Spare and her family; in Washington, D.C., Seraj and Abir Assi; and in Freilassing, Germany, Gerhard and Anke Walcher. During my stay in the United Kingdom, I enjoyed the generous hospitality of Niall Sayers and Ben Zvi in Aberdeen, and Chris Hall in London.

This book could not have been written but for a very special man who worked with me on the basic idea more than fifteen years ago: the late Itzik Meron (Mitrani), my former history teacher at Galili High School, Kfar-Saba, Israel. As my adviser for a high school term paper on the German resistance to Hitler, Itzik taught me the basic methods of historical research, from reading sources critically to writing footnotes. Most of all, he taught me to love history. Unfortunately, he did not have the opportunity to witness the publication of *The Plots Against Hitler*. This book is dedicated to his memory.

All of the people mentioned here have a share in the merits of this book. The responsibility for any faults or errors, however, is exclusively my own.

# NOTES

## Abbreviations

BA: Bundesarchiv, Berlin

BA-MA: Bundesarchiv-Militärarchiv, Freiburg

CAC: Churchill Archives Center, Cambridge, U.K.

DRYV: Department of the Righteous Archive, Yad Vashem Holocaust Memorial Authority, Jerusalem

GARF: Gosudarstvennii Arhiv Rossikei Federatsi (State Archive of the Russian Federation), Moscow

GEAH: Georg-Elser-Arbeitskreis Heidenheim (online archive, http://www .georg-elser-arbeitskreis.de/gearchiv.htm)

HULL: Harvard University Lamont Library, Cambridge, Massachusetts

IfZ: Institut für Zeitgeschichte, Munich

KA: Risto Rytin arkisto (Finnish National Archive), Helsinki

NA: National Archives, Kew, London

NARA: National Archives and Records Administration, Washington, D.C.

*Nuremberg Blue: International Military Tribunal: Trial of the Major War Criminals Before the International Military Tribunal* (Nuremberg, 1947). 42 vols.

*Nuremberg Green: Trials of the Major War Criminals Before the Nuremberg Military Tribunals Under Control Council Law No. 10, October 1946–April 1949* (Washington, D.C.: GPO, 1953). 15 vols.

*Nuremberg Red:* Office of the U.S. Chief Counsel for the Prosecution of Axis Criminality, *Nazi Conspiracy and Aggression* (Washington, D.C.: GPO, 1946). 8 vols. plus 3 suppl. vols.

NWHA: Nordrhein-Westfälisches Hauptstaatsarchiv, Düsseldorf

SAL: Stadtarchive Leipzig, Leipzig

UMA: Ulkoasiainministeriön Arkisto (Archive of the Ministry for Foreign Affairs of Finland), Helsinki

UPEN-RBML: University of Pennsylvania, Rare Book and Manuscript Library, Philadelphia

USAMHI: Army Heritage and Education Center Archive, Carlisle, Pennsylvania

WC-TAU: Wiener Collection, Tel Aviv University

## Introduction

1. *"confront the dark forces of the age"*: Hans Rothfels, *The German Opposition to Hitler: An Assessment*, trans. Lawrence Wilson (London: Wolff, 1970), 71–72.

2. *"revolt of conscience"*: Eckart Conze, "Aufstand des preußischen Adels: Marion Gräfin Dönhoff und das Bild des Widerstands gegen den Nationalsozialismus in der Bundesrepublik Deutschland," *Vierteljahrshefte für Zeitgeschichte* 51, no. 4 (2003): 499.

3. *"life and the preservation of life"*: Peter Hoffmann, *The History of the German Resistance, 1933–1945*, trans. Richard Barry (Montreal: McGill-Queen's University Press, 1985), x.

4. *They may have slowly learned:* Hans Mommsen, "Beyond the Nation State: The German Resistance Against Hitler and the Future of Europe," in *Working Towards the Führer: Essays in Honour of Sir Ian Kershaw*, ed. Anthony McElligott and Tim Kirk (Manchester, U.K.: Manchester University Press, 2003), 246–57; Hans Mommsen, *Alternative zu Hitler—Studien zur Geschichte des deutschen Widerstandes* (Munich: Beck, 2000), 7–9.

5. *They may have been against:* Christoph Dipper, "Der Widerstand und die Juden," in *Der Widerstand gegen den Nationalsozialismus: Die deutsche Gesellschaft und der Widerstand gegen Hitler*, ed. Jürgen Schmädecke and Peter Steinbach (Munich: Piper, 1985), 598–616.

6. *The sad truth was:* Christian Gerlach, "Männer des 20 Juli und der Krieg gegen die Sowjetunion," in *Vernichtungskrieg—Verbrechen der Wehrmacht 1941 bis 1944*, ed. Hannes Heer and Klaus Naumann (Hamburg: Hamburger Edition, 1995), 439–41.

7. *In ten years of research:* Danny Orbach, *Valkyrie: Ha-Hitnagdut Ha-Germanit Le-Hitler* (Or Yehuda, Isr.: Yedioth Ahronot Press, 2009).

8. *The representation of the resistance:* See my critical assessment of Christoph Dipper, Christian Gerlach, and others in Danny Orbach, "Criticism Reconsidered: The German Resistance to Hitler in Critical German Scholarship," *Journal of Military History* 75 (April 2011): 1–25.

9. *"The question of what really motivates"*: Aviad Kleinberg, *Flesh Made Word: Saints' Stories and the Western Imagination* (Cambridge, Mass.: Belknap Press of Harvard University Press, 2008), 88.

10. *almost none of them . . . have adequately analyzed:* There is one important exception. Linda von Keyserlingk, a PhD candidate from Postdam University, is working in her dissertation on a quantitative network analysis of the German resistance. An abstract of her much-expected prospective research was published as Linda von Keyserlingk, "Erkenntnisgewinn durch die historische Netzwerkforschung: Eine qualitative und quantitative Analyse des Beziehungsgeflechts von zivilem und militärischem Widerstand, 1938–1944," in *Das ist Militärgeschichte! Probleme — Projekte — Perspektiven*, ed. Christian Th. Müller and Matthias Rogg (Paderborn: Ferdinand Schöningh, 2013), 464–68.

## 1. Opposition in Flames

1. *In the evening of February 27, 1933:* Benjamin Carter Hett, *Burning the Reichstag: An Investigation into the Third Reich's Enduring Mystery* (New York: Oxford University Press, 2014), 14.

2. *"The guilty are the Communist revolutionaries"*: Rudolf Diels, *Lucifer ante Portas — Zwischen Severing und Heydrich* (Zurich: Interverlag, 1949), 143.

3. *"AGAINST MURDERERS, ARSONISTS"*: Ian Kershaw, *Hitler, 1889–1936: Hubris* (New York: Norton, 1999), 460.

4. *"So the Communists had burned down"*: Sebastian Haffner, *Defying Hitler: A Memoir*, trans. Oliver Pretzel (London: Weidenfeld & Nicolson, 2002), 126.

5. *Hitler had yet to win support:* Wolfgang Michalka, ed., *Das Dritte Reich: Dokumente zur Innen- und Außenpolitik* (Munich: Deutscher Taschenbuch Verlag, 1985), 1:291.

6. *"The feelings of most Germans"*: Kershaw, *Hubris*, 461.

7. *Scholars have debated this question ever since:* The best and most updated study on the Reichstag fire is Hett, *Burning the Reichstag*.

8. *"Was it the Reichstag alone?"*: Hans B. Gisevius, *To the Bitter End*, trans. Richard Winston and Clara Winston (New York: Da Capo Press, 1998), 3.

9. *"A Communist attack"*: Haffner, *Defying Hitler*, 101.

10. *its leaders were fettered:* Peter Hoffmann, *Widerstand, Staatsstreich, Attentat — der Kampf der Opposition gegen Hitler* (Munich: Piper, 1985), 18–19.

11. *The Communist Party, said a Russian diplomat:* Friedrich Stampfer, *Erfahrungen und Erkenntnisse — Aufzeichnungen aus meinem Leben* (Cologne: Verlag für Politik und Wirtschaft, 1957), 264.

12. *"We, the German Social Democrats"*: Michalka, *Das Dritte Reich*, 1:34.

13. *"You are late, but still you come!"*: Max Domarus, *Hitler: Reden und Proklama-*

*tionen, 1932–1945: Kommentiert von einem deutschen Zeitgenossen* (Würzburg: Schmidt, Neustadt a.d. Aisch, 1962), 1:242–46.

14. *"The German National Socialist Workers' party"*: Michalka, *Das Dritte Reich*, 1:34.

15. *"marched thickly surrounded"*: Lucas Erhard, *Vom Scheitern der deutschen Arbeiterbewegung* (Basel: Stroemfeld, 1983), 164–65; *Nuremberg Blue* (USA-238, 392-PS), 25:534–36.

16. *"It cannot be denied, he has grown"*: Erich Ebermayer, *Denn heute gehört uns Deutschland: Persönliches und politisches Tagebuch*, trans. Sally Winkle (Hamburg: Zsolnay, 1959), 46–47.

17. *The turnout was massive:* Dieter Nohlen and Philip Stöver, eds., *Elections in Europe: A Data Handbook* (Baden-Baden: Nomos, 2010), 762.

18. *"I swear by God this holy oath"*: Hoffmann, *Widerstand, Staatsstreich, Attentat*, 46.

19. *a massive decrease in unemployment: Statistiches Jahrbuch für das deutsche Reich, 1938* (Berlin: Puttkammer & Mühlbrecht), 371, http://www.digizeitschrift en.de/. For a visual representation of the development of unemployment, see Statista 2015, ed., "Anzahl der Arbeitslosen in der Weimarer Republik in den Jahren 1926 bis 1935," http://de.statista.com/statistik/daten/studie/277373/umfrage/historische-arbeitslosenzahl-in-der-weimarer-republik/. For the development in real wages, see U. Pfister, "Deutsche Wirtschaft seit 1850: Die Wirtschaft in der Ära des Nationalsozialismus, 1933–1939," http://www.wiwi.uni-muenster.de/wisoge/md/personen/pfister/Vorlesungsdatei en/Deutsche_Wirtschaft_seit_1850/S02-NS-Folien.pdf.

20. *"The effect [of the propaganda]"*: Haffner, *Defying Hitler*, 128–29.

21. *the cooperation of the public:* Ian Kershaw, *Hitler, the Germans, and the Final Solution* (Jerusalem: Yad Vashem Press; New Haven, Conn.: Yale University Press, 2008), 248.

22. *"Every one of these classes"*: Haffner, *Defying Hitler*, 146.

23. *"Please dear God, make me mute"*: Rudolph Herzog, *Heil Hitler, das Schwein ist tot!: Lachen unter Hitler: Komik und Humor im dritten Reich* (Frankfurt am Main: Eichborn, 2006), 72. This black-humor ditty puns on a German children's prayer: *Lieber Gott, mach mich fromm, / dass ich in den Himmel komm* ("Please dear God, make me pious, so I can go to heaven").

24. *there were relatively few professional Gestapo agents:* Robert Gallately, "The Political Policing of Nazi Germany," in *Germans Against Nazism: Nonconformity, Opposition, and Resistance in the Third Reich: Essays in Honour of Peter Hoffmann*, ed. Francis R. Nicosia and Lawrence D. Stokes (New York: St. Martin's Press, 1990), 27–31.

25. "the period of large-scale underground activity": Peter Hoffmann, *The History of the German Resistance, 1933–1945*, trans. Richard Barry (Montreal: McGill-Queen's University Press, 1985), 22.

## 2. "That Damned Mare!": The Army Top-Brass Scandal

1. *As scandal followed scandal:* Karl-Heinz Janssen and Fritz Tobias, *Der Sturz der Generäle: Hitler und die Blomberg-Fritsch Krise, 1938* (Munich: Beck, 1994), 24.
2. *the development of an embryonic network:* Klaus-Jürgen Müller, "Die Blomberg-Fritsch Krise, 1938: Elemente eines politisch-militärischen Skandals," in *Der politische Skandal,* ed. Julius H. Schoeps (Stuttgart: Burg, 1992), 129–31.
3. *Far from being the moderate:* Franz Halder, "Zu den Aussagen des Dr. Gisevius in Nürnberg, 24. Bis 26.4.1946," BA-MA BAarch N/124/10. See also Ian Kershaw, *Hitler, 1889–1936: Hubris* (New York: Norton, 1999), 391.
4. *"He was crazy about me":* Janssen and Tobias, *Der Sturz der Generäle,* 24.
5. *Göring was quick to translate:* Müller, "Die Blomberg-Fritsch Krise," 116–17; Abschrift Huppenkothen, 11.7.1947, IfZ, 0249-1, pp. 8–10, http://www.ifz -muenchen.de/archiv/zs/zs-0249_1.pdf.
6. *"inconceivable that the first officer in the army":* Nicholas Reynolds, *Treason Was No Crime: Ludwig Beck, Chief of the German General Staff* (London: Kimber, 1976), 132; Janssen and Tobias, *Der Sturz der Generäle,* 56–63.
7. *"Wait, you pigs":* Janssen and Tobias, *Der Sturz der Generäle,* 129.
8. *"biggest expert on the homosexual scene":* Harold C. Deutsch, *The Conspiracy Against Hitler in the Twilight War* (Minneapolis: University of Minnesota Press, 1970), 140; Abschrift Huppenkothen, 11.7.1947, IfZ 0249-1, p. 3.
9. *The Schmidt file, never burned:* Müller, "Die Blomberg-Fritsch Krise," 123–27; Kershaw, *Hubris,* 396–98.

## 3. The Officer, the Mayor, and the Spy

1. *The investigation against Fritsch:* Klaus-Jürgen Müller, "Die Blomberg-Fritsch Krise, 1938: Elemente eines politisch-militärischen Skandals," in *Der politische Skandal,* ed. Julius H. Schoeps (Stuttgart: Burg, 1992), 129–30; Abschrift Huppenkothen, 11.7.1947, IfZ 0249-1, p. 4.
2. *A senior officer in the Amt Ausland/Abwehr:* Franz Xaver Sonderegger, to Freiherr von Siegler, to Dr. Helmut Krausnick, and to Dr. Hermann Mau, 14.10.1952, IfZ, ZS-303-1, p. 43, http://www.ifz-muenchen.de/archiv/zs/zs 0303_1.pdf.
3. *the "frail, multi-party state":* Hans A. Jacobsen, ed., *"Spiegelbild einer Verschwörung": Die Opposition gegen Hitler und der Staatsstreich vom 20. Juli 1944 in der SD-Berichterstattung: Geheime Dokumente aus dem ehemaligen Reichssicherheitshauptamt* (Stuttgart: Seewald, 1984), 1:302.
4. *"I feel responsible before God":* Terry Parssinen, *The Oster Conspiracy of 1938: The Unknown Story of the Military Plot to Kill Hitler and Avert World War II* (New York: HarperCollins, 2003), 7.

5. *"gang of brigands"*: Jacobsen, *"Spiegelbild einer Verschwörung,"* 1:451.

6. *In his first two years of service:* Heinz Höhne, *Canaris*, trans. J. Maxwell Brownjohn (London: Secker & Warburg, 1979), 260–63.

7. *Canaris ordered that nothing would be done:* Ibid., 303; see also Helmut Krausnick's interview with Franz Maria Liedig (date unknown), 1, 15–16, Harold C. Deutsch Papers, USAMHI, series 4, box 15, Liedig. For a much less flattering description, see General Halder's testimony: Halder an Deutsch, 23.10.1954, 2–3, Halder an Krausnick, 28.4.1955, 2(11), Deutsch Papers, series 3, box 2.

8. *"His appearance was as stiff"*: Walter Laqueur and Richard Breitman, *Breaking the Silence: The German Who Exposed the Final Solution* (Hanover, N.H.: University Press of New England for Brandeis University Press, 1994), 168.

9. *"A friend described him"*: Ibid., 169–70.

10. *he "went in formal dress"*: Peter Hoffmann, *Carl Goerdeler and the Jewish Question, 1933–1942* (Cambridge: Cambridge University Press, 2011), 42; letter to Gauleiter Mutschmann in the name of Bruno Basarke (author name unclear), 19.9.1933, BA, PK/A201, pp. 2724–27.

11. *Deputy Mayor Haacke's pressure:* Peter Hoffmann, "The Persecution of the Jews as a Motive for Resistance Against National-Socialism," in *The Moral Imperative: New Essays on the Ethics of Resistance in National Socialist Germany, 1933–1945*, ed. Andrew Chandler (Boulder, Colo.: Westview Press, 1998), 86.

12. *"[Goerdeler said that] the foremost German problem"*: Harold C. Deutsch, *The Conspiracy Against Hitler in the Twilight War* (Minneapolis: University of Minnesota Press, 1970), 11.

13. *Goerdeler's wife, "who is known"*: Wolf an Kunz, 7.12.1936, SAL, Kap 10 G Nr.685 Bd.1, 270R.

14. *"The Mendelssohn monument affair"*: Haacke an Mutschmann, 4.12.1936, SAL Kap 10 G Nr.685 Bd.1, 267R–268; Marianne Meyer-Krahmer, *Carl Goerdeler—Mut zum Widerstand: Eine Tochter erinnert sich* (Leipzig: Leipziger Universitätsverlag, 1998), 143–44.

15. *in order to "spare the lord mayor"*: Sabine Gillmann and Hans Mommsen, eds., *Politische Schriften und Briefe Carl Friedrich Goerdelers* (Munich: Saur, 2003), 2:1223.

16. *"Thus I decided without hesitation"*: Meyer-Krahmer, *Carl Goerdeler,* 144; Ines Reich, *Carl Friedrich Goerdeler: Ein Oberbürgermeister gegen den NS-Staat* (Cologne: Böhlau, 1997), 266–73; SAL Kap 10 G Nr.685 Bd.1, 263, 65.

17. *"an informal association of people"*: W. Lloyd Warner and Paul S. Lunt, *The Social Life of a Modern Community* (New Haven, Conn.: Yale University Press, 1941), 32, 110. For more discussion on the definition of a clique, see also John Scott, *Social Network Analysis: A Handbook* (London: SAGE, 2009), 20–21.

18. *"The recruitment of new members":* Jacobsen, *"Spiegelbild einer Verschwörung,"* 1:523.

19. *"an insurgency can more easily attach":* David Knoke, *Political Networks: The Structural Perspective* (Cambridge: Cambridge University Press, 1990), 68. Paul Staniland studies this phenomenon in detail in his new book, *Networks of Rebellion: Explaining Insurgent Cohesion and Collapse* (Ithaca, NY: Cornell University Press, 2014), p. 9.

20. *the SS and the Gestapo were not allowed:* Jacobsen, *"Spiegelbild einer Verschwörung,"* 1:525–7; Abschrift Huppenkothen, 11.7.1947, IfZ ZS 0249-1, p. 7. A study of the indictments in the various July 20, 1944, trials indicates that many of the accused neither participated in the conspiracy nor supported it; they were just acquainted with leading connectors of the conspiracy, such as Goerdeler or Leuschner, or belonged to the same social circles. Even if they disagreed politically with the conspirators, all of them were reluctant to turn over comrades to the authorities. For one example among many, see Anklageschrift gegen Richter, Lenz, Zitzewitz, and Korsch, 18.11.1944, Eberhard Zeller Papers, IfZ ED 88/3, pp. 371–90.

21. *Generally speaking, the club was an ideal venue:* Jacobsen, *"Spiegelbild einer Verschwörung,"* 1:117.

22. *Goerdeler and Oster were "salesmen":* Malcolm Gladwell, *The Tipping Point: How Little Things Can Make a Big Difference* (Boston: Back Bay Books, 2002), 30–89.

23. *In winter 1938, the network was mainly intended:* Helmut Krausnick's interview with Franz Maria Liedig (date unknown), 1, Deutsch Papers, series 4, box 15, Liedig; Jacobsen, *"Spiegelbild einer Verschwörung,"* 1:430.

24. *"Conspiracy and mutiny do not exist":* Nicholas Reynolds, *Treason Was No Crime: Ludwig Beck, Chief of the German General Staff* (London: Kimber, 1976), 135. Compare Salmuth an Krausnick, 7.8.1955, 1–2, Deutsch Papers, series 3, box 3, round 1 Material.

25. *Whatever the results of his trial might be:* Niederschrift der Unterredung zwischen Herrn Ministerialdirigent Dr. v. Etzdorf und Herrn Dr. H. Krausnick im Auftrage des Instituts für Zeitgeschichte München, durchgeführt am 26.9.1953 in Bonn, 6, Deutsch Papers, series 3, box 2, Material on Groscurth.

26. *Simultaneously with Brauchitsch's appointment:* Reynolds, *Treason Was No Crime*, 128; *Nuremberg Red* (3704-PS), 6:419–20.

27. *"obsequious to his seniors":* Constantine FitzGibbon, *The Shirt of Nessus* (London: Cassell, 1956), 25.

28. *Hitler used the opportunity:* Abschrift Huppenkothen, 11.7.1947, IfZ 0249-1, p. 8.

29. *The central actor in the cell:* Eckart Conze et al., *Das Amt und die Vergangenheit: Deutsche Diplomaten im Dritten Reich und in der Bundesrepublik* (Munich: Karl Blessing Verlag, 2010), 155, 296.

30. *Hassell, too, supported Hitler:* Gregor Schöllgen, *Ulrich von Hassell, 1881–1944: Ein Konservativer in der Opposition* (Munich: Beck, 1990), 89–90.

31. *Kleist . . . was an implacable enemy:* Ewald von Kleist-Schmenzin, "Selbsterlebte wichtige Begebenheiten aus den Jahren 1933 und 1934," Bodo Scheurig Papers, IfZ ZS/A 31-8, pp. 64–68.

32. *one of few members of the German National People's Party:* Schlabrendorff to Scheurig (interview, 19.9.1965), Scheurig Papers, IfZ ZS/A 31-8, http://www.ifz-muenchen.de/archiv/zsa/ZS_A_0031_08.pdf, pp. 11, 17; Ewald von Kleist-Schmenzin, "Adel und Preußentum," *Süddeutsche Monatshefte* 51 (August 23, 1926): 378–84.

33. *National Socialism . . . was bound to destroy Germany:* Wetzel to Scheurig, 29.4.1965, Scheurig Papers, IfZ ZS/A 31-8, http://www.ifz-muenchen.de/archiv/zsa/ZS_A_0031_08.pdf, p. 35; Ewald von Kleist-Schmenzin, *Der Nationalsozialismus: Eine Gefahr* (Berlin-Britz: Werdermann, 1932).

34. *Hitler and his followers were a new reincarnation:* Ewald von Kleist-Schmenzin, "Glaubt ihr nicht, so bleibt ihr nicht," in Bodo Scheurig, *Ewald von Kleist-Schmenzin: Ein Konservativer gegen Hitler* (Oldenburg: Stalling, 1968), 265 and also 140.

35. *Kleist's hatred of fellow conservatives:* Ibid., 132, 144; Ewald von Kleist-Schmenzin, "Selbsterlebte wichtige Begebenheiten aus den Jahren 1933 und 1934," Scheurig Papers, IfZ ZS/A 31-8, http://www.ifz-muenchen.de/archiv/zsa/ZS_A_0031_08.pdf, pp. 64–68; Fabian von Schlabrendorff, *The Secret War Against Hitler,* trans. Hilda Simon (Boulder, Colo.: Westview Press, 1994), 41–45. Between 1933 and 1944, Kleist was frequently arrested by the authorities. During one of his arrests, SA thugs tried to storm his castle in order to fly the swastika over it. They were blocked, however, by Kleist's loyal villagers, who barricaded themselves in the castle. In the end, the local party leader wisely decided to give up in order to avoid a scandal. On Kleist's ideology, see also Ekkehard Klause, "Ewald von Kleist-Schmenzin (1890–1945): Ein altpreußischer Konservativer im Widerstand gegen den Nationalsozialismus," *Forschungen zur Brandenburgischen und Preußischen Geschichte* 19, no. 2 (2009): 243–55.

36. *"Until our last breath":* Michael Balfour, *Withstanding Hitler in Germany, 1933–1945* (London: Routledge, 1988), 163.

37. *Hitler expressed his personal sympathy:* Ibid., 147; Abschrift Huppenkothen, 11.7.1947, IfZ 0249-1, p. 8.

38. *"Hitler is Germany's fate":* Ulrich von Hassell, *Die Hassell-Tagebücher, 1938–1944: Aufzeichnungen vom anderen Deutschland,* ed. Friedrich Freiherr Hiller von Gärtringen (Munich: Goldmann, 1994), 71; Salmuth an Krausnick, 7.8.1955, 2, Deutsch Papers, series 3, box 3, round 1 Material; Franz Halder, "Zu den Aussagen des Dr. Gisevius in Nürnberg 24. Bis 26.4.1946," BA-MA BAarch N/124/10, pp. 1–2. Fritsch repeated the same words to Halder. See

Halder's testimony, "Protokoll der öffentlichen Sitzung der Spruchkammer Muenchen X, BY 11/47, am 15.9.1948," p. 4(68).

## 4. "In the Darkest Colors": The Decision of General Beck

1.  *suffering from incessant feuds:* R. W. Seton-Watson, *A History of the Czechs and Slovaks* (Hamden, Conn.: Archon, 1965), 325.

2.  *The party chairman . . . summarized his agenda:* Johann W. Brügel, *Tschechen und Deutsche, 1918–1938* (Munich: Nymphenburger Verlagshandlung, 1967), 332.

3.  *"It is my [Hitler's] irrevocable decision":* Walther Hofer, ed., *Der Nationalsozialismus: Dokumente, 1933–1945* (Frankfurt am Main: Fischer Taschenbuch Verlag, 1957), 204.

4.  *Beck had praised the 1933 takeover:* Klaus-Jürgen Müller, *Generaloberst Ludwig Beck: Eine Biographie* (Paderborn: Schöningh, 2008), 100.

5.  *he felt like a military Cassandra:* Ludwig Beck, *Studien*, ed. Hans Speidel (Stuttgart: K. F. Koehler, 1955), 119; Nicholas Reynolds, *Treason Was No Crime: Ludwig Beck, Chief of the German General Staff* (London: Kimber, 1976), 148–59; Müller, *Generaloberst Ludwig Beck*, 319–21, 375–76.

6.  *Beck had expressed opposition to the invasion:* Reynolds, *Treason Was No Crime*, 99–100.

7.  *"The three nations share Europe":* Beck, *Studien*, 119; Klaus-Jürgen Müller, *Armee und Drittes Reich, 1933–1939: Darstellung und Dokumentation* (Paderborn: Schöningh, 1987), 73–82; Müller, *Generaloberst Ludwig Beck*, 332–33.

8.  *"although Czechoslovakia in its current boundaries":* Peter Hoffmann, *Widerstand, Staatsstreich, Attentat: Der Kampf der Opposition gegen Hitler* (Munich: Piper, 1985), 98–99; Wolfgang Foerster, *Ein General kämpft gegen den Krieg: Aus nachgelassenen Papieren des Generalstabchefs Ludwig Beck* (Munich: Münchener Dom-Verlag, 1949), 94.

9.  *For years Beck had been an advocate:* Müller, *Generaloberst Ludwig Beck*, 320, 322–23, 377.

10. *"Critical decisions about the future of the nation":* Foerster, *Ein General kämpft*, 103.

11. *"For the Führer":* Ibid., 106.

12. *Caught up in his idealism:* Müller, *Generaloberst Ludwig Beck*, 319–21; Franz Halder, "Zu den Aussagen des Dr. Gisevius in Nürnberg 24. Bis 26.4.1946," BA-MA BAarch N/124/10, p. 2; Halder, "Protokoll der öffentlichen Sitzung der Spruchkammer Muenchen X, BY 11/47, am 15.9.1948," BA-MA Msg 2/213, p. 5(69).

13. *"Brauchitsch [has] left me in the lurch":* Halder, "Zu den Aussagen," BA-MA BAarch N/124/10, p. 2; Reynolds, *Treason Was No Crime*, 168, 171, 181; Helmut Groscurth, *Tagebücher eines Abwehroffiziers, 1938–1940: Mit weiteren Dokumenten zur Militäropposition gegen Hitler*, ed. Helmut Krausnick and

Harold C. Deutsch (Stuttgart: Deutsche Verlags-Anstalt, 1970), 168; Müller, *Generaloberst Ludwig Beck*, 377, 386–87.

14. *Oster visited Beck again and again:* Reynolds, *Treason Was No Crime*, 181; Halder an H. von Witzleben, 6.9.1952, Deutsch Papers, series 4, box 9, General Opposition.

15. *It is uncertain whether Beck gave his consent:* Historians disagree over whether Beck was involved in the 1938 attempt at a coup and, if so, to what extent. Klaus-Jürgen Müller, Beck's newest biographer, believes that he was not involved (*Generaloberst Ludwig Beck*, 368). However, there is convincing evidence pointing in the other direction. Franz Halder, for one, told historian Helmut Krausnick that Beck was involved. It is hard to believe that Halder, who despised Beck, wanted to protect his posthumous reputation. See Halder an Krausnick, 1952, 3–4, Deutsch Papers, series 4, box 9, Plot to Assassinate Hitler.

## 5. The Bird and Its Cage:
## First Attempt at Coup d'État, September 1938

1. *"When I rang the doorbell":* Hans B. Gisevius, *To the Bitter End*, trans. Richard Winston and Clara Winston (New York: Da Capo Press, 1998), 288.

2. *"That madman, that criminal":* Ibid., 289; Klaus-Jürgen Müller, *Generaloberst Ludwig Beck: Eine Biographie* (Paderborn: Schöningh, 2008), 381–82. The animosity, it seems, was mutual. In his later testimony, Halder denied the mere existence of this meeting and admitted to having met Gisevius only once, on September 26. According to Halder, Schacht brought Gisevius to a meeting without asking his permission beforehand, and he (Halder) was "very angry" about it. See Halder an Krausnick, 28.4.1955, 2(10), Deutsch Papers, series 3, box 3, round 1; Franz Halder, "Zu den Aussagen des Dr. Gisevius in Nürnberg 24. Bis 26.4.1946," BA-MA BAarch N/124/10, p. 3.

3. *When Hitler ordered the army:* Erich Kordt, *Nicht aus der Akten* (Stuttgart: Union deutsche Verlagsgesellschaft, 1950), 244; Hans B. Gisevius, *Bis zum bittern Ende* (Zurich: Fretz & Wasmuth, 1946), 329.

4. *"no third side will be so reckless": Akten zur deutschen auswärtigen Politik, 1918–1945* (Baden-Baden: Impr. Nationale, 1950–95), 2:421.

5. *He promised his associates:* Gisevius, *Bis zum bittern Ende*, 339–40.

6. *Oster, though, was not content:* Erich Kordt, "Kommentar zu einer Erklärung von Lord Vansittart," 2–3, Deutsch Papers, series 3, box 3, round 1 Material.

7. *The first volunteer was Dr. Carl Goerdeler:* Gerhard Ritter, *Carl Goerdeler und die deutsche Widerstandsbewegung* (Stuttgart: Deutsche Verlags-Anstalt, 1954), 158–61.

8. *"The National Socialists were masters of propaganda":* Marianne Meyer-Krahmer, *Carl Goerdeler—Mut zum Widerstand: Eine Tochter erinnert sich* (Leipzig: Leipziger Universitatsverlag, 1998), 149.

9. *"Goerdeler impressed us all"*: Arthur P. Young, *X Documents* (London: Deutsch, 1974), 24.

10. *"X [Goerdeler] fears catastrophe"*: Ibid., 139. Goerdeler mentioned the Jewish question several times during his talks with Young, and even demanded that England stop all discussion about "crucial questions" with Germany as long as the persecution of the Jews was going on. See ibid., 59, 136, 139, 161, 177.

11. *"I showed the document"*: Chaim Weizmann, *Trial and Error: The Autobiography of Chaim Weizmann* (New York: Harper, 1949), 411.

12. *Goerdeler's mission ended in failure*: Andrea Mason, "Opponents of Hitler in Search of Foreign Support: The Foreign Contacts of Dr. Carl Goerdeler, Ludwig Beck, Ernst von Weizsäcker, and Adam von Trott zu Solz" (master's thesis, McGill University, 2002), 50–51, available at http://digitool.library. mcgill.ca/webclient/StreamGate?folder_id=0&dvs=1340873715337~113.

13. *The prime minister wanted above all*: For the debate on appeasement, see Andrew D. Stedman, *Alternatives to Appeasement: Neville Chamberlain and Hitler's Germany* (New York: Tauris, 2011), 232–47; Sidney Aster, "Guilty Men: The Case of Neville Chamberlain," in *Origins of the Second World War*, ed. Patrick Finney (New York: St. Martin's Press, 1997), 62–78. For a survey of the debate, see Mason, "Opponents of Hitler," 6–15.

14. *Alexander Cadogan . . . wrote in his diary*: *The Diaries of Sir Alexander Cadogan, O.M., 1938–1945*, ed. David Dilks (London: Cassell, 1971), 123–24, 128–29. For Goerdeler's view on the Sudeten question, see Sabine Gillmann and Hans Mommsen, *Politische Schriften und Briefe Carl Friedrich Goerdelers* (Munich: Saur, 2003), 2:1151, 1179–80.

15. *Kleist told the British explicitly*: "Notiz über ein Gespräch zwischen Sir R. Vansittart und Herrn von Kleist," C/8520/1941/18 (18.8.1938), Scheurig Papers, IfZ ZS-1 31-8, pp. 40–45.

16. *"I take it that von Kleist"*: "Note of Conversation at Chartwell Between Monsieur de K. and Mr. Winston Churchill," 19.8.1938, Sir Winston Churchill Papers, reel 534, CHAR 2/340 B, HULL; David Faber, *Appeasement and World War II* (New York: Simon & Schuster, 2008), 226.

17. *"The interview was a stormy one"*: Gisevius, *To the Bitter End*, 298.

18. *All three gave their full consent*: For Thomas's version of his own motives, see Georg Thomas, "20. Juli 1944," 20.7.1945, BA-MA Msg 2/213, pp. 4–6.

19. *In conversations with other officers*: Hans A. Jacobsen, ed., *"Spiegelbild einer Verschwörung": Die Opposition gegen Hitler und der Staatsstreich vom 20. Juli 1944 in der SD-Berichterstattung: Geheime Dokumente aus dem ehemaligen Reichssicherheitshauptamt* (Stuttgart: Seewald, 1984), 1:366.

20. *"Witzleben was a refreshingly uncomplicated man"*: Gisevius, *To the Bitter End*, 304.

21. *The real difference between Halder and Witzleben*: Peter Hoffmann, *Widerstand, Staatsstreich, Attentat: Der Kampf der Opposition gegen Hitler* (Munich: Piper, 1985), 118; Halder an Deutsch, 28.4.1952, 1, Deutsch Papers, series 3, box 2.

22. *Dr. Schacht, who would take it upon himself:* Based on Gisevius's version. Halder denied after the war that he ever proposed the Reich chancellorship to Schacht. See Franz Halder, "Zu den Aussagen," 24. Bis 26.4.1946," BA-MA BAarch N/124/10, p. 4.

23. *According to one version:* Heinrich Bücheler, *Generaloberst Erich Hoepner und die Militäropposition gegen Hitler* (Berlin: Landeszentrale für politische Bildungsarbeit, 1981), 9–10; Halder, "Protokoll der öffentlichen Sitzung der Spruchkammer München X, BY 11/47, am 15.9.1948," BA-MA Msg 2/213, p. 6(70); and compare with the version of Hoepner's son, who believed (perhaps erroneously) that his father's mission was to block SS reinforcements from Munich; see Joachim Hoepner to Peter Hoffmann, 3.4.1964, IfZ ZS-2121, p. 2, http://www.ifz-muenchen.de/archiv/zs/zs-2121.pdf.

24. *"My God, . . . he's given us everything!":* Hugh Ragsdale, *The Soviets, the Munich Crisis, and the Coming of World War II* (Cambridge: Cambridge University Press, 2004), 48–49.

25. *"A splinter of a nation":* Hermann Göring, *Reden und Aufsätze* (Munich: F. Eher Nachf, 1938), 387; Max Domarus, *Hitler: Reden und Proklamationen, 1932–1945: Kommentiert von einem deutschen Zeitgenossen* (Würzburg: Schmidt, Neustadt a.d. Aisch, 1962), 888–89.

26. *both train station and airport "were full of Jews":* William L. Shirer, *The Rise and Fall of the Third Reich: A History of Nazi Germany* (New York: Simon & Schuster, 1960), 1:383.

27. *"In view of the increasingly critical situation":* Keith Feiling, *The Life of Neville Chamberlain* (London: Macmillan, 1970), 363.

28. *the Führer kept his belligerent mood:* Ibid., 367; compare to the testimony of Paul Schmidt, Hitler's personal interpreter; see Paul Schmidt, *Statist auf diplomatischer Bühne, 1923–1945: Erlebnisse des Chefdolmetschers im Auswärtigen Amt mit den Staatsmännern Europas* (Bonn: Athenäum Verlag, 1949), 396–97; "2.Teil, Fortsetzung der Befragung Professor Deutsch von Botho von Wussow [und Gräfin Schwerin]" (undated), pp. 4–6, Deutsch Papers, series 3, box 3, round 1 Material.

29. *"The Führer told Chamberlain yesterday": Akten zur deutschen auswärtigen Politik*, 2:648; Horace Wilson, Report on Berchtesgaden, 17.9.1938, Papers of Neville Chamberlain, HULL, reel 45, NC8/26/2.

30. *"The putsch and the assassination":* Halder, "Protokoll," BA-MA Msg 2/213, p. 86(62); for similar complaints, see Halder, "Zu den Aussagen des Dr. Gisevius in Nürnberg 24. Bis 26.4.1946," BA-MA BAarch N/124/10, pp. 2, 4.

31. *Dohnanyi had a slightly different plan:* Halder an Deutsch, 23.10.1954, 3, Deutsch Papers, series 3, box 2; Franz Halder, "Zu den Aussagen des Dr. Gisevius in Nürnberg 24. Bis 26.4.1946," BA-MA BAarch N/124/10, p. 5.

32. *Its job was to arrest Hitler:* Susanne Meiml, *Nationalsozialisten gegen Hitler: Die nationalrevolutionäre Opposition um Friedrich Wilhelm Heinz* (Berlin: Siedler, 2000), 283–98. In Liedig's testimony on the shock troops, he is wrong in

dating them 1939, which is one year later. However, the fact that this scheme was born in 1938 becomes clear at p. 10 ("these plans took a systematic shape already in 1938"). See Hauptquartier, Streitkräfte der Vereinigten Staaten, Europäische Abteilung, Zentrum des militärischen Geheimdienstes APO 757, Sonderbericht seiner Vernehmung (CSIR) No. 6, Ereignisse des Monats Juli 1944, Franz Maria Liedig, 7, 10, Deutsch Papers, series 4, box 9, General Opposition.

33.  *only three people were privy to the plot:* Meiml, *Nationalsozialisten gegen Hitler,* 292–93.

34.  *"It was a disgusting day":* Unterhaltung mit Frau Ursula von Witzleben, 10.2.1970, 2, Deutsch Papers, series 3, box 3, round 1 Material.

35.  *he used to boast of his ties:* Ted Harrison, "'Alter Kämpfer' im Widerstand: Graf Helldorff, die NS-Bewegung, und die Opposition gegen Hitler," *Vierteljahrshefte für Zeitgeschichte* 45, no. 3 (July 1997): 385–423; SD report, 11.8.1944, GARF Fond R-9401, Opis 2, Del 97, p. 208. SS prosecutor Walther Huppenkothen, who was deeply involved in the investigations following July 20, 1944, related after the war that the conspirators planned to replace Helldorff with Tresckow because of the former's "bad reputation." See Abschrift Huppenkothen, IfZ ZS 0249-1, p. 51.

36.  *Now, he promised Oster:* There is an interesting eyewitness testimony on Schulenburg's involvement in the 1938 conspiracy. The witness, Countess Schwerin von Schwanenfeld, confirming her memories with her sister's diary, told Harold Deutsch that on September 17 (probably a mistake; it must have been a few days earlier, before the Berchtesgaden summit), she and her husband were traveling with the Schulenburgs in their car. When they passed a military convoy, Schulenburg told her, "Soon this army will liberate us from Hitler and all of his associates." Her testimony is supported by the unrelated account of Charlotte, Schulenburg's wife, also to Harold Deutsch; see "2.Teil, Fortsetzung der Befragung Professor Deutsch von Botho von Wussow [und Gräfin Schwerin]" (undated), pp. 3–4, Deutsch Papers, series 3, box 3, round 1 Material.

37.  *Arthur Nebe . . . was and remains an unsolved mystery:* After the war, some of the surviving conspirators, most prominently Gisevius, Gersdorff, and Schlabrendorff, opened a posthumous campaign to clear Nebe's name. They argued that Nebe helped them in the conspiracy against Hitler and also tried to do his best to mitigate the massacres in the east. Historical research has not been kind to these arguments. Indeed, they seem to be poorly supported. Schlabrendorff himself was cynically asked by the prosecutor in the government ministries trial at Nuremberg "how many millions of Jews" it was acceptable to kill if the "final goal is to overthrow Hitler." Not even one, answered Schlabrendorff, and the prosecutor rested his case. See *Nuremberg Green,* 13:402.

38. *Witzleben decided to send Gisevius:* Gisevius, *To the Bitter End*, 320.

39. *Oster met privately with Captain Heinz:* Hoffmann, *Widerstand, Staatsstreich, Attentat*, 121; Meiml, *Nationalsozialisten gegen Hitler*, 290-93; Terry Parssinen, *The Oster Conspiracy of 1938: The Unknown Story of the Military Plot to Kill Hitler and Avert World War II* (New York: HarperCollins, 2003), 132–35.

40. *"Hitler was in a highly nervous state":* Shirer, *Rise and Fall of the Third Reich*, 1:391.

41. *These were days of immense pressure:* "2.Teil, Fortsetzung der Befragung Professor Deutsch von Botho von Wussow, [und Gräfin von Schwerin]" (undated), pp. 6–7, Deutsch Papers, series 3, box 3, round 1 Material.

42. *"With the most profound regret":* Paul Schmidt, *Hitler's Interpreter*, ed. R. H. C. Steed (New York: Macmillan, 1951), 101.

43. *"The bird . . . has to come back to its cage":* Romedio G. Grav von Thun-Hohenstein, *Der Verschwörer: General Oster und die Militäropposition* (Berlin: Severin & Sielder, 1982), 113.

44. *Foreign Secretary Halifax had a serious conversation:* Halifax Papers, CAC, HLFX I/3/3.6, A4.410.3.7, p. 3; Cadogan, *Diaries*, 105–6.

45. *"so long as Nazism lasted":* Cabinet Papers, NA CAB 23/95, pp. 198–200.

46. *"The complete change of view":* Halifax Papers, CAC, HLFX I/3/3.6, A4.410.3.7, pp. 1–2. In the introduction to the relevant section of his papers, Halifax was not able to recall the exact date when the notes were exchanged, only that it was during the height of the Sudeten crisis. However, a comparison with the description of the same incident in the diary of Alexander Cadogan (see note 44), and the cabinet minutes of September 25 (see note 45), shows that 25.9.1938 is most probably the right date, as Parssinen argues (*Oster Conspiracy of 1938*, 146).

47. *Another surprising turn took place:* Halifax Papers, CAC, HLFX I/3/3.6, A4.410.3.7., p. 6; Cabinet Papers, NA, CAB/23/95, pp. 234–35.

48. *"if France, in fulfillment of her treaty obligations":* Schmidt, *Statist auf diplomatischer Bühne*, 409; for the agreed-upon text of Wilson's message, see Cabinet Papers, NA, CAB 23/95.

49. *"he would have liked best":* Gisevius, *To the Bitter End*, 324.

50. *"I had not been standing long":* William L. Shirer, *Berlin Diary: The Journal of a Foreign Correspondent, 1934–1941* (London: Hamilton, 1943), 27.9.1943, p. 119; compare with the versions of Gisevius (*To the Bitter End*, 324) and Ruth Andreas-Friedrich, who witnessed the parade: *Schauplatz Berlin: Ein deutsches Tagebuch* (Munich: Rheinsberg Verlag G. Lentz, 1962), 27.9.1943, pp. 5–6.

51. *"How horrible, fantastic, incredible it is":* Chamberlain Papers, HULL Roll 31, NC 4/5/24: 2, 6–7, 42:3.

52. *"The silence of predawn Berlin":* Parssinen, *Oster Conspiracy of 1938*, 161.

53. *Oster gave Gisevius the Führer's reply:* Gisevius, *To the Bitter End*, 325.

54. *"Gisevius, the time has come!":* Ibid.

55. *"I have something further to say"*: Feiling, *Life of Neville Chamberlain*, 374.
56. *Chamberlain probably continued to believe*: Chamberlain Papers, HULL, NC 4/5/40, 7–8.
57. *"We, the German Führer and Chancellor"*: Chamberlain Papers, HULL, NC 4/5/29, NC 4/5/30, 13.
58. *"We are in the presence of a disaster"*: Chamberlain Papers, HULL, NC 13-11-274-811; Winston S. Churchill, *Into Battle: Speeches by the Right Hon. Winston Churchill*, ed. Randolph S. Churchill (London: Cassell, 1941), 42–53.
59. *"We are abandoned"*: Robert Kee, *Munich: The Eleventh Hour* (London: Hamilton, 1988), 204.
60. *"Never, since 1933, . . . was there such a good chance"*: Erich Kordt, *Wahn und Wirklichkeit* (Stuttgart: Union deutsche Verlagsgesellschaft, 1947), 126.
61. *Now the heartbroken conspirators met*: Halder, "Protokoll der öffentlichen Sitzung der Spruchkammer München X, BY 11/47, am 15.9.1948," BA-MA Msg 2/213, p. 8(71).
62. *"I had already passed the order to Witzleben"*: *Nuremberg Green*, 12:1083.
63. *"It is clear from the chain of events"*: Hjalmar Schacht, Abrechnung mit Hitler, WC-TAU N4F SCHA.
64. *Gisevius and Oster had to quietly dissolve*: Gerhard Ringshausen, *Hans-Alexander von Voss: Generalstabsoffizier im Widerstand, 1907–1944* (Berlin: Lukas Verlag, 2008), 37–38.
65. *"The impossible had happened"*: Gisevius, *To the Bitter End*, 326.

## 6. Without a Network: The Lone Assassin

1. *Until the end of 1944*: Peter Steinbach and Johannes Tuchel, *Georg Elser: Der Hitler Attentäter* (Berlin: Be. Bra Wissenschaft, 2008), 108–27; Walter Uslepp (interview, 10.5.1964), Bürgerbräuattentat, IfZ ZS/A 17-4, http://www.ifz-muenchen.de/archiv/zsa/ZS_A_0017_04.pdf, pp. 42, 84, 86–89, 137. Elser lived in similar conditions at his second, and last, place of internment—the concentration camp of Dachau. There, too, he was held in strict isolation but given carpentry tools and his old zither. See Franz Lechner (interview, 5.12.1959), Bürgerbräuattentat, IfZ ZS/A 17-2, http://www.ifz-muenchen.de/archiv/zsa/ZS_A_0017_02.pdf, pp. 20–21.
2. *"He does not have a typically criminal face"*: *Völkischer Beobachter*, November 22, 1939. As Elser left hardly any writings, there is only one major primary source on his life and activities: his detailed Gestapo interrogation, which can be seen as an autobiography of sorts. This chapter is based mainly on this source, as well as on other documents and testimonies kept in IfZ, BA, and GEAH. For a published version of the interrogation, analysis, and juxtaposition, see Georg J. Elser, *Autobiographie eines Attentätters: Der Anschlag auf Hitler in Bürgerbräukeller, 1939*, ed. Lothar Gruchmann (Stuttgart: Deutsche Verlags-Anstalt, 1989), 22.

3. *Georg Elser was born in 1903:* Anton Egetemaier (interview, undated), Bürgerbräuattentat, IfZ ZS/A 17-1, http://www.ifz-muenchen.de/archiv/zsa/ZS_A_0017_01.pdf, p. 48.

4. *Georg was interested in little:* Ibid., pp. 51–52; Leonhard Elser (interrogation, undated), Friedrich Grupp (interview, undated), Elsa Votteler (interview, 28.7.1950), Bürgerbräuattentat, IfZ ZS/A 17-1, http://www.ifz-muenchen.de/archiv/zsa/ZS_A_0017_01.pdf, pp. 61–63, 102–6; Bürgerbräuattentat, IfZ ZS/A 17-3, http://www.ifz-muenchen.de/archiv/zsa/ZS_A_0017_03.pdf, p. 15. On Elser's time in Switzerland, see the replies of the Swiss police to the inquires of the Gestapo, 1.2.1940: BA, E 4320 (B) 1970/25 Bd 1–4, Dossier C.2.102, Ermittlungsbericht VI.

5. *Elser's family . . . came close to the brink:* Hilda Wetzel (interview, undated), Bürgerbräuattentat, IfZ ZS/A 17-3, http://www.ifz-muenchen.de/archiv/zsa/ZS_A_0017_03.pdf, p. 140.

6. *Elser related to his Gestapo interrogators:* Elser, *Autobiographie*, 80.

7. *"I believe that God made the world":* Ibid., 75–74, 79, 80.

8. *"I am convinced that the Munich Agreement will not hold":* Ibid., 81; compare with Otto Kessler (interrogation, 15.8.1950), Bürgerbräuattentat, IfZ ZS/A 17-1, www.ifz-muenchen.de/archiv/ed_0088.pdf, p. 141.

9. *"My hope was to prevent a bigger bloodshed":* Elser, *Autobiographie*, 75, 84.

10. *Elser was never "normal":* Leonhard Elser (interrogation, undated), Bürgerbräuattentat, IfZ ZS/A 17-1, http://www.ifz-muenchen.de/archiv/zsa/ZS_A_0017_01.pdf, p. 61–63.

11. *"So I decided to kill the leadership myself":* Elser, *Autobiographie*, 84–85.

12. *"Here in this gathering":* Peter Hoffmann, *Hitler's Personal Security* (London: Macmillan, 1979), 106–7. See also Resch to Hoch (18.1.1966), Schmitt to Hoch (29.3.1966), Bürgerbräuattentat, IfZ ZS/A 17-2, http://www.ifz-muenchen.de/archiv/zsa/ZS_A_0017_02.pdf, p. 147; ZS/A 17-3, http://www.ifz-muenchen.de/archiv/zsa/ZS_A_0017_03.pdf, p. 33.

13. *the two veterans responsible for the security inside:* Maria Strobl (interview, 15.10.1959), Bürgerbräuattentat, IfZ ZS/A 17-3, http://www.ifz-muenchen.de/archiv/zsa/ZS_A_0017_03.pdf, pp. 63–64.

14. *"I went from the entrance to the middle of the hall":* Elser, *Autobiographie*, 87.

15. *During the nights, he sneaked unnoticed:* Wilhelm Rauschenberger (interrogation, 9.8.1950), Bürgerbräuattentat, IfZ ZS/A 17-2, http://www.ifz-muenchen.de/archiv/zsa/ZS_A_0017_02.pdf, p. 135.

16. *Quickly, he found that the great hall could be reached:* Maria Strobl (interview, 15.10.1959), Bürgerbräuattentat, IfZ ZS/A 17-3, http://www.ifz-muenchen.de/archiv/zsa/ZS_A_0017_03.pdf, p. 64.

17. *he planned a highly sophisticated bomb:* Eugen Elser (interview, undated), Bürgerbräuattentat, IfZ ZS/A 17-1, http://www.ifz-muenchen.de/archiv/zsa/ZS_A_0017_01.pdf, p. 58.

18. *"From that moment, . . . I lived only for one purpose":* Elser, *Autobiographie*, 104;

Karoline Schmauder (interview, undated), Bürgerbräuattentat, IfZ ZS/A 17-3, http://www.ifz-muenchen.de/archiv/zsa/ZS_A_0017_03.pdf, p. 21.

19. *Again he rented an apartment close to the beer hall:* Ibid.; Rauschenberger (interrogation, 9.8.1950), Bürgerbräuattentat, IfZ ZS/A 17-2, http://www.ifz-muenchen.de/archiv/zsa/ZS_A_0017_02.pdf, p. 135.

20. *"When the hall was opened . . .":* Elser, *Autobiographie,* 126.

21. *Many of his generals deemed the plan:* See chapter 8.

22. *"During my short stay at Stuttgart":* Elser, *Autobiographie,* 38; compare with Karl's version: Karl Hirth (interview, 5.8.1950), Bürgerbräuattentat, IfZ ZS/A 17-1, www.ifz-muenchen.de/archiv/ed_0088.pdf, p. 111.

23. *"Immediately upon my arrival at the hall":* Elser, *Autobiographie,* 152.

24. *"The lies of that time [1914] are identical":* Max Domarus, *Hitler: Reden und Proklamationen, 1932–1945: Kommentiert von einem deutschen Zeitgenossen* (Würzburg: Schmidt, Neustadt a.d. Aisch, 1962), 1406.

25. *This time chance betrayed him:* Hoffmann, *Hitler's Personal Security,* 107–8; Steinbach and Tuchel, *Georg Elser,* 74–75.

26. *The pillar exploded:* Steinbach and Tuchel, *Georg Elser,* 76–77; Maria Strobl (interview, 15.10.1959), Bürgerbräuattentat, IfZ ZS/A 17-3, http://www.ifz-muenchen.de/archiv/zsa/ZS_A_0017_03.pdf, pp. 67–68; Elser, *Autobiographie,* 8–9. Quote taken from an anonymous eyewitness account, translated by the British Foreign Office, "The Black Night of Munich," Der Bund No.532, 14.11.1939, NA, FO 371/23012, p. 112.

27. *"I stopped right away":* Elser, *Autobiographie,* 154; compare with the version of the guards: Xaver Rieger (interrogation, 23.10.1950), Bürgerbräuattentat, IfZ ZS/A 17-2, http://www.ifz-muenchen.de/archiv/zsa/ZS_A_0017_02.pdf, pp. 146–49.

28. *The policemen searched him:* See the official reports on Elser's arrest: Xaver Rieger and Othmar Zipperer "Schilderung des Aufgriffs des Georg Elser," 15.12.1939, Bürgerbräuattentat, IfZ ZS/A 17-5, http://www.ifz-muenchen.de/archiv/zsa/ZS_A_0017_05.pdf, pp. 29–33; compare with Otto Grethe (interview, 30.4.1964), Bürgerbräuattentat, IfZ ZS/A 17-1, http://www.ifz-muenchen.de/archiv/ed_0017_01.pdf, pp. 92–100; Karl Metzen an den Generalstaatsanwalt bei dem Oberlandesgericht München, 16.10.1956, Bürgerbräuattentat, IfZ ZS/A 17-2, http://www.ifz-muenchen.de/archiv/zsa/ZS_A_0017_02.pdf, pp. 77–80.

29. *Göring and his other close associates congratulated him:* Joseph Goebbels, *Tagebücher, 1924–1945,* ed. Ralf Georg Reuth, 2nd ed. (Munich: Piper, 1992), entry 9.11.1939, 3:1346–47.

30. *This true statement was accepted by Nebe:* Paul Bässler (interview, 18.8.1950), Bürgerbräuattentat, IfZ, http://www.ifz-muenchen.de/archiv/zsa/ZS_A_0017_01.pdf, p. 12; Steinbach and Tuchel, *Georg Elser,* 96.

31. *two British intelligence operatives were kidnapped:* Abschrift Huppenkothen, 11.7.1947, IfZ ZS 0249-1, p. 17; BA, E 4320 (B) 1970/25 Bd 1–4, Dossier C.2.102, available also online in GEAH, http://www.georg-elser-arbe itskreis.de/texts/schweiz.htm; Wilhelm Rauschenberger (interrogation, 9.8.1950), Bürgerbräuattentat, IfZ ZS/A 17-2, http://www.ifz-muenchen.de/ archiv/zsa/ZS_A_0017_02.pdf, p. 135.

32. *When the Gestapo officials confronted him with his mother:* Maria Elser (interrogation, 19.6.1950), Karl Hirth (interview, 5.8.1950), Bürgerbräuattentat, IfZ ZS/A 17-1, http://www.ifz-muenchen.de/archiv/zsa/ZS_A_0017_01.pdf, pp. 80, 112; Elser, *Autobiographie*, 75, 119.

33. *"I wanted to kill the leadership":* Elser, *Autobiographie*, 23, 156–57.

34. *He enjoyed relatively good conditions in return:* For photographs of the reconstructed bomb, see Bürgerbräuattentat, IfZ ZS/A 17-5, http://www .ifz-muenchen.de/archiv/zsa/ZS_A_0017_05.pdf, pp. 6–15; Steinbach and Tuchel, *Georg Elser*, pp. 70–71, 108–9.

35. *"I do not regret what I did":* For a moving testimony on Elser's last days, see Lechner (interview), Bürgerbräuattentat, IfZ ZS/A 17-2, http://www.ifz -muenchen.de/archiv/zsa/ZS_A_0017_02.pdf, pp. 26, 39–40 (the quote is taken from p. 26).

## 7. The Point of No Return: Pogrom and War

1. *Among them were the Grynszpans:* Martin Gilbert, *Kristallnacht: Prelude to Destruction* (London: HarperPress, 2006), 23–25.

2. *Goebbels gave a speech of incitement:* Leni Yahil, *The Holocaust: The Fate of European Jewry* (New York: Oxford University Press, 1990), 110.

3. *"A pogrom that burgeoned into a mass frenzy":* Ibid., 111.

4. *For the first time, Jews were incarcerated: Nuremberg Blue* (USA-261, 1816-PS), 28:499–540.

5. *Others were deeply disappointed:* General Halder confessed after the war that the high command was completely indifferent to the pogrom and its consequences. This, probably, was also true of his own attitude. See Halder to Krausnick, 28.4.1955, 3/11, Deutsch Papers, series 3, box 3, round 1.

6. *Hitler . . . was "beyond redemption":* Arthur P. Young, *X Documents* (London: Deutsch, 1974), 153.

7. *"We loved Germany":* Gerhard Ritter, *Carl Goerdeler und die deutsche Widerstandsbewegung* (Stuttgart: Deutsche Verlags-Anstalt, 1954), 200–201; compare with Sabine Gillmann and Hans Mommsen, *Politische Schriften und Briefe Carl Friedrich Goerdelers* (Munich: Saur, 2003), 2:819–20.

8. *Prof. Johannes Popitz, for example:* Hans A. Jacobsen, ed., *"Spiegelbild einer Verschwörung": Die Opposition gegen Hitler und der Staatsstreich vom 20. Juli*

*1944 in der SD-Berichterstattung: Geheime Dokumente aus dem ehemaligen Reichssicherheitshauptamt* (Stuttgart: Seewald, 1984), 1:449.

9. *"Germany is controlled by 10,000 of its worst elements"*: Young, *X Documents*, 152–53, 158–61.

10. *the "persecution of the Jews will continue"*: Ibid., 153.

11. *"I write under the gloomy impression"*: Ulrich von Hassell, *Die Hassell-Tagebücher, 1938–1944: Aufzeichnungen vom anderen Deutschland*, ed. Friedrich Freiherr Hiller von Gärtringen (Munich: Goldmann, 1994), 62. Beck's response was very similar. See Klaus-Jürgen Müller, *Generaloberst Ludwig Beck: Eine Biographie* (Paderborn: F. Schöningh, 2008), 375–76.

12. *"A small bureaucrat"*: Albert Krebs, *Fritz-Dietlof Graf von der Schulenburg: Zwischen Staatsraison und Hochverrat* (Hamburg: Leibniz-Verlag, 1964), 172–73.

13. *Luck did not favor the conspirators:* Peter Hoffmann, *Widerstand, Staatsstreich, Attentat: Der Kampf der Opposition gegen Hitler* (Munich: Piper, 1985), 132.

14. *"The provinces of Bohemia and Moravia"*: Max Domarus, *Hitler: Reden und Proklamationen, 1932–1945: Kommentiert von einem deutschen Zeitgenossen* (Würzburg: Schmidt, Neustadt a.d. Aisch, 1962), 1908.

15. *Foreign Minister Halifax, already skeptical about appeasement:* John Charmley, *Churchill, the End of Glory: A Political Biography* (New York: Harcourt Brace, 1993), 360.

16. *"In the event of any action"*: E. L. Woodward and Rohan Butler, eds., *Documents on British Foreign Policy, 1919–1939*, 3rd ser. (London: Oxford University Press, 1949), 4:553.

17. *His own private notes reveal the distress:* Chamberlain Papers, HULL, NC 4/5/29, NC 4/5/30, 1.

18. *the British were rearming:* For data on British rearmament, see Mark Thomas, "Rearmament and Economic Recovery in the Late 1930s," *Economic History Review*, n.s., 36, no. 4 (November 1983): 554–55. For more general discussion, see Andrea Mason, "Opponents of Hitler in Search of Foreign Support: The Foreign Contacts of Dr. Carl Goerdeler, Ludwig Beck, Ernst von Weizsäcker, and Adam von Trott zu Solz" (master's thesis, McGill University, 2002), 9–15.

19. *General Beck was following events by radio:* Nicholas Reynolds, *Treason Was No Crime: Ludwig Beck, Chief of the German General Staff* (London: Kimber, 1976), 181–82. For Goerdeler's view, see Gillmann and Mommsen, *Goerdelers*, 2:1176–78.

20. *The new recruit was the anti-Nazi jurist:* Abschrift Huppenkothen, IfZ ZS 0249-1, p. 24.

21. *he in fact devoted all his time to underground activity:* Marikje Smid, *Hans von Dohnanyi, Christine Bonhoeffer: Eine Ehe im Widerstand gegen Hitler* (Gütersloh: Gütersloher Verlagshaus, 2002), 145–46; Hoffmann, *Widerstand, Staats-*

*streich, Attentat,* 159; Abschrift der Aufzeichnungen von Frau Christine v. Dohnanyi geb. Bonhoeffer (post war, undated), 1, Deutsch Papers, series 3, box 3, round 1 Material.

22. *A triumph for Hitler . . . was for him intolerable:* Harold C. Deutsch, *The Conspiracy Against Hitler in the Twilight War* (Minneapolis: University of Minnesota Press, 1970), 82–84; Hoffmann, *Widerstand, Staatsstreich, Attentat,* 165–67; Etzdorf an Deutsch, 14.11.1947, Deutsch Papers, series 3, box 2.

23. *"Dr. Müller, you are now in the central headquarters":* Helmut Krausnick's inverview with Josef Müller, 1958, 5–6, Deutsch Papers, series 3, box 1, Müller interviews.

24. *Accordingly, he told Goerdeler, active support:* Hoffmann, *Widerstand, Staatsstreich, Attentat,* 132–33.

25. *the tortures he endured gave him the ability:* Dorothea Beck, *Julius Leber: Sozialdemokrat zwischen Reform und Widerstand* (Berlin: Siedler, 1983), 155, 161.

26. *In 1939, there were no concrete plans: Nuremberg Blue,* 12:548–49; *Nuremberg Green,* 12:1087–88.

27. *The best the emissaries could get:* Harold C. Deutsch's interview with Josef Müller, 1958, 8–10, Deutsch Papers, series 3, box 1, Müller interviews; Hedva Ben Israel, "Matarot Mitstalvot: Ha-Teguvot Ha-Beritiyot La-Hitnagdut Ha-Anti-Nazit be-Germania," in *Ha-Hitnagdut La-Nazism,* ed. Moshe Zimmermann (Jerusalem: Koebner Institute for German History, 1984), 66–76.

28. *no one would agree to revolt:* On April 12, 1939, Halder had approached the American envoy in Berlin and told him that the "German army dreaded a European war, but would march if ordered to do so by Herr Hitler." See NA, FO 371/22969, p. 89.

29. *"That is the end of Germany":* Hans B. Gisevius, *Bis zum bittern Ende* (Zurich: Fretz & Wasmuth, 1946), 139; *Nuremberg Blue,* 2:445, 3:25.

30. *The resistance of the Polish army:* Christopher Browning, *Origins of the Final Solution: The Evolution of Nazi Jewish Policy, September 1939–March 1942* (Jerusalem: Yad Vashem Press; Lincoln: University of Nebraska Press, 2004), 15–25; compare with the description of the Einsatzgruppen's evolution and their role in Abschrift Huppenkothen, 11.7.1947, IfZ 0249-1, pp. 4–7. This account is detailed but apologetic (for the SS), and has to be read with extreme caution.

31. *"Unless the German Government are prepared":* Woodward and Butler, *Documents on British Foreign Policy,* 7:488.

32. *General Beck . . . was expecting the worst:* Reynolds, *Treason Was No Crime,* 181–82.

33. *"I have accordingly the honor to inform you":* Woodward and Butler, *Documents on British Foreign Policy,* 7:535.

## 8. The Spirit of Zossen: When Networks Fail

1. *they were completely unprepared:* See Goerdeler's message to a British emissary (Dr. Shairer), 28.8.1939, NA, FO/37122981, pp. 155–59.

2. *to "demonstrate the military might":* Fabian von Schlabrendorff, *The Secret War Against Hitler,* trans. Hilda Simon (Boulder, Colo.: Westview Press, 1994), 105; Kunrat Freiherr von Hammerstein, *Spähtrupp* (Stuttgart: Govert, 1963), 79–80.

3. *"it became my job to inform the British":* Schlabrendorff, *Secret War Against Hitler,* 106.

4. *"most uncomfortable moments":* Ibid. On September 2, an informant in the General Staff suggested to the British military attaché, in veiled language, that an imminent overthrow of the regime was possible (NA, FO 371/22981, p. 56). Yet I was unable to find direct references to Hammerstein's plot, or to the conversation between Schlabrendorff and Forbes, either in Forbes's private papers (located at Aberdeen University) or in NA. Forbes, probably, did not find time or reason to report it during the hectic days after the outbreak of the war. It is clear, though, that he did not take the German opposition seriously, and he stressed that believing in a military coup d'état was a "dangerous fallacy. If and when Herr Hitler decides that a war with Britain is necessary, the Germans, extremists and moderates, will with their characteristic discipline follow him to a man, and any would-be opposition will be promptly and ruthlessly dealt with by the SS. It will be a long time and only after much reciprocal destruction that opposition will show its head with effect." Still, rumors of an anti-Nazi military underground reached the British Foreign Office, through other quarters, on September 9 and 27. See Forbes to Viscount Halifax, 3.1.1939, NA, FO 371/22960, pp. 230–31. For the other sources of information mentioned here, see pp. 151, 162–63.

5. *"These people turn me . . . into an anti-militarist":* Rudolf Pechel, *Deutscher Widerstand* (Zurich: Rentsch, 1947), 154; Ulrich von Hassell, *Die Tagebücher, 1938–1944: Aufzeichnungen vom anderen Deutschland,* ed. Friedrich Freiherr Hiller von Gärtringen (Munich: Goldmann, 1994), 68; Peter Hoffmann, *The History of the German Resistance, 1933–1945,* trans. Richard Barry (Montreal: McGill-Queens University Press, 1985), 113.

6. *"Uprooting whole generations . . . could be done":* Helmuth Stieff, Brief HQ/u, 21.11.1939, *Vierteljahrshefte für Zeitgeschichte* (July 1954), 300. For similar remarks of Stieff about the Holocaust, see his letters quoted in Scheurig Papers, IfZ ZS/A 0031-3, http://www.ifz-muenchen.de/archiv/zsa/ZS_A_0031_03 .pdf, p. 119.

7. *"The army is hungry for pillage":* Hermann Kaiser, *Mut zum Bekenntnis: Die geheimen Tagebücher des Hauptmanns Hermann Kaiser, 1941, 1943,* ed. Peter M. Kaiser (Berlin: Lukas Verlag, 2010), 29.5.1941, 203–4.

8. *"These acts will be stopped only through shooting":* Based on an interview with

Axel von dem Bussche, 7.3.1947, in Detlef Graf von Schwerin, *Dann sind's die besten Köpfe, die man henkt: Die junge Generation im deutschen Widerstand* (Munich: Piper, 1991). Bussche gave similar testimony in a lecture delivered three weeks beforehand. See Axel von dem Bussche, "Eid und Schuld," in *Axel von dem Bussche*, ed. Gevinon von Medem (Mainz: Hase & Koehler, 1994), 137.

9. *"not to burden them with details"*: Peter Hoffmann, *Widerstand, Staatsstreich, Attentat: Der Kampf der Opposition gegen Hitler* (Munich: Piper, 1985), 194; Klaus-Jürgen Müller, *Generaloberst Ludwig Beck: Eine Biographie* (Paderborn: F. Schöningh, 2008), 377; Aufzeichnungen von Frau Inga Haag, Frankfurt A.M, 4.4.1948, 1, Halder an Krausnick, 1952, 3, Deutsch Papers, series 3, box 2, Material on Groscurth, series 4, box 9, Plot to Assassinate Hitler.

10. *"There is just no point"*: Aktenvermerk über die Besprechung im Führerzug am 12.9.1939 in Illnau. 14.9.1939, NARA, Rg. 238/3047-PS (US-80); Helmut Krausnick and Hans H. Wilhelm, *Die Truppe des Weltanschauungskrieges: Die Einsatzgruppen der Sicherheitpolizei und des S.D.* (Stuttgart: Deutsche Verlags-Anstalt, 1981), 64; Hassell, *Tagebücher*, 147.

11. *"If, in the near future"*: Max Domarus, *Hitler: Reden und Proklamationen, 1932–1945: Kommentiert von einem deutschen Zeitgenossen* (Würzburg: Schmidt, Neustadt a.d. Aisch, 1962), 1394.

12. *Most generals in the high command:* Ankara Embassy to Viscount Halifax, 30.11.1939, NA, FO 371/23014, p. 149, as well as FO 371/23012, pp. 208–10; Harold C. Deutsch, *The Conspiracy Against Hitler in the Twilight War* (Minneapolis: University of Minnesota Press, 1970), 72–75, 210.

13. *General Halder gave his final okay:* Halder, "Protokoll der öffentlichen Sitzung der Spruchkammer München X, BY 11/47, am 15.9.1948," BA-MA Msg 2/213, p.55(31); Hoffmann, *Widerstand, Staatsstreich, Attentat*, 173.

14. *Erich Kordt was even ready to assassinate Hitler:* Deutsch, *Conspiracy Against Hitler*, 224; Hoffmann, *Widerstand, Staatsstreich, Attentat*, 176–77; Erwin Lahousen, "Zur Vorgeschichte des Anschlages vom 20. Juli 1944," 2, Deutsch Papers, series 4, box 9, Halder Franz. Again, rumors reached the British on November 10, this time through Greek diplomats. See NA, FO 371/23012, p. 33.

15. *When Thomas tried to brief him:* Georg Thomas, "20. Juli 1944," BA-MA Msg 2/213, p. 8.

16. *The conspirators believed they had reasons to be optimistic:* Deutsch, *Conspiracy Against Hitler*, 226–27.

17. *In his fury, Hitler said that he was well familiar:* Ibid., 228; Hoffmann, *Widerstand, Staatsstreich, Attentat*, 177; Halder an Deutsch, 28.4.1952, 3, Deutsch Papers, series 3, box 2; Halder, "Protokoll," BA-MA Msg 2/213, p. 41(17).

18. *"It is not possible to avert the western offensive"*: Hoffmann, *Widerstand, Staats-*

*streich, Attentat,* 178; Helmut Groscurth, *Tagebücher eines Abwehroffiziers, 1938–1940: Mit weiteren Dokumenten zur Militäropposition gegen Hitler,* ed. Helmut Krausnick and Harold C. Deutsch (Stuttgart: Deutsche Verlags-Anstalt, 1970), 225; Frau Inga Haag an Deutsch (date unknown), Aufzeichnungen von Frau Inga Haag, Frankfurt A.M, 4.4.1948, 2, Deutsch Papers, series 3, box 2, Material on Groscurth.

19. *"The baleful character of the regime":* Hassell, *Tagebücher,* 16.6.1940, 167.

20. *Beck was reluctant:* Müller, *Generaloberst Ludwig Beck,* 407–8.

21. *an "exercise in name calling":* Nicholas Reynolds, *Treason Was No Crime: Ludwig Beck, Chief of the German General Staff* (London: Kimber, 1976), 198. Halder, it seems, was unforgiving even after the war. In his later testimonies, he portrayed Beck and Goerdeler as having lost touch with reality. Never had they understood, he wrote time and again, the practical difficulties of staging a coup d'état. In a letter sent on September 6, 1952, Halder even called Beck "an utter fool" (*reiner Tor*). See Halder an Deutsch, 23.10.1954, 2–3, Abschrift Aussage Huppenkothen Der 20. Juli 1944, 6, Halder an Krausnick, 1952, 3–4, Halder an H. von Witzleben, 6.9.1952, 2, Deutsch Papers, series 4, box 9, General Opposition, series 3, box 2, Material on Halder, Huppenkothen, series 4, box 9, Plot to Assassinate Hitler; Franz Halder, "Zu den Aussagen des Dr. Gisevius in Nürnberg 24. Bis 26.4.1946," BA-MA BAarch N/124/10, p. 1.

22. *Beck and Halder parted on the "worst of terms":* Reynolds, *Treason Was No Crime,* 198; Müller, *Generaloberst Ludwig Beck,* 407–10.

23. *The last chance appeared to have gone:* Eidesstattliche Erklärung Erwin Lahousen, 1.7.1947, 1, Deutsch Papers, series 3, box 2, round 2 (revision); Georg Thomas, "20. Juli 1944," 20.7.1945, BA-MA Msg 2/213, p. 5.

24. *After a few meetings, an interview:* Summary of Events, 18.11.1939, NA, FO 371/23107, pp. 25–28. Also available in GEAH, http://www.georg -elser-arbeitskreis.de/texts/venloakte.htm; *Nuremberg Green,* 12:1178–79.

25. *Now, the British were ever more careful:* Cable to Bland, 30.11.1939, NA, FO 371/23013 (C19889), pp. 97–98. Even Goerdeler, who kept cordial ties with many members of the British elite until the outbreak of the war (see, for example, Arthur P. Young, *X Documents* [London: Deutsch, 1974], 148–49), was disregarded. "It is not intended to make any use of this man," advised the Foreign Office in May 1941. See NA, HS9/593/6; and also FO 371/23107, pp. 29–31; and Situation in Germany, October 1939, 16.11.1939, Chamberlain Papers, HULL, reel 45, NC8/29/1, 3.

26. *More and more conspirators accepted Oster's opinion:* Allen W. Dulles (OSS Bern) to OSS director William J. Donovan, 20.7.1944, in *American Intelligence and the German Resistance to Hitler,* ed. Jürgen Heideking and Christof Mauch (Boulder, Colo.: Westview Press, 1996), 233; Klaus-Jürgen Müller, "Über den 'militärischen Widerstand,'" in *Widerstand gegen den Nationalsozialismus,* ed. Peter Steinbach and Johannes Tuchel (Berlin: Akademie

Verlag, 1994), 277; Gotthard von Falkenhausen, "Bericht über Vorgänge in Paris am 20 Juli" (undated), Zeller Papers, IfZ ED 88/1, pp. 45–47.

27. *"One may say I am a traitor to my country"*: Helmut Krausnick's interview with Franz Maria Liedig (date unknown), 5, Deutsch Papers, series 4, box 15, Liedig. English translation taken from Deutsch, *Conspiracy Against Hitler*, 99–100. There is also a basis to assume that Oster, probably through Goerdeler, tipped off the British about the impending Nazi-Soviet pact. Sir Robert Vansittart, who was in constant touch with Goerdeler and other resistance fighters, sent an urgent dispatch on May 18, 1939, to this effect, clearly specifying that the "reliable source" for his information was the "German General Staff." See NA, FO 371/22972, pp. 145–47.

28. *Both the Dutch and the Belgians refused to believe:* Deutsch, *Conspiracy Against Hitler*, 94–98.

29. *"I have seen the man"*: Reynolds, *Treason Was No Crime*, 207–8.

30. *His eyes were wet with tears:* Hassel, *Tagebücher*, 127.

## 9. Signs in the Darkness: Rebuilding the Conspiracy

1. *"The last time we met, Hans"*: Dorothy Thompson, *Listen, Hans* (Boston: Houghton Mifflin, 1942), 137–38.

2. *Some of them were even bribed:* Norman J. W. Goda, "Black Marks: Hitler's Bribery of His Senior Officers During World War II," *Journal of Modern History* 72, no. 2 (June 2000): 413–52.

3. *"No one can deny the magnitude"*: Ulrich von Hassell, *Die Hassell-Tagebücher, 1938–1944: Aufzeichnungen vom anderen Deutschland*, ed. Friedrich Freiherr Hiller von Gärtringen (Munich: Goldmann, 1994), 199.

4. *"In October 1941, an old friend of mine"*: Beria to Stalin, 19.9.1944, GARF Fond R-9401, Opis 2, Del 66, pp. 297–98.

5. *"Discussing practical issues about the organization"*: Ibid., p. 319.

## 10. On the Wings of Thought: Networks of Imagination

1. *The first proposal for an "alternative governmental structure"*: For the full document, see Ulrich von Hassell, *Die Hassell-Tagebücher, 1938–1944: Aufzeichnungen vom anderen Deutschland*, ed. Friedrich Freiherr Hiller von Gärtringen (Munich: Goldmann, 1994), 305–8. For Hassell's view of foreign policy, see p. 105, as well as his important memorandum "Germany Between West and East" ("Deutschland zwischen West und Ost"), in Gregor Schöllgen, *Ulrich von Hassell, 1881–1944: Ein Konservativer in der Opposition* (Munich: Beck, 1990), 207–18. For analysis, see Schöllgen, 138–54, and Peter Hoffmann, *Widerstand, Staatsstreich, Attentat: Der Kampf der Opposition gegen Hitler* (Munich: Piper, 1985), 233–39, 261–63. A similar, though more moderate, plan had been drafted in 1939 by Beck and Groscurth. According to

this plan, the future of Austria and the Sudetenland would be decided by a referendum. See Aufzeichnungen von Frau Inga Haag, Frankfurt A.M, 4.4.1948, 2, Deutsch Papers, series 3, box 2, Material on Groscurth.

2. *Goerdeler's vision was liberal:* The full document is reproduced in Wilhelm R. von Schramm, *Beck und Goerdeler: Gemeinschaftsdokumente für den Frieden, 1941–1944* (Munich: Müller, 1965). For analysis, see Hoffmann, *Widerstand, Staatsstreich, Attentat*, 239–46; Hans Mommsen, *Alternative zu Hitler: Studien zur Geschichte des deutschen Widerstandes* (Munich: Beck, 2000), 159–207; and Marianne Meyer-Krahmer, *Carl Goerdeler—Mut zum Widerstand: Eine Tochter erinnert sich* (Leipzig: Leipziger Universitatsverlag, 1998), 222–23. For the tension between divine and earthly authorities, see Sabine Gillmann and Hans Mommsen, *Politische Schriften und Briefe Carl Friedrich Goerdelers* (Munich: Saur, 2003), 2:1226; and for Goerdeler's criticism on German ultranationalism, see 2:1178.

3. *Some scholars have argued that there was no real difference:* Klemens von Klemperer has skillfully criticized these radical views, while contending with the question of the perceived similarity with National Socialist ideas. See Klemens von Klemperer, "Der deutsche Widerstand gegen den Nationalsozialismus im Lichte der konservativen Tradition," in *Demokratie und Diktatur: Geist und Gestalt politischer Herrschaft in Deutschland und Europa; Festschrift für Karl Dietrich Bracher*, ed. Manfred Funke (Düsseldorf: Droste, 1987), 277.

4. *Almost all conspirators . . . agreed to liberate:* Hans A. Jacobsen, ed., *"Spiegelbild einer Verschwörung": Die Opposition gegen Hitler und der Staatsstreich vom 20. Juli 1944 in der SD-Berichterstattung: Geheime Dokumente aus dem ehemaligen Reichssicherheitshauptamt* (Stuttgart: Seewald, 1984), 1:66–67, 140–42, 147–56, 199–203.

5. *all laws enacted by the National Socialist Party:* Hassell, "Programm für erste Maßnahmen bei einem Umsturz," in Hassell, *Die Hassell-Tagebücher*, 454.

6. *"On January 19 and 27 [1942]":* Gillmann and Mommsen, *Goerdelers*, 2:846–47; "Der Weg," in Schramm, *Beck und Goerdeler*, 217. The emphasis is Goerdeler's.

7. *in the prewar years even the Third Reich:* The exception was Polish and Romanian Jews, as their respective countries showed little interest in protecting their Jewish citizens abroad. See Fritz Kieffer, "Carl Friedrich Goerdelers Vorschlag zur Gründung eines jüdischen Staates," *Zeitschrift der Savigny-Stiftung für Rechtsgeschichte* 125 (2008): 487–88.

8. *Goerdeler never called for the expulsion of Jews:* Gillmann and Mommsen, *Goerdelers*, 2:895–97; "Das Ziel," in Schramm, *Beck und Goerdeler,* 105–7. For Christoph Dipper's arguments, see "Der Widerstand und die Juden," in *Der Widerstand gegen den Nationalsozialismus: Die deutsche Gesellschaft und der Widerstand gegen Hitler*, ed. Jürgen Schmädecke and Peter Steinbach (Munich: Piper, 1985), 598–616. For critical research refuting Dipper, see Kief-

fer, "Carl Friedrich Goerdelers Vorschlag," 474–500. For further evidence on the regime's hesitancy to persecute Jews with foreign passports, even in the wake of Kristallnacht, see *Nuremberg Blue* (USA-261, PS-1816), 27:507, 521–23; as well as NA, T 188/226, pp. 133–60. Another important question is the correct timing of "Das Ziel" (The Goal). The study of Sabine Gillmann and Hans Mommsen, the most up-to-date and in-depth study written so far, dates it from December 1941 to January 1942 (*Goerdelers*, 2:873). This is also a key to contextualizing Goerdeler's Jewish clause. His proposal to establish a Jewish state was written as a reaction to the Nazi plan to exterminate European Jewry. For the debate about dating, see Kieffer, "Carl Friedrich Goerdelers," 475–76.

9. *"The vegetable fields and fruit orchards"*: Gillmann and Mommsen, *Goerdelers*, 1:628, 632.

10. *"It often appeared as though the ordinary pleasure of life"*: Helmuth James von Moltke, *A German of the Resistance: The Last Letters of Count Helmuth James von Moltke* (London: Oxford University Press, 1946), 15. Moltke was similarily described in a report of the American intelligence service OSS; see "OSS Biographical Files: Personal Data of Helmuth James Graf von Moltke, 2.11.1943," in *American Intelligence and the German Resistance to Hitler*, ed. Jürgen Heideking and Christof Mauch (Boulder, Colo.: Westview Press), 362–63.

11. *he did not want to find shelter abroad*: Ger van Roon, *Neuordnung im Widerstand: Der Kreisauer Kreis innerhalb der deutschen Widerstandsbewegung* (Munich: Oldenbourg, 1967), 32, 102–6.

12. *Moltke had no illusions*: See interview with Freya von Moltke in the documentary of Hava Kohav Beller, *The Restless Conscience: Resistance to Hitler inside Nazi Germany, 1933–1945* (1992; Los Angeles: New Video Group, 2009), DVD.

13. *he even went to the Viennese Gestapo*: Roon, *Neuordnung im Widerstand*, 67.

14. *His group . . . all the while maintained*: Ibid., 68–74, 212–15; Fugger-Gloett to Zeller (undated), Zeller Papers, IfZ ED 88/1, p. 70.

15. *Now, the two small groups united*: The Kreisau Circle was also in touch with a like-minded Bavarian group called the Augsburg Circle; see Fugger-Gloett to Zeller (undated), Zeller Papers, IfZ ED 88/1, p. 71. Fugger-Gloett maintained that Moltke was expected to be the first post-Nazi prime minister, but I was unable to find corroboration for this argument in other sources.

16. *"all laws and acts discriminating against"*: Helmuth James von Moltke, "Erste Weisung an die Landesverweser," in Roon, *Neuordnung im Widerstand*, 568.

17. *the Kreisau plan departed radically*: The full text of the remaining segments from the Kreisau draft is reproduced in Roon, *Neuordnung im Widerstand*, 561–71.

18. *still their Christian idealism prevented them*: Theodore S. Hamerow, *On the*

*Road to Wolf's Lair: German Resistance to Hitler* (Cambridge, Mass.: Belknap Press of Harvard University Press, 1997), 367; Constantine FitzGibbon, *The Shirt of Nessus* (London: Cassell, 1956), 104–5.

19. *"I am not and could never be a Nazi"*: Hans-Adolf Jacobsen and Erich Zimmermann, eds., *20 Juli 1944* (Bonn: Berto Verlag, 1960), 173; Jacobsen, *"Spiegelbild einer Verschwörung,"* 1:181; English translation taken from Peter Hoffmann, *The History of the German Resistance, 1933–1945*, trans. Richard Barry (Montreal: McGill-Queens University Press, 1985), 526.

20. *"We are ready to help you to win"*: Peter Hoffmann, "The Question of Western Allied Cooperation with the German Anti-Nazi Conspiracy, 1938–1944," *Historical Journal* 34, no. 2 (1991): 459.

21. *It is possible that the detailed information on the atrocities*: According to Gerhard Ringshausen (*Hans-Alexander von Voss: Generalstabsoffizier im Widerstand, 1907–1944* [Berlin: Lukas Verlag, 2008], 75–76), Witzleben initially declined to kill Hitler, pointing out that legality could not be reachieved through an illegal act and that he was a field marshal, not a murderer. However, at the same time, he silently authorized the plans to kill Hitler without being personally involved; see also Hoffmann, *Widerstand, Staatsstreich, Attentat*, 325–26; Erwin Lahousen, "Erklärung," 1–2, 30.1.1953, Deutsch Papers, series 4, box 9, Halder Franz. Lahousen testified that among all high commanders of the Wehrmacht, Witzleben was the only one who drew practical conclusions (namely, about the need for a coup) based on the atrocities report given to him by Canaris in 1940. According to Fromm's testimony, Witzleben remained steadfast in his belief that Germany would lose the war even at the height of the Third Reich's military success (Jacobsen, *"Spiegelbild einer Verschwörung,"* 1:366).

22. *Again, a coup was not . . . planned*: Crome testifies that there were some preparations for a revolt, but Witzleben was skeptical about its prospects. The organization, he said, was just "too weak." See Beria to Stalin, 19.9.1944, GARF Fond R-9401, Opis 2, Del 66, p. 317.

23. *Schwerin belonged to the tiny minority*: Bengt von zur Mühlen, ed., *Die Angeklagten des 20. Juli vor dem Volksgerichtshof* (Berlin: Chronos, 2001), 302.

24. *Witzleben, he wrote, was like his father*: Ringshausen, *Hans-Alexander von Voss*, 62–74.

25. *He was usually reluctant to visit the fronts*: As Ringshausen writes (ibid., 75), Voss's farewell letters, written in November 1941, are a strong indication that the assassination attempt was imminent. Considering his safe desk position in France, he had little chance to die on the front. The precise date of this assassination attempt is unclear. Some date it to early 1942, such as Ringshausen, ibid., 74–94. Hans Crome's testimony, Beria to Stalin, GARF, pp. 312–17, dates Voss's attempt to December 1941 but Beck's decision to assassinate Hitler to early February 1942. Inga Haag, Groscurth's confidante, dates the attempt to February 1942. Schwerin's wife,

by contrast, dates it to late 1940: Aufzeichnungen von Frau Inga Haag, Frankfurt A.M, 4.4.1948, 2–3, Deutsch Papers, series 3, box 2, Material on Groscurth. In any case, the sources on the 1941 plot are all hazy and confused. Juxtaposing all of them, I believe that Schwerin and Voss's attempt was probably scheduled for late 1941, but this is only an educated guess. See "2.Teil, Fortsetzung der Befragung Professor Deutsch von Botho von Wussow [und Gräfin von Schwerin]" (undated), 8, Deutsch Papers, series 3, box 3, round 1 Material.

26.  *"Who will save us?"*: Hermann Kaiser, *Mut zum Bekenntnis: Die geheimen Tagebücher des Hauptmanns Hermann Kaiser, 1941, 1943*, ed. Peter M. Kaiser (Berlin: Lukas Verlag, 2010), 127.

27.  *the opposition was merely a medley of disgruntled citizens*: Toivo M. Kivimäki to Marshal Mannerheim, 6.5.1942, KA, kotelo 24.

28.  *In January 1942, they agreed, with Witzleben's consent*: GARF Fond R-9401, Opis 2, Del 66, p. 313.

29.  *One such list proposed Witzleben*: Ibid.

## 11. Brokers on the Front Line: The New Strategy

1.  *"In 1939 the Reich government sought"*: *Akten zur deutschen auswärtigen Politik, 1918–1945* (Baden-Baden: Impr. Nationale, 1950–95), 2:2, 887–89.

2.  *"I believe . . . that we are talking about war"*: "Beceda Narkoma Inostrantsih Del SSSR V. M. Molotova s Posolom Germanii v SSSR F. Shulenbergom," in *Rossia XX Vek: Dokumenti, 1941 God v 2-x Knigah*, ed. A. N. Yakovlev et al. (Moscow: Mezhdunarodniy Fond "Demokratiya," 1998), 2:432.

3.  *The broker's job is to bridge remote groups*: The most important measure for an actor's function as a broker is his or her "betweenness," defined as "the extent to which a particular point [actor] lies between the various other points in the graph." In practice, the meaning of "betweenness" is "the extent to which an agent can play the part of a 'broker' or 'gatekeeper' with a potential of control over others." See John Scott, *Social Network Analysis: A Handbook* (London: SAGE, 2009), 86–87. A UCINET analysis in March 2012 of German resistance networks, based on the connections described in the primary sources and the memoir literature, shows that in-betweenness, Schlabrendorff and Kaiser were leading by far (59.13 and 29.374, respectively), followed by the two leaders Beck and Goerdeler (14.995 each), Tresckow (13.554), and Oster (13.551).

4.  *Under the pretext of frequent work trips*: Hermann Kaiser, *Mut zum Bekenntnis: Die geheimen Tagebücher des Hauptmanns Hermann Kaiser, 1941, 1943*, ed. Peter M. Kaiser (Berlin: Lukas Verlag, 2010), 347.

5.  *Kaiser was not only a liaison*: Ibid., 20.11.1941, p. 312.

6.  *he had access to a generous supply*: Ibid., 42.

7.  *"As an enthusiastic idealist and devout Christian"*: Friedrich Meinecke, *Die*

*deutsche Katastrophe: Betrachtungen und Erinnerungen* (Wiesbaden: Brockhaus, 1946), 144–46.

8. *Later, he was disgusted by atrocities:* Kaiser, *Mut zum Bekenntnis,* 230, 269, 452.

9. *"not one day is to be lost":* Ibid., 91–92, 266–69. Like many others, Beck is mentioned in Kaiser's diary under several code names, including Generaloberst von v.d. RhH and Generoberst X. However, at the end of the entry, he is mentioned as B., and his quoted words are similar to, almost verbatim, Beck's famous memoranda from summer 1938. These clues, probably, led Ger van Roon to argue that RhH is the code name for Beck. See Ger van Roon, "Hermann Kaiser und der deutsche Widerstand," *Vierteljahrshefte für Zeitgeschichte,* 24, no. 3 (July 1976): 267.

10. *an implacable enemy of Hitler:* Tresckow had abandoned his opposition to Hitler after the occupation of France. He wrote to an acquaintance, Luise Jodl, that all of his doubts were now gone as a result of the "astounding achievements" and the high hopes for a favorable peace. However, Hitler's failure to obtain a peace agreement and the German mistreatment of the French had quickly turned him back into an anti-Nazi. As for the Jewish question, Tresckow opposed not only violence against the Jews but also the "legal" anti-Semitism of the Nuremberg Laws. For testimonies about his motives, see Margarethe von Hardenberg (Oven) to Bodo Scheurig (interview, 2.5.1969), Luise Jodl (undated), Fabian von Schlabrendorff (interview, 17.6.1967), Schmidtke to Hesse, 21.3.1966, Erika von Tresckow (interview, 1.5.1969), Scheurig Papers, IfZ ZS/A 0031-2, http://www.ifz-muenchen.de/archiv/zsa/ZS_A_0031_02.pdf, pp.165, 209–12; ZS/A 0031-3, http://www.ifz-muenchen.de/archiv/zsa/ZS_A_0031_03.pdf, pp. 75, 93, 136–37.

11. *"A leader one would wish to have":* Peter von der Groeber to Bodo Scheurig (interview, 4.6.1970), Scheurig Papers, IfZ ZS/A 0031-2, http://www.ifz-muenchen.de/archiv/zsa/ZS_A_0031_02.pdf, p. 149; "Henning von Tresckow—Beurteilung," March 1944, BA-MA BAarch PERS 6/1980.

12. *"He had a personality that simply bowled you over":* Dorothee von Meding, *Courageous Hearts: Women and the Anti-Hitler Plot of 1944,* trans. Michael Balfour and Volker R. Berghahn (Providence, R.I.: Berghahn Books, 1997), 60–61.

13. *He promised Schlabrendorff:* Fabian von Schlabrendorff, *The Secret War Against Hitler,* trans. Hilda Simon (Boulder, Colo.: Westview Press, 1994), 135. Compare with Kurt von Hesse to Bodo Scheurig (interview, 12.10.1969), Scheurig Papers, IfZ ZS/A 0031-2, http://www.ifz-muenchen.de/archiv/zsa/ZS_A_0031_02.pdf, p. 183.

14. *"one of National Socialism's natural enemies":* Schlabrendorff, *Secret War Against Hitler,* 123. See also Rudolf-Christoph Freiherr von Gersdorff, "History of the Attempt on Hitler's Life (20 Jul. 1944)," Historical Division Headquarters, United States Army Europe, Foreign Military Studies Branch, USAMHI D739, D6713 No.A-855 Fgn Ms, 9.

15. *"a synthesis of duty and freedom"*: The quote is taken from a speech given by Tresckow in the confirmation ceremony of his sons, their official admission into the Protestant church. For the full text of the speech, see Sigrid Grabner and Hendrik Röder, eds., *Ich bin der ich war: Henning von Tresckow; Texte und Dokumente* (Berlin: Lukas Verlag, 2001), 52.

16. *"The German army attacking Russia"*: Ibid., 42; Gersdorff, "History of the Attempt," 5.

17. *"We, the younger people, respected and revered"*: Eberhard von Breitenbuch, "Erinnerungen an Generalmajor von Tresckow," Scheurig Papers, IfZ ZS/A 0031-2, http://www.ifz-muenchen.de/archiv/zsa/ZS_A_0031_02.pdf, p. 54.

18. *The group liked to shut themselves up:* Alexander Stahlberg, *Die verdammte Pflicht* (Berlin: Ullstein, 1988), 220–24. Compare with Albrecht Eggert to Bodo Scheurig (interview, 7.10.1968), Scheurig Papers, IfZ ZS/A 0031-2, http://www.ifz-muenchen.de/archiv/zsa/ZS_A_0031_02.pdf, p. 82.

## 12. War of Extermination:
## The Conspirators and the Holocaust

1. *"This war is a war between worldviews"*: Max Domarus, *Hitler: Reden und Proklamationen, 1932–1945: Kommentiert von einem deutschen Zeitgenossen* (Würzburg: Schmidt, Neustadt a.d. Aisch, 1962), 2:1682; compare to the testimonies of Erwin Lahousen, *Nuremberg Blue*, 2:454; and Franz Halder, "Protokoll der öffentlichen Sitzung der Spruchkammer München X, BY 11/47, am 15.9.1948," BA-MA Msg 2/213, p. 73(49).

2. *Field Marshal Wilhelm Keitel . . . issued a second order:* Nuremberg Blue (USA-554, 050-C), 34:254.

3. *"Gersdorff, if we don't succeed"*: Rudolf-Christoph Freiherr von Gersdorff, *Soldat im Untergang* (Frankfurt am Main: Ullstein, 1977), 87.

4. *"Fedi, . . . I've had your plane made ready"*: Ibid., 88.

5. *"What if he dismisses us?"*: Ibid.

6. *"Have it be noted, gentlemen"*: Ibid., 89.

7. *"When we arrived at the place"*: Israel Gutman and Chaim Shatzker, *Ha-Sho'ah ve-Mashma'utah* (Jerusalem: Merkaz Zalman Shazar, 1987), 106–9. Compare with the testimony of Erwin Lahousen, *Nuremberg Blue*, 2:454–56.

8. *Gen. Franz Halder . . . bore the largest measure:* Christopher Browning, *Origins of the Final Solution: The Evolution of Nazi Jewish Policy, September 1939–March 1942* (Jerusalem: Yad Vashem Press, 2004), 15–25, 216–22.

9. *"the severe but justified acts of revenge"*: Nuremberg Blue, 20:642–46; (USA-927, 4064-PS), 34:131; (USA-556, 411-D), 35:85; Gerd R. Ueberschär, ed., *NS Verbrechen und der militärische Widerstand gegen Hitler* (Darmstadt: Primus, 2000), 185. For a thorough discussion of Wehrmacht and Einsatzgruppen relations in the Barbarossa Operation, see Hans-Heinrich Wilhelm Helmut

Krausnick, *Die Truppe des Weltanschauungskrieges: Die Einsatzgruppen der Sicherheitpolizei und des SD, 1938–1942* (Stuttgart: Deutsche Verlags-Anstalt, 1981), 223–43.

10. *Wehrmacht units supplied logistical assistance:* Anthony Beevor, *Stalingrad* (London: Viking, 1998), 58.

11. *Credible evidence shows that Tresckow, Gersdorff, and the others:* Tresckow's attitude toward war crimes in his sector is one of the most controversial questions in the history of the German resistance to Hitler. While all historians agree that Tresckow was well informed, some believe that he was indifferent until the Borisov Massacre, on October 20, whereas others think that he resisted the atrocious orders even beforehand. For the former opinion, see Johannes Hürter, "Auf dem Weg zur Militäropposition: Tresckow, Gersdorff, der Vernichtungskrieg, und der Judenmord; Neue Dokumente über das Verhältnis der Heeresgruppe Mitte zur Einsatzgruppe B im Jahr 1941," *Vierteljahrshefte für Zeitgeschichte* 3 (2004): 527–62; Johannes Hürter and Felix Römer, "Alte und neue Geschichtsbilder von Widerstand und Ostkrieg: Zu Hermann Gramls Beitrag 'Massenmord und Militäropposition,'" *Vierteljahrshefte für Zeitgeschichte* 54, no. 2 (April 2006): 300–322. For the latter opinion, see Hermann Graml, "Massenmord und Militäropposition: Zur jüngsten Diskussion über den Widerstand im Stab der Heeresgruppe Mitte," *Vierteljahrshefte für Zeitgeschichte* 54, no. 1 (2006): 1–26; Günther Gillessen, "Tresckow und der Entschluß zum Hochverrat: Eine Nachschau zur Kontroverse über die Motive," *Vierteljahrshefte für Zeitgeschichte* 58, no. 3 (2010): 364–86. And for my own assessment and interpretation of the evidence, see Danny Orbach, "The Other Prussia: General von Tresckow, Resistance to Hitler, and the Question of Charisma," *Tel Aviver Jahrbuch für deutsche Geschichte* (October 2016).

12. *The SS men drove to Barysaw:* Gersdorff, *Soldat im Untergang*, 98.

13. *"This must not happen again":* Bodo Scheurig, *Henning von Tresckow: Ein Preuße gegen Hitler; Biographie* (Berlin: Propyläen, 1987), 126; Berg to Scheurig, 16.3.1970, Schlabrendorff (interview, 28.9.1970), Scheurig Papers, IfZ ZS/A 0031-2, http://www.ifz-muenchen.de/archiv/zsa/ZS_A_0031_02.pdf, pp. 9–15, 0031-3, http://www.ifz-muenchen.de/archiv/zsa/ZS_A_0031_03 .pdf, p. 85.

14. *"I shall not tolerate any attack":* Fabian von Schlabrendorff, *The Secret War Against Hitler,* trans. Hilda Simon (Boulder, Colo.: Westview Press, 1994), 136.

15. *"because it is not clear whether it is possible":* This line of interpretation is supported by the Gestapo reports; see Hans A. Jacobsen, ed., *"Spiegelbild einer Verschwörung": Die Opposition gegen Hitler und der Staatsstreich vom 20. Juli 1944 in der SD-Berichterstattung: Geheime Dokumente aus dem ehemaligen Reichssicherheitshauptamt* (Stuttgart: Seewald, 1984), 1:425. A report from 29.9.1944, based on the interrogation of Admiral Canaris, reads as follows:

"In Army Group Center it was believed that the SS impeded the pacification of the hinterland . . . and in consideration of the general state of affairs in the east, this political momentum played a significant role in the wider clique of 20.7 conspirators." See also Horst Mühleisen, "Patrioten im Widerstand: Carl-Hans Graf von Hardenbergs Erlebnisbericht," *Vierteljahrshefte für Zeitgeschichte* 14, no. 3 (January 1993): 450. Tresckow's attempts to reduce as far as possible the number of Einsatzgruppen units in Army Group Center's rear are documented in a report by SS officer Kurt Knoblauch to one of his commanders, although the latter did not suspect Tresckow's motives and was oblivious to his resistance activities. See Kommandostab RF-SS, Der Chef des Stabes an Jüttner 19.6.41, BA-MA SF-02/37542. Christian Gerlach, a historian who has implicated Tresckow in war crimes, presented this document misleadingly and incorrectly in one of his articles, arguing that "Tresckow and Knoblauch agreed to the deployment of Einsatzgruppen units." In fact, the decision to allow the units to deploy was taken at much higher levels, as required by the second Wagner-Heydrich agreement. Tresckow and Knoblauch met only to coordinate the deployment's technical side. Tresckow nevertheless managed to reduce the number of Einsatzgruppen in his area. Gerlach does not mention this. See Christian Gerlach, "Männer des 20 Juli und der Krieg gegen die Sowjetunion," in *Vernichtungskrieg: Verbrechen der Wehrmacht, 1941 bis 1944*, ed. Hannes Heer and Klaus Naumann (Hamburg: Hamburger Edition, 1995), 439–40.

16. *"During all the long talks I conducted"*: Maj. I. G. Freiherr von Gersdorff, "Abschrift, 9.12.1941," Scheurig Papers, IfZ 0031-4, http://www.ifz-muenchen. de/archiv/zsa/ZS_A_0031_04.pdf, p. 186. It is interesting that Gersdorff forgot this report after the war and had to be reminded by a historian who found it by chance. See Krausnick to Gersdorff, 29.10.1956, and Gersdorff's reply, 30.10.1956, IfZ ZS-0047-2, pp. 105–8. On Heinz's order of the day against the massacre of the Jews of Lvov, see Susanne Meiml, *Nationalsozialisten gegen Hitler: Die nationalrevolutionäre Opposition um Friedrich Wilhelm Heinz* (Berlin: Siedler, 2000), 318–19.

17. *"Should we wonder that there are partisans?"*: Bogislaw von Bonin to Bodo Scheurig (interview), 25.9.1970, Scheurig Papers, IfZ ZS/A 0031-2, http://www.ifz-muenchen.de/archiv/zsa/ZS_A_0031_02.pdf, p. 50.

## 13. "Flash" and Liqueur Bottles: Assassination Attempts in the East

1. *"If we do not make a resolute advance to Moscow"*: Bodo Scheurig, *Henning von Tresckow: Ein Preuße gegen Hitler; Biographie* (Berlin: Propyläen, 1987), 130; Alexander Stahlberg, *Die verdammte Pflicht* (Berlin: Ullstein, 1988), 222.

2. *"The German soldier of the winter war"*: Rudolf-Christoph Freiherr von Gersdorff, *Soldat im Untergang* (Frankfurt am Main: Ullstein, 1977), 114.

3. *"This war that you still believe has a chance"*: Scheurig, *Henning von Tresckow*, 152–53; Stahlberg, *Die verdammte Pflicht*, 224.

4. *when confronted with the notion of absolute obedience*: Hermann Kaiser, *Mut zum Bekenntnis: Die geheimen Tagebücher des Hauptmanns Hermann Kaiser, 1941, 1943*, ed. Peter M. Kaiser (Berlin: Lukas Verlag, 2010), 487.

5. *he was still not considered a full-fledged member*: Helena Schrader, *Codename Valkyrie: General Friedrich Olbricht and the Plot Against Hitler* (Sparkford, U.K.: Haynes, 2009), 171–211.

6. *Olbricht was "very careful"*: Kaiser, *Mut zum Bekenntnis*, 306; compare with Hans A. Jacobsen, ed., *"Spiegelbild einer Verschwörung": Die Opposition gegen Hitler und der Staatsstreich vom 20. Juli 1944 in der SD-Berichterstattung: Geheime Dokumente aus dem ehemaligen Reichssicherheitshauptamt* (Stuttgart: Seewald, 1984), 1:369.

7. *Olbricht finally joined the conspiracy*: Kaiser, *Mut zum Bekenntnis*, 287–88.

8. *the "strong man of the home front"*: Bernhard R. Kroener, *Generaloberst Friedrich Fromm: Der starke Mann im Heimatkriegsgebiet; Eine Biographie* (Paderborn: Schöningh, 2005), 412–13. For one example, see the testimony of Maj. Hans-Ludwig Bartram, 1954, "20. Juli 1944," BA-MA Msg 2/214, p. 1. Among other praises, Bartram wrote that "Fromm as a personality will always be my role model." He described Fromm as a commander who "excelled spiritually, and was superior to anyone in knowledge and competence. And still, he always cared and shared in the personal issues of his subordinates."

9. *it was Fromm's reluctance to commit himself*: Kaiser, *Mut zum Bekenntnis*, 307; Johannes Rohowsky, "Stellungnahme zur Kennes-Kritik bezügl. Müller-Broschüre," 18.5.48, BA-MA N/124/10.

10. *"Maybe he has some higher calling"*: Kaiser, *Mut zum Bekenntnis*, 134.

11. *he kept playing his double game*: Ibid., 424–25.

12. *"Germany has never been in better shape"*: Ibid., 306–7.

13. *"the threads of the entire plot"*: Fabian von Schlabrendorff, *The Secret War Against Hitler*, trans. Hilda Simon (Boulder, Colo.: Westview Press, 1994), 225. On Olbricht's critical role in the conspiracy's management, see also the testimony of Franz Maria Liedig, Hauptquartier, Streitkräfte der Vereinigten Staaten, Europäische Abteilung, Zentrum des militärischen Geheimdienstes APO 757, Sonderbericht einer Vernehmung (CSIR) No. 6, Ereignisse des Monats Juli 1944, Franz Maria Liedig, 19, Deutsch Papers, series 4, box 9, General Opposition.

14. *Witzleben was extremely pessimistic*: Schlabrendorff, *Secret War Against Hitler*, 144; Ulrich von Hassell, *Die Hassell-Tagebücher, 1938–1944: Aufzeichnungen vom anderen Deutschland*, ed. Friedrich Freiherr Hiller von Gärtringen (Munich: Goldmann, 1994), 297; GARF Fond R-9401, Opis 2, Del 66, pp. 318–19; Unterhaltung mit Frau Ursula von Witzleben, 10.2.1970, 11, Deutsch Papers, series 3, box 3, round 1 Material.

15. *"One has to resort to active revolutionary means"*: Horst Mühleisen, "Patrioten im Widerstand: Carl-Hans Graf von Hardenbergs Erlebnisbericht," *Viertel-jahrshefte für Zeitgeschichte* 14, no. 3 (January 1993): 449–50.

16. *"is it really so negative"*: Stahlberg to Scheurig (interview, 15.9.1965), Scheurig Papers, IfZ ZS/A 0031-3, http://www.ifz-muenchen.de/archiv/zsa/ ZS_A_0031_03.pdf, pp. 111–14. For a slightly different version, see the interview with Philipp von Boeselager in Hava Kohav Beller's documentary film *The Restless Conscience: Resistance to Hitler Within Germany, 1933–1945* (1992; Los Angeles: New Video Group, 2009), DVD; Mühleisen, "Patrioten im Widerstand," 451. For Manstein's version, see *Nuremberg Blue* 20:624–25; Joachim Kuhn, "Eigenhändige Aussagen des Majors der deutschen Wehr-macht Ioachim Kuhn, 2.9.1944," in Peter Hoffmann, *Stauffenbergs Freund: Die tragische Geschichte des Widerstandskämpfers Joachim Kuhn* (Munich: Ver-lag C. H. Beck, 2007), 202–3. See also Gersdorff to Krausnick, 19.10.1956, IfZ ZS-0047-2, pp. 10–11. For a discussion of Manstein's heavy responsibil-ity for Nazi war crimes, see Michael Schröder, "Erich von Manstein—Ein unpolitischer Soldat?," *Forum "Barbarossa,"* no. 3 (2004), http://www.histo risches-centrum.de/forum/schroeders04-2.html.

17. *Tresckow did better with his immediate superior*: Fabian von Schlabrendorff, *Offiziere gegen Hitler* (Zurich: Europa Verlag, 1946), 57; Berg an Scheurig, 16.3.1970, Scheurig Papers, IfZ ZS/A 0031-2, http://www.ifz-muenchen.de/ archiv/zsa/ZS_A_0031_02.pdf, pp. 9–15. When Breitenbuch urged Kluge to protest, at least, against the murder of the Jews, the field marshal flatly refused. He noted that either Goebbels would throw his protest letter in the dustbin or Hitler would force him to resign. In any case, he, Kluge, com-manded more divisions and troops than any one person in history, and he would never forsake his troops and responsibility for the sake of empty pro-tests. When Breitenbuch tried to offer counterarguments, he was promptly ordered to leave the room. See Eberhard von Breitenbuch, *Erinnerungen eines Reserveoffiziers, 1939–1945: Aufgeschrieben zur Kenntnis meiner Kinder* (Norderstedt: Books on Demand, 2011), 87.

18. *"O [Olbricht] is on vacation"*: Kaiser, *Mut zum Bekenntnis*, 347.

19. *Oster was reluctant to rely on the communication network*: Ibid., 436; compare with Jacobsen, "Spiegelbild einer Verschwörung," 1:370.

20. *Witzleben . . . agreed to lead the Wehrmacht*: Hans Crome testified on the preparations for a coup in 1942 but did not know of the assassination at-tempt. See GARF Fond R-9401, Opis 2, Del 66, p. 318. On Witzleben, see Kaiser, *Mut zum Bekenntnis*, 438. Witzleben was depressed, unhealthy, and isolated at the time, and was updated on developments in the outside world by Count Schwerin, his contact in the conspiracy ("Spiegelbild einer Ver-schwörung," 1:366).

21. *"Boeselager, . . . you heard what the Führer said"*: Philipp Freiherr von Boese-lager, "Mein Weg zum 20. Juli 1944 (Vortrag gehalten am 20. Juli 2002 bei

den Johannitern in Wasserburg/Bayern)" (unpublished manuscript, 2002), 20–23.

22. *Kluge's avarice overcame him:* Peter Hoffmann, *Widerstand, Staatsstreich, Attentat: Der Kampf der Opposition gegen Hitler* (Munich: Piper, 1985), 338.

23. *A single bullet . . . was likely to miss:* Philipp von Boeselager to Peter Hoffmann, 19.11.1964, IfZ ZS-2118, p. 2, http://www.ifz-muenchen.de/archiv/zs/zs-2118.pdf; Gersdorff to Scheurig, 28.3.1972, http://www.ifz-muenchen.de/archiv/zsa/ZS_A_0031_02.pdf, p. 131.

24. *Boeselager put together an elite cavalry force:* Boeselager to Hoffmann, IfZ, p. 3; Kuhn, "Eigenhändige Aussagen," 202; Schlabrendorff, *Secret War Against Hitler*, 269; Gersdorff, *Soldat im Untergang*, 126; *Nuremberg Green*, 13:397.

25. *"they died so that Germany could continue to live":* Anthony Beevor, *Stalingrad* (London: Viking, 1998), 333.

26. *"I wondered . . . whether I was signing my own death warrant":* Gersdorff, *Soldat im Untergang*, 119–20.

27. *"Tresckow spoke with me with utter frankness":* Ibid., 121–22. See also Rudolf-Christoph Freiherr von Gersdorff, "History of the Attempt on Hitler's Life (20 Jul. 1944)," Historical Division Headquarters, United States Army Europe, Foreign Military Studies Branch, USAMHI, pp. 11–12.

28. *"One is ready to act only when commanded":* Kaiser, *Mut zum Bekenntnis*, 420–22, 439, 445.

29. *"to do everything possible to reinforce his resolution":* Ibid., 434.

30. *"Not to lose even one day":* Ibid., 419, 433.

31. *"Is it not horrifying":* Gersdorff, *Soldat im Untergang*, 129; Scheurig, *Henning von Tresckow*, 202.

32. *"there is no point, as Himmler will not be there":* Boeselager to Hoffmann, 19.11.1964, IfZ ZS-2118, p. 3.

33. *On March 3, he sent a message to Olbricht:* Hoffmann, *Widerstand, Staatsstreich, Attentat*, 347; Klaus-Jürgen Müller, *Generaloberst Ludwig Beck: Eine Biographie* (Paderborn: F. Schöningh, 2008), 465; Kaiser, *Mut zum Bekenntnis*, 459; Gersdorff, *Soldat im Untergang*, 126; Gersdorff, *History*, USAMHI, pp. 10–11. On the decision to assassinate Hitler, see also "Verräter vor dem Volksgericht, Teil II, Rolle 4, Ton/ 294m/ 10,45 min," in Bengt von zur Mühlen, ed., *Die Angeklagten des 20 Juli vor dem Volksgerichtshof* (Berlin: Chronos, 2001), 257–58. Hans Crome dates Beck's decision to sanction the assassination to the end of 1942; see GARF Fond R-9401, Opis 2, Del 66, p. 313.

34. *"Hitler was served a special meal":* Schlabrendorff, *Secret War Against Hitler*, 76–77.

35. *"I waited until Hitler had dismissed the officers":* Ibid., 235.

36. *"In order to free Germany and the world":* Scheurig, *Henning von Tresckow*, 144–45; Gersdorff, *History*, USAMHI, p. 14; and see a similar position in Hardenberg's testimony, Mühleisen, "Patrioten in Widerstand," 457–58.

37. *"After waiting more than two hours"*: Schlabrendorff, *Secret War Against Hitler*, 236.
38. *Schlabrendorff . . . seriously feared a belated explosion:* Ibid.
39. *"I could see that the condition of the explosive"*: Ibid., 237–38.
40. *Apparently, he would need to blow himself up:* Gersdorff, *Soldat im Untergang*, 128–29.
41. *"I spent March 20 at the Armory"*: Ibid., 130.
42. *"I arrived at the Armory on the late morning"*: Ibid., 131.
43. *Fifty seconds later, the radio announced:* FBIS, NARA, Rg.263, SA 190, R 23, C 34, S7, box 58, pp. 1–7. American intelligence analysts counted fifty seconds between the announcement that Hitler had entered the museum and the announcement of his exit (p. 7). Gersdorff's account of the speech is inaccurate, which is unsurprising, given the circumstances and the great mental pressure he was under. Hitler made no explicit mention of *Götterdämmerung*, the "twilight of the gods," although he did speak of the utter obliteration of the Western Allies and the eradication of their culture in a Communist revolution.
44. *"So the window of opportunity for the assassination closed"*: Rudolf Pechel, *Deutscher Widerstand* (Zurich: Rentsch, 1947), 164; compare with Gersdorff's testimony to the U.S. Army's Center of Military History, Gersdorff, *History*, USAMHI, pp. 17–18.
45. *"Only now his importance becomes clear"*: Kaiser, *Mut zum Bekenntnis*, 463, 465–66.
46. *The room for maneuvering was diminishing quickly:* See chapter 17.

## 14. Code Name U-7: Rescue and Abyss

1. *His extraordinary ability to play:* Abschrift Huppenkothen, IfZ ZS 0249-1, p. 32.
2. *Inside the Abwehr, he was known:* Heinz Höhne, *Canaris*, trans. J. Maxwell Brownjohn (London: Secker & Warburg, 1979), 168–69.
3. *"one of the people to whom Franco owed his power"*: Kruglov to Beria, 6.5.1946, GARF Fond R-9401, Opis 2, Del 136, pp. 256–97; Helmut Krausnick's interview with Franz Maria Liedig (date unknown), 19–20, Deutsch Papers, series 4, box 15, Liedig.
4. *"I require you to stand foursquare"*: Höhne, *Canaris*, 213; *Nuremberg Blue*, 3:26.
5. *The notorious anti-Semitic newspaper* Der Stürmer: *Der Stürmer* (Nuremberg), no. 37, September 1937.
6. *"The scenes of devastation in Poland"*: Höhne, *Canaris*, 361–62.
7. *"Canaris was a pure intellect"*: *Nuremberg Blue*, 2:443; Helmut Krausnick's interview with Franz Maria Liedig (date unknown), 21, Deutsch Papers, series 4, box 15, Liedig.
8. *"While visiting Poznan"*: Höhne, *Canaris*, 362–63.

9. *Very few people, then and now, have known:* Rachel Altein, ed., *Out of the Inferno: The Efforts That Led to the Rescue of Rabbi Yosef Yitzchak Schneersohn of Lubavitch from War-Torn Europe in 1939–1940* (New York: Kehot Publication Society, 2002), 14–15, 31–37; Winfried Meyer, *Unternehmen Sieben: Eine Rettungsaktion für vom Holocaust Bedrohte aus dem Amt Ausland/Abwehr im Oberkommando der Wehrmacht* (Frankfurt am Main: Hain, 1993), 129–38; Saul S. Deutsch, "Me-Varsha Le-New York Dereh Berlin, Riga Ve-Stockholm: Giluyim Hadashim al Parashat Ha-Hatsala shel Kevod Kedushat Admor Harayats," *Kefar Chabad*, 9 Adar, February 1993. For a book-length study of the affair, see Bryan Rigg, *Rescued from the Reich: How One of Hitler's Soldiers Saved the Lubavitcher Rebbe* (New Haven, Conn.: Yale University Press, 2004).

10. *Canaris's agent carried his Great War medal:* Meyer, *Unternehmen Sieben*, 137–38.

11. *Some say that he did so:* Ibid., 83–84, 88, 120; Gabrielle Lindemann to Dr. Winfried Meyer, 29.11.1985 (Privatbesitz Dr. Winfried Meyers), p. 1.

12. *Canaris spoke out against German crimes:* Helmut Krausnick and Hans-Heinrich Wilhelm, *Die Truppe des Weltanschauungskrieges: Die Einsatzgruppen der Sicherheitpolizei und des SD, 1938–1942* (Stuttgart: Deutsche Verlags-Anstalt, 1981), 64; Aktenvermerk über die Besprechung im Führerzug am 12.9.1939 in Illnau 14.9.1939, NARA, Rg.238/3047-PS (US-80); Meyer, *Unternehmen Sieben*, 102–13; *Nuremberg Blue*, 2:447–48, 454–62, 471–73.

13. *Formally, he was under Canaris:* Meyer, *Unternehmen Sieben*, 102–7, 338–37; Christopher Browning, *Origins of the Final Solution: The Evolution of Nazi Jewish Policy, September 1939–March 1942* (Jerusalem: Yad Vashem Press, 2004), 289; Gert Buchheit, *Die Anonyme Macht: Aufgaben, Methoden, Erfahrungen von Geheimdienste* (Frankfurt am Main: Akademische Verlagsgesellschaft Athenaion, 1969), 85; Abschrift Huppenkothen, IfZ ZS 0249-1, p. 38. On the Secret Field Police, see also NARA 1188885 6.18.

14. *"Thank you for the cigars you've sent me":* Meyer, *Unternehmen Sieben*, 212, 214.

15. *Schulze-Bernett himself confessed:* Ibid., 216.

16. *"Recently, during deportation transports":* Adolf Eichmann an die Geheime Staatspolizei Düsseldorf, 2.12.1941, NWHA, Düsseldorf, RW 58/74234, p. 12.

17. *The letter was likely a ploy:* Meyer, *Unternehmen Sieben*, 237, 239.

18. *the key figure in U-7 was . . . Dr. Hans von Dohnanyi:* Dohnanyi was recently recognized by Yad Vashem, the Israeli Holocaust Memorial Authority, as a "righteous among the nations," an honor reserved for non-Jews who saved Jews for humanitarian reasons during the war.

19. *"Nazi treatment of the Jews and the church":* Hans A. Jacobsen, ed., *"Spiegelbild einer Verschwörung": Die Opposition gegen Hitler und der Staatsstreich vom 20. Juli 1944 in der SD-Berichterstattung: Geheime Dokumente aus dem ehemaligen Reichssicherheitshauptamt* (Stuttgart: Seewald, 1984), 1:519.

20.  *as a resistance fighter and a "better German"*: Marikje Smid, *Hans von Dohnanyi, Christine Bonhoeffer: Eine Ehe im Widerstand gegen Hitler* (Gütersloh: Gütersloher Verlagshaus, 2002), 141; Abschrift der Aufzeichnungen von Frau Christine v. Dohnanyi geb. Bonhoeffer (postwar, undated), 1, Deutsch Papers, series 3, box 3, round 1 Material.

21.  *Dohnanyi also helped to record the crimes*: Aufzeichnungen Christine von Dohnanyis, 1–6, Deutsch Papers, series 3, box 3, round 1 Material.

22.  *an unusual guest came to Abwehr headquarters*: Meyer, *Unternehmen Sieben*, 63; Bericht Fritz Arnolds A, DRYV, p. 3. This document, part of the Dohnanyi file at the Department of the Righteous, Yad Vashem Holocaust Memorial Authority, Jerusalem, was given to me with the courtesy of its former director Dr. Mordechai Paldiel.

23.  *Around that time, probably, he made up his mind*: Meyer, *Unternehmen Sieben*, 63, 69.

24.  *"The Reich Main Security Office has found out"*: Ibid., 68–69.

25.  *he proposed to smuggle Arnold, Fliess, and their families*: Ibid., 69.

26.  *Dohnanyi even asked Arnold to help*: Bericht Fritz Arnolds A, DRYV, p. 4.

27.  *"Admiral Canaris, with whom I spoke only twice"*: Meyer, *Unternehmen Sieben*, 98.

28.  *their intentions "to employ Jewish agents in Switzerland"*: Ibid., 243, 257–59.

29.  *"Did you hear, Langer?"*: Ibid., 256–57.

30.  *he gave the refugees one million goldmarks*: Ibid., 303; Niederschrift Manfred Roeder, 3 and 4 December 1951, IfZ, ZS-0124, p. 30, http://www.ifz -muenchen.de/archiv/zs/zs-0124.pdf.

31.  *Years later, she admitted that Arnold*: Dorothee Fliess, "Geschichte Einer Rettung," in *20 Juli 1944: Annäherung an den geschichlichen Augenblick*, ed. Rüdiger von Boss and Günther Neske (Pfullingen: Neske, 1984), 74.

32.  *Nazi authorities discovered the illegal monetary transfer*: Sonderegger to Mattmer, 17.10.1952, IfZ, ZS-0303-1, http://www.ifz-muenchen.de/archiv/zs/zs -0303_1.pdf, p. 32.

33.  *The Gestapo caught Josef Müller*: The best and most reliable description is Roeder's; see Niederschrift Manfred Roeder, December 3 and 4, 1951, IfZ, ZS-0124, http://www.ifz-muenchen.de/archiv/zs/zs-0124.pdf, pp. 24–30; see also Abschrift Huppenkothen, IfZ ZS 0249-1, pp. 22–25. For detailed description and historical analysis, see Meyer, *Unternehmen Sieben*, 336–83.

34.  *The real nature of Operation U-7 had been exposed*: Niederschrift Manfred Roeder, IfZ, p. 30.

35.  *a Gestapo agent infiltrated a tea party*: "Abschrift des Oberreichsanwalts beim Volksgerichtshof 2 J 243/44g Rs. 1 L 214/44, Anklageschrift gegen Elisabeth von Thadden und anderen, 22.6.1944," in Bengt von zur Mühlen, *Die Angeklagten des 20 Juli vor dem Volksgerichtshof* (Berlin: Chronos, 2001), 318–27; Abschrift Huppenkothen, IfZ ZS 0249-1, pp. 27–30; Lagi

Countess Ballestrem-Solf, "Tea Party," in *We Survived: Fourteen Stories of the Hidden and Hunted of Nazi Germany*, ed. Eric H. Boehm (Santa Barbara, Calif.: ABC-Clio Information Services, 1985), 135; Fugger-Gloett to Zeller (undated), Zeller Papers, IfZ ED 88/1, p. 71.

36. *The Abwehr . . . was dissolved:* Abschrift Huppenkothen, IfZ ZS 0249-1, pp. 41–42.

## 15. Count Stauffenberg: The Charismatic Turn

1. *Wasn't that proved by the destructive power:* Peter Hoffmann, *Stauffenberg: A Family History, 1905–1944* (Cambridge: Cambridge University Press, 1995), 6.

2. *Even as a child, he said that he wanted:* Ibid., 3, and see also 25.

3. *"I often feel I must draw plans":* Ibid., 26.

4. *"His glowing eyes clearly expressed":* Eberhard Zeller, *Oberst Claus Graf Stauffenberg: Ein Lebensbild* (Paderborn: Schöningh, 1994), 14–15.

5. *"My Germany cannot perish":* Ibid., 8.

6. *"the saddest day in my entire life":* Ibid., 5; Christian Graf von Krockow, *Eine Frage der Ehre: Stauffenberg und das Hitler-Attentat vom 20. Juli 1944* (Berlin: Rowohlt, 2004), 28.

7. *they were never among the supporters:* Christian Müller, *Oberst i. G. Stauffenberg: Eine Biographie* (Düsseldorf: Droste, 1971), 42–43. See also the testimony of Manfred von Brauchitsch, cited in Wolfgang Venohr, *Stauffenberg, Symbol der deutschen Einheit: Eine politische Biographie* (Frankfurt am Main: Ullstein, 1986), 61.

8. *"bathed in a mystic, luminous haze":* Hoffmann, *Stauffenberg*, 30.

9. *He won a great honor:* Dorothee von Meding, *Mit dem Mut des Herzens — Die Frauen des 20 Juli* (Berlin: Siedler, 1992), 293; Müller, *Oberst i. G. Stauffenberg*, 51–52.

10. *"in the name of Secret Germany":* Hoffmann, *Stauffenberg*, 31–32.

11. *"How can I orient my life":* Zeller, *Oberst Claus Graf Stauffenberg*, 12–13.

12. *"We believe in the future of the Germans":* The oath is reproduced in full in Hoffmann, *Stauffenberg*, 293–94.

13. *"painful birth of a new Germany":* Zeller, *Oberst Claus Graf Stauffenberg*, 14.

14. *he wrote a friend from the George circle:* Ibid., 20–22.

15. *"I manage well with subordinates":* Müller, *Oberst i. G. Stauffenberg*, 78.

16. *he preferred Hitler for president:* Zeller, *Oberst Claus Graf Stauffenberg*, 26; Hoffmann, *Stauffenberg*, 69.

17. *he and his younger brother "accepted National Socialist principles":* Hans A. Jacobsen, ed., *"Spiegelbild einer Verschwörung": Die Opposition gegen Hitler und der Staatsstreich vom 20. Juli 1944 in der SD-Berichterstattung: Geheime Dokumente aus dem ehemaligen Reichssicherheitshauptamt* (Stuttgart: Seewald, 1984), 1:450.

18. *"Do you mind that I'm Jewish?"*: Zeller, *Oberst Claus Graf Stauffenberg*, 34; see also Hoffmann, *Stauffenberg*, 81, 105.

19. *At first, Nina kept her distance*: Venhor, *Stauffenberg*, 57; Konstanze von Schulthess, *Nina Schenk Gräfin von Stauffenberg: Ein Porträt* (Munich: Pendo, 2008), 50–51.

20. *"to marry is to be on duty"*: Krockow, *Eine Frage der Ehre*, 50; Hoffmann, *Stauffenberg*, 55; Schulthess, *Nina Schenk Gräfin von Stauffenberg*, 60.

21. *Berthold . . . said that the "best part" of his life*: Hoffmann, *Stauffenberg*, 88–89; Schulthess, *Nina Schenk Gräfin von Stauffenberg*, 50–51, 63, 74–75; Guido Knopp, *Stauffenberg: Die wahre Geschichte* (Munich: Pendo, 2008), 72, 78.

22. *"iron will, discretion, extraordinary spiritual qualities"*: Venohr, *Stauffenberg*, 75–76.

23. *"He hated German nationalist arrogance"*: Zeller, *Oberst Claus Graf Stauffenberg*, 42.

24. *He told one of his friends*: Müller, *Oberst i. G. Stauffenberg*, 143.

25. *"If the Western world did not disintegrate"*: Zeller, *Oberst Claus Graf Stauffenberg*, 45.

26. *"That lunatic will make war"*: Hoffmann, *Stauffenberg*, 111. Such unproven stories tend to project Stauffenberg's later career as a resistance fighter onto his earlier days. For the legend, see Constantine FitzGibbon, *The Shirt of Nessus* (London: Cassell, 1956), 40, though this author admits that it is not a fact but guesswork. More insistent was Hoepner's son, who claimed that Stauffenberg was "undoubtedly" initiated by his father. Though Stauffenberg indeed served under Hoepner's command, he almost certainly knew nothing about the coup plans. See Hoepner to Hoffmann, 3.4.1964, IfZ ZS-2121, p. 2.

27. *"high aim of self-preservation"*: Hoffmann, *Stauffenberg*, 117.

28. *Stauffenberg lectured her enthusiastically*: C. Schulenburg, in Hava Kohav Beller, *The Restless Conscience: Resistance to Hitler Within Germany, 1933–1945* (1992; Los Angeles: New Video Group, 2009), DVD.

29. *"This man's father was not a petty bourgeois"*: Hoffmann, *Stauffenberg*, 132.

30. *"The inhabitants are an unbelievable rabble"*: Ibid., 115.

31. *Stauffenberg told some friends*: Ibid., 117; Müller, *Oberst i. G. Stauffenberg*, 167; Meding, *Mit dem Mut des Herzens*, 275.

32. *"great organizational talent"*: Hoffmann, *Stauffenberg*, 119.

33. *"Stauffenberg, tall, slender, agile"*: Müller, *Oberst i. G. Stauffenberg*, 180.

34. *"The entire existing organization"*: Ibid., 183. Hoffmann, *Stauffenberg*, 130.

35. *A victory . . . must be capitalized on*: Müller, *Oberst i. G. Stauffenberg*, 192; FitzGibbon, *Shirt of Nessus*, 42.

36. *He even blamed Hitler for giving up*: Müller, *Oberst i. G. Stauffenberg*, 198, 204.

37. *"we will purge the brown plague"*: Ibid., 215–16; Hans Bentzien, *Claus Schenk Graf von Stauffenberg: Der Täter und seine Zeit* (Berlin: Das Neue Berlin, 2004), 182. Stauffenberg spoke similarly in a conversation with Hasso von

Etzdorf. When the latter told him that Hitler had to be shot, Stauffenberg disagreed. Only Himmler, he said, had to executed, along with some of the gauleiters. See Niederschrift der Unterredung zwischen Herrn Ministerialdirigent Dr. v. Etzdorf und Herrn Dr. H. Krausnick im Auftrage des Instituts für Zeitgeschichte München, durchgeführt am 26.9.1953 in Bonn, 6, Deutsch Papers, series 3, box 2, Material on Groscurth.

38.  *The destruction, in his mind: Nuremberg Blue* (USA-556, 411-D), 35:85–86.

39.  *Orders issued by Keitel practically allowed:* Ibid., (USA-554, 050-C), 34:254.

40.  *He warned, again and again:* Müller, *Oberst i. G. Stauffenberg,* 223–24, 227, 235; Hoffmann, *Stauffenberg,* 150.

41.  *the rate of desertions from the Red Army:* For statistics and analysis, see Mark Solonin, *22 Iunya: Anatomiya Katastrofi* (Moscow: Iuza Eskmo, 2008), 359–70.

42.  *he "expressed outrage at the brutal treatment":* Hoffmann, *Stauffenberg,* 151.

43.  *ignore the "little bomb throwers":* Ibid.

44.  *"You seem to believe that I am engaged":* "Bericht von Urban Thiersch über seine Begegnungen mit Oberst Graf Stauffenberg im Juli 1944," Zeller Papers, IfZ ED 88/2, pp. 355–56. For additional testimony on Stauffenberg's attempts to win over high officers in 1942, see Sönke Neitzel, *Abgehört: Deutsche Generäle in britischer Kriegsgefangenschaft 1942–1945* (Berlin: Propyläen, 2005), pp. 336, 339.

45.  *"The daily staff reports":* Kuhn, "Eigenhändige Aussagen," 190.

46.  *"they are shooting Jews in masses":* Hoffmann, *Stauffenberg,* 152; Müller, *Oberst i. G. Stauffenberg,* 257; Rudolf-Christoph Freiherr von Gersdorff, "History of the Attempt on Hitler's Life (20 Jul. 1944)," Historical Division Headquarters, United States Army Europe, Foreign Military Studies Branch, USAMHI, p. 20; Hans Herwarth von Bittenfeld, "Meine Verbindung mit Graf Stauffenberg" (newspaper clipping, 18.7.1969), Deutsch Papers, series 3, box 2, rounds 3 and 4 Material.

47.  *his remarks about the legitimacy of tyrannicide:* Speer an den Chef der Securite Publique, 18.10.1945, Zeller Papers, IfZ ED 88/2, p. 301; Kurt Finker, *Stauffenberg und der 20 Juli 1944* (Berlin: Union Verlag, 1967), 74; Bentzien, *Claus Schenk Graf von Stauffenberg,* 212; Joachim Kramarz, *Claus Graf Stauffenberg: 15. November 1907—20 Juli 1944; Das Leben eines Offiziers* (Frankurt am Main: Bernard & Graefe, 1965), 113.

48.  *"We are sowing hatred":* Müller, *Oberst i. G. Stauffenberg,* 255.

49.  *Many officers in the high command:* Bericht Thiersch, Zeller Papers, IfZ ED 88/2, p. 356; Finker, *Stauffenberg,* 76–77; Kramarz, *Claus Graf Stauffenberg,* 114.

50.  *Tresckow and others watched him:* Stahlberg to Scheurig (interview, 15.9.1965), Scheurig Papers, IfZ ZS/A 0031-3, http://www.ifz-muenchen.de/archiv/zsa/ZS_A_0031_03.pdf, p. 111.

51. *The officer who reprimanded him:* Bericht Thiersch, Zeller Papers, IfZ ED 88/2, p. 356; Finker, *Stauffenberg*, 154.

52. *"How refreshing it is to visit [the front]":* The letter is reproduced in full in Kramarz, *Claus Graf Stauffenberg*, 226 (appendix). For Broich's anti-Nazi attitude and positive evaluation of Stauffenberg, see Neitzel, *Abgehört*, p. 336.

53. *"Stauffenberg's uniforms had not yet been bleached":* Hoffmann, *Stauffenberg*, 164.

54. *Late that morning, Stauffenberg took leave:* Ibid., 178–79.

55. *Thus, a hole opened:* Otto John, *Twice Through the Lines: The Autobiography of Otto John*, trans. Richard Barry (London: Macmillan, 1972), 117, 139; Jacobsen, *"Spiegelbild einer Verschwörung,"* 1:178, 364–65.

56. *"If the generals have not achieved anything":* Hoffmann, *Stauffenberg*, 183; Meding, *Mit dem Mut des Herzens*, 275.

57. *"The struggle against National Socialism":* Kuhn, "Eigenhändige Aussagen," 191.

58. *"Any chance, be it the slightest":* Based on the testimony of Olga von Saucken, Üxküll's daughter, reproduced in Kramarz, *Claus Graf Stauffenberg*, 245. See also Üxküll's own testimony at the People's Court: "Verräter vor dem Volksgericht, Teil II, Rolle 4, Ton / 294 m / 10,45 min," in Bengt von zur Mühlen, ed., *Die Angeklagten des 20 Juli vor dem Volksgerichtshof* (Berlin: Chronos, 2001), 257.

## 16. Thou Shalt Kill: The Problem of Tyrannicide

1. *the decision to assassinate him ... was difficult:* Gotthard von Falkenhausen, "Bericht über Vorgänge in Paris am 20 Juli" (undated), Zeller Papers, IfZ ED 88/1, pp. 42–44.

2. *He rejected assassination:* Ibid., p. 42; Hans B. Gisevius, *To the Bitter End*, trans. Richard Winston and Clara Winston (New York: Da Capo Press, 1998), 526–27; compare with Hans A. Jacobsen, ed., *"Spiegelbild einer Verschwörung": Die Opposition gegen Hitler und der Staatsstreich vom 20. Juli 1944 in der SD-Berichterstattung: Geheime Dokumente aus dem ehemaligen Reichssicherheitshauptamt* (Stuttgart: Seewald, 1984), 1:175.

3. *Ulrich von Hassell continued to prefer:* Ulrich von Hassell, *Die Hassell-Tagebücher, 1938–1944: Aufzeichnungen vom anderen Deutschland*, ed. Friedrich Freiherr Hiller von Gärtringen (Munich: Goldmann, 1994), 297.

4. *"crimes taking place behind the army's back":* Nicholas Reynolds, *Treason Was No Crime: Ludwig Beck, Chief of the German General Staff* (London: Kimber, 1976), 216; Jacobsen, *"Spiegelbild einer Verschwörung,"* 1:201; compare with G. Falkenhausen, "Bericht," Zeller Papers, IfZ ED 88/1, pp. 45–47.

5. *"in case of failure":* Niederschrift Manfred Roeder, 3 and 4 December 1951, IfZ, ZS-0124, http://www.ifz-muenchen.de/archiv/zs/zs-0124.pdf., p. 24.

Roeder had seen evidence for this plan in the documents confiscated from Dohnanyi on April 3, 1943. Unfortunately, this stack of documents, which could have been a major historical source on the German resistance movement, did not survive the war. Roeder's testimony backs up and complements Crome's deposition; see following note.

6. *At the end of January 1942 . . . there was a conspiratorial meeting:* Beria to Stalin, 19.9.1944, GARF Fond R-9401, Opis 2, Del 66, pp. 297–98, 320.

7. *in February 1943, the leader of the resistance:* Klaus-Jürgen Müller, *Generaloberst Ludwig Beck: Eine Biographie* (Paderborn: Schöningh, 2008), 465; Reynolds, *Treason Was No Crime*, 216.

8. *Beck fully supported Tresckow's attempt:* Hermann Kaiser, *Mut zum Bekenntnis: Die geheimen Tagebücher des Hauptmanns Hermann Kaiser, 1941, 1943,* ed. Peter M. Kaiser (Berlin: Lukas Verlag, 2010), 438.

9. *"Hitler is the source of all misery":* Ibid., 434; Gersdorff to Scheurig, 9.11.1970, Scheurig Papers, IfZ ZS/A 0031-2, http://www.ifz-muenchen.de/archiv/zsa/ZS_A_0031_02.pdf, p. 130; Rudolf-Christoph Freiherr von Gersdorff, *Soldat im Untergang* (Frankfurt am Main: Ullstein, 1977), 129.

10. *The fact that young officers . . . became enthusiastic supporters:* Peter von der Groeben to Bodo Scheurig (interview, 4.6.1970), Adolf Heusinger to Scheurig (interview, 5.5.1970), Scheurig Papers, IfZ ZS/A 0031-2, http://www.ifz-muenchen.de/archiv/zsa/ZS_A_0031_02.pdf, pp. 148, 83.

11. *A coup destined to bring about a moral regeneration:* Sabine Gillmann and Hans Mommsen, *Politische Schriften und Briefe Carl Friedrich Goerdelers* (Munich: Saur, 2003), 2:1199, 1241; Peter Hoffmann, *The History of the German Resistance, 1933–1945,* trans. Richard Barry (Montreal: McGill-Queens University Press, 1985), 370; Jacobsen, *"Spiegelbild einer Verschwörung,"* 1:101.

12. *"Goerdeler countered time and again":* Jacobsen, *"Spiegelbild einer Verschwörung,"* 1:535.

13. *he "does not want to wait any longer":* Kaiser, *Mut zum Bekenntnis,* 419.

14. *The shift from unrelenting, conscious rejection:* Hoffmann, *History of the German Resistance,* 371.

15. *"You do not have anyone who could do it right":* Cited in Theodore S. Hamerow, *On the Road to Wolf's Lair: German Resistance to Hitler* (Cambridge, Mass.: Belknap Press of Harvard University Press, 1997), 367.

16. *"I can't stand that fellow Helmuth Moltke":* Peter Hoffmann, "The Question of Western Allied Cooperation with the German Anti-Nazi Conspiracy, 1938–1944," *Historical Journal* 34, no. 2 (1991): 459; Peter Hoffmann, *Stauffenberg: A Family History, 1905–1944* (Cambridge: Cambridge University Press, 1995), 194.

17. *"I was and am still uninvolved in violence":* Helmuth James von Moltke, *Briefe an Freya, 1933–1945* (Munich: Beck, 2005), 616, 23; Klemens von Klemperer, *German Resistance to Hitler: The Search for Allies Abroad* (Oxford: Oxford

University Press, 1992), 327–40; Hoffmann, *History of the German Resistance*, 372.

18. *Bonhoeffer . . . believed that political assassination counted as murder:* Dietrich Bonhoeffer, *Ethics*, vol. 6 of *Dietrich Bonhoeffer Works*, ed. Clifford J. Green, trans. Reinhard Krauss, Charles C. West, and Douglas W. Stott (Minneapolis: Fortress Press, 2005), 248–49.

19. *"Responsible action . . . takes place":* Ibid., 284.

20. *"'The shooting itself would have no significance'":* Based on a firsthand testimony of Bonhoeffer's friend the theologian Wolf-Dieter Zimmermann, reproduced in his book *Wir nannten ihn Bruder Bonhoeffer: Einblicke in ein hoffnungsvolles Leben* (Berlin: Wichern Verlag, 1995), 112–13.

## 17. A Wheel Conspiracy: The Stauffenberg Era

1. *"joint, violent action against the Führer":* Ger van Roon, "Hermann Kaiser und die deutsche Widerstandsbewegung," *Vierteljahrshefte für Zeitgeschichte* 24, no. 3 (July 1976): 284.

2. *"Although the two of us":* Joachim Kuhn, "Eigenhändige Aussagen," in Peter Hoffmann, *Stauffenbergs Freund: Die tragische Geschichte des Widerstandskämpfers Joachim Kuhn* (Munich: Verlag C. H. Beck, 2007), 195.

3. *From the outset, Stauffenberg endorsed:* Rudolf Fahrner, "Geschehnisse um 20. Juli 1944," in *Gesammelte Werke*, ed. Stefano Bianca and Bruno Pieger (Cologne: Böhlau Verlag, 2008), 254.

4. *"Kaiser was a confidant and mediator":* Roon, "Hermann Kaiser," 284.

5. *Even if one does not believe the unfounded theories:* For such conspiracy theories, see, for example, Hedwig Meyer, "Die SS und der 20. Juli 1944," *Vierteljahrshefte für Zeitgeschichte* 14, no. 3 (July 1966): 299–316. Gotthard von Falkenhausen assumed after the war that the evidence gathered against Goerdeler and Oster led the Gestapo astray, shifting its attention from the truly dangerous group around Stauffenberg. See Gotthard von Falkenhausen to Eberhard Zeller, 29.11.1945, Zeller Papers, IfZ ED 88/1, p. 32.

6. *Prof. Johannes Popitz . . . recklessly tried to win over Himmler:* Abschrift Huppenkothen, 11.7.1947, IfZ ZS 0249-1, pp. 17–19, 35. The best source for the bizarre Himmler-Popitz "negotiations" is the secret indictment against Popitz. However, this source has to be read critically, as Popitz overstated the support he received from some people in the resistance for his SS overtures. It is highly unlikely that Tresckow and Witzleben, with their well-known hatred of the SS, supported such plans, and even less reasonable that Goerdeler did not object at the very beginning. Even Popitz conceded that he was virtually ostracized by everyone after his meeting with Himmler. The entire document is reproduced in Allen W. Dulles, *Germany's Underground* (New York: Macmillan, 1947), 151–62; about Kaiser's arrest, see Roon, "Hermann Kaiser," 285.

7. *"Never mention names"*: Dorothee von Meding, *Courageous Hearts: Women and the Anti-Hitler Plot of 1944*, trans. Michael Balfour and Volker R. Berghahn (Providence, R.I.: Berghahn Books, 1997), 53, 56.

8. *only around February 1943 was he informed:* Hermann Kaiser, *Mut zum Bekenntnis: Die geheimen Tagebücher des Hauptmanns Hermann Kaiser, 1941, 1943,* ed. Peter M. Kaiser (Berlin: Lukas Verlag, 2010), 424, 434–35; Hans A. Jacobsen, ed., *"Spiegelbild einer Verschwörung": Die Opposition gegen Hitler und der Staatsstreich vom 20. Juli 1944 in der SD-Berichterstattung: Geheime Dokumente aus dem ehemaligen Reichssicherheitshauptamt* (Stuttgart: Seewald, 1984), 1:522; Berg to Scheurig, 16.3.1970, Scheurig Papers, IfZ ZS/A 0031-2, http://www.ifz-muenchen.de/archiv/zsa/ZS_A_0031_02.pdf, pp. 9–15.

9. *Stauffenberg considerably tightened:* Stauffenberg did not disclose many operational details to members of the Social Democratic group, for example, and even Goerdeler was partially kept in the dark. See Jacobsen, *"Spiegelbild einer Verschwörung,"* 1:212–13, 217.

10. *"spotless National Socialist worldview"*: Gotthard von Falkenhausen to Eberhard Zeller, 29.11.1945, Zeller Papers, IfZ ED 88/1, p. 32; Oberleutnant a.D. Herber, "Was ich am 20.7.1944 in der Bendlerstrasse erlebte," BA-MA Msg 2/214, pp. 4–5; GARF Fond R-9401, Opis 2. Del 66, pp. 293–322; Rudolf-Christoph Freiherr von Gersdorff, "History of the Attempt on Hitler's Life (20 Jul. 1944)," Historical Division Headquarters, United States Army Europe, Foreign Military Studies Branch, USAMHI, 2–3, 8; "Von Tresckow, Henning: Beurteilung," BA-MA BAarch PERS 6/1980.

11. *Even a sharp observer:* Kivimäki's report from Berlin, 12.2.1943, UMA, UM 5 C. See also Errki Kouri, "Das Bild der Finnen vom deutschen Widerstand gegen Hitler," in *Die deutsche Widerstand: Wahrnehmung und Wertung in Europa und den USA,* ed. Gerd R. Ueberschär (Darmstadt: Wissenschafliche Buchgesellschaft, 2002), 191–92.

12. *To use terminology taken from criminal-law theory:* Gregory D. Lee, *Conspiracy Investigations: Terrorism, Drugs, and Gangs* (Upper Saddle River, N.J.: Pearson Prentice Hall, 2005), 31.

13. *"Stauffenberg was considered the person"*: Jacobsen, *"Spiegelbild einer Verschwörung,"* 1:523; compare with pp. 177–78.

14. *The count . . . did not know every individual:* For indications of the relative autonomy of Goerdeler in the network, see ibid., 177–78. Goerdeler played a predominant connecting role in the civilian oppositional networks. For a summary of his connections with civilian networks, see ibid., 350–52.

15. *Stauffenberg distrusted Gisevius and Helldorff:* Gisevius, *Bis Zum bittern Ende* (Zurich: Fretz & Wasmuth,1946), 446–47, 468–69, 471–74; Jacobsen, ibid., 177–78, 217, 362; Konstanze von Schulthess, *Nina Schenk Gräfin von Stauffenberg: Ein Porträt* (Munich: Pendo, 2008), 80; Fahrner, "Geschehnisse," 254. On Stauffenberg's hostility to Helldorff, see "Bericht von Urban Thiersch

über seine Begegnungen mit Oberst Graf Stauffenberg im Juli 1944," Zeller Papers, IfZ ED 88/2, p. 335.

16. *"I am sending tens of thousands"*: Peter Hoffmann, *Stauffenberg: A Family History, 1905–1944* (Cambridge: Cambridge University Press, 1995), 192.

17. *"I was nervous"*: Meding, *Courageous Hearts*, 53.

18. *Oven realized that she was privy*: Ibid.; Hoffmann, *Stauffenberg*, 197; Peter Hoffmann, "Oberst i. G. Henning von Tresckow und die Staatsstreichpläne im Jahr 1943," *Vierteljahrshefte für Zeitgeschichte* 55, no. 2 (2007): 344.

19. *Stauffenberg knew, too, that masses of people*: Christian Müller, *Oberst i. G. Stauffenberg: Eine Biographie* (Düsseldorf: Droste, 1971), 382.

20. *a poem written by his spiritual mentor*: Hoffmann, *Stauffenberg*, 197–98. Hans von Bittenfeld had also testified that Stauffenberg radiated with "sacred fire" and believed that he was a "divine tool" in the fight against National Socialism. See Bittenfeld, "Meine Verbindung mit Graf Stauffenberg" (newspaper clipping, 18.7.1969), Deutsch Papers, series 3, box 2, rounds 3 and 4 Material.

21. *"those responsible in Germany"*: Hoffmann, *Stauffenberg*, 283–84.

22. *"In our Dubno garrison"*: Axel von dem Bussche, "Eid und Schuld," *Axel von dem Bussche*, ed. Gevinon von Medem (Mainz: Hase & Koehler, 1994), 138. In his full report, Bussche argued that he was promised by the authorities that the remaining women at least would be kept alive, because around fifty Jews were needed for forced labor. However, that protection was valid only for a limited period of time, and finally all survivors of the massacre were deported to Auschwitz. See Axel von dem Bussche, Ns v.18.6.1948, betr. Massenerschießungen v. Juden Ghetto Dubno 1942, IfZ ZS-1827, pp. 7–12.

23. *At Dubno, Bussche had witnessed*: Bussche, "Eid und Schuld," 139–40, 150–53; Peter Hoffmann, *Widerstand, Staatsstreich, Attentat: Der Kampf der Opposition gegen Hitler* (Munich: Piper, 1985), 399–401.

24. *"These days . . . were illuminated"*: Bussche, "Eid und Schuld," 141.

25. *When Beck . . . visited Olbricht*: Helena Page, *General Friedrich Olbricht: Ein Mann des 20. Juli* (Bonn: Bouvier, 1994), 192.

26. *Originally, the Valkyrie orders were designed*: The original Valkyrie orders were drafted in October 1941. See Allgemeines Heeresamt, Abt. Demob. Nr. 350/42 g.Kdos, "Herstellung einsatzfähiger Verwenungsbereitschaft des Ersatzheeres," 5.2.1942, Chef der Heeresrüstung und Befehlshaber des Ersatzheeres, AHA Ia VII Nr. 1160/42 g.Kdos., "Betr.: Walküre II," 21.3.1942, BA-MA RH/12/21, 7, pp. 128–42, 204–12; Stellv. Generalkommando XX.A.K (Wehrkreiskommando XX), Abt. Ib/Org, "Betr. Einsatz Walküre," 14.5.1942, BA-MA RH/53/20, 27, pp. 78–84. The phantom of a mass uprising of foreign workers, which was later to become associated with the plan in the resistance literature, can be traced to autumn 1943. See Kommandeur

der Panzertruppen XVII, Wien, 10.9.1943, "An die Herrn Kommandeure," BA-MA RH/53/17, 143.

27. *"the preparations must be carried through"*: Chef der Heeresrüstung und Befehlshaber des Ersatzheeres, AHA/Ia (I), Nr. 3830/43 g.Kdos, "Betr.: Walküre," 31.7.1943, BA-MA RH/12/21, 56, pp. 171–79 (hereafter this source is cited as Valkyrie 31.7.43); another, more formal copy can be found in BA-MA RH/53/17, 39). The orders were revised again on 6.10.1943 so as to put all troops that happened to be in Germany at that moment under the command of the Home Command. See Walküre, 6.10.1943, BA-MA RH/53/17, 39. For a summary report on the drills and rehearsals, see, for example, Wehrkreis Kommando XVII, Wien, 1.9.1943, "Verwendungsbereitschaft des Ersatzheeres," BA-MA RH/53/17, 143. The stringent secrecy measures were inherited from Valkyrie II, 5.2.1942, and the version from 23.6.1942, BA-MA RH/53/20, 27, p. 100. In this version, it is maintained that cooperation with SS and police should take place only under explicit orders covered by a different code name (Neptun). For a concise discussion on the evolution of the orders, see Hoffmann, *Stauffenberg*, 198–200.

28. *The idea was, of course, to keep the prying eyes*: Indeed, in a plan against enemy paratroopers drafted in January 1944, which orchestrated close cooperation between army, Luftwaffe, SS, and police forces, Valkyrie was not mentioned even once. If the drafters of such a comprehensive plan did not know about coeval measures intended to achieve the same purpose, it seems that even the "legitimate," military part of Valkyrie was hidden quite well. See Wehrkreiskommando XVII (Stellv. Gen. Kdo. XVII A.K.), Wien, 12.1.1944, "Grundsätzlicher Befehl für die Abwehr feindlicher Einzelspringer, Fallschirmjäger und Luftlandetruppen," BA-MA RH/53/17, 39.

29. *The leaders of the resistance decided*: For the full distribution list, see Valkyrie 31.7.1943, BA-MA RH/12/21, 56, p. 175.

30. *The first communiqué would disclose*: Kuhn, "Eigenhändige Aussagen," 199–200; Horst Mühleisen, "Patrioten im Widerstand: Carl-Hans Graf von Hardenbergs Erlebnisbericht," *Vierteljahrshefte für Zeitgeschichte* 14, no. 3 (January 1993): 452. According to SS prosecutor Walther Huppenkothen, Helldorff was supposed to lead the police on the first day and then be replaced by Tresckow. The conspirators, according to Huppenkothen, wanted to remove Helldorff because of his "bad reputation." See Abschrift, Anlage zur Aussage Huppenkothen zum 20. Juli 1944, 51, Deutsch Papers, series 3, box 2, material on Huppenkothen.

31. *Stauffenberg and Tresckow had worked on detailed operational plans*: "Maßnahmenkalender," in Hoffmann, "Oberst i. G. Henning von Tresckow"; Hoffmann, *Stauffenbergs Freund*, 171–82; Kuhn, "Eigenhändige Aussagen," 200–201.

32. *it was probably written by Stauffenberg:* Hoffmann, *Stauffenberg*, 210–11.
33. *"Germans! . . . The tyranny of Hitler is broken!":* Jacobsen, *"Spiegelbild einer Verschwörung,"* 1:140–42.
34. *"above all we have to act":* Ibid., 201; Roon, "Hermann Kaiser," 275.
35. *the charismatic leader Carlo Mierendorff:* Emil Henk, *Die Tragödie des 20 Juli 1944: Ein Beitrag zur politischen Vorgeschichte* (Heidelberg: Rausch, 1946), 46–52.
36. *Even if such a network did exist:* Exilvorstand der Sozialdemokratischen Partei Deutschlands (SOPADE), *Sozialistische Mitteilungen: Newsletter, herausgegeben vom 1939–1948.* Hefte Nr.45, 3–9, Nr.47, 5, Nr.49, 3–8, Nr.52 p. 19, Beilage 2: I–XII, Nr.53/4, 1–5, Nr. 55/6, 7–15, Nr.57, 4–9, Nr.58/9, 1–14, Nr.62, 20, Nr.63/4, Beilage 2: I–XVI.
37. *the conspirators hoped to reach a truce:* Agent "Dogwood" to U.S. Military Attaché General Richard D. Tindall (Ankara), 29.12.1943; Report of the OSS Planning Group, 3.4.1944; OSS assistant director G. Edward Buxton to Secretary of State Cordell Hull, 16.5.1944; OSS director William J. Donovan to President FDR, 22.7.1944; Wallace R. Deuel (OSS-Washington) to OSS director William J. Donovan, 24.7.1944, all in *American Intelligence and the German Resistance to Hitler*, ed. Jürgen Heideking and Christof Mauch (Boulder, Colo.: Westview Press, 1996), 177–80, 204–5, 219–22, 245–46, 251; Bengt von zur Mühlen, *Die Angeklagten des 20 Juli vor dem Volksgerichtshof* (Berlin: Chronos, 2001), 252–54.
38. *Even the attempts of Allen Dulles:* Dulles himself was initially hostile to the conspirators. Then, he became more sympathetic, but Gisevius's doubts about the resolution of the generals did not encourage him. For the development of Dulles's approach to the resistance, see Allen W. Dulles (COI New York) to Colonel William J. Donovan, 8.5.1942; Dulles (OSS Bern) to OSS Washington, 13.1.1943, 8.11.1943, 27.1.1944, 12.7.1944, in Heideking and Mauch, *American Intelligence*, pp. 24, 38–9, 152–53, 192–93, 244. As for Gisevius's doubts (he is not mentioned, but his identity is clear from context), see Buxton to Cordell Hull, 16.5.1944, Heideking and Mauch, 219–22.
39. *Stauffenberg had been able to get in touch:* Nuremberg Blue, 15:403; Gotthard von Falkenhausen to Eberhard Zeller, 29.11.1945, Zeller Papers, IfZ, ED 88/1, p. 34. Rommel's true commitment to the coup has always been controversial. The tapped testimony of General Eberbach (in British captivity) suggests that Rommel at least thought about a coup d'état and an assassination at the time, giving more credence to the possibility of his involvement. See Sönke Neitzel, *Abgehört: Deutsche Generäle in britischer Kriegsgefangenschaft 1942–1945* (Berlin: Propyläen, 2005), pp. 351, 353, 372.
40. *According to the operational procedure:* Valkyrie 31.7.1943, BA-MA RH/12/21, 56.

41. *The general continued to play that game:* Hoffmann, *Stauffenberg,* 201; Unterhaltung mit Frau Ursula von Witzleben, 10.2.1970, 3, Deutsch Papers, series 3, box 3, round 1 Material.

42. *he told Olbricht and Stauffenberg "not to forget":* Hoffmann, *Stauffenberg,* 201, and compare with Mühleisen, "Patrioten im Widerstand," 460.

43. *Hoepner, denounced by Gisevius:* Hans B. Gisevius, *To the Bitter End,* trans. Richard Winston and Clara Winston (New York: Da Capo Press, 1998), 519; Hans Mommsen, *Alternative zu Hitler: Studien zur Geschichte des deutschen Widerstandes* (Munich: Beck, 2000), 375–76.

44. *he was even mentioned as part of the unrealistic plan:* Niederschrift Manfred Roeder, 3 and 4 December 1951, IfZ, ZS-0124, p. 24, http://www.ifz -muenchen.de/archiv/zs/zs-0124.pdf.

45. *Hoepner had been forbidden . . . to wear uniform:* Kaiser, *Mut zum Bekenntnis,* 500.

46. *Bussche was notified by telephone:* Bussche, "Eid und Schuld," 141.

47. *"It was January 1944":* Ewald-Heinrich von Kleist, interviewed by Nicholas Netteau, 13.1.1998; given to the present author with the courtesy of Nicholas Netteau; compare with Kleist's interview to Eberhard Zeller, 14.2.1946, Zeller Papers, IfZ ED 88/2, p. 223.

48. *According to the young man's testimony:* Bodo Scheurig, *Ewald von Kleist-Schmenzin: Ein Konservativer gegen Hitler* (Oldenburg: Stalling, 1968), 184–85; Hoffmann, *Stauffenberg,* 230–31; Klaus J. Müller, "Prussian Elements in the German Resistance," in *The Moral Imperative: New Essays on the Ethics of Resistance in National Socialist Germany, 1933–1945,* ed. Andrew Chandler (Boulder, Colo.: Westview Press, 1998), 63.

49. *"Tresckow took me to my private room":* Breitenbuch to Scheurig, 28.3.1970, Scheurig Papers, IfZ ZS/A 0031-2, http://www.ifz-muenchen.de/archiv/zsa/ ZS_A_0031_02.pdf, p. 55.

50. *Breitenbuch was ready to sacrifice his own life:* Eberhard von Breitenbuch, *Erinnerungen eines Reserveoffiziers, 1939–1945: Aufgeschrieben zur Kenntnis meiner Kinder* (Norderstedt: Books on Demand, 2011), 121.

51. *Breitenbuch swore that he would never go through:* Ibid., 123–24. For a slightly different version of the events, see Fabian von Schlabrendorff, *The Secret War Against Hitler,* trans. Hilda Simon (Boulder, Colo.: Westview Press, 1994), 295; compare with Alexander Stahlberg, *Bounden Duty: The Memoirs of a German Officer, 1932–1945,* trans. Patricia Crampton (London: Macmillan, 1990), 298. Stahlberg is clearly mistaken about the date, as Breitenbuch's attempt took place in March 1944. His (Stahlberg's) testimony might have been adversely affected by the passage of time.

52. *Some . . . were moved by the Normandy invasion:* These debates are echoed in the OSS memoranda; see OSS director William J. Donovan to President FDR, 22.7.1944, in Heideking and Mauch, *American Intelligence,* 244, and in Hardenberg's testimony, Mühleisen, "Patrioten im Widerstand," 253. See

also Harold C. Deutsch's interview with Botho von Wussow and Gräfin Schwerin von Schwanenfeld, 27.6.1970, 12–13, Deutsch Papers, series 3, box 3, round 1 Material; and the testimony of Albrecht Fischer on his conversations with Goerdeler in spring 1944: Albrecht Fischer, "Erlebnisse vom 20. Juli 1944 bis 8. April 1945," 9.10.1961, IfZ, ZS-1758, p. 3.

53. *"The assassination of Hitler must take place"*: Hoffmann, *Stauffenberg*, 238. The text is slightly different in each of the following accounts: Eberhard Zeller, *Geist der Freiheit: Der Zwanzigste Juli* (Munich: Rhinn, 1952), 358–59; Schlabrendorff, *Secret War Against Hitler*, 277; Gerd R. Ueberschär, *Stauffenberg: Der 20 Juli 1944* (Frankfurt am Main: Fischer, 2004), 39; Meding, *Mit dem Mut des Herzens: Die Frauen des 20 Juli* (Berlin: Siedler, 1992), 118; compare with the version of Margarethe von Hardenberg (Oven) in an interview with Bodo Scheurig, 2.5.1969, Scheurig Papers, IfZ ZS/A 0031-2, http://www.ifz-muenchen.de/archiv/zsa/ZS_A_0031_02.pdf, p. 166.

54. *"during and preceding this war"*: For the Stauffenberg quote, see Schulthess, *Nina Schenk Gräfin von Stauffenberg*, 81. Beck is quoted by Theodore S. Hamerow, *On the Road to Wolf's Lair: German Resistance to Hitler* (Cambridge, Mass.: Belknap Press of Harvard University Press, 1997), 350. See also Friedrich Meinecke, *Die deutsche Katastrophe: Betrachtungen und Erinnerungen* (Wiesbaden: Brockhaus, 1946), 149; Meding, *Mit dem Mut des Herzens*, 273. Goerdeler's letter is reproduced in full as an appendix to Helena P. Page's biography of Olbricht, *General Friedrich Olbricht*; see Goerdeler an Olbricht/Zeitzler, 15.05.1943. For similar evidence, see the Kaltenbrunner reports in Jacobsen, *"Spiegelbild einer Verschwörung,"* 1:201.

55. *"The most terrible thing . . . is knowing"*: Hoffmann, *Stauffenberg*, 243; Mühleisen, "Patrioten im Widerstand," 456.

56. *Stauffenberg decided to kill Hitler himself*: Hoffmann, *Stauffenberg*, 152.

57. *Major General Stieff, the only other conspirator*: Fahrner, "Geschehnisse," 255; Hoffmann, *Stauffenberg*, 226.

58. *In his diary, Hermann Kaiser used clumsy code names*: Kaiser, *Mut zum Bekenntnis*, 436; Jacobsen, *"Spiegelbild einer Verschwörung,"* 1:57, 352, 461; Peter Hoffmann, *The History of the German Resistance, 1933–1945*, trans. Richard Barry (Montreal: McGill-Queens University Press, 1985), 378. In his testimony at the Nuremberg Trials, Schlabrendorff disclosed that some conspirators shied away from Hassell, because he was known as a reckless speaker; see *Nuremberg Green*, 13:391. In July 1944, Goerdeler was also considered so "compromised" and exposed to Gestapo eyes that even Beck tried to avoid his company in the days before July 20 (Jacobsen, *"Spiegelbild einer Verschwörung,"* 1:362). For Tresckow's words, see Kaiser, *Mut zum Bekenntnis*, 422.

59. *Stauffenberg . . . hesitated at first*: Hoffmann, *Stauffenberg*, 196; Henk, *Die Tragödie*, 52–54.

60. *The Communists accepted, in principle*: Hoffmann, *Stauffenberg*, 196.

61. *Schulenburg sent a short message to Leber's wife:* Dorothea Beck, *Julius Leber: Sozialdemokrat zwischen Reform und Widerstand* (Berlin: Siedler, 1983), 199.

62. *Oven was carrying the operational plan of the coup:* Mühleisen, "Patrioten im Widerstand," 457; Meding, *Courageous Hearts*, 53–54.

63. *He and Beck had agreed in advance:* Gotthard von Falkenhausen, "Bericht über Vorgänge in Paris am 20 Juli" (undated), Zeller Papers, IfZ ED 88/1, pp. 54–55; Hoffmann, *Widerstand, Staatsstreich, Attentat,* 469–70.

64. *General Olbricht had activated the Valkyrie orders:* Page, *General Friedrich Olbricht,* 206–8.

65. *Next time, Olbricht said, he would activate the orders:* Ueberschär, *Stauffenberg,* 41; Jacobsen, *"Spiegelbild einer Verschwörung,"* 1:91; Otto Hitzfeld to Gerd Buchheit, 5.7.66, IfZ ZS-1858, http://www.ifz-muenchen.de/archiv/zs/zs-1858.pdf, p. 1.

66. *Adam von Trott zu Solz . . . reported that he had some basis:* Jacobsen, *"Spiegelbild einer Verschwörung,"* 1:101, 175.

67. *the conspirators lost the most powerful:* On the influence of Rommel's injury on the coup at the western front, see Gotthard von Falkenhausen to Eberhard Zeller, 29.11.1945, Zeller Papers, IfZ, ED 88/1, p. 34.

68. *Arthur Nebe . . . gave them a tip:* Gisevius, *Bis Zum bittern Ende,* 497; Gerhard Ritter, *Carl Goerdeler und die deutsche Widerstandsbewegung* (Stuttgart: Deutsche Verlags-Anstalt, 1954), 408. I was not able to find evidence that such an arrest warrant was in fact issued. Most of the relevant Gestapo documents were destroyed in 1945, but in the Kaltenbrunner Reports (Jacobsen, *"Spiegelbild einer Verschwörung,"* 1:524) only the warning given to Goerdeler by his friends is mentioned, not an actual warrant. It is highly improbable that such a document was unbeknownst to Kaltenbrunner and his officials, had it existed. Nebe's information was based either on a decision to publish a warrant or on rumors about such a decision. In any case, the Gestapo probably did not have the time to issue any arrest order until after July 20. In his interrogation, Goerdeler did not elaborate on the real reasons behind his escape on July 18, most probably in order not to incriminate his first host, Baron Palombini. See Jacobsen, "Spiegelbild einer Verschwörung," 1:217.

69. *After a "jolly party" with his family:* Interview with Charlotte von der Schulenburg, in Hava Kohav Beller, *The Restless Conscience: Resistance to Hitler Within Germany, 1933–1945* (1992; Los Angeles: New Video Group, 2009), DVD.

70. *A chance visitor in the Bendlerstrasse:* Jacobsen, *"Spiegelbild einer Verschwörung,"* 1:92; Meding, *Courageous Hearts*, 58; Hoffmann, *Widerstand, Staatsstreich, Attentat,* 485.

## 18. The Final Showdown: July 20, 1944

1. *"an impregnable lair of reinforced concrete":* Abakumov to Beria, 22.2.1945, GARF Fond R-9401, Opis 2, Del 93, p. 6.

2. *Stauffenberg probably knew:* Eberhard Zeller, *Geist der Freiheit: Der Zwanzigste Juli* (Munich: Rhinn, 1952), 381.

3. *Fellgiebel became involved in the conspiracy:* Helmuth Arnz, "Abschrift einer Niederschrift über den General der Nachrichtentruppen Erich Fellgiebel," Zeller Papers, IfZ ED 88/1, pp. 2–3; Beria to Stalin, 19.9.1944, GARF Fond R-9401, Opis 2, Del 66, p. 317; Peter Hoffmann, *Widerstand, Staatsstreich, Attentat: Der Kampf der Opposition gegen Hitler* (Munich: Piper, 1985), 415; Joachim Kuhn, "Eigenhändige Aussagen," in Peter Hoffman, *Stauffenbergs Freund: Die tragische Geschichte des Widerstandskämpfers Joachim Kuhn* (Munich: Verlag C. H. Beck, 2007), 199; Hermann Kaiser, *Mut zum Bekenntnis: Die geheimen Tagebücher des Hauptmanns Hermann Kaiser, 1941, 1943*, ed. Peter M. Kaiser (Berlin: Lukas Verlag, 2010), 436, 478. There are some indications that Fellgiebel became involved, at least indirectly, in winter 1942. See Stahlberg to Scheurig (interview, 15.9.1965), Scheurig Papers, IfZ ZS/A 0031-3, http://www.ifz-muenchen.de/archiv/zsa/ZS_A_0031_03.pdf, p. 111.

4. *After briefing Fellgiebel one last time:* Arnz, "Abschrift," Zeller Papers, IfZ ED 88/1, pp. 3–4.

5. *Stauffenberg believed that the meeting:* Hoffmann, *Widerstand, Staatsstreich, Attentat*, 487.

6. *Stauffenberg suddenly asked for permission:* Hans A. Jacobsen, ed., *"Spiegelbild einer Verschwörung": Die Opposition gegen Hitler und der Staatsstreich vom 20. Juli 1944 in der SD-Berichterstattung: Geheime Dokumente aus dem ehemaligen Reichssicherheitshauptamt* (Stuttgart: Seewald, 1984), 1:85.

7. *Peeping through the half-opened door:* Peter Hoffmann, *Stauffenberg: A Family History, 1905–1944* (Cambridge: Cambridge University Press, 1995), 265.

8. *Hitler nodded in response:* Jacobsen, *"Spiegelbild einer Verschwörung,"* 1:85.

9. *"The Russian . . . is strongly advancing":* Zeller, *Geist der Freiheit*, 381.

10. *Stauffenberg ordered the driver:* Jacobsen, *"Spiegelbild einer Verschwörung,"* 1:86; Karl Fischer, *Ich Fuhr Stauffenberg: Erinnerungen an die Kriegsjahre, 1939–1945* (Angermünde: Spiegelberg Verlag, 2008), 97.

11. *"Thank you very much, and wish us luck":* Fischer, *Ich Fuhr Stauffenberg*, 97; Jacobsen, *"Spiegelbild einer Verschwörung,"* 1:86.

12. *Inside the Third Ring, in Hitler's briefing hut:* Hoffmann, *Widerstand, Staatsstreich, Attentat*, 495. For an additional firsthand testimony, see Walter Warlimont, *Im Hauptquartier der deutschen Wehrmacht, 1939–1945* (Frankfurt am Main: Bernard & Graefe, 1962), 471.

13. *"I always knew . . . that I am surrounded":* Hoffmann, *Widerstand, Staatsstreich, Attentat*, 496.

14. *"Something terrible happened":* Arnz, "Abschrift," Zeller Papers, IfZ ED 88/1, p. 4.

15. *In Hitler's headquarters, there was still great confusion:* Hoffmann, *Widerstand, Staatsstreich, Attentat*, 504; "Ernennung Himmlers zum Befehlshaber des Ersatzheeres, 20.7.1944" (Doc. 340), in *Führer-Erlasse, 1939–1940*, ed. Mar-

tin Holl (Stuttgart: Steiner, 1997), 433; firsthand testimony: "Der 20. Juli 1944 im Führerhauptquartier," 4, Deutsch Papers, series 4, box 9, Halder Franz. Another indication can be found in Goebbels's radio broadcast from 26.7.1944; see FBIS, NARA, Rg.263, SA 190, R 23, C 34, S7, box 93, H4.

16. *"Mussolini was absolutely horrified"*: Paul Schmidt, *Hitler's Interpreter*, ed. and trans. R. H. C. Steed (New York: Macmillan, 1951), 275–76.

17. *During dinner, the Nazi leaders were still busy:* Max Domarus, *Hitler: Reden und Proklamationen, 1932–1945: Kommentiert von einem deutschen Zeitgenossen* (Würzburg: Schmidt, Neustadt a.d. Aisch, 1962), 2127; Zeller, *Geist der Freiheit*, 422–23.

18. *"It begins! . . . I have heard from Olbricht"*: Hans B. Gisevius, *Bis zum bittern Ende* (Zurich: Fretz & Wasmuth, 1946), 510. On Hase, see Roland Kopp, *Paul von Hase von der Alexander-Kaserne nach Plötzensee: Eine deutsche Soldatenbiographie, 1885–1944* (Münster: Lit, 2001), 268–69.

19. *The rumors about the blast in Wolf's Lair:* Wilhelm R. von Schramm, *Aufstand der Generale: Der 20 Juli in Paris* (Munich: Kindler, 1964), 82–83.

20. *At 3:45 p.m., Stauffenberg disembarked:* Gisevius, *Bis zum bittern Ende*, 517–18; see also the interview with Ludwig von Hammerstein in Hava Kohav Beller, *The Restless Conscience: Resistance to Hitler Within Germany, 1933–1945* (1992; Los Angeles: New Video Group, 2009), DVD, 1:20.

21. *"There was an assassination attempt"*: Hoffmann, *Widerstand, Staatsstreich, Attentat*, 513–14; Gisevius, *Bis zum bittern Ende*, 518–19; H. L. Bartram, "20. Juli 1944," BA-MA Msg 2/214, p. 2. For a more sympathetic view of Fromm, see Bernhard Kroener, *Generaloberst Friedrich Fromm: Der starke Mann im Heimatkriegsgebiet; Eine Biographie* (Paderborn: Schöningh, 2005), 682–701.

22. *Lieutenant General Hase ordered the guard battalion:* "Befehl für den Berliner Wehrmachtkommandanten, 20.7.1944," reproduced in Kopp, *Paul von Hase*, plate 35.

23. *Olbricht was hardly out of Fromm's office:* Gisevius, *Bis zum bittern Ende*, 519; "Stenogram der ersten Volksgerichtshofverhandlung vom 7/8 August 1944," in *Die Angeklagten des 20 Juli vor dem Volksgerichtshof*, ed. Bengt von zur Mühlen (Berlin: Chronos, 2001), appendix, 76.

24. *Here, the conspirators entered a dangerous mental loop:* Eugen Gerstenmaier, "Der 20. Juli 1944," BA-MA Msg 2/213, p. 5(26).

25. *Beck, however, was doubtful:* Gisevius, *Bis zum bittern Ende*, 514; Nicholas Reynolds, *Treason Was No Crime: Ludwig Beck, Chief of the German General Staff* (London: Kimber, 1976), 264; Jacobsen, *"Spiegelbild einer Verschwörung,"* 1:191; "Stenogram," 122.

26. *Stauffenberg's next move:* Walter Bargatzky, "Persönliche Erinnerungen an die Aufstandsbewegung des 20. Juli 1944 in Frankreich," 20.10.1945, IfZ, ZS-203, p. 10.

27. *"General, . . . the Gestapo is trying to stage a coup"*: Schramm, *Aufstand der*

*Generale*, 84, 86–87; Andreas von Klewitz, "General d. Inf. Carl-Heinrich von Stülpnagel und der 20 Juli 1944 in Paris," in Mühlen, *Angeklagten*, 107.

28. *"It should be welcomed":* Schramm, *Aufstand der Generale*, 84, 86–87.

29. *"I sat in my office in Majestic":* Walter Bargatzky, "Letzte Runde in Paris," in *20 Juli 1944*, ed. Hans A. Jacobsen and Erich Zimmermann (Bonn: Berto Vaerlag, 1960), 154.

30. *Soon afterward, Hofacker rushed:* Schramm, *Aufstand der Generale*, 103; Hans Freiherr von Boineburg-Langsfeld, "Als Kommandant von Groß-Paris am 20.Juli 1944," in *Der 20. Juli 1944 in Paris: Verlauf, Hauptbeteiligte, Augenzeugen*, ed. Bengt von zur Mühlen and Frank Bauer (Berlin: Chronos, 1995), 198.

31. *"I think that the Führer is alive":* Hoffmann, *Widerstand, Staatsstreich, Attentat*, 514, 519–20; H. L. Bartram, "20. Juli 1944," BA-MA Msg 2/214, p. 2; Gisevius, *Bis zum bittern Ende*, 519; "Stenogram," 77; Kleist (interview with Zeller,14.2.1946), "Augenzeugenbericht," Zeller Papers, IfZ ED 88/2, p. 225; compare with Hardenberg's testimony in "Patrioten im Widerstand: Carl-Hans Graf von Hardenbergs Erlebnisbericht," *Vierteljahrshefte für Zeitgeschichte* 14, no. 3 (January 1993): 461. For a slightly different version, see Kroener, *Generaloberst Friedrich Fromm*, 682–86.

32. *Two hours earlier, Mertz had sent them:* Jacobsen, *"Spiegelbild einer Verschwörung,"* 1:63.

33. *"The Führer Adolf Hitler is dead":* Ibid., 1:25–26.

34. *At 4:30 p.m., after arresting Fromm:* Herber, Oberleutnant a.D. Herber, "Was ich am 20.7.1944 in der Bendlerstrasse erlebte," BA-MA Msg 2/214, pp. 1–2; Oberst von Roell, "Über die Ereignisse des Nachm. und Abends des 20.7.1944," 21.7.1944, BA-MA Msg 2/213, p. 1.

35. *Stauffenberg sent one of his men:* Mühleisen, "Patrioten im Widerstand," 462; Herber, "Was ich erlebte," BA-MA Msg 2/214, pp. 1–2; Roell, "Ereignisse," BA-MA Msg 2/213, pp. 2–3; Cords to Zeller, 23.8.1951, Otto John, "Ein Augenzeugenbericht vom 20. Juli 1944" (undated), Zeller Papers, IfZ ED 88/1, p. 6, ED 88/2, pp. 211–12.

36. *At around 4:15 p.m., . . . the conspirators had other prominent visitors:* Gisevius, *Bis zum bittern Ende*, 512–14; compare with Helldorff's apologetic testimony and also with the more detailed account offered by Bismarck, in Mühlen, *Angeklagten*, 225–26, 283–85.

37. *A few minutes after 5:00 p.m., the conspirators had to cope:* Hans B. Gisevius, *To the Bitter End*, trans. Richard Winston and Clara Winston (New York: Da Capo Press, 1998), 551; Jacobsen, *"Spiegelbild einer Verschwörung,"* 1:22; Reynolds, *Treason Was No Crime*, 262–63; Mühlen, *Angeklagten*, 235. See also Herber, "Was ich erlebte," BA-MA Msg 2/214, p. 3; "Tagebuch des Stabsgefreiten Karl Berlin," in Daniil E. Melnikov, *20 Juli 1944: Legende und Wirklichkeit*, trans. Fritz Rehak (Berlin: Deutscher Verlag der Wissen-

schaften, 1964), 275–76; Cords to Zeller, 23.8.1951, Zeller Papers, IfZ, ED 88/1, p. 6.

38.  *he ordered his troops to march west:* Philipp Freiherr von Boeselager, "Mein Weg zum 20. Juli 1944 (Vortrag gehalten am 20. Juli 2002 bei den Johannitern in Wasserburg/Bayern) (unpublished manuscript, 2002), 39–40; Boeselager to Hoffmann, 19.11.1964, IfZ ZS-2118.

39.  *Lt. Gen. Otto Hitzfeld, was away at a funeral:* Otto Hitzfeld to Wolfgang Müller, 18.10.1966, Müller to Hitzfeld, 15.10.1966, IfZ ZS-1858, pp. 4–7, http://www.ifz-muenchen.de/archiv/zs/zs-1858.pdf.

40.  *Jacob ... was ignorant of the correct communication procedures:* Hoffmann, *Widerstand, Staatsstreich, Attentat,* 531–32; Allen W. Dulles (OSS Bern) to Brigadier General Thomas J. Betts (London), 21.7.1944, in *American Intelligence and the German Resistance to Htiler,* ed. Jürgen Heideking and Christof Mauch (Boulder, Colo.: Westview Press, 1996), 236.

41.  *ordered "a relentless attack on the SS":* Wolfgang Müller, *Gegen eine neue Dolchstoßlüge: Ein Erlebnisbericht zum 20 Juli 1944* (Hannover: Verlag "Das andere Deutschland," 1947), 44; Hitzfeld to Müller, 18.10.1966, Müller to Hitzfeld, 15.10.1966, IfZ ZS-1858, pp. 4–7.

42.  *Gisevius, though, was uneasy:* Gisevius, *Bis zum bittern Ende,* 527–28.

43.  *Many obeyed the counterorders:* FBIS, NARA, Rg.263, SA 190, R 23, C 34, S7, box 92, CCB1; Herber, "Was ich erlebte," BA-MA Msg 2/214, pp. 2–3; Jacobsen, *"Spiegelbild einer Verschwörung,"* 1:104–8.

44.  *One of the deputies of General Esebeck:* Ludwig Jedlinka, *Das Einsame Gewissen: Der 20 Juli in Österreich* (Vienna: Verlag Herold, 1966), 56; Hoffmann, *Widerstand, Staatsstreich, Attentat,* 575.

45.  *Major General Brehmer ... led the occupation:* Schramm, *Aufstand der Generale,* 139–40.

46.  *Soldiers from the security regiment:* Walter Bargatzky, "Zwei Stunden und eine verratene Chance," in Mühlen and Bauer, *Der 20. Juli 1944 in Paris,* 214. For Hitler's own view of the "unprecedented" nature of the events in Paris, see Felix Gilbert, ed., *Hitler Directs His War: The Secret Records of His Daily Military Conferences* (New York: Oxford University Press, 1950), 104. Bargatzky probably began collecting the material in 1943. See the editor's introduction in Mühlen and Bauer, 9; and Teuchert's testimony in the same collection, 183, 187.

47.  *"a very moral man, staunch German patriot":* Quoted in Schramm, *Aufstand der Generale,* 25. For the French version, see Henri Navarre, *Le temps des vérités* (Paris: Plon, 1979), 150–51.

48.  *For a while, it seemed as though the conspirators:* Hoffmann, *Widerstand, Staatsstreich, Attentat,* 535.

49.  *Major Remer now turned to the most important task:* Jacobsen, *"Spiegelbild einer Verschwörung,"* 2:639–40; Domarus, *Hitler,* 2126. Remer's own testimony,

apologetic through and through, has to be read with caution. Contrary to his self-serving version of the events, he did comply with the orders of the conspirators until his conversation with the Führer. In his radio broadcast on July 26, Goebbels brought forth a more accurate version of that conversation, but he skipped the inconvenient fact that Remer initially threatened to arrest him. See FBIS, NARA, Rg.263, SA 190, R 23, C 34, S7, box 93, H4.

50. *Around 7:00 p.m., Field Marshal Witzleben finally arrived:* Gisevius, *To the Bitter End*, 558–59; Hoffmann, *Widerstand, Staatsstreich, Attentat*, 615–16; compare Otto John's testimony to U.S. intelligence, reported in William A. Kimbel (OSS Washington) to OSS Director William J. Donovan, 15.9.1944, in Heideking and Mauch, *American Intelligence*, 285.

51. *"You must hold firm":* Gisevius, *To the Bitter End*, 555. Compare with Otto John's account of these telephone conversations: "Augenzeugenbericht," Zeller Papers, IfZ ED 88/2, p. 217.

52. *The hesitancy, even timidity, of Hoepner:* Gisevius, *To the Bitter End*, 558–59; "Stenogram," 81, 122.

53. *Shortly afterward, Beck called Kluge:* Schramm, *Aufstand der Generale*, 110.

54. *In a last attempt to find out the truth:* Ibid., 116–20.

55. *"My hands are tied":* Ibid., 130–31; Gotthard von Falkenhausen, "Bericht über Vorgänge in Paris am 20 Juli" (undated), Zeller Papers, IfZ ED 88/1, p. 57. Falkenhausen heard about the conversation from Hofacker on July 21 at 3:00 a.m.

56. *"This denial, Stülpnagel knew, was untrue":* Constantine FitzGibbon, *The Shirt of Nessus* (London: Cassell, 1956), 208.

57. *the officers sat at a silent candlelit dinner:* Hans Speidel, *We Defended Normandy*, trans. Ian Colvin (London: Jenkins, 1951), 132.

58. *Stülpnagel . . . told Kluge that he had already ordered:* Schramm, *Aufstand der Generale*, 133, 135.

59. *We climbed the stairs to room 405:* Bargatzky, "Letzte Runde in Paris," 155.

60. *Even then, Stülpnagel briefly considered:* Ibid.; Boineburg-Langsfeld, "Als Kommandant," 162; Zeller, *Geist der Freiheit*, 413. Some of the younger, more radical conspirators in Paris wanted even then to radicalize the putsch with summary executions of the captive SS leaders, but Stülpnagel did not agree. Even Hofacker was reluctant to execute such a radical plan. See Bargatzky, "Erinnerungen," IfZ, ZS-203, p. 13; compare with Falkenhausen, "Bericht," Zeller Papers, IfZ ED 88/1, pp. 57–58.

61. *Around midnight, Stülpnagel finally surrendered:* Bargatzky, "Letzte Runde in Paris," 156; Schramm, *Aufstand der Generale*, 170–75.

62. *The telephone, wrote Gisevius, still worked:* Gisevius, *To the Bitter End*, 569.

63. *Ironically, Colonel Müller from Döberitz showed up:* Müller, *Gegen eine neue Dolchstoßlüge*, 45–46.

64. *Most of the guards at the Bendlerstrasse:* Cords to Zeller, 23.8.1951, Zeller Pa-

pers, IfZ ED 88/1, p. 6; Friedrich Georgi, "Abschrift-Bernau, 21.7.1944, 00.10," in Helena P. Page, *General Friedrich Olbricht: Ein Mann des 20. Juli* (Bonn: Bouvier, 1994), appendix.

65. *The clock struck eleven:* "Tagebuch des Stabsgefreiten Karl Berlin," 276; Herber, "Was ich erlebte," BA-MA Msg 2/214, p. 7; Cords to Zeller, 23.8.1951, Friedrich Georgi, Abschrift, 26.9.1947, Zeller Papers, IfZ ED 88/1, pp. 6, 91–92; Gerstenmaier, "Der 20. Juli 1944," BA-MA Msg 2/213, p. 6(27); Delia Ziegler, "Wer schoss auf Stauffenberg," *Die Welt*, BA-MA Msg 2/213 (last page).

66. *General Fromm . . . faced the conspirators:* The description is based on a synthesis of several eyewitness accounts: Herber, "Was ich erlebte," BA-MA Msg 2/214, p. 7; H. L. Bartram, "20. Juli 1944," BA-MA Msg /2/214, p. 6; "Stenogram," 117–18; Hoffmann, *Widerstand, Staatsstreich, Attentat*, 622–23; Zeller, *Geist der Freiheit*, 398. On Fromm's intentions, see also Sönke Neitzel, *Abgehört: Deutsche Generäle in britischer Kriegsgefangenschaft 1942–1945* (Berlin: Propyläen, 2005), p. 351.

67. *Beck asked for permission:* There are multiple versions of this exchange between Beck and Fromm, but the description of the events is essentially similar. For some of the versions, see Zeller, *Geist der Freiheit*, 398; "Tagebuch des Stabsgefreiten Karl Berlin," 277; H. L. Bartram, "20. Juli 1944," BA-MA Msg /2/214, p. 6.

68. *Fromm was ready for his next move:* "Stenogram," 118; Dr. Ing. Werner Kennes, "Stellungnahme zu Wolfgang Müller: 'Gegen eine neue Dolchstoßlüge,'" 27.8.1947, BA-MA BAarch PERS N/124/10; H. L. Bartram, "20. Juli 1944," BA-MA Msg /2/214, p. 6.

69. *Eyewitnesses said that the four stood calmly:* Zeller, *Geist der Freiheit*, 399.

70. *A short while later:* Otto Skorzeny, *Skorzeny's Special Missions: The Memoirs of the Most Dangerous Man in Europe* (London: Robert Hale, 1957), 116–17; Herber, "Was ich erlebte," BA-MA Msg 2/214, p. 9.

71. *"For the third time an attempt on my life has been planned":* The full text of the speech was published in several Western newspapers on July 21. The English translation quoted here is from the British *Times*, 21.7.1944. For the German original, see Jacobsen and Zimmermann, *20 Juli 1944*, 185–89, and compare to a U.S. intelligence report on the speech: FBIS, NARA, Rg.263, SA 190, R 23, C 34, S7, box 92, CCA1-2.

72. *The assassination attempt . . . "failed due to amateurish dilettantism":* Frank Stern, "Wolfsschanze versus Auschwitz: Widerstand als deutsches Alibi?," *Zeitschrift für Geschichtswissenschaft* 42, no. 7 (1997): 645.

73. *"[Maj. Bernhard] Klamroth said":* Jacobsen, *"Spiegelbild einer Verschwörung,"* 1:483 (emphasis in original). Gotthard von Falkenhausen, by contrast, mentioned three reasons for the coup's failure: Hitler did not die on July 20; Rommel was injured on July 17; and Kluge was weak and undecided. See

Gotthard von Falkenhausen to Eberhard Zeller, 29.11.1945, Zeller Papers, IfZ ED 88/1, p. 34.

74. *Operation Valkyrie was planned methodically:* For the secrecy measures embedded in "Valkyrie," see Stellv. Generalkommando XX.A.K (Wehrkreiskommando XX), Abt. Ib/Org. Nr. 217/42 g.Kdos, "Betr. Einsatz Walküre," 14.5.1942, BA-MA RH/53/20, 27, p. 83. They were not overwritten in subsequent versions of the order.

## 19. The Shirt of Nessus

1. *"Now they will all fall upon us":* Fabian von Schlabrendorff, *The Secret War Against Hitler,* trans. Hilda Simon (Boulder, Colo.: Westview Press, 1994), 294–95.

2. *"You know, . . . as Beck's subordinate":* Joachim Kuhn, "Eigenhändige Aussagen," in Peter Hoffmann, *Stauffenbergs Freund: Die tragische Geschichte des Widerstandskämpfers Joachim Kuhn* (Munich: Verlag C. H. Beck, 2007), 186–87.

3. *Even at this hour . . . he felt responsible:* Bodo Scheurig, *Henning von Tresckow: Ein Preuße gegen Hitler; Biographie* (Berlin: Propyläen, 1987), 218. The records of Tresckow's phone conversations indicate that he left for his last journey at around 10:00 a.m. on July 21. See "Ferngespräche von 21.7.1944," Scheurig Papers, IfZ ZS-1 0031-4, http://www.ifz-muenchen.de/archiv/zsa/ZS_A_0031_04.pdf, pp. 149–52.

4. *"I do not wish to give our enemy the pleasure":* Eberhard von Breitenbuch, "Erinnerungen," Scheurig Papers, IfZ ZS/A 0031-2, http://www.ifz-muenchen.de/archiv/zsa/ZS_A_0031_02.pdf, p. 54; compare with Breitenbuch's later version in his memoirs, *Erinnerungen eines Reserveoffiziers, 1939–1945: Aufgeschrieben zur Kenntnis meiner Kinder* (Norderstedt: Books on Demand, 2011), 157–59.

5. *Tresckow entered a staff car:* Scheurig, *Tresckow,* 219.

6. *Most of the conspirators present in the Bendlerstrasse:* Peter Hoffmann, *Widerstand, Staatsstreich, Attentat: Der Kampf der Opposition gegen Hitler* (Munich: Piper, 1985), 627; Detlef Graf von Schwerin, *Dann sind's die besten Köpfe, die man henkt: Die junge Generation im deutschen Widerstand* (Munich: Piper, 1991), 413.

7. *"Had we believed in eternity":* Helmuth Arnz, "Abschrift einer Niederschrift über den General der Nachrichtentruppen Erich Fellgiebel," Zeller Papers, IfZ ED 88/1, p. 5.

8. *Gen. Karl-Heinrich von Stülpnagel . . . knew that his hour:* Walter Bargatzky, "Persönliche Erinnerungen an die Aufstandsbewegung des 20. Juli 1944 in Frankreich," 20.10.1945, IfZ, ZS-203, p. 14.

9. *Hermann Kaiser . . . was arrested on July 21:* Huppenkothen trial, 37–38, Deutsch Papers, USAMHI, series 1, box 3, folder 2.

10. *The conspirators were not left in peace:* Hans A. Jacobsen, ed., *"Spiegelbild einer Verschwörung": Die Opposition gegen Hitler und der Staatsstreich vom 20. Juli 1944 in der SD-Berichterstattung: Geheime Dokumente aus dem ehemaligen Reichssicherheitshauptamt* (Stuttgart: Seewald, 1984), 1:16–17, 19, 399–404. It is almost unbelievable, but some scholars have taken Schlabrendorff's fictitious testimony seriously. See, for example, Ronald Rathert, *Verbrechen und Verschwörung: Arthur Nebe; Der Kripochef des Dritten Reiches* (Münster: Lit, 2001), 117.

11. *Yet the conspirators were broken one by one:* Horst Mühleisen, "Patrioten im Widerstand": Carl-Hans Graf von Hardenbergs Erlebnisbericht," *Vierteljahrshefte für Zeitgeschichte* 14, no. 3 (January 1993): 467.

12. *Life in the Gestapo prison was hard:* Wolfgang Müller, *Gegen eine neue Dolchstoßlüge: Ein Erlebnisbericht zum 20 Juli 1944* (Hannover: Verlag "Das andere Deutschland," 1947), 113–17; Dorothee von Meding, *Courageous Hearts: Women and the Anti-Hitler Plot of 1944*, trans. Michael Balfour and Volker R. Berghahn (Providence, R.I.: Berghahn Books, 1997), 62; Huppenkothen trial, 1VT: 129–138, 2VT: 102–1, 28–30, 62–5, VT3: 3–13, 18, Deutsch Papers, series 1, box 3, folder 2.

13. *"This time, ... the trials will be quickly concluded":* Wilhelm Scheidt, "Gespräche mit Hitler," *Echo der Woche*, 9.9.1949; compare with Joseph Goebbels, *Tagebücher, 1924–1945*, ed. Ralf Georg Reuth, 2nd ed. (Munich: Piper, 1992), 23.7.1944, 5:2084–86.

14. *Through "Courts of Honor":* "Von Tresckow, Henning," BA-MA BArch PERS 6/301112; "Bildung eines Ehrenhofes zur Überprüfung der Beteiligten am Attentat vom 20.7.1944 (2.8.1944, doc. 346)," in *Führer-Erlasse, 1939–1940*, ed. Martin Holl (Stuttgart: Steiner, 1997), 439; Heinz Guderian, *Erinnerungen eines Soldaten* (Heidelberg: Vowinckel, 1951), 313–14. On the proceedings of the courts of honor, see the taped testimony of Lieutenant General Kirchheim in British captivity, though as a member of the court, he was naturally apologetic: Sönke Neitzel, *Abgehört: Deutsche Generäle in britischer Kriegsgefangenschaft 1942–1945* (Berlin: Propyläen, 2005), pp. 370–77.

15. *The president of the tribunal was Dr. Roland Freisler:* Helmut Ortner, *Der Hinrichter: Roland Freisler, Mörder im Dienste Hitlers* (Vienna: Zsolnay, 1995), 132–33, 136.

16. *"If you deny [that you're a swine,]":* "Stenogram der ersten Volksgerichtshofverhandlung vom 7/8 August 1944," in *Die Angeklagten des 20 Juli vor dem Volksgerichtshof*, ed. Bengt von zur Mühlen (Berlin: Chronos, 2001), 83.

17. *Freisler was not an independent judge:* Ortner, *Der Hinrichter*, 127–28; Ian Kershaw, *Hitler, 1936–1945: Nemesis* (New York: Norton, 2000), 10–11, 22.

18. *these ends were intimately tied:* Ortner, *Der Hinrichter*, 107, 136.

19. *"the court has only one duty":* "Stenogram," 53, 97, 99–103. Only one of the lawyers, Hagne's attorney Dr. Gustav Schwarz, courageously tried to do

his duty in good faith. During the trial, he did almost everything possible to save his client from the rope. For discussion on the role of the defense attorneys and the difficulties they faced, see Arnim Ramm, *Der 20 Juli vor dem Volksgerichtshof* (Berlin: Gaudig & Veit, 2007), 236–41.

20. *"Witzleben . . . was revealed in the trial"*: Jacobsen, *"Spiegelbild einer Verschwörung,"* 1:180.

21. *"He pushed back the thought"*: Ibid., 1:181; Huppenkothen trial, 173–74, Deutsch Papers USAMHI, series 1, box 3, folder 2.

22. *When asked by Freisler why he failed to join:* Hans A. Jacobsen and Erich Zimmermann, eds., *20 Juli 1944* (Bonn: Berto Verlag, 1960), 173; Jacobsen, *"Spiegelbild einer Verschwörung,"* 1:181. English translation from Peter Hoffmann, *The History of the German Resistance, 1933–1945,* trans. Richard Barry (Montreal: McGill-Queens University Press, 1985), 526.

23. *"In the name of the German People!"*: "Stenogram," 119.

24. *The conspirators were hanged slowly:* Brigitte Oleschinski, *Plötzensee Memorial Center* (Berlin: Gedenkstätte deutscher Winderstand, 2002), 5.

25. *"Hitler put on his spectacles"*: Bernd Freytag von Loringhoven, with François d'Alançon, *In the Bunker with Hitler, 23.7.1944–29.4.1945* (London: Weidenfeld & Nicolson, 2006), 68–69.

26. *"We took this deed upon ourselves"*: Mühlen, *Angeklagten,* 302. The protocol of Schulenburg's trial is probably lost for good. The only information we have on the trial is based on a letter by a German journalist who was able to speak with one of those present, an SS guard. He submitted his findings (in code) to Schulenburg's wife. See Ulrich Heinemann, *Ein Konservativer Rebell: Fritz-Dietlof Graf von der Schulenburg und der 20. Juli* (Berlin: Siedler, 1990), 171–72.

27. *"Soon you will be in hell"*: Jacobsen and Zimmermann, *20 Juli 1944,* 175.

28. *Moltke wrote . . . that he stood before Freisler:* Helmuth James von Moltke, *A German of the Resistance: The Last Letters of Count Helmuth James von Moltke* (London: Oxford University Press, 1946), 39–40, 49. On American attempts to save Moltke, see OSS director Charles S. Cheston to Secretary of State Edward R. Stettinius, 20.1.1945, in *American Intelligence and the German Resistance to Hitler,* ed. Jürgen Heideking and Christof Mauch (Boulder, Colo.: Westview Press, 1996), 360–61.

29. *"You should look at the Germanic Sagas"*: Jacobsen and Zimmermann, *20 Juli 1944,* 172; Huppenkothen trial, pp. 138–42, Deutsch Papers, series 1, box 3, folder 2.

30. *"By the fence in front of my window"*: Meding, *Courageous Hearts,* 187; Konstanze von Schulthess, *Nina Schenk Gräfin von Stauffenberg: Ein Porträt* (Munich: Pendo, 2008), 25, 36, 80.

31. *Nina was not the only one to be arrested:* Felicitias von Aretin, *Die Enkel des 20 Juli 1944* (Leipzig: Faber & Faber, 2004), 30; Schulthess, *Nina Schenk Gräfin von Stauffenberg,* 25, 36, 80.

32. *In fact, the Gestapo had been planning for a long time:* For example, see "Underground Organizations in the Wismar and Hamburg Areas, Germany, 8/44," NARA 110903 S, 6.19.

33. *"I suddenly saw Ambassador Ulrich von Hassell":* Hans B. Gisevius, *To the Bitter End*, trans. Richard Winston and Clara Winston (New York: Da Capo Press, 1998), 582.

34. *In early August 1944 . . . Hassell heard a knock:* Ibid., 584–85.

35. *The SS uniform of Nebe would no longer protect him:* The evidence suggests that SS authorities, at least initially, were at odds about Nebe's disappearance, or at the very least attempted to keep the suspicions against him secret to avoid public embarrassment. He was formally expelled from the SS only on November 30, 1944. See Himmler to Herff, 30.11.1944, BA, SSO/345A, pp. 142–43, 144–45, 148–49; see also Huppenkothen trial, 158–59, Anklageschrift gegen Dr. Hans Böhm und andere, 23.3.1945, 3–14, Deutsch Papers, series 1, box 3, series 3, box 2, rounds 3 and 4 Material.

36. *Gisevius was still roaming around Germany:* Goerdeler's network of friends and shelterers, by contrast, relied on former resistance fighters, and was therefore discovered and eliminated in the days following July 20. See Reinhard Gördeler, "Die letzten Tage meines Vater," Zeller Papers, IfZ ED 88/1, pp. 167–68.

37. *Temporarily, he took refuge with friends:* National Socialist authorities were completely oblivious to Gisevius's presence in Berlin. On August 8, Klaterbrunner reported to Bormann that he managed to escape to Switzerland two days after the failure of the coup (July 22). This fact explains why Gisevius was hunted less rigorously than Goerdeler. See Jacobsen, *"Spiegelbild einer Verschwörung,"* 1:174.

38. *Dr. Carl Goerdeler . . . moved from one acquaintance to another:* Ibid., 167–68, 217–23; Albrecht Fischer, "Erlebnisse vom 20. Juli 1944 bis 8. April 1945," 9.10.1961, IfZ, ZS-1758, p. 5.

39. *The Nazi press promised one million marks: Völkischer Beobachter,* 3.8.1944.

40. *While Goerdeler was waiting for his meal:* Jacobsen, *"Spiegelbild einer Verschwörung,"* 1:222–23. For the Schwarzel affair, see the verdict in her trial in *Justiz und NS-Verbrechen: Sammlung deutscher Strafurteile, wegen nationalsozialistischer Tötungsverbrechen, 1945–1999*, ed. Fritz Bauer (Amsterdam: University Press Amsterdam, 1968), vol. 1, http://www1.jur.uva.nl/junsv/Excerpts/032inhalt.htm.

41. *In a series of lengthy confessions:* Franz Xaver Sonderegger to Freiherr von Siegler, Dr.Helmut Krausnick, and Dr. Hermann Mau, 14.10.1952, IfZ, ZS-0303-1, p. 43, http://www.ifz-muenchen.de/archiv/zs/zs-0303_1.pdf; Jacobsen, *"Spiegelbild einer Verschwörung,"* 1:232.

42. *"In his eyes it was not a coup d'état":* Gerhard Ritter, *Carl Goerdeler und die deutsche Widerstandsbewegung* (Stuttgart: Deutsche Verlags-Anstalt, 1954), 415.

43. *"His [the attorney's] defense was a disgrace":* Sabine Gillmann and Hans Momm-

sen, *Politische Schriften und Briefe Carl Friedrich Goerdelers* (Munich: Saur, 2003), 2:1152.

44. *"All that he had striven for"*: Klemens von Klemperer, *German Resistance to Hitler: The Search for Allies Abroad* (Oxford: Clarendon Press), 395.

45. *"God knows . . . that I risked everything"*: Gillmann and Mommsen, *Politische Schriften und Briefe*, 2:1248.

46. *"How much pain did I cause my beloved wife"*: Ibid., 2:1226.

47. *"I hereby implore the statesmen"*: Ibid., 2:1229.

48. *"This war was criminal"*: Ibid., 2:1127–29, 1236–37. The emphasis is Goerdeler's.

49. *"Tomorrow I go to the hangman"*: Ludwig Rosenberg, "Wilhelm Leuschner," in *Das Zwanzigste Juli: Alternative zu Hitler?*, ed. Hans J. Schultz (Stuttgart: Kreuz Verlag, 1997), 165.

50. *"I fought for Germany"*: Dr. Ing. Werner Kennes, "Stellungnahme zu Wolfgang Müller: 'Gegen eine neue Dolchstoßlüge,'" 27.8.1947, BA-MA BAarch PERS N/124/10. Goebbels was deeply suspicious of Fromm already on July 23; see Goebbels, *Tagebücher*, 23.7.1944, 5:2084.

51. *"I have come to say goodbye"*: Desmond Young, *Rommel* (London: Collins, 1972), 235.

52. *"I saw Rommel in the back seat"*: Niederschrift über die Aussage des Heinrich Doose, vor CIC 101 30.5.1945, Berchtesgaden Records, UPEN-RBML.

53. *"a vicious hand, my Führer"*: Kluge's speech was quoted in FBIS, NARA, Rg.263, SA 190, R 23, C 34, S7, box 92, CCA1 CCC1. For the National Socialist suspicions against him, see Schreiben Bormann, Führerhauptquartier, 17.8.1944, Scheurig Papers, IfZ ZS/A 0031-4, http://www.ifz-muenchen.de/archiv/zsa/ZS_A_0031_04.pdf, p. 128.

54. *Colonel Gersdorff . . . turned up at the headquarters:* Rudolf-Christoph Freiherr von Gersdorff, *Soldat im Untergang* (Frankfurt am Main: Ullstein, 1977), 151–52.

55. *"Both of us, Rommel and I"*: Bengt von zur Mühlen and Frank Bauer, eds., *Der 20. Juli 1944 in Paris: Verlauf, Hauptbeteiligte, Augenzeugen* (Berlin: Chronos, 1995), 242.

56. *At the Nuremberg Trials, General Jodl recalled: Nuremberg Blue*, 15:403–4; Felix Gilbert, ed., *Hitler Directs His War: The Secret Records of His Daily Military Conferences* (New York: Oxford University Press, 1950), 101.

57. *On July 27, the National Socialists "took care" of the scattered remnants:* Schlabrendorff, *Secret War Against Hitler*, 311–12.

58. *"I have committed treason"*: Scheurig, *Ewald von Kleist-Schmenzin*, 192; Schlabrendorff, *Secret War Against Hitler*, 324–25; compare with the testimony of Schlabrendorff on April 26–27, 1966, in a West German court: "Zeugenaussage Fabian von Schlabrendorffs im Rahmen des Ermittlungsverfahrens gegen Hans-Joachim Rehse vom 26./27. April 1966," in Ramm, *Der 20. Juli*, 499.

59. *One of the lawyers turned:* Gerhard Ringshausen, *Widerstand und christlicher Glaube angesichts des Nationalsozialismus* (Berlin: Lit, 2008), 229; Schlabrendorff, *Secret War Against Hitler,* 325.

60. *"After I finished speaking":* "Zeugenaussage Fabian von Schlabrendorffs," 500–502.

61. *Still, after Schlabrendorff was led back:* Schlabrendorff, *Secret War Against Hitler,* 328.

62. *"No one gets out of here alive":* Georg Thomas, "20 Juli 1944," BA-MA Msg 2/213, p. 12.

63. *Gisevius, as usual, had been luckier:* Gisevius, *To the Bitter End,* 591.

64. *he raised his arm "limply in response":* Ibid., 596.

65. *Canaris was still fighting a pitched battle:* Jacobsen, "*Spiegelbild einer Verschwörung,*" 1:407; Franz Sonderegger, "Ermittlungsverfahren gegen Walter Huppenkoth," 14.1.1951, IfZ, ZS-0303-1, p. 10, http://www.ifz-muenchen.de/archiv/zs/zs-0303_1.pdf.

66. *But in April, the Gestapo commissioners searched:* A detailed list of the contents of the Zossen safe can be found in Sonderegger, "Ermittlungsverfahren," 14.1.1951, IfZ, ZS-0303-1; see also Abschrift Huppenkothen, IfZ ZS 0249-1, p. 35; Georg Thomas, "20. Juli 1944," 20.7.1945, BA-MA Msg 2/213, p. 8.

67. *the man who combined the "purity of a dove":* Naval Attaché, Stockholm to D.N.I., 16.8.1945, "Fate of Admiral Canaris," NA, FO 371/47341; Huppenkothen trial, VT1 144–50, 56–57, VT5, 54, Deutsch Papers. Kaltenbrunner was proud of his part in the exposure of Canaris to his last day; see his testimony at Nuremberg, *Nuremberg Blue,* 22:378.

68. *he swallowed poisoned food:* Dohnanyi to his wife, 8.3.1945, Zeller Papers, IfZ ED 88/1, pp. 26–27.

69. *Canaris's Danish neighbor later testified:* Heinz Höhne, *Canaris,* trans. J. Maxwell Brownjohn (London: Secker & Warburg, 1979), 596; Ramm, *Der 20 Juli,* 343–44; Huppenkothen trial, VT1 163–66, VT2 113–14, 138–41, 53–54, VT5, 54–56, Deutsch Papers, series 1, box 3, folder 2; Ringshausen, *Widerstand und christlicher Glaube,* 230.

70. *Schlabrendorff was supposed to die with them:* Halder, "Protokoll der öffentlichen Sitzung der Spruchkammer München X, BY 11/47, am 15.9.1948," BA-MA Msg 2/213.

71. *As he entered the hotel:* Fabian von Schlabrendorff, *Revolt Against Hitler: The Personal Account of Fabian von Schlabrendorff,* trans. and ed. Gero von Gaevernitz (London: Eyre & Spottiswoode, 1948), 23–25.

72. *Maj. Joachim Kuhn was released:* Peter Hoffmann, *Stauffenbergs Freund: Die tragische Geschichte des Widerstandskämpfers Joachim Kuhn* (Munich: Verlag C. H. Beck, 2007), 161–67.

73. *Countess Nina von Stauffenberg gave birth:* Schulthess, *Nina Schenk Gräfin von Stauffenberg,* 80–86.

## 20. Motives in the Twilight

1. *Many observers and scholars have argued:* Shlomo Aharonson, "Hitler: Ha-Ketsinim Ha-Shotim" in *Ha-Hitnagdut La-Nazism* (Jerusalem: Koebner Institute for German History, 1984), 63–64; Hannsjoachim W. Koch, *In the Name of the Volk: Political Justice in Hitler's Germany* (London: Tauris, 1989), 212.

2. *"During the war's first two years":* Sabine Gillmann and Hans Mommsen, *Politische Schriften und Briefe Carl Friedrich Goerdelers* (Munich: Saur, 2003), 2:1241.

3. *Recall that Stauffenberg was certain:* Joachim Kuhn, "Eigenhändige Aussagen," in Peter Hoffmann, *Stauffenbergs Freund: Die tragische Geschichte des Widerstandskämpfers Joachim Kuhn* (Munich: Verlag C. H. Beck, 2007), 190; Peter Hoffmann, *Stauffenberg: A Family History, 1905–1944* (Cambridge: Cambridge University Press, 1995), 152; Christian Müller, *Oberst i. G. Stauffenberg: Eine Biographie* (Düsseldorf: Droste, 1971), 256–57; Rudolf-Christoph Freiherr von Gersdorff, "History of the Attempt on Hitler's Life (20 Jul. 1944)," Historical Division Headquarters, United States Army Europe, Foreign Military Studies Branch, USAMHI, p. 20; Hans Herwarth von Bittenfeld, "Meine Verbindung mit Graf Stauffenberg" (newspaper clipping, 18.7.1969), Deutsch Papers, series 3, box 2, rounds 3 and 4 Material.

4. *A third common argument holds:* Johannes Hürter's controversial article is the newest publication in this school of thought. See Johannes Hürter, "Auf dem Weg zur Militäropposition: Tresckow, Gersdorff, der Vernichtungskrieg, und der Judenmord; Neue Dokumente über das Verhältnis der Heeresgruppe Mitte zur Einsatzgruppe B im Jahr 1941," *Vierteljahrshefte für Zeitgeschichte* 3 (2004): 527–62.

5. *As was noted long ago by Quentin Skinner:* Quentin Skinner, "Meaning and Understanding," *History and Theory* 8, no. 1 (1969): 8–12.

6. *Some of them, for example, believed that several of the principles:* Hans A. Jacobsen, ed., *"Spiegelbild einer Verschwörung": Die Opposition gegen Hitler und der Staatsstreich vom 20. Juli 1944 in der SD-Berichterstattung: Geheime Dokumente aus dem ehemaligen Reichssicherheitshauptamt* (Stuttgart: Seewald, 1984), 1:447–57.

7. *Gersdorff argued that the primary impetus:* Gersdorff, *History*, USAMHI, p. 7; Axel von dem Bussche, "Eid und Schuld," in *Axel von dem Bussche*, ed. Gevinon von Medem (Mainz: Hase & Koehler, 1994), 135.

8. *Resistance fighters like Hans von Dohnanyi:* Winfried Meyer, *Unternehmen Sieben: Eine Rettungsaktion für vom Holocaust Bedrohte aus dem Amt Ausland/Abwehr im Oberkommando der Wehrmacht* (Frankfurt am Main: Hain, 1993), 309–10; Gerhard Ritter, *Carl Goerdeler und die deutsche Widerstandsbewegung* (Stuttgart: Deutsche Verlags-Anstalt, 1954), 211–12; Ulrich von

Hassell, *Die Hassell-Tagebücher, 1938–1944: Aufzeichnungen vom anderen Deutschland*, ed. Friedrich Freiherr Hiller von Gärtringen (Munich: Goldmann, 1994), 62.

9.  *the conspirators made no distinction:* Such dichotomies unfortunately exist even in new, otherwise sophisticated studies. See, for example, Eckart Conze et al., *Das Amt und die Vergangenheit: Deutsche Diplomaten im Dritten Reich und in der Bundesrepublik* (Munich: Karl Blessing Verlag, 2010), 296.

10. *"The morality that motivated the resistance fighters":* Klaus-Jürgen Müller, "Über den 'militärischen Widerstand,'" in *Widerstand gegen den Nationalsozialismus*, ed. Peter Steinbach and Johannes Tuchel (Berlin: Akademie Verlag, 1994), 275; Ger van Roon, "Hermann Kaiser und der deutsche Widerstand," *Vierteljahrschefte für Zeitgeschichte* 24, no. 3 (July 1976): 273.

11. *Most conspirators were not exclusively patriots:* Jacobsen, "Spiegelbild einer Verschwörung," 1:431.

12. *Dr. Carl Goerdeler wrote how tormented he was:* Ritter, *Carl Goerdeler*, 211–12.

13. *In the diary of Ulrich von Hassell:* Hassell, *Tagebücher*, 14, 15, 16, 19, 79, 100, 104, 114, 115, 120, 152, 156, 221, 227, 365.

14. *Stauffenberg indicated that the "treatment of the Jews":* Kuhn, "Eigenhändige Aussagen," 190; Hoffmann, *Stauffenberg*, 152; Müller, *Oberst i. G. Stauffenberg*, 382; Gersdorff, *History*, USAMHI, p. 20; Bittenfeld, "Meine Verbindung" (newspaper clipping, 18.7.1969), Deutsch Papers, series 3, box 2, rounds 3 and 4 Materials.

15. *"Morality . . . is the most profound basis":* Roon, "Hermann Kaiser," 273.

16. *"Dead tired, but I did not sleep all night":* Hermann Kaiser, *Mut zum Bekenntnis: Die geheimen Tagebücher des Hauptmanns Hermann Kaiser, 1941, 1943*, ed. Peter M. Kaiser (Berlin: Lukas Verlag, 2010), 474.

17. *Kaiser wrote that Goerdeler had reported:* Ibid., 446, and compare with 230.

18. *the feeling of misery pervading his journal:* Ibid., 292.

19. *"I could not overcome my humiliation":* Ibid.

20. *"I believe that Kleist did not know":* Schlabrendorff to Scheurig (interview, 19.9.1965), Scheurig Papers, IfZ ZS/A 31-8, http://www.ifz-muenchen.de/archiv/zsa/ZS_A_0031_08.pdf, p. 5.

21. *In fact he opposed them:* Meyer, *Unternehmen Sieben*, 457–58.

22. *Virulently anti-Semitic, violent, and corrupt:* Ted Harrison, "'Alter Kämpfer' im Widerstand: Graf Helldorff, die NS-Bewegung und die Opposition gegen Hitler," *Vierteljahrshefte für Zeitgeschichte* 45, no. 3 (July 1997): 385–423.

23. *Helldorff told the Gestapo that he agreed:* Jacobsen, "Spiegelbild einer Verschwörung," 1:449, 451, 453.

24. *this SS officer was nothing but an opportunist:* Ronald Rathert, *Verbrechen und Verschwörung: Arthur Nebe; Der Kripochef des Dritten Reiches* (Münster: Lit, 2001), 194.

25. *"The military obedience . . . finds its limits":* Wolfgang Foerster, *Ein General*

*kämpft gegen den Krieg: Aus nachgelassenen Papieren des Generalstabchefs Ludwig Beck* (Munich: Münchener Dom-Verlag, 1949), 103.

26. *"What good are our tactical and other capabilities":* Bodo Scheurig, *Henning von Tresckow: Ein Preuße gegen Hitler; Biographie* (Berlin: Propyläen, 1987), 201–2.

27. *Tresckow indeed disobeyed the Commissar Order:* Fabian von Schlabrendorff, *The Secret War Against Hitler,* trans. Hilda Simon (Boulder, Colo.: Westview Press, 1994), 124. On Tresckow's opposition to the Commissar Order, see also Engel to Scheurig, 4.5.1972, Karl-Heinz Wirsing, "Bericht" (December 1970), Scheurig Papers, IfZ ZS/A 0031-2, http://www.ifz-muenchen. de/archiv/zsa/ZS_A_0031_02.pdf, p. 103, ZS/A 0031-3, http://www.ifz -muenchen.de/archiv/zsa/ZS_A_0031_03.pdf, p. 211.

28. *"The German Resistance Movement was not a profession":* Nuremberg Green, 13:398. Tresckow had a very similar approach; see Eggert to Scheurig, Scheurig Papers, IfZ ZS/A 0031-2, http://www.ifz-muenchen.de/archiv/zsa/ ZS_A_0031_02.pdf, p. 82; Gersdorff to Scheurig (interview), 17.3.1970, IfZ ZS/A 0031-2, http://www.ifz-muenchen.de/archiv/zsa/ZS_A_0031_02.pdf, p. 141.

29. *contrary to the story told by Count Boeselager:* Philipp von Boeselager, interview with the author, 15.7.2003; and his book (with Florence Fehrenbach and Jerome Fehrenbach), *Valkyrie: The Story of the Plot to Kill Hitler by Its Last Member,* trans. Steven Rendall (New York: Vintage, 2010), 124.

30. *he . . . did not willingly cooperate with the murderers:* Christian Streit, "Angehörige des militärischen Widerstands und der Genozid an den Juden im Südabschnitt der Ostfront," in *NS Verbrechen und der militärische Widerstand gegen Hitler,* ed. Gerd R. Ueberschär (Darmstadt: Primus, 2000), 99. Streit refers to a minimum number of 6,329 victims, most of them murdered after Stülpnagel was replaced by Hoth. For comparison, 55,000 and 57,000 victims were murdered at the same time in Manstein's and Reichenau's territories, respectively.

31. *Stülpnagel's children claim that their father:* Bengt von zur Mühlen and Frank Bauer, eds., *Der 20. Juli 1944 in Paris: Verlauf, Hauptbeteiligte, Augenzeugen* (Berlin: Chronos, 1995), 151–52.

32. *Axel von dem Bussche, for example:* For that matter, it is worthwhile to compare the testimonies of two Israelis who met Bussche after the war in different circumstances: the composer Josef Tal and the Israeli ambassador in Germany Avi Primor. In a conference talk he gave at Tel Aviv University (May 13, 2002), Primor related that Bussche wondered how an Israeli was willing to speak with a person such as him. Tal testified that Bussche tried to avoid him in order not to "force" an Israeli to speak with a former Wehrmacht officer. Even after the two became friends, Bussche refrained from speaking about the war or about his experience in the German resistance. See Josef Tal, "Ein Mensch-zu-Mensch Erlebnis im Wissenschaftskolleg Berlin," in Medem, *Axel von dem Bussche,* 126.

33.	*"We became silent witnesses":* Cited in Peter Steinbach, *Claus von Stauffenberg: Zeuge im Feuer* (Leinfelder-Echterdingen: DRW, 2007), 8.

34.	*Tresckow, a proud scion of a Prussian noble family:* For more details on the dynastic mythology of the Tresckows and their self-perception as bearers of Prussian heritage, see Heinrich von Tresckow and Hans-Heinrich von Tresckow, *Familiengeschichte derer von Tresckow* (Potsdam, 1920/1953), Scheurig Papers, IfZ ZS/A 0031-01, http://www.ifz-muenchen.de/archiv/zsa/ZS_A_0031_01.pdf, pp. 62–129.

35.	*"I stood before [People's Court president] Freisler":* Helmuth James von Moltke, *A German of the Resistance: The Last Letters of Count Helmuth James von Moltke* (London: Oxford University Press, 1946), 39–40, 49. On the importance of religion, see also Jacobsen, *"Spiegelbild einer Verschwörung,"* 1:435–36.

36.	*Germany was home . . . "to plenty of believing Christians":* Klaus von Dohnanyi, introduction to Meyer, *Unternehmen Sieben*, xi.

37.	*"I don't understand . . . how people who are not fierce opponents":* Erika von Tresckow to Bodo Scheurig (interview, 1.5.1969), Scheurig Papers, IfZ ZS-1 0031-3, http://www.ifz-muenchen.de/archiv/zsa/ZS_A_0031_03.pdf, p. 151.

38.	*"Every ideal, whether or not based on reality":* Based on some surviving excerpts from a diary written by Tresckow on July 10, 1920; see Scheurig Papers, IfZ ZS/A 0031-01, http://www.ifz-muenchen.de/archiv/zsa/ZS_A_0031_01.pdf, p. 15.

## 21. Networks of Resistance

1.	*Evan Mawdsley, for example, argues:* Evan Mawdsley, *Thunder in the East: The Nazi-Soviet War* (London: Oxford University Press, 2005), 397–407.

2.	*and 1944, respectively:* The model below partly corresponds with that of Paul Staniland in his new study, *Networks of Rebellion: Explaining Insurgent Cohesion and Collapse* (Ithaca, NY: Cornell University Press, 2014). Though Staniland focused on open insurgencies more than on clandestine groups of conspirators inside the state's apparatus, his model may provide useful insights for our subject as well. Staniland divides insurgent networks into four types, according to the strength of their central leadership and local cadres. Integrated networks, the strongest ones, have both formidable central leadership and effective local cadres. Vanguard networks have a strong leadership core but weak influence in the field, while parochial networks sport strong local cells but weak leaderships. Fragmented networks, which have weak centers and ineffective local cadres, are doomed to failure if unable to change. The vanguard model corresponds with our analysis of the Berlin clique of 1938, and the parochial model with Tresckow's connected cliques of 1942–43. Staniland indeed emphasizes the importance of brokerage in such groups, and also, as we do, the problem of tenuous cooperation and internal feuds (pp. 30–31). Stauffenberg's wheel conspiracy may be the closest configuration to Staniland's model of "integrated network," though the strength of its local cadres, as we explain, was at least partially illusory.

3. *Top commanders, field marshals:* Halder, "Protokoll der öffentlichen Sitzung der Spruchkammer München X, BY 11/47, am 15.9.1948," BA-MA Msg 2/213, p. 18(78c).

4. *The most effective strategy for winning cooperation:* For one example among many of the strategy of "surrounding," see Peter Hoffmann, *Stauffenberg: A Family History, 1905–1944* (Cambridge: Cambridge University Press, 1995), 231, as well as Eberhard von Breitenbuch, "Erinnerungen an Generalmajor von Tresckow," Scheurig Papers, IfZ ZS/A 0031-2, http://www.ifz-muenchen.de/archiv/zsa/ZS_A_0031_02.pdf, p. 53.

5. *Erika von Tresckow related:* Erika von Tresckow to Bodo Scheurig (interview, 1.5.1969), Scheurig Papers, IfZ ZS-1 0031-3, http://www.ifz-muenchen.de/archiv/zsa/ZS_A_0031_03.pdf, p. 138.

6. *According to Gerhard Ringshausen:* Gerhard Ringshausen, *Hans-Alexander von Voss: Generalstabsoffizier im Widerstand, 1907–1944* (Berlin: Lukas Verlag, 2008), 85.

7. *The early 1943 entries in Kaiser's diary:* Hermann Kaiser, *Mut zum Bekenntnis: Die geheimen Tagebücher des Hauptmanns Hermann Kaiser, 1941, 1943,* ed. Peter M. Kaiser (Berlin: Lukas Verlag, 2010), 420–22, 439, 445.

8. *"both the Wehrmacht and the civilian population":* H. L. Bartram, "20. Juli 1944," BA-MA Msg 2/214, p. 5.

## Epilogue

1. *"The Jewish heroes were not knights":* Yehuda Bauer, *Jews for Sale?: Nazi-Jewish Negotiations, 1933–1945* (New Haven, Conn.: Yale University Press, 1994), 328.

2. *Dohnanyi forbade his wife:* Marikje Smid, *Hans von Dohnanyi, Christine Bonhoeffer: Eine Ehe im Widerstand gegen Hitler* (Gütersloh: Gütersloher Verlagshaus, 2002), 57–58.

3. *Goerdeler was, in the minds of many:* See, for example, Stauffenberg's opinion on Goerdeler (chap. 17, n. 15).

4. *And Hase . . . condemned deserters to death:* Roland Kopp, *Paul von Hase von der Alexander-Kaserne nach Plötzensee: Eine deutsche Soldatenbiographie, 1885–1944* (Münster: Lit, 2001), 177–99.

5. *"Responsible action . . . takes place":* Dietrich Bonhoeffer, "Ethics," vol. 6 of *Dietrich Bonhoeffer Works,* ed. Clifford J. Green, trans. Reinhard Krauss, Charles C. West, and Douglas W. Stott (Minneapolis: Fortress Press, 2005), 284.

# SELECT BIBLIOGRAPHY

Note: In many cases, I have used the German originals of texts for indirect references and existing English translations for quotations. In such cases, both the original and the translation appear in the bibliography.

## Unpublished and Archival Sources

Abakumov to Beria (report on Wolf's Lair), 22.2.1945, GARF Fond R-9401, Opis 2, Del 93, 6–15.

Aktenvermerk über die Besprechung im Führerzug am 12.9.1939 in Illnau. 14.9.1939, NARA, Rg. 238/3047-PS (US-80).

Allgemeines Heeresamt, Abt. Demob. Nr. 350/42 g.Kdos, "Herstellung einsatzfähiger Verwenungsbereitschaft des Ersatzheeres," 5.2.1942, Chef der Heeresrüstung und Befehlshaber der Ersatzheeres, AHA Ia VII Nr. 1160/42 g.Kdos., "Betr.: Walküre II," 21.3.1942, BA-MA RH/12/21.

Arnold, Fritz, Bericht A, 3, DRYV.

Bartram, Hans-Ludwig, 1954, "20. Juli 1944," BA-MA Msg 2/214.

Beria to Stalin, 19.9.1944 (see Crome, Hans [testimony] below).

Boeselager, Philipp Freiherr von, Mein Weg zum 20. Juli 1944 (Vortrag gehalten am 20. Juli 2002 bei den Johannitern in Wasserburg/Bayern).

———, to Peter Hoffmann, 19.11.1964, IfZ ZS-2118, p. 2, http://www.ifz -muenchen.de/archiv/zs/zs-2118.pdf.

Bürgerbräuattentat, IfZ, ZS/A 17 1–11.

Bussche, Axel von dem, Ns v.18.6.1948, betr. Massenerschießungen v. Juden im Ghetto Dubno 1942, IfZ ZS-1827, pp. 7–12.

Cabinet Papers, Great Britain, NA, CAB/23/95.

Chamberlain, Neville, Papers of Neville Chamberlain, HULL.

Chef der Heeresrüstung und Befehlshaber des Ersatzheeres, AHA/Ia (I), Nr. 3830/43 g. Kdos, "Betr.: Walküre," 31.7.1943, BA-MA RH/12/21, 56.

Churchill, Winston, Sir Winston Churchill Papers, HULL.

Crome, Hans (testimony), Beria to Stalin, 19.9.1944, GARF Fond R-9401, Opis 2, Del 66, pp. 297–98.

Deutsch, Harold C., Harold C. Deutsch Papers, USAMHI.

Eichmann, Adolf, an die Geheime Staatspolizei Düsseldorf, 2.12.1941, NWHA, RW 58/74234, 12.

Fischer, Albrecht, Erlebnisse vom 20. Juli 1944 bis 8. April 1945, 9.10.1961, IfZ, ZS-1758, http://www.ifz-muenchen.de/archiv/zs/zs-1758.pdf.

Foreign Broadcast Intelligence Service (FBIS), Federal Communications Commission, Daily Report, Foreign Radio Broadcasts, NARA, Rg.263, SA 190, R 23, C 34, S7, box 58.

Gersdorff to Krausnick, 19.10.1956, IfZ ZS-0047-2.

Goerdeler, Anneliese, Abschrift, Protokoll, in dem Spruchkammerverfahren gegen Dr. Strölin, 27.10.1948, IfZ, ZS-0580, http://www.ifz-muenchen.de/archiv/zs/zs-0580.pdf.

Goerdeler, Carl Friedrich (personal file), NA, HS9/593/6.

Haacke an Mutschmann, 4.12.1936, SAL Kap 10 G Nr.685 Bd.1, 267R-268.

Halder, Franz, testimony in "Protokoll der öffentlichen Sitzung der Spruchkammer München X, BY 11/47, am 15.9.1948," BA-MA BAarch N/124/10.

———, "Zu den Aussagen des Dr. Gisevius in Nürnberg 24. bis 26.4.1946," BA-MA BAarch N/124/10.

Halifax, First Earl of (Edward F. L. Wood), Halifax Papers, CAC, HLFX I/3/3.6.

Herber (Oberleutnant a.D.), "Was ich am 20.7.1944 in der Bendlerstraße erlebte," BA-MA Msg 2/214.

Hitzfeld, Otto, to Gerd Buchheit, 5.7.66, IfZ ZS-1858, http://www.ifz-muenchen.de/archiv/zs/zs-1858.pdf.

Hoepner, Joachim, to Peter Hoffmann, 3.4.1964, IfZ ZS-2121, p. 2.

Huppenkothen, Walther, "Abschrift," 11.7.1947, IfZ 0249-1, pp. 8–10, http://www.ifz-muenchen.de/archiv/zs/zs-0249_1.pdf.

Kivimäki, Toivo M., report from Berlin, 12.2.1943, UMA, UM 5 C.

———, to Marshal Mannerheim, 6.5.1942, KA, kotelo 24.

Kommandeur der Panzertruppen XVII, Wien, 10.9.1943, "An die Herrn Kommandeure," BA-MA RH/53/17, 143.

Kommandostab RF-SS, Der Chef des Stabes an Jüttner 19.6.41, BA-MA SF-02/37542 SD report, 11.8.1944, GARF Fond R-9401, Opis 2, Del 97, p. 208.

Krausnick to Gersdorff, 29.10.1956, and Gersdorff's reply, 30.10.1956, IfZ ZS-0047-2, pp. 105-8.

Kruglov to Beria, 6.5.1946, GARF Fond R-9401, Opis 2, Del 136, pp. 256-97.

Lindemann, Gabrielle, to Winfried Meyer, 29.11.1985 (Privatbesitz Winfried Meyers).

Müller an Weiter, 5.4.1945, EA-GEAH http://www.georg-elser-arbeitskreis.de/texts/ermordung.htm.

Naval Attaché, Stockholm to D.N.I, 16.8.1945, "Fate of Admiral Canaris," NA, FO 371/47341.

Roeder, Manfred, 3 and 4 December 1951, IfZ, ZS-0124, p. 30, http://www.ifz-muenchen.de/archiv/zs/zs-0124.pdf.

Rohowsky, Johannes, "Stellungnahme zur Kennes-Kritik bezügl. Müller-Broschüre," 18.5.48, BA-MA N/124/10.

Scheurig, Bodo, Bodo Scheurig Papers, IfZ ZS-A 0031-1–0031-11.

Secret Field Police, NARA 1188885 6.18.

Sonderegger, Franz X., to Freiherr von Siegler, Dr. Helmut Krausnick, and Dr. Hermann Mau, 14.10.1952, IfZ, ZS-0303-1, p. 43, http://www.ifz-muenchen.de/archiv/zs/zs-0303_1.pdf.

———, to Mattmer, 17.10.1952, IfZ, ZS-0303-1, p. 32, http://www.ifz-muenchen.de/archiv/zs/zs-0303_1.pdf.

Stellv. Generalkommando XX.A.K (Wehrkreiskommando XX), Abt. Ib/Org, "Betr. Einsatz Walküre," 14.5.1942, BA-MA RH/53/20, 27, pp. 78–84.

Swiss Federal Police, BA, E 4320 (B) 1970/25 Bd 1–4, Dossier C.2.102, available also online in GEAH, http://www.georg-elser-arbeitskreis.de/texts/schweiz.htm.

Swiss Federal Police, replies to Gestapo inquiries, 1.2.1940: BA, E 4320 (B) 1970/25 Bd 1–4, Dossier C.2.102, Ermittlungsbericht VI.

Thomas, Georg, "20. Juli 1944," 20.7.1945, BA-MA Msg 2/213.

"Tresckow, Henning von: Beurteilung," BA-MA BAarch PERS 6/1980.

Wehrkreis Kommando XVII, Wien, 1.9.1943, "Verwendungsbereitschaft des Ersatzheeres," BA-MA RH/53/17, 143.

Wehrkreiskommmando XVII (Stellv. Gen. Kdo. XVII A.K.), Wien, 12.1.1944, "Grundsätzlicher Befehl für die Abwehr feindlicher Einzelspringer, Fallschirmjäger und Luftlandetruppen," BA-MA RH/53/17, 39.

Wolf an Kunz, 7.12.1936, SAL Kap 10 G Nr.685 Bd.1, 270R.

Zeler, Eberhard, Eberhard Zeller Papers, IfZ ED-88/1–3.

## Published Memoirs, Interviews, and Primary Sources

*Akten zur deutschen auswärtigen Politik, 1918–1945* (Baden-Baden: Impr. Nationale, 1950–95).

Andreas-Friedrich, Ruth, *Schauplatz Berlin: Ein deutsches Tagebuch* (Munich: Rheinsberg Verlag G. Lentz, 1962).

Aretin, Felicitias von, *Die Enkel des 20 Juli 1944* (Leipzig: Faber & Faber, 2004).

Ballestrem-Solf, Lagi Countess, "Tea Party," in *We Survived: Fourteen Stories of the Hidden and Hunted of Nazi Germany*, ed. Eric H. Boehm (Santa Barbara, Calif.: ABC-Clio Information Services, 1985).

Bauer, Fritz, ed., *Justiz und NS-Verbrechen: Sammlung deutscher Strafurteile, wegen nationalsozialistischer Tötungsverbrechen, 1945–1999* (Amsterdam: University Press Amsterdam, 1968).

Beck, Ludwig, *Ein General kämpft gegen den Krieg: Aus nachgelassenen Papieren des Generalstabchefs Ludwig Beck*, ed. Wolfgang Foerster (Munich: Münchener Dom-Verlag, 1949).

———, *Studien*, ed. Hans Speidel (Stuttgart: K. F. Koehler, 1955).

Bethge, Eberhard, ed., *Auf dem Wege zur Freiheit: Gedichte und Briefe aus der Haft*, by Dietrich Bonhoeffer and Klaus Bonhoeffer (Berlin: Lettner Verlag, 1954).

Boeselager, Philipp von, with Florence Fehrenbach and Jerome Fehrenbach, *Valkyrie: The Story of the Plot to Kill Hitler by Its Last Member*, trans. Steven Rendall (New York: Vintage, 2010).

Bonhoeffer, Dietrich, *Dietrich Bonhoeffer Werke*, ed. Eberhard Bethge et al. (Munich: Chr. Kaiser, 1986–1999).

———, *Dietrich Bonhoeffer Works* (Minneapolis: Fortress Press, 1996–2014). 16 vols.

Breitenbuch, Eberhard von, *Erinnerungen eines Reserveoffiziers, 1939–1945: Aufgeschrieben zur Kenntnis meiner Kinder* (Norderstedt: Books on Demand, 2011).

Cadogan, Alexander, *The Diaries of Sir Alexander Cadogan, O. M, 1938–1945*, ed. David Dilks (London: Cassell, 1971).

Churchill, Winston, *Into Battle: Speeches by the Right Hon. Winston Churchill*, ed. Randolph S. Churchill (London: Cassell, 1941).

Diels, Rudolf, *Lucifer ante Portas: Zwischen Severing und Heydrich* (Zurich: Interverlag, 1949).

Domarus, Max, *Hitler: Reden und Proklamationen, 1932–1945: Kommentiert von einem deutschen Zeitgenossen* (Würzburg: Schmidt, Neustadt a.d. Aisch, 1962). 2 vols.

Ebermayer, Erich, *Denn heute gehört uns Deutschland: Persönliches und politisches Tagebuch*, trans. Sally Winkle (Hamburg: Zsolnay, 1959).

Elser, Georg J., *Autobiographie eines Attentätters: Der Anschlag auf Hitler in Bürgerbräukeller 1939*, ed. Lothar Gruchmann (Stuttgart: Deutsche Verlags-Anstalt, 1989).

Fahrner, Rudolf, "Geschehnisse um 20. Juli 1944," in *Gesammelte Werke*, ed. Stefano Bianca and Bruno Pieger (Cologne: Böhlau Verlag, 2008).

Fischer, Karl, *Ich Fuhr Stauffenberg: Erinnerungen an die Kriegsjahre, 1939–1945* (Angermünde: Spiegelberg Verlag, 2008).

Fliess, Dorothee, "Geschichte Einer Rettung," in *20. Juli 1944: Annäherung an den geschichlichen Augenblick*, ed. Rüdiger von Boss and Günther Neske (Pfullingen: Neske, 1984).

Foerster, Wolfgang, *Ein General kämpft gegen den Krieg: Aus nachgelassenen Papieren des Generalstabchefs Ludwig Beck* (Munich: Münchener Dom-Verlag, 1949).

Gerlach, Christian, "Männer des 20 Juli und der Krieg gegen die Sowjetunion," in *Vernichtungskrieg: Verbrechen der Wehrmacht, 1941 bis 1944*, ed. Hannes Heer and Klaus Naumann (Hamburg: Hamburger Edition, 1995).

Gersdorff, Rudolf-Christoph Freiherr von, *Soldat im Untergang* (Frankfurt am Main: Ullstein, 1977).

Gilbert, Felix, ed., *Hitler Directs His War: The Secret Records of His Daily Military Conferences* (New York: Oxford University Press, 1950).

Gillmann, Sabine, and Hans Mommsen, *Politische Schriften und Briefe Carl Friedrich Goerdelers* (Munich: Saur, 2003). 2 vols.

Gisevius, Hans B., *Bis zum bittern Ende* (Zurich: Fretz & Wasmuth, 1946).

———, *To the Bitter End*, trans. Richard Winston and Clara Winston (New York: Da Capo Press, 1998).

Goebbels, Joseph, *Tagebücher, 1924–1945*, ed. Ralf Georg Reuth, 2nd ed. (Munich: Piper, 1992).

Göring, Hermann, *Reden und Aufsätze* (Munich: F. Eher Nachf, 1938).

Groscurt, Helmut, *Tagebücher eines Abwehroffiziers, 1938–1940: Mit weiteren Dokumenten zur Militäropposition gegen Hitler*, ed. Helmut Krausnick and Harold C. Deutsch (Stuttgart: Deutsche Verlags-Anstalt, 1970).

Guderian, Heinz, *Erinnerungen eines Soldaten* (Heidelberg: Vowinckel, 1951).

Haffner, Sebastian, *Defying Hitler: A Memoir*, trans. Oliver Pretzel (London: Weidenfeld & Nicolson, 2002).

Hammerstein, Kunrat Freiherr von, *Spähtrupp* (Stuttgart: Govert, 1963).

Hassell, Ulrich von, *Die Hassell-Tagebücher, 1938–1944: Aufzeichnungen vom anderen Deutschland*, ed. Friedrich Freiherr Hiller von Gärtringen (Munich: Goldmann, 1994).

Heideking, Jürgen, and Christof Mauch, eds., *American Intelligence and the German Resistance to Hitler* (Boulder, Colo.: Westview Press, 1996).

Henk, Emil, *Die Tragödie des 20. Juli 1944: Ein Beitrag zur politischen Vorgeschichte* (Heidelberg: Rausch, 1946).

Hofer, Walther, ed., *Der Nationalsozialismus: Dokumente, 1933–1945* (Frankfurt am Main: Fischer Taschenbuch Verlag, 1957).

Holl, Martin, ed., *Führer-Erlasse, 1939–1940* (Stuttgart: Steiner, 1997).

Jacobsen, Hans A., ed., *"Spiegelbild einer Verschwörung": Die Opposition gegen Hitler und der Staatsstreich vom 20. Juli 1944 in der SD-Berichterstattung; Geheime Dokumente aus dem ehemaligen Reichssicherheitshauptamt* (Stuttgart: Seewald, 1984).

Jacobsen, Hans A., and Erich Zimmermann, eds., *20. Juli 1944* (Bonn: Berto Verlag, 1960).

John, Otto, *Twice Through the Lines: The Autobiography of Otto John*, trans. Richard Barry (London: Macmillan, 1972).

Kaiser, Hermann, *Mut zum Bekenntnis: Die geheimen Tagebücher des Hauptmanns Hermann Kaiser 1941, 1943*, ed. Peter M. Kaiser (Berlin: Lukas Verlag, 2010).

Kleist-Schmenzin, Ewald von, "Adel und Preußentum," *Süddeutsche Monatshefte* 51 (23 August 1926): 378–84.

———, *Der Nationalsozialismus: Eine Gefahr* (Berlin-Britz: Werdermann, 1932).

Kopp, Roland, *Paul von Hase von der Alexander-Kaserne nach Plötzensee: Eine deutsche Soldatenbiographie, 1885–1944* (Münster: Lit, 2001).

Kordt, Erich, *Nicht aus den Akten* (Stuttgart: Union deutsche Verlagsgesellschaft, 1950).

Kuhn, Joachim, "Eigenhändige Aussagen." In Hoffmann, Peter, *Stauffenbergs Freund.*

Loringhoven, Bernd Freytag von, with François d'Alançon, *In the Bunker with Hitler, 23.7.1944–29.4.1945* (London: Weidenfeld & Nicolson, 2006).

Medem, Gevinon von, ed., *Axel von dem Bussche* (Mainz: Hase & Koehler, 1994).

Meding, Dorothee von, *Courageous Hearts: Women and the Anti-Hitler Plot of 1944*, trans. Michael Balfour and Volker R. Berghahn (Providence, R.I.: Berghahn Books, 1997).

——— , *Mit dem Mut des Herzens: Die Frauen des 20 Juli* (Berlin: Siedler, 1992).

Meinecke, Friedrich, *Die deutsche Katastrophe: Betrachtungen und Erinnerungen* (Wiesbaden: Brockhaus, 1946).

Meyer-Krahmer, Marianne, *Carl Goerdeler—Mut zum Widerstand: Eine Tochter erinnert sich* (Leipzig: Leipziger Universitatsverlag, 1998).

Michalka, Wolfgang, ed., *Das Dritte Reich: Dokumente zur Innen- und Außenpolitik* (Munich: Deutscher Taschenbuch Verlag, 1985). Vol. 1.

Moltke, Helmuth James von, *Briefe an Freya, 1933–1945* (Munich: Beck, 2005).

——— , *A German of the Resistance: The Last Letters of Count Helmuth James von Moltke* (London: Oxford University Press, 1946).

Mühlen, Bengt von zur, ed., *Die Angeklagten des 20 Juli vor dem Volksgerichtshof* (Berlin: Chronos, 2001).

Mühlen, Bengt von zur, and Frank Bauer, eds., *Der 20. Juli 1944 in Paris: Verlauf, Hauptbeteiligte, Augenzeugen* (Berlin: Chronos, 1995).

Müller, Wolfgang, *Gegen eine neue Dolchstoßlüge: Ein Erlebnisbericht zum 20 Juli 1944* (Hannover: Verlag "Das andere Deutschland," 1947).

Navarre, Henri, *Le temps des vérités* (Paris: Plon, 1979).

Neitzel, Sönke, *Abgehört: Deutsche Generäle in britischer Kriegsgefangenschaft 1942–1945* (Berlin: Propyläen, 2005).

Nohlen, Dieter, and Philip Stöver, eds., *Elections in Europe: A Data Handbook* (Baden-Baden: Nomos, 2010).

Pechel, Rudolf, *Deutscher Widerstand* (Zürich: Rentsch, 1947).

Schacht, Hjalmar, Abrechnung mit Hitler (WC-TAU, N4F SCHA).

Schlabrendorff, Fabian von, *Offiziere gegen Hitler* (Zurich: Europa Verlag, 1946).

——— , *Revolt Against Hitler: The Personal Account of Fabian von Schlabrendorff*, trans. and ed. Gero von Gaevernitz (London: Eyre & Spottiswoode, 1948).

——— , *The Secret War Against Hitler*, trans. Hilda Simon (Boulder, Colo.: Westview Press, 1994).

Schmidt, Paul, *Hitler's Interpreter*, ed. and trans. R. H. C. Steed (New York: Macmillan, 1951).

——— , *Statist auf diplomatischer Bühne, 1923–1945: Erlebnisse des Chefdolmetschers im Auswärtigen Amt mit den Staatsmännern Europas* (Bonn: Athenäum Verlag, 1949).

Schramm, Wilhelm R. von, *Beck und Goerdeler: Gemeinschaftsdokumentefür den Frieden, 1941–1944* (Munich: Müller, 1965).

Shirer, William L., *Berlin Diary: The Journal of a Foreign Correspondent, 1934–1941* (London: Hamilton, 1943).

Skorzeny, Otto, *Skorzeny's Special Missions: The Memoirs of the Most Dangerous Man in Europe* (London: Robert Hale, 1957).

SOPADE (Exilvorstand der Sozialdemokratischen Partei Deutschlands), sozialistische Mitteilungen—Newsletter, herausgegeben 1939–1948. Hefte Nr. 45, 3–9, Nr. 47, 5, Nr. 49, 3–8, Nr. 52, p.19, Beilage 2: I-XII, Nr. 53/4, 1–5, Nr. 55/6, 7–15, Nr. 57, 4–9, Nr. 58/9, 1–14, Nr. 62, 20, Nr. 63/4, Beilage 2: I-XVI.

Speidel, Hans, *We Defended Normandy*, trans. Ian Colvin (London: Jenkins, 1951).

Stahlberg, Alexander, *Bounden Duty: The Memoirs of a German Officer, 1932–1945*, trans. Patricia Crampton (London: Macmillan, 1990).

——— , *Die verdammte Pflicht: Erinnerungen 1932 bis 1945* (Berlin: Ullstein, 1988).

Stampfer, Friedrich, *Erfahrungen und Erkenntnisse: Aufzeichnungen aus meinem Leben* (Cologne: Verlag für Politik und Wirtschaft, 1957).

Statista 2015, ed., "Anzahl der Arbeitslosen in der Weimarer Republik in den Jahren 1926 bis 1935," http://de.statista.com/statistik/daten/studie/277373/umfrage/historische-arbeitslosenzahl-in-der-weimarer-republik/.

*Statistiches Jahrbuch für das deutsche Reich*, Berlin: Puttkammer & Mühlbrecht, 1938, http://www.digizeitschriften.de.

Stieff, Helmuth, "Brief HQ/u, 21.11.1939," *Vierteljahrshefte für Zeitgeschichte* (July 1954).

Thompson, Dorothy, *Listen, Hans* (Boston: Houghton Mifflin, 1942).

Warlimont, Walter, *Im Hauptquartier der deutschen Wehrmacht, 1939–1945* (Frankfurt am Main: Bernard & Graefe, 1962).

Weizmann, Chaim, *Trial and Error: The Autobiography of Chaim Weizmann* (New York: Harper, 1949).

Woodward, E. L., and Rohan Butler, eds., *Documents on British Foreign Policy, 1919–1939*, 3rd Series (London, 1949).

Yakovlev, A. N., et al., eds., *Rossia XX Vek: Dokumenti, 1941*, God v 2-x Knigah (Moscow: Mezhdunarodniy Fond "Demokratiya," 1998).

Young, Arthur P., *X Documents* (London: Deutsch, 1974).

Zimmermann, Wolf-Dieter, *Wir nannten ihn Bruder Bonhoeffer: Einblicke in ein hoffnungsvolles Leben* (Berlin: Wichern Verlag, 1995).

## Published Secondary Sources

Altein, Rachel, ed., *Out of the Inferno: The Efforts That Led to the Rescue of Rabbi Yosef Yitzchak Schneersohn of Lubavitch from War-Torn Europe in 1939–40* (New York: Kehot Publication Society, 2002).

Aster, Sidney, "Guilty Men: The Case of Neville Chamberlain," in *Origins of the Second World War*, ed. Patrick Finney (New York: St. Martin's, 1997).

Balfour, Michael, *Withstanding Hitler in Germany, 1933–1945* (London: Routledge, 1988).

Bauer, Yehuda, *Jews for Sale?: Nazi-Jewish Negotiations, 1933–1945* (New Haven, Conn.: Yale University Press, 1994).

Beck, Dorothea, *Julius Leber: Sozialdemokrat zwischen Reform und Widerstand* (Berlin: Siedler, 1983).

Beevor, Anthony, *Stalingrad* (London: Viking, 1998).

Bentzien, Hans, *Claus Schenk Graf von Stauffenberg: Der Täter und seine Zeit* (Berlin: Das Neue Berlin, 2004).

Bethge, Eberhard, *Dietrich Bonhoeffer: Theologe, Christ, Zeitgenosse: Eine Biographie*, 9th ed. (Gütersloh: Gütersloher Verlagshaus, 2005).

Browning, Christopher, *Origins of the Final Solution: The Evolution of Nazi Jewish Policy, September 1939–March 1942* (Jerusalem: Yad Vashem Press, 2004).

Brügel, Johann W., *Tschechen und Deutsche, 1918–1938* (Munich: Nymphenburger Verlagshandlung, 1967).

Bücheler, Heinrich, *Generaloberst Erich Hoepner und die Militäropposition gegen Hitler* (Berlin: Landeszentrale für politische Bildungsarbeit, 1981).

Buchheit, Gert, *Die Anonyme Macht: Aufgaben, Methoden, Erfahrungen der Geheimdienste* (Frankfurt am Main: Akademische Verlagsgesellschaft Athenaion, 1969).

Chandler, Andrew, ed., *The Moral Imperative: New Essays on the Ethics of Resistance in National Socialist Germany, 1933–1945* (Boulder, Colo.: Westview Press, 1998).

Charmley, John, *Churchill, the End of Glory: A Political Biography* (New York: Harcourt Brace, 1993).

Conze, Eckart, et al., *Das Amt und die Vergangenheit: Deutsche Diplomaten im Dritten Reich und in der Bundesrepublik* (Munich: Karl Blessing Verlag, 2010).

Deutsch, Harold C., *The Conspiracy Against Hitler in the Twilight War* (Minneapolis: University of Minnesota Press, 1970).

Deutsch, Saul S., "Me-Varsha Le-New York Dereh Berlin, Riga Ve-Stockholm: Giluyim Hadashim al Parashat Ha-Hatsala shel Kevod Kedushat Admor Harayats," *Kefar Chabad* (9 Adar, February 1993).

Dosenrode, Soren, ed., *Christianity and Resistance in the 20th Century: From Kaj Munk and Dietrich Bonhoeffer to Desmond Tutu* (Leiden: Brill, 2009).

Dulles, Allen W., *Germany's Underground* (New York: Macmillan, 1947).

Erhard, Lucas, *Vom Scheitern der deutschen Arbeiterbewegung* (Basel: Stroemfeld, 1983).

Faber, David, *Appeasement and World War II* (New York: Simon & Schuster, 2008).

Feiling, Keith, *The Life of Neville Chamberlain* (London: Macmillan, 1970).

Fest, Joachim, *Plotting Hitler's Death: The German Resistance to Hitler, 1933–1945*, trans. Bruce Little (London: Weidenfeld & Nicolson, 1996).

Finker, Kurt, *Stauffenberg und der 20. Juli 1944* (Berlin: Union Verlag, 1967).

FitzGibbon, Constantine, *The Shirt of Nessus* (London: Cassell, 1956).

Gallately, Robert, "The Political Policing of Nazi Germany," in *Germans Against Nazism: Nonconformity, Opposition, and Resistance in the Third Reich: Essays in Honour of Peter Hoffmann*, ed. Francis R. Nicosia and Lawrence D. Stokes (New York: St. Martin's Press, 1990).

Gilbert, Martin, *Kristallnacht: Prelude to Destruction* (London: HarperPress, 2006).

Gillessen, Günther, "Tresckow und der Entschluß zum Hochverrat: Eine Nachschau zur Kontroverse über die Motive," *Vierteljahrshefte für Zeitgeschichte* 58, no. 3 (2010): 364–86.

Gladwell, Malcolm, *The Tipping Point: How Little Things Can Make a Big Difference* (Boston: Back Bay Books, 2002).

Goda, Norman J. W., "Black Marks: Hitler's Bribery of His Senior Officers During World War II," *Journal of Modern History* 72, no. 2 (June 2000): 413–52.

Grabner, Sigrid, and Hendrik Röder, eds., *Ich bin der ich war: Henning von Tresckow; Texte und Dokumente* (Berlin: Lukas Verlag, 2001).

Graml, Hermann, "Massenmord und Militäropposition: Zur jüngsten Diskussion über den Widerstand im Stab der Heeresgruppe Mitte," *Vierteljahrshefte für Zeitgeschichte* 54, no. 1 (2006): 1–26.

Gutman, Israel, and Chaim Shatzker, *Ha-Sho'ah ve-Mashma'utah* (Jerusalem: Merkaz Zalman Shazar, 1987).

Hamerow, Theodore S., *On the Road to Wolf's Lair: German Resistance to Hitler* (Cambridge, Mass.: Belknap Press of Harvard University Press, 1997).

Harrison, Ted, "'Alter Kämpfer' im Widerstand: Graf Helldorff, die NS-Bewegung, und die Opposition gegen Hitler," *Vierteljahrshefte für Zeitgeschichte* 45, no. 3 (July 1997).

Heinemann, Ulrich, *Ein Konservativer Rebell! Fritz Dietlof Graf von der Schulenberg und der 20. Juli* (Berlin: Siedler, 1990).

Herzog, Rudolph, *Heil Hitler, das Schwein ist tot! Lachen unter Hitler; Komik und Humor im dritten Reich* (Frankfurt am Main: Eichborn, 2006).

Hoffmann, Peter, *Carl Goerdeler and the Jewish Question, 1933–1942* (Cambridge: Cambridge University Press, 2011).

———, *The History of the German Resistance, 1933–1945*, trans. Richard Barry (Montreal: McGill-Queens University Press, 1985).

———, *Hitler's Personal Security* (London: Macmillan, 1979).

———, "Oberst i. G. Henning von Tresckow und die Staatsstreichpläne im Jahr 1943," *Vierteljahrshefte für Zeitgeschichte* 55, no. 2 (2007).

———, "The Question of Western Allied Cooperation with the German Anti-Nazi Conspiracy, 1938–1944," *Historical Journal* 34, no. 2 (1991): 437–64.

———, *Stauffenberg: A Family History, 1905–1944* (Cambridge: Cambridge University Press, 1995).

———, *Stauffenbergs Freund: Die tragische Geschichte des Widerstandskämpfers Joachim Kuhn* (Munich: Verlag C. H. Beck, 2007).

———, *Widerstand, Staatsstreich, Attentat: Der Kampf der Opposition gegen Hitler* (Munich: Piper, 1985).

Höhne, Heinz, *Canaris*, trans. J. Maxwell Brownjohn (London: Secker & Warburg, 1979).

Howe, Harald, et al., eds., *75 Jahre Walther-Rathenau-Oberschule—Gymnasium—(vormals Grunewald Gymnasium): 1903–1978* (Berlin: Rimbach Beratungs- und Verl. GmbH, 1978).

Hürter, Johannes, "Auf dem Weg zur Militäropposition: Tresckow, Gersdorff, der Vernichtungskrieg, und der Judenmord; Neue Dokumente über das Verhältnis der Heeresgruppe Mitte zur Einsatzgruppe B im Jahr 1941," *Vierteljahrshefte für Zeitgeschichte* 3 (2004): 527–62.

Hürter, Johannes, and Felix Römer, "Alte und neue Geschichtsbilder von Widerstand und Ostkrieg: Zu Hermann Gramls Beitrag 'Massenmord und Militäropposition,'" *Vierteljahrshefte für Zeitgeschichte* 54, no. 2 (April 2006): 300–322.

Janssen, Karl-Heinz, and Fritz Tobias, *Der Sturz der Generäle: Hitler und die Blomberg-Fritsch Krise, 1938* (Munich: Beck, 1994).

Jedlinka, Ludwig, *Das Einsame Gewissen: Der 20 Juli in Österreich* (Vienna: Verlag Herold, 1966).

Kee, Robert, *Munich: The Eleventh Hour* (London: Hamilton, 1988).

Kershaw, Ian, *Hitler, 1889–1936: Hubris* (New York: Norton, 2000).

———, *Hitler, 1936–1945: Nemesis* (New York: Norton, 2000).

———, *Hitler, the Germans, and the Final Solution* (Jerusalem: Yad Vashem Press; New Haven, Conn.: Yale University Press, 2008).

Keyserlingk, Linda von, "Erkenntnisgewinn durch die historische Netzwerkforschung. Eine qualitative und quantitative Analyse des Beziehungsgeflechts von zivilem und militärischem Widerstand, 1938–1944," in *Das ist Militärgeschichte! Probleme—Projekte—Perspektiven*, ed. Christian Th. Müller and Matthias Rogg (Paderborn: Ferdinand Schöningh), 464–68.

Kieffer, Fritz, "Carl Friedrich Goerdelers Vorschlag zur Gründung eines jüdischen Staates," *Zeitschrift der Savigny-Stiftung für Rechtsgeschichte* 125 (2008): 474–500.

Klause, Ekkehard, "Ewald von Kleist-Schmenzin (1890–1945): Ein altpreußischer Konservativer im Widerstand gegen den Nationalsozialismus," *Forschungen zur Brandenburgischen und Preußischen Geschichte* 19, no. 2 (2009): 243–55.

Kleinberg, Aviad, *Flesh Made Word: Saints' Stories and the Western Imagination* (Cambridge, Mass.: Belknap Press of Harvard University Press, 2008).

Klemperer, Klemens von, "Der deutsche Widerstand gegen den Nationalsozialismus im Lichte der konservativen Tradition," in *Demokratie und Diktatur: Geist und Gestalt politischer Herrschaft in Deutschland und Europa; Festschrift für Karl Dietrich Bracher*, ed. Manfred Funke (Düsseldorf: Droste, 1987).

———, *German Resistance to Hitler: The Search for Allies Abroad* (Oxford: Oxford University Press, 1992).

Knoke, David, *Political Networks: The Structural Perspective* (Cambridge: Cambridge University Press, 1990).

Knopp, Guido, *Stauffenberg: Die wahre Geschichte* (Munich: Pendo, 2008).

Koch, Hannsjoachim W., *In the Name of the Volk: Political Justice in Hitler's Germany* (London: Tauris, 1989).

Kordt, Erich, *Wahn und Wirklichkeit* (Stuttgart: Union deutsche Verlagsgesellschaft, 1947).

Kramarz, Joachim, *Claus Graf Stauffenberg: 15. November 1907—20. Juli 1944; Das Leben eines Offiziers* (Frankurt am Main: Bernard & Graefe, 1965).

Krausnick, Helmut, and Hans-Heinrich Wilhelm, *Die Truppe des Weltanschauungskrieges: Die Einsatzgruppen der Sicherheitpolizei und des SD, 1938–1942* (Stuttgart: Deutsche Verlags-Anstalt, 1981).

Krebs, Albert, *Fritz-Dietlof Graf von der Schulenburg: Zwischen Staatsraison und Hochverrat* (Hamburg: Leibniz-Verlag, 1964).

Krockow, Christian Graf von, *Eine Frage der Ehre: Stauffenberg und das Hitler-Attentat vom 20. Juli 1944* (Berlin: Rowohlt, 2004).

Kroener, Bernhard, *Generaloberst Friedrich Fromm: Der starke Mann im Heimatkriegsgebiet; Eine Biographie* (Paderborn: Schöningh, 2005).

Laqueur, Walter, and Richard Breitman, *Breaking the Silence: The German Who Exposed the Final Solution* (Hanover, N.H.: University Press of New England for Brandeis University Press, 1994).

Lee, Gregory D., *Conspiracy Investigations: Terrorism, Drugs, and Gangs* (Upper Saddle River, N.J.: Pearson Prentice Hall, 2005).

Mason, Andrea, "Opponents of Hitler in Search of Foreign Support: The Foreign Contacts of Dr. Carl Goerdeler, Ludwig Beck, Ernst von Weizsäcker, and Adam von Trott zu Solz" (master's thesis, McGill University, 2002), http://digitool.library.mcgill.ca/webclient/StreamGate?folder_id=0&dvs=1340873715337~113.

Mawdsley, Evan, *Thunder in the East: The Nazi-Soviet War* (London: Oxford University Press, 2005).

Meiml, Susanne, *Nationalsozialisten gegen Hitler: Die nationalrevolutionäre Opposition um Friedrich Wilhelm Heinz* (Berlin: Siedler, 2000).

Melnikov, Daniil E., *20 Juli 1944: Legende und Wirklichkeit*, trans. Fritz Rehak (Berlin: Deutscher Verlag der Wissenschaften, 1964).

Meyer, Hedwig, "Die SS und der 20. Juli 1944," *Vierteljahrshefte für Zeitgeschichte* 14, no. 3 (July 1966): 299–316.

Meyer, Winfried, *Unternehmen Sieben: Eine Rettungsaktion für vom Holocaust Bedrohte aus dem Amt Ausland/Abwehr im Oberkommando der Wehrmacht* (Frankfurt am Main: Hain, 1993).

Mommsen, Hans, *Alternative zu Hitler: Studien zur Geschichte des deutschen Widerstandes* (Munich: Beck, 2000).

Mühleisen, Horst, "Patrioten im Widerstand: Carl-Hans Graf von Hardenbergs Erlebnisbericht," *Vierteljahrshefte für Zeitgeschichte* 14, no. 3. (January 1993).

Müller, Christian, *Oberst i. G. Stauffenberg: Eine Biographie* (Düsseldorf: Droste, 1971).

Müller, Klaus-Jürgen, *Armee und Drittes Reich, 1933–1939: Darstellung und Dokumentation* (Paderborn: Schöningh, 1987).

———, "Die Blomberg-Fritsch Krise, 1938: Elemente eines politisch-militärischen Skandals," in *Der politische Skandal,* ed. Julius H. Schoeps (Stuttgart: Burg, 1992).

———, *Generaloberst Ludwig Beck: Eine Biographie* (Paderborn: Schöningh, 2008).

Oleschinski, Brigitte, *Plötzensee Memorial Center* (Berlin: Gedenkstätte deutscher Winderstand, 2002).

Orbach, Danny, "Criticism Reconsidered: The German Resistance to Hitler in Critical German Scholarship," *Journal of Military History* 75 (April 2011): 1–25.

———, "The Other Prussia: General von Tresckow, Resistance to Hitler, and the Question of Charisma," *Tel Aviver Jahrbuch für deutsche Geschichte* (October 2016).

———, *Valkyrie: Ha-Hitnagdut Ha-Germanit Le-Hitler* (Or Yehuda, Isr.: Yedioth Ahronot Press, 2009).

Ortner, Helmut, *Der Hinrichter: Roland Freisler, Mörder im Dienste Hitlers* (Vienna: Zsolnay, 1995).

Page, Helena P., *General Friedrich Olbricht: Ein Mann des 20. Juli* (Bonn: Bouvier, 1994). *See also* Schrader, Helena.

Parssinen, Terry, *The Oster Conspiracy of 1938: The Unknown Story of the Military Plot to Kill Hitler and Avert World War II* (New York: HarperCollins, 2003).

Pfister, U., "Die Wirtschaft in der Ära des Nationalsozialismus 1933–1939" (PowerPoint presentation), October 28, 2008, http://www.wiwi.uni-muenster.de/wisoge/md/personen/pfister/Vorlesungsdateien/Deutsche_Wirtschaft_seit_1850/So2-NS-Folien.pdf.

Pritchard, John R., *Reichstag Fire: Ashes of Democracy* (New York: Ballantine, 1972).

Ragsdale, Hugh, *The Soviets, the Munich Crisis, and the Coming of World War II* (Cambridge: Cambridge University Press, 2004).

Ramm, Arnim, *Der 20 Juli vor dem Volksgerichtshof* (Berlin: Gaudig & Veit, 2007).

Rathert, Ronald, *Verbrechen und Verschwörung: Arthur Nebe; Der Kripochef des Dritten Reiches* (Münster: Lit, 2001).

Reich, Ines, *Carl Friedrich Goerdeler: Ein Oberbürgermeister gegen den NS-Staat* (Cologne: Böhlau, 1997).

Reynolds, Nicholas, *Treason Was No Crime: Ludwig Beck, Chief of the German General Staff* (London: Kimber, 1976).

Rigg, Bryan, *Rescued from the Reich: How One of Hitler's Soldiers Saved the Lubavitcher Rebbe* (New Haven, Conn.: Yale University Press, 2004).

Ringshausen, Gerhard, "Hans-Alexander von Voss (1907–1944): Offizier im Widerstand," *Vierteljahrshefte für Zeitgeschichte* 52, no. 3 (2004): 377–87.

———, *Hans-Alexander von Voss: Generalstabsoffizier im Widerstand, 1907–1944* (Berlin: Lukas Verlag, 2008).

———, *Widerstand und christlicher Glaube angesichts des Nationalsozialismus* (Berlin: Lit, 2008).

Ritter, Gerhard, *Carl Goerdeler und die deutsche Widerstandsbewegung* (Stuttgart: Deutsche Verlags-Anstalt, 1954).

Roon, Ger van, "Hermann Kaiser und der deutsche Widerstand," *Vierteljahrshefte für Zeitgeschichte* 24, no. 3 (July 1976): 259–86.

———, *Neuordnung im Widerstand: Der Kreisauer Kreis innerhalb der deutschen Widerstandsbewegung* (Munich: Oldenbourg, 1967).

Rosen, Chaim, "Opozitsyah le'umit shamranit ba-Raykh ha-shelishi" [National Conservative Opposition in the Third Reich] (Ph.D. dissertation, Hebrew University of Jerusalem, 1997).

Scheurig, Bodo, *Ewald von Kleist-Schmenzin: Ein Konservativer gegen Hitler* (Oldenburg: Stalling, 1968).

———, *Henning von Tresckow: Ein Preuße gegen Hitler; Biographie* (Berlin: Propyläen, 1987).

Schmädecke, Jürgen, and Peter Steinbach, eds., *Der Widerstand gegen den Nationalsozialismus: Die deutsche Gesellschaft und der Widerstand gegen Hitler* (Munich: Piper, 1985).

Schöllgen, Gregor, *Ulrich von Hassell, 1881–1944: Ein Konservativer in der Opposition* (Munich: Beck, 1990).

Scholtyseck, Joachim, *Robert Bosch und der liberale Widerstand gegen Hitler, 1933 bis 1945* (Munich: Beck, 1999).

Schrader, Helena, *Codename Valkyrie: General Friedrich Olbricht and the Plot Against Hitler* (Sparkford, UK: Haynes, 2009). *See also* Page, Helena P.

Schramm, Wilhelm R. von, *Aufstand der Generale: Der 20 Juli in Paris* (Munich: Kindler, 1964).

Schröder, Michael, "Erich von Manstein: Ein unpolitischer Soldat?," *Forum "Barbarosa,"* no. 3 (2004), http://www.historisches-centrum.de/forum/schroeders04-2.html.

Schulthess, Konstanze von, *Nina Schenk Gräfin von Stauffenberg: Ein Porträt* (Munich: Pendo, 2008).

Schultz, Hans J., ed., *Der Zwanzigste Juli: Alternative zu Hitler?* (Stuttgart: Kreuz Verlag, 1997).

Schwerin, Detlef Graf von, *Dann sind's die besten Köpfe, die man henkt: Die junge Generation im deutschen Widerstand* (Munich: Piper, 1991).

Scott, John, *Social Network Analysis: A Handbook* (London: SAGE, 2009).

Segev, Tom, *Soldiers of Evil: The Commandants of the Nazi Concentration Camps* (New York: McGraw-Hill, 1987).

Seton-Watson, R. W., *A History of the Czechs and Slovaks* (Hamden, Conn.: Archon, 1965).

Shirer, William L., *The Rise and Fall of the Third Reich: A History of Nazi Germany* (New York: Simon & Schuster, 1960). 2 vols.

Skinner, Quentin, "Meaning and Understanding," *History and Theory* 8, no. 1 (1969).

Smid, Marikje, *Hans von Dohnanyi, Christine Bonhoeffer: Eine Ehe im Widerstand gegen Hitler* (Gütersloh: Gütersloher Verlagshaus, 2002).

Solonin, Mark, *22 Iunya: Anatomiya Katastrofi* (Moscow: Iuza Eskmo, 2008).

Staniland, Paul, *Networks of Rebellion: Explaining Insurgent Cohesion and Collapse* (Ithaca, NY: Cornell University Press, 2014).

Stedman, Andrew D., *Alternatives to Appeasement: Neville Chamberlain and Hitler's Germany* (New York: Tauris, 2011).

Steinbach, Peter, *Claus von Stauffenberg: Zeuge im Feuer* (Leinfelder-Echterdingen: DRW, 2007).

Steinbach, Peter, and Johannes Tuchel, *Georg Elser: Der Hitler Attentäter* (Berlin: Be. Bra Wissenschaft, 2008).

——— , eds., *Widerstand gegen den Nationalsozialismus* (Berlin: Akademie Verlag, 1994).

Stern, Frank, "Wolfsschanze versus Auschwitz: Widerstand als deutsches Alibi?," *Zeitschrift für Geschichtswissenschaft* 42, no. 7 (1997).

Thomas, Mark, "Rearmament and Economic Recovery in the Late 1930s," *Economic History Review*, n.s., 36, no. 4 (November 1983).

Thun-Hohenstein, Romedio G. Graf von, *Der Verschwörer: General Oster und die Militäropposition* (Berlin: Severin & Siedler, 1982).

Ueberschär, Gerd R., ed., *Der deutsche Widerstand gegen Hitler: Wahrnehmung und Wertung in Europa und den USA* (Darmstadt: Wissenschafliche Buchgesellschaft, 2002).

——— , ed., *NS Verbrechen und der militärische Widerstand gegen Hitler* (Darmstadt: Primus, 2000).

——— , *Stauffenberg: Der 20. Juli 1944* (Frankfurt am Main: Fischer, 2004).

Venohr, Wolfgang, *Stauffenberg, Symbol der deutschen Einheit: Eine politische Biographie* (Frankfurt am Main: Ullstein, 1986).

Warner, W. Lloyd, and Paul C. Lunt, *The Social Life of a Modern Community* (New Haven, Conn.: Yale University Press, 1941).

Yahil, Leni, *The Holocaust: The Fate of European Jewry* (New York: Oxford University Press, 1990).

Young, Desmond, *Rommel* (London: Collins, 1972).

Zeller, Eberhard, *Geist der Freiheit: Der Zwanzigste Juli* (Munich: Rhinn, 1952).

——— , *Oberst Claus Graf Stauffenberg: Ein Lebensbild* (Paderborn: Schöningh, 1994).

Zimmermann, Moshe, ed., *Ha-Hitnagdut La-Nazism* (Jerusalem: Koebner Institute for German History, 1984).

## Press and Newspapers

*Der Stürmer* (Nuremberg)
*Echo der Woche*
*London Times*
*New York Times*
*Pravda* (Moscow)
*Völkischer Beobachter* (Munich)

## Visual Media

Kohav Beller, Hava, *The Restless Conscience: Resistance to Hitler Within Germany*, *1933–1945* (1992; Los Angeles: New Video Group, 2009), DVD.

## Interviews

Author with Philipp Freiherr von Boeselager, Kreuzberg, Germany, 15.7.2003.
Nicholas Netteau with Ewald-Heinrich von Kleist, Munich, Germany, 13.1.1998
(given to author by the courtesy of Nicholas Netteau).

# INDEX